Tribal Sovereignty and the Historical Imagination

TRIBAL SOVEREIGNTY
and the
HISTORICAL IMAGINATION

CHEYENNE-ARAPAHO POLITICS

Loretta Fowler

UNIVERSITY OF NEBRASKA PRESS
LINCOLN AND LONDON

Publication of this volume was assisted by
The Virginia Faulkner Fund,
established in memory of Virginia Faulkner,
editor-in-chief of the University of Nebraska Press.

Library of Congress Cataloging-in-Publication Data

Fowler, Loretta, 1944–
Tribal sovereignty and
the historical imagination :
Cheyenne-Arapaho politics /
Loretta Fowler.
p. cm.
Includes bibliographical references and index.
ISBN 0-8032-2013-8 (cloth : alk. paper)
1. Arapaho Indians—Oklahoma—Politics and government.
2. Cheyenne Indians—Oklahoma—Politics and government.
3. Arapaho Indians—Government relations.
4. Cheyenne Indians—Government relations. I. Title.
E99.A7 F69 2002
323.1'1973—dc21
2001045690

Contents

Plates

Figures, Maps, and Tables

Preface

Among the protagonists in the partisan conflicts during President Bill Clinton's second term was a small group of Cheyenne and Arapaho men who gained access to the besieged president and others in his administration and who, in so doing, became targets themselves. Hoping to gain the support of key congressmen and officials in Clinton's administration for the return of a few acres of tribal land in Oklahoma, the elected representatives of the Cheyenne and Arapaho Tribes donated a relatively small amount of money from tribal business enterprises to the Democratic National Committee and ventured to Washington in the midst of impeachment hearings and investigations of campaign financing. Caught up in the battle between the national political parties, they found themselves accused of making an illegal contribution and threatened with criminal prosecution. Just as noteworthy was that a few Cheyenne and Arapaho individuals suggested to the national media that these elected representatives did not have the confidence of their people and that they had acted in violation of the Cheyenne and Arapaho constitution. The national media generally portrayed the Cheyenne and Arapaho delegates as duped innocents and ignored the historical and contemporary circumstances that led these Native Americans to divert thousands of dollars from services for needy tribal members to an attempt to participate in the national political process. Media within the state of Oklahoma generally characterized the elected officials as corrupt and incompetent. The land recovery effort was derailed, and its proponents subsequently adopted a defensive posture as their rivals at home ridiculed their foray into national politics. These characterizations of the Southern Cheyenne and Arapaho peoples have considerable historical depth. My recognition of this longstanding pattern and its social implications helped shape the interpretations in this book.

I began fieldwork in 1984 as the third phase of a controlled comparison of the three Arapaho divisions (associated with the northern, central, and southern plains and settled, respectively, in Montana, Wyoming, and Oklahoma) suggested to me by Fred Eggan when I was still a graduate student. The conditions I found in Oklahoma differed significantly from the circumstances of life on the reservations in Wyoming and Montana. In Oklahoma, where the Southern Arapahos and Cheyennes ceded most of their reservation, I was particularly struck and profoundly disturbed by the intensity of the assault on Cheyenne and Arapaho economic resources and political institutions. Without a reservation land base and social insulation, which the Arapahos had in Montana and Wyoming and the Cheyennes had in Montana, Southern Cheyennes and Arapahos were routinely subjected to demeaning encounters with their non-Indian neighbors as well as to the devastating economic exploitation so clearly revealed in the work of Donald Berthrong. This book represents my efforts to understand the effect of these glaring power differentials on relations between Native Americans and whites in

Oklahoma and also on the Arapahos' and Cheyennes' courageous struggle to play a meaningful role in the sociocultural transformations they experienced and to challenge characterizations of that struggle by their federal trustees and their more powerful neighbors.

I have a profound debt to the hundreds of Arapahos and Cheyennes who welcomed me into their community and who generously supported my research. Elders and others with keen historical sensibilities helped me to learn something of the way Cheyennes and Arapahos view the relationship between historical events and present-day circumstances. Tribal employees and elected officials patiently explained the intricacies of tribal government today and provided letters of support for my work at archives. Community members allowed me to accompany them to court proceedings and other political events. It is my heartfelt hope that this book will contribute toward the struggle of Arapahos and Cheyennes to obtain fair treatment from the wider society and better appreciation of their immense contribution to western Oklahoma.

While I worked on this manuscript I was fortunate in receiving comments and suggestions from colleagues at the University of Oklahoma, and I particularly want to thank Circe Sturm as well as Ross Hassig and Margaret Bender. Tom Biolsi also provided helpful comments and suggestions on the manuscript. I benefited from the comments of colleagues at colloquia and conferences where I presented papers: Clara Sue Kidwell's session, "Tribal Sovereignty and Survival in the Twentieth Century," at the American Society of Ethnohistory meetings in 1999; Garrick Bailey's symposium on Native American sovereignty in 1994; and Ray DeMallie's seminar series at the American Indian Studies Research Institute at Indiana University.

The National Institute of Aging and the National Endowment for the Humanities provided research grants for archival and field research on Southern Arapaho and Cheyenne society during the periods 1984–87 and 1993–94, respectively. I am also grateful to the Research Foundation of the City University of New York for grants during the period 1988–90 that enabled me to extend my studies to the cultural history of peoples in western Oklahoma generally and to the use of Indian imagery in this region. A grant from the Sandoz Foundation for Gerontological Research in 1993–94 also supported my research in Oklahoma.

To William Welge, director of archives at the Oklahoma Historical Society, I owe thanks for help in locating documents that made this study possible. Meg Hacker and Barbara Rust provided generous assistance during my many trips to the regional federal archives in Fort Worth. I also thank John Lovett at the Western History Collections at the University of Oklahoma for his help.

I am grateful to Darrell Rice of the *Watonga Republican* for providing photographs; Chester Cowen at the Oklahoma Historical Society and Joanna Scherer at the Office of the Handbook of North American Indians, Smithsonian Institution, for assistance in locating photographs; Bea Thompson for her work on the figures; Christine Schultz for drawing the maps; and Ann Morris for help in producing the manuscript. John Moore provided me with a copy of a map of Cheyenne and Arapaho allotments and engaged me in informative discussions of ethnological problems concerning Cheyennes. Julia Jordan gave me generous assistance during my first field trip to Oklahoma.

Introduction

When explaining the nature of tribal politics or trying to sway opinion in a political context, Cheyennes and Arapahos often tell or allude to the story of two fishermen, one white and one Indian. The following is one man's version: "An Indian fisherman met a white fisherman. They each had a bucket of crabs. The white man's kept getting away. The white man said, 'Mine are getting away; why not yours?' The Indian said, 'These are Indian crabs—every time one tries to get away, the rest pull him down.' That's what's happening. That's tribal politics." The Cheyennes and Arapahos are native peoples of the Plains who reside in west-central Oklahoma in an area that formerly was their reservation. The Cheyenne and Arapaho Tribes and their constitutional government are federally recognized, and the tribes have taken liberal advantage of the provisions of the Indian Self-Determination and Educational Assistance Act of 1975 to contract for the administration of federal programs. In fact, when Cheyennes and Arapahos use the term "tribal politics," they are referring to post-1975 transformations in tribal government. In linking the image of struggling crabs in a bucket to contemporary tribal politics, Cheyennes and Arapahos make the point that this struggle is not so much to achieve a particular goal as it is to prevent others from distinguishing themselves. The story also conveys the view of many Cheyenne and Arapaho people that intrasocietal rivalry adversely affects the tribes' struggle for greater sovereignty—that is, the competition among individuals prevents the tribes from escaping the constraints facing tribal governments and native peoples in the United States and from exploring new opportunities for economic and political development. A recent example of the unfortunate effects of this rivalry is the futile attempt of tribal officials to obtain the Clinton administration's help in land recovery, described in the preface.

In the crab story, the comparison between Indian and white reflects an ambivalence about Indian society and about the nature of Indians. On the one hand, Indians are portrayed as a category distinct from whites, defined in part by a tendency to stick together and, in so doing, to outmaneuver whites; after all, the Indian fisherman is able to continue fishing while the white fisherman must try to retrieve his crabs. On the other hand, in the context of tribal politics, the Indian way of doing things is perceived to be a disadvantage. The narrator suggests that, although native people cooperate with each other, they also compete in a socially disruptive way.

The themes in the story reflect issues about Cheyenne-Arapaho politics that I confront in this study, questions about the processes by which Cheyennes and Arapahos are mobilized, or not, to work toward political goals in various contexts. On one level, my objective is to explain why, since the 1970s, there has been disabling confrontation and contention in this community (as in many other Native American communities) and a general disenchantment with the Self-Determination Act. More broadly, I look for a relationship between local-level politics and the course of the sovereignty movement in Fourth World settings generally, and I pursue more far-reaching questions about hegemony and consciousness in colonial and post-colonial societies.

Tribal Politics and the Self-Determination Act

There are puzzling contradictions about politics in Native American communities today. Namely, at a moment in time when there is arguably more potential for tribal sovereignty, why is it that memberships challenge their tribal government's efforts to act on that sovereignty, and, more specifically, why is there often a prevailing demand for tribal assets to be distributed on a per capita basis when the potential for economic development through investment seemingly outweighs the temporary benefits the small payments would provide individuals? Further, why do the avowal of tribal unity and the demonstration of widespread political co-operation exist in the ritual sphere (particularly in the organization of powwows and dances), yet, in the context of tribal government, these same ritual participants commit themselves to contest political acts and undermine each other's efforts? These developments characterize Cheyenne-Arapaho tribal politics during the Self-Determination Act era. Here, as in other Native American communities, both tribal and federal courts and the Department of the Interior have been flooded with petitions to overturn elections, remove or prosecute tribal officials, overturn decisions made by elected tribal officials, and so on. Whether or how this activity is related to the Self-Determination Act and associated legislative and judicial developments is a matter of speculation, for no local-level studies have examined this question. Nor have scholars provided a perspective on tribal politics that includes and accounts for political behavior in both tribal government and ritual life.

The Self-Determination Act, passed by Congress on 4 January 1975 is arguably the most important legislation affecting Native American tribal governments since the Indian Reorganization Act of 1934. It gave new legal responsibilities to tribal officials and introduced a discourse into Indian affairs that suggested the promise of sovereignty, or greater sovereignty, for tribal communities. Specifically, the act (Public Law 93-638) directed the secretary of the interior, "upon the request of any Indian tribe, to enter into a contract or contracts with any tribal organization of any such Indian tribe to plan, conduct, and administer programs or portions thereof." The secretary of health, education, and welfare also was directed to enter into contracts in the same manner. This legislation was designed to improve economic, social, and medical programs for native peoples and to strengthen tribal governments by providing training and support to enable them to adequately plan and operate these programs, which had formerly been managed by the federal bureaucracy. The act specified that the transfer of program funds would be done in a speedy fashion so as to minimize the time elapsing between the transfer of funds from the federal government and their disbursement by the tribal organization. It also specified that the amount of funds provided "shall not be less than the appropriate Secretary would have otherwise provided for his direct operation of the programs."[1]

In my simultaneous consideration of the realms of ritual leadership and tribal government, I define tribal politics broadly. There is a large literature on political conflict in native North America that focuses on one or the other of these realms and that applies a factionalism model to the analysis of that conflict. In fact, George Esber suggests that the self-determination legislation has had the effect of institutionalizing divisiveness and reinforcing conservative or progressive factionalism in local communities, ultimately favoring progressive factions. In the late 1960s and 1970s, political anthropologists focused on the study of factions and defined factionalism as local-level conflict between noncorporate groups competing over the use of public power in the pursuit of the maximization of power or material resources. Attention to local-level politics was overshadowed in the late 1970s by other concerns, particularly world system theories, but the terms "faction" and "factionalism" continued to be used to describe the political process, and this view has influenced much of the public, as well as the scholarly, characterization of tribal politics in native North America. In accounting for the patterns of both intrasocietal cooperation and conflict and identifying both what is agreed upon and what is contested, this study takes a broader approach.[2]

Historical perspective is central to this analysis as well: first, in comparing pre– and post–Self-Determination Act eras; second, in viewing peoples' characterizations of social conflict as historical constructions that change over time and that are part of the political process; and third, in situating local-level politics within wider processes of colonialism as these developed in the western Oklahoma context. I view the Self-Determination Act and its implementation as products of these processes of colonization.[3]

The Self-Determination Act specified new responsibilities for tribal officials. It also detailed the limits, more than the opportunities, of self-determination. The federal government determined whether a tribal group was eligible for participation, and the contracting party (tribal organization) had to be the federally "recognized governing body." Recipients of the funds had to keep "such records as the appropriate Secretary shall prescribe." The secretary of the interior or the secretary of health, education, and welfare could decline to enter into a contract requested by an Indian tribe if he or she determined that the contracting party would not manage the program satisfactorily. The secretaries were authorized to make "such rules and regulations as may be necessary and proper" and to determine whether or not the tribal organization's performance under the contract agreement was competent; if the performance was deemed negligent or funds were mismanaged, the contract could be rescinded. No penalties were specified for federal negligence or mismanagement.

By implication, the language of the act put the burden of satisfactory contracting solely on the tribal organization. Moreover, by this legislation Congress declared that it gave Indians the "full opportunity to develop leadership skills crucial to the realization of self-government," and "an effective voice in the planning and implementation of programs for the benefit of Indians." In this act, Congress declared its commitment to "an orderly transition from Federal domination" of programs for Indians to "effective and meaningful participation by the Indian people" in the operation of those programs. The implication was that Indians lacked leadership skills before the legislation and that Congress now had met its obligation to give Indians a voice in their own affairs.[4]

The apparent contradiction between the clear congressional control of the contracting process and the characterization of it as the realization of self-determination gives rise to several issues about domination and how it is experienced in colonial and postcolonial contexts. In this study, I am particularly interested in exploring how these issues are reflected in Cheyenne and Arapaho constructions of history and how these constructions bear on contemporary tribal politics.

Local Histories in Colonial Context: The Colonization of Consciousness and the Consciousness of Colonization

That external forces of domination shape the lives of subordinated people is not in question. Much of the literature on native peoples in Fourth World settings focuses on the determining aspects of global, regional, and national forces and considers intrasocietal conflict a product of imposed structures. Research among indigenous peoples emphasizes how imposed categories of identity (in Canada, for example, the categories of status and nonstatus, Métis, Indian, and Inuit) precipitate new political divisions and controversies, especially when political representivity, as well as access to state services, becomes linked to these imposed identities. Similarly, there are studies of how state funding of political action groups has generated conflict by challenging and subverting native agendas and political values. Scholars also have examined how the penetration of corporations in alliance with the state has set native groups against each other in competition for scarce resources or provoked challenges to leaders' political positions.[5]

What kinds of constraints did the Cheyenne and Arapaho people face once they settled on their reservation in Indian Territory and thereafter? The Cheyennes' and Arapahos' settlement on the reservation came just five years after many were massacred at Sand Creek and one year after General George Custer led a surprise attack on a Cheyenne camp on the Washita River. The Cheyennes and Arapahos had every reason to expect more attacks from the army, even to fear genocide.

Moreover, the threat of coercion aside, with the impending extermination of the buffalo, rations provided by the federal government were essential, and the federal agent on the reservation could withhold rations to sanction behavior. The behavior of which the agents disapproved included political institutions such as the military societies and tribal religious ceremonies that helped mobilize cooperation among Cheyennes and among Arapahos. Food also was withheld for refusal to cooperate with the agents' farming programs and to send children to boarding school. In 1891, on the heels of congressional legislation that provided for the allotment of reservation land to individuals (with the title held in trust by the United States) and the end of a tribal or communal land base, the Cheyennes and Arapahos faced a new set of constraints. Most of their reservation was settled by Americans, who gradually stripped the Cheyennes and Arapahos of their property and made them even more dependent on federal support. In the early twentieth century, Congress passed legislation to further erode the land base of Native Americans. Cheyenne and Arapaho allotments could be sold and the money from the sale and lease of allotments controlled by the federal agent. Chiefs, who hitherto had been able to use resources at their disposal to help support a following, now became as poor as other Cheyennes and Arapahos. By the 1930s the federal government was discouraging the participation of chiefs in negotiations over Cheyenne and Arapaho land and property, instead working to establish an elective, representative government yet withholding control of tribal resources or adequate funding for the programs that the tribal government was expected to operate. In 1975 the self-determination legislation and a new Cheyenne-Arapaho constitution reinforced the supervisory powers of the federal government.

Subordinated peoples in colonial and neocolonial situations not only contend with social institutions of dominance. They also face symbolic dominance, for example, ideologies that reflect cultural constructions of the dominant order and that rationalize that order. These rationalizations may come to be unconsciously accepted (an experience John and Jean Comaroff refer to as the "colonization of consciousness"). It is important here to distinguish between ideology and hegemonic constructs as components of culture (or of a cultural field). Hegemony refers to the dominant conception of the world that has come to be taken for granted or naturalized (hidden in everyday forms of life). In the process of hegemony, dominant conceptions of the world acquire symbolic power so as to shape the unconscious thoughts and actions of the subordinate. In this context, governing practices, including bureaucratic policies and procedures that the governed find virtually impossible to challenge, may be rationalized, justified, and legitimated as efficient, effective, and in the collective interest. In contrast, articulated conscious beliefs are ideologies, used by both dominant and subordinated groups to rationalize behavior or challenge the social order. With what kinds of symbolic dominance did Cheyennes and Arapahos contend?[6]

After Cheyennes and Arapahos settled on the reservation, federal agents, missionaries, and settlers portrayed control over them as necessary to their "civilization," then later to their "progress." In agency circulars, newspaper interviews, personal encounters, and correspondence with Cheyenne and Arapaho individuals and groups, Indians are portrayed as incapable of managing their own resources or of educating their children to function as adults. They are described as lacking leadership institutions and clinging irrationally to primitive ritual traditions—shortcomings that adversely affected their ability to survive in their changed circumstances. Therefore, according to federal and settler discourse, control and supervision were necessary, and settler expropriation of Cheyenne and Arapaho resources provided lessons in civilization and progress. Federal officials described self-determination legislation in the 1930s and 1970s as adequate for a competent leadership to equip themselves to improve Cheyenne and Arapaho living conditions. Similarly, program regulations were presented as promoting the best interests of the community. Like the economic and political sanctions at the disposal of agents and settlers, the characterizations that rationalized the subordination of Cheyenne and Arapaho peoples became an impediment to these peoples' effort to change their societies on their own terms.[7]

While it is the case that external forces have worked to limit the options of subordinated peoples, constraint is but one dimension of colonization. Subordinated peoples do not accept dominant economic, political, and religious structures passively. They may accommodate imposed institutions and absorb them into a reinvented tradition. They also may reconstruct dominant social institutions in ways that are locally meaningful and that serve local ends. And they may contest and overtly resist dominant structures. As John and Jean Comaroff have written, local systems "affect the course of history at the same time as they are remade by it." Subordinated peoples are "determined, yet determining in their own history." Given the kinds of federal and settler controls over Cheyennes and Arapahos, in what ways could they be determining in their own history? In what ways were they determined?[8]

The Cheyennes and Arapahos, like subordinated peoples elsewhere, have dealt in practical ways with social institutions of dominance by cooperating or by resisting either overtly or through "everyday forms of resistance," as James Scott puts it. They also have had to contend with symbolic dominance, either accepting the cultural constructs of the dominant social sector (the colonization of consciousness) or rejecting them through a process referred to as the "consciousness of colonization." Hegemony is intrinsically unstable, for subordinated peoples may become aware of contradictions between the world as represented in dominant ideology and the world as lived experience. They develop a consciousness of colonization. When what is natural becomes negotiable, the colonization of consciousness is mediated by "good sense" understandings of the changing social world, understandings that draw on a subordinated people's sense of their own history and culture. In other words, subordinated ideologies may come to conflict with hegemonic or "common sense" constructs and challenge them.[9]

Subjected peoples may internalize some alien cultural messages while taking issue with others, and transparent and mystified modes of dominance are not mutually exclusive. Oppressed peoples may react to the world as hegemonically conditioned with a mixture of acquiescence at one level and expressions of resistance at another. Or, as Charles Hale puts it, hegemonic processes can involve different spheres of inequity (such as legal rights, educational institutions, and employment opportunities). At particular points in time, each sphere may generate a combination of resistance and accommodation, or resistance may focus on one sphere while the premises of another sphere may be accepted. Antihegemonic consciousness may or may not lead to social forms of resistance. And that subordinated people experience a polyvalent cultural field and have differential access to power can result in conflicts as well as collective efforts at transformation or reconstruction of the social world.[10]

I explore several questions in this study: in what ways did Cheyennes and Arapahos accept or challenge the demeaning characterizations of themselves, and to what extent did imposed social forms become institutionalized? Were challenges broadly based or were there conflicts among Cheyennes and Arapahos over the transformations of Cheyenne and Arapaho life? Were some spheres of inequity more easily resisted than others? How can we account for what was accepted and what was resisted over time? How did the specific historical experiences of the Cheyennes and Arapahos and their understandings of those experiences influence contemporary tribal politics, such as the electoral process in tribal government, the 1975 constitution, the implementation of Self-Determination Act legislation, and dance and powwow leadership institutions since the 1960s?

This book is organized chronologically to address issues of dominance and resistance from the time of Cheyenne and Arapaho settlement on the reservation in 1869 through the 1990s. The southern bands of the Cheyenne and Arapaho people were forced out of most of their hunting territory in Colorado and Kansas by the westward expansion of the United States in the 1860s. Determined to minimize armed resistance of native peoples to the immigration process, President Ulysses Grant opted for a pacification policy that stressed offering tribes federal guarantees of safety and provisions in return for peace and settlement on reservations. After President Grant's peace commission negotiated the Medicine Lodge Creek Treaty,

Brinton Darlington, a Quaker agent, was given charge of the Southern Cheyennes and Arapahos in July 1869. At that time most of the Cheyennes had not arrived at Camp Supply in Indian Territory to receive supplies, and the Arapahos there refused to occupy the reservation established by the treaty in Kansas, arguing that the boundaries were different from those to which they had agreed. A presidential commission arrived at Camp Supply for negotiations in August 1869.

The Arapaho chief Little Raven acted as intermediary between the commissioners and the Arapahos and the Cheyennes, who both refused the reservation defined in the Medicine Lodge Creek Treaty. That same month President Grant created by executive order a new 4,297,771-acre reservation in Indian Territory, utilizing lands ceded by the Creek, Seminole, Chickasaw, and Choctaw Nations. Darlington first built an agency on Pond Creek, a tributary of the Salt Fork of the Arkansas River, but, at the urging of the army, the agency was moved in May 1870 to a location on the North Canadian River, farther from American settlement. Little Raven rejected the "civilization" program of Agent Darlington but was more convincing than the Cheyennes as to his people's peaceful intent. Avoiding the new agency, many Cheyennes and most of the Arapahos remained in the vicinity of Camp Supply with the consent of army officers, who were at odds with the agent. Buffalo were plentiful near Camp Supply, so neither Arapahos nor Cheyennes were dependent on the agent at first. Gradually, as game disappeared from the Camp Supply area, the agency on the North Canadian River became the focal point of Arapaho and Cheyenne reservation life.[11]

Chapter 1 covers the reservation period (1869–91) and the first ten years after the reservation was subdivided into individual allotments and opened to the settlement of Americans. I show how the more powerful sectors of Oklahoma society exploited Cheyenne and Arapaho laborers, expropriated Indian lands and property, and challenged the legitimacy of the Cheyenne and Arapaho way of life. I argue that in reorganizing their society to cope with these pressures Cheyennes and Arapahos perpetuated an authority structure headed by chiefs and ritual authorities and a supporting system of economic relations that encouraged individuals to cooperate with one another. And, while their dependent position necessitated some conformity to federal and missionary agendas, they rejected the demeaning ideology that supported their subordination.

As chapter 2 opens, Congress has passed legislation to provide for the sale of allotments of deceased allottees. During these years (1903–27) most of the Cheyenne and Arapaho lands were sold to settlers, and the federal government increasingly withdrew support and protection and, at the same time, ostensibly to supervise the Cheyennes' and Arapahos' expenditures of cash income from the leasing and sale of land by individual allottees or their heirs, became more intrusive in the personal lives of individuals. Cheyennes and Arapahos faced a discourse, both intensified and elaborated, about Indians that at once rationalized the expropriation of their resources and demeaned them as individuals and peoples. I argue that, on the one hand, Cheyennes and Arapahos continued to resist the institutions of dominance by engaging in communal activities underpinned by religious ideals that reinforced cooperation; yet, on the other hand, individuals began to pursue personal goals by appropriating some aspects of the dominant ideology, particularly ideas about kinship and inheritance. By 1928 there was a shift in progress, not yet complete, from an authority tradition in which individuals located themselves with reference to particular extrafamilial groups (districts) to one that provided opportunities for and encouraged individuals as independent political operatives.

Chapter 3 examines the 1928–76 era, during which the federal government pressured the Cheyenne and Arapaho peoples to accept a new form of constitutional, representative tribal government and (in the 1950s) to migrate to urban areas away from the rural homeland. The rural communities declined, and, over time, ceremonial activity became more diffused and intertribal. I argue that in transforming ritual life, Cheyennes and Arapahos gave expression to the new social reality that reflected both the wane of rural, district-oriented community life and the celebration of native identity generally. I also show how "the claim" (a lawsuit against the United States for violating the 1851 Fort Laramie Treaty) replaced "the treaty" as a pervasive political symbol for most Cheyennes and Arapahos. For some tribal members in rural communities, the claim was a link between contemporary elected leadership and chieftainship. But as individuals became economically independent of the rural communities, they openly challenged not only federal policy and local discrimination but also the competence of tribal government and the concept of "tribe" as corporate identity. One outcome was the adoption of a new constitution in 1975.

In part 2, I draw on my fieldwork during the years 1984–94 and newspaper and archival sources to provide an analysis of contemporary tribal government, political mobilization, and political discourse. This self-determination era has resulted in the transformation of the physical and social landscape of Cheyenne-Arapaho country through the tribes' expansion of economic opportunities for members. Tribal government officials are responsible for overseeing the tribes' property and managing social and economic programs for the Cheyenne and Arapaho community. Today Cheyennes and Arapahos are settled primarily in small towns throughout the former reservation area, which was ceded in 1891. Now the area is subdivided into eight counties. This is a country of reddish loam and clay soil, prairie grass, and gently rolling hills. The Canadian River flows through the area northwest to east. The Washita River flows through the southwestern portion, and the Cimarron River abuts the northeastern corner of the former reservation. There were 10,173 Cheyenne-Arapaho tribal members in May 1993. Of these, 4,727 were living within the former reservation boundaries; 2,833 were outside the former reservation but within the state of Oklahoma; and 2,613 lived outside the state. In Canadian County were 1,006 Cheyenne-Arapahos, most of whom lived in El Reno, a town of 15,414, located thirty miles west of Oklahoma City. In Custer County, to the west, were 1,025 tribal members, over half of whom lived in the town of Clinton, with a population of almost 10,000, and about a fourth of whom lived in the smaller town of Weatherford. In Blaine County, there were 1,090 Cheyennes and Arapahos, living primarily in small towns: over 400 in Watonga, over 300 in Geary, and about 200 in Canton. The remainder of the tribal members lived in other counties in the small towns of Hammon, Seiling, and Kingfisher as well as along country roads in this very rural part of the northwest quadrant of the state. Only El Reno, Clinton, and Weatherford are accessible by the interstate highway. The state and county roads that traverse the area are in poor condition, and many homes can be reached only by gravel or dirt roads.[12]

Economic opportunities in the rural communities are limited to seasonal agricultural labor. There are jobs in restaurants and motels along the interstate, but few Cheyennes and Arapahos have these kinds of jobs. The leading employer is the Cheyenne and Arapaho Tribes. The Indian Health Service (I H S) and the Bureau of Indian Affairs (B I A) also employ largely Cheyennes and Arapahos. A tribal survey administered in 1987 found an unemployment rate within the former reservation boundaries, referred to as the service area, of 62 percent. The B I A arrived at essentially the same figure. In 1987, about two-thirds of the Cheyenne and Arapaho households received either food stamps or commodities; 20 percent were receiving Aid for Families with Dependent Children. The tribal survey found that 56 percent of the households were headed by a married couple, 38 percent by a female, and 6 percent by a male. Thirty-six percent of the households were extended families; that is, relatives other than parents and children were included in the household.

The Cheyenne and Arapaho Tribes administer programs, operate business enterprises, and own land. The tribes' jurisdiction includes the eight-county (and part of a ninth) service area, which amounts to seventy thousand square miles. In addition, some of the programs operated by the tribes cover a larger area: B I A-funded programs serve eleven counties and I H S-funded programs serve eighteen counties. Most tribal members depend on I H S for medical and dental care. The I H S operates a hospital in Clinton that does not handle serious cases requiring long-term hospitalization. I H S also has health clinics in Watonga and El Reno. For surgery, obstetrical services, and matters requiring specialized medical attention, patients are referred elsewhere, depending on the financial resources of I H S.

The tribes own 10,358 acres, which are divided among tribal reserves at Concho, Clinton, Watonga, Canton, and Colony (a small rural community in Washita County) and in the Watonga area where the tribes purchased land. The Cheyenne

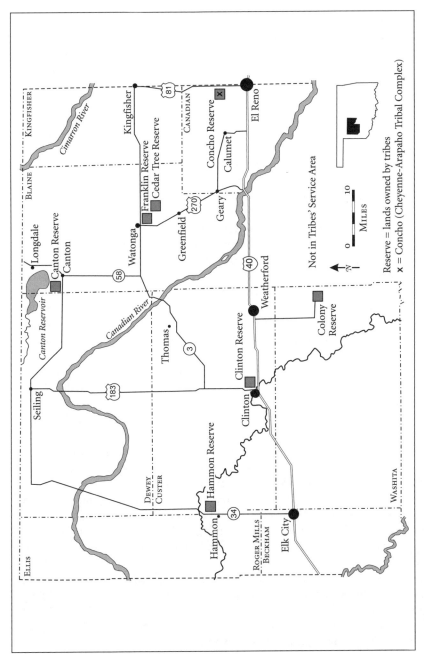

1. Cheyenne and Arapaho Lands and Communities, 1995.

and Arapaho Tribes lease about 4,000 acres of the tribes' land for farming and most of the remainder for grazing; the subsurface is leased for gas and oil extraction. Also on these tribal lands are federal housing projects and community halls. And, at Watonga, Clinton, and Concho (five miles north of El Reno) are Cheyenne-Arapaho bingo operations and retail stores as well as I H S facilities and tribal administrative offices.

Chapter 4 is an overview of the organization of Cheyenne-Arapaho government. I discuss the ways in which the contracting of programs encouraged by the Self-Determination Act, the establishment of tribally owned businesses, the creation of a tribal court, and the imposition of tribal taxes have affected government operations. I argue that while recent federal initiatives have enabled tribal government to develop culturally sensitive programs and policies and to be a more aggressive advocate for the tribal members, federal supervisory institutions and media characterizations of tribal officials predispose tribal governments to have difficulty accomplishing goals of self-determination and convincing constituents of the tribal government's legitimacy and effectiveness.

Chapter 5 reviews the considerable accomplishments of business committees since 1976, particularly as these figure in the self-determination movement. Also analyzed here are patterns of conflict between the incumbent officials and the newly elected ones, who serve concurrently, and the ways the conflict has been expressed. I argue that business committee members use a discourse in political struggles that, on the one hand, takes the federal government to task for paternalism, economic exploitation, and employing an ideology that demeans native peoples and, on the other hand, appropriates elements of this ideology to discredit rival business committee members and other opponents.

Chapter 6 explains the pattern of political opposition to the business committees, including the use of recalls, lawsuits, and local media. This opposition has tried to undermine the efforts of the business committees to pursue greater tribal sovereignty, while at the same time protesting local discrimination and the paternalism of the federal government. I argue that Cheyennes and Arapahos use a discourse in political confrontations that takes the surrounding society to task for using demeaning Indian imagery and partaking in social discrimination, yet appropriates an ideology that promotes individualism—specifically, that the individual is more important than the tribe—and questions the competence of leaders who are native Cheyennes and Arapahos.

Chapter 7 focuses on the organization of Cheyenne and Arapaho dance and powwow activities. These rituals are both political act and expressive culture. They are the product of cooperative political activity in which authority roles have broad community acceptance and in which contributions of others are publicly acknowledged without challenge. I argue that powwow and dance rituals present a critique of the Euro-American discourse that demeaned and continues to demean the Cheyenne and Arapaho way of life. Specifically, the rituals give expression to the conviction that an extended network of kin is preferable to the Euro-American model of kinship, that generosity and sharing are preferable to the materialism prevalent in American society, that unlike Euro-Americans Cheyennes and Arapahos value egalitarian social relations, and that—contrary to the Euro-American characterization of native rituals as pagan—dancing is a legitimate way of praying.

If we are to understand why constituents resist tribal officials' efforts to attain greater sovereignty and why there is such disparity between the politics of ritual and politics in the tribal government sphere, we must examine how local historical experiences and peoples' interpretations of them have articulated over time with wider processes of colonialism, including ideologies of dominance. In the concluding chapter, I argue that Cheyenne and Arapaho experiences led to a local focus on personal valuation or self-validation that found expression in both political individualism and ritual communalism. The seeming preoccupation of Cheyennes and Arapahos with personal valuation can be understood by situating them within the local, western Oklahoma context, wherein Indians and whites have lived as neighbors, interacted daily, and maintained a public dialogue and wherein Cheyennes and Arapahos have been demeaned on virtually a daily basis. In the sphere of tribal government, political discourse is framed in terms of resistance to personal devaluation through confrontation; defense of personal value is linked to the ideal of political reform. In the ritual sphere, discourse is framed in terms of personal value and linked to the ideal of social and spiritual unity. Small victories in prior decades kept alive a nonhegemonic tradition that lends support to the sovereignty movement, and officials attempt to draw on this tradition, but hegemonic influences also gained a foothold in the sphere of tribal government. At the same time, Cheyennes and Arapahos developed new rituals through which they rejected ideologies of the dominant society. Given the historical constraints of the colonial experience, ritual cooperation and public protest against tribal and nontribal officials coexisted, and both came to serve as vehicles of personal valuation.

Cheyenne and Arapaho political history, as I understand it, makes clear that these people, though subordinate to larger national forces, never completely acquiesced to domination and that the larger society did not succeed in completely quashing nationalist aspirations or cultural orientations that conflict with those of American society generally. At the same time, Cheyenne and Arapaho culture and society were transformed, often in ways that forced social reorganization and reinforced ideologies about Native Americans that were exploitative. This study of Cheyenne and Arapaho politics is intended to contribute to a trend in postcolonial studies only recently embraced in studies of native North America, that of examining the complex process wherein both dominance and resistance, and both hegemonic and counter-hegemonic processes, are simultaneously at work in social and cultural transformations.[13]

The Cheyenne-Arapaho case also shows how political representatives are constrained by constituents' views of the sovereignty movement and suggests the need to situate sovereignty movements locally, to contextualize them in relations between constituents and the leaders who take responsibility for articulating tribal or Fourth World goals to the state. In the concluding chapter I argue that the strategies, goals, commitment, and potential success of leaders are as constrained by their relations with constituents as they are by the state and that this dimension of the sovereignty movement should receive more attention from scholars.

Abbreviations

AAG	Assistant Adjutant General
AFDC	Aid to Families with Dependent Children
AVT	Adult Vocational Training
BIA	Bureau of Indian Affairs
CDIB	Certification Degree of Indian Blood
CETA	Comprehensive Employment and Training Act
CFR	Code of Federal Regulations
CHR	Community Health Representative
CIA	Commissioner of Indian Affairs
DHS	Department of Human Services
DOL	Department of Labor
EDA	Economic Development Act
EEOC	Equal Employment Opportunity Commission
EMS	Emergency Medical Service
EOT	Employment Opportunities and Training Services
EPA	Environmental Protection Agency
FBI	Federal Bureau of Investigation
FEMA	Federal Emergency Management Agency
HHS	Health and Human Services
HIP	Housing Improvement Program
HUD	Department of Housing and Urban Development
ICW	Indian Child Welfare
IHS	Indian Health Service
IIM	Individual Indian Money
JOBS	Job Opportunity and Basic Skills
JTPA	Job Training Partnership Act
NAGPRA	Native American Graves Protection and Repatriation Act
OIG	Office of the Inspector General
OIWA	Oklahoma Indian Welfare Act
TERO	Tribal Employment Rights Organization
TWEP	Tribal Work Experience Program

Tribal Sovereignty and the Historical Imagination

1
HISTORICAL TRANSFORMATIONS

1

"To Be Friendly with Everybody"

COMMUNITY AND AUTHORITY, 1869–1902

The Cheyenne and Arapaho peoples lived in family clusters or bands allied by crosscutting ties of kinship during the time they occupied the reservation and for about ten years after a portion of that reservation was allotted to them and the remainder was opened for settlement by American citizens. Individuals sustained themselves economically and had an influence on group decisions at various levels in two ways: by cooperating with and providing generous assistance to other people in the bands and by conforming to the norms promoted by ritual leaders. In facing increasingly pervasive modes of dominance on the part of federal officials and others, the Cheyenne and Arapaho peoples put forth a multifaceted resistance that, in large part, was facilitated and bolstered by the social and cultural institutions in place at the time of reservation settlement. This chapter focuses on the interplay of the institutions of dominance and the strategies of resistance during what I am calling the reservation (1869–91) and the allotment (1892–1902) eras.

Reservation Life

For the first few years after they came to the reservation, the bands hunted buffalo and moved their camps accordingly. After 1876, subsistence by buffalo hunting was no longer feasible, but the band socioeconomic organization was adapted to wage work and small-scale farming. Political intermediaries (chiefs), who interacted with federal officials on behalf of the Cheyennes and Arapahos, were both constrained and supported by band membership and ritual ties.

Band Organization, 1869–76

The men in a band hunted buffalo cooperatively on horseback, and women, often working in groups, processed the meat and the hides. Hides could be made into clothing and tepee covers and also could be traded for supplies, including ammunition (yet, due to the high volume of trade, cloth increasingly was substituted for hide clothing and tepee lining and covers). The meat was shared, even with families who did not have the means to hunt or whose horses were too few to hunt very successfully.

This socioeconomic organization was buttressed by kinship networks that were both expansive and flexible. Not only were kinsmen expected to share food and labor cooperatively, but in-laws helped each other as well. Even American men who married Cheyenne or Arapaho women were expected to follow custom; the army officer in charge of the troops stationed on the reservation at Camp Cantonment

3

(later Canton Reserve) in 1880 noted that "White men who marry Indian women, marry the whole family, generally the whole band."[1] Kinship was based on bilateral descent, with consanguineal relatives categorized on the basis of generation and gender and with collateral and lineal relatives classed together. Respect among kinsmen was central to Cheyenne and Arapaho social organization. An important way in which respect was expressed and relationships affirmed was through gift-giving ceremonies in which one relative honored another or by gift exchange.

Key to Cheyenne and Arapaho social organization was the sibling relationship. Sibling relationships between males were very close; they worked together and protected each other. The sibling relationship between females was similar. These women worked together, and sometimes two or three might marry the same man. Siblings of the opposite gender were deferential in each other's presence, avoiding close contact, and very solicitous, not only of each other but of each other's children as well. Elder siblings were solicitous toward and had some authority over younger ones. The attitudes and behaviors toward an individual's parents' children were extended to the sons and daughters of parents' siblings (that is, to individuals referred to in English as "cousins") and could be extended to sons and daughters of parents' parents' children's children. The terms for "brother" and "sister" in each language were extended to these classificatory siblings.

Parent-child relations ideally involved mutual duties that involved training on the part of the parent and attentiveness on the part of the child. Children could expect parents' siblings of the same gender (that is, the mother's sisters and the father's brothers) to treat them as they treated their own sons and daughters. The terms for mother and father were extended to these classificatory relatives. There was an extension of a child's attitudes and behaviors toward parents to classificatory parents (and potentially, depending on the closeness of the personal relationship, to a "parent's" spouse, that is "mother's" husband and "father's" wife). The father's sisters had a wide range of duties toward their brother's children and were expected to be affectionate helpmates who had specific responsibilities during important moments in a child's life. The mother's brothers similarly attended to the interests of their sister's children. The terms used for mother's brothers and father's sisters were different than for mother's sisters and father's brothers in each language.

A particularly intense emotional bond was that between grandparent and grandchild, who treated each other with affection and defended and aided each other. The attitudes and behaviors associated with the grandparent-grandchild relationship potentially extended beyond the mother's father, mother's mother, father's mother, and father's father to collateral relatives. Thus, relations between children and the siblings of their mother's parents and father's parents also could be very supportive and close emotionally. Children used the same kinship term for all these older relatives.

4

Considerable attention was given to creating ties of respect between affines as well. The families of husband and wife exchanged gifts not only at the time of the marriage but throughout the couple's time together. After children were born, the relationship became even closer, as both the father's and the mother's relatives took an interest in and had obligations toward the children, even if the marriage dissolved. Ceremonial gift giving was expected between the wife and her husband's parents and between the husband and his wife's parents. After marriage, a couple could join the household of the groom's parents or the bride's parents. The choice depended on the circumstances of the families or individuals involved. Thus, a young man with poor prospects might ally himself with his wife's prosperous father. Or an older or prosperous man might bring his new wife to his household. Individuals could marry within or outside their band; individuals might even live with more than one band during their lifetimes. Ties between families were maintained and strengthened not only through gift giving but through the importance placed on the relationship between "brothers-in-law" (a term extended to classificatory relatives) as well. A man and his wife's brother and his sister's husband cooperated in work activity and protected each other; tensions ideally were dissipated in "rough" teasing and gift giving. "Sisters-in-law" (a woman and her brother's wife and her husband's sister) were expected to be helpful to each other. Publicly approved joking, often of a sexual nature, ideally worked to mitigate tension surrounding the relationship between men and their "sisters-in-law" (a man and his wife's sister and his brother's wife), who were potential spouses.

The expected behavior between relatives could be extended to very distant relatives or even nonrelatives (who could be "adopted" as relatives). The symbols surrounding the respect relationship could be used or manipulated by individuals to establish ties with or influence the behavior of others. In other words, symbols of kinship also were political symbols. Thus, social relationships in general and, as we shall see, ritual relations as well were expressed in the idiom of kinship. During the years in which the Cheyennes and Arapahos settled and lived on the reservation, the activities in the household and band were organized on the basis of these social roles and the ideas associated with them.[2]

During the 1870s the Arapaho bands stayed away from the agency to the northwest and the Cheyenne bands scattered to the northwest and southwest of the agency for most of the year. Occasionally they would send a small party to the agency for supplies, including luxuries such as sugar and coffee, from the annual issue of goods guaranteed them by treaty. In the fall and winter, when the buffalo hair was thickest, the bands were eager to hunt, and the traders visited the hunting camps to trade for the hides. In the late spring most of the bands returned to the agency, in part to avoid contact with troops who were pursuing hostile parties of Kiowa and Northern Cheyenne warriors and in part to get supplies. In late summer they left again, sometimes leaving behind small numbers of the aged and infirm who were unable to travel—generally these would be people from poor families who owned only a small number of horses, too few to provide transportation for all their members (the "poorer class," as Agent John Miles, Brinton Darlington's successor, described them).[3]

In February 1873 the 357 families of Cheyennes (2,142 in number) were located hunting in eight bands or camps forty miles northeast of Camp Supply on the banks of the Cimarron River. The seven named headmen were Little Robe, Mahniniicoco (Eagle Head), White Antelope, Spotted Horse, Big Horse, Bear Tongue, and Ben Clark (an American married to a Cheyenne woman). The eighth band was the Dog Soldier band. The Arapahos numbered 1,578. Six bands were formed by 263 families. Little Raven's people (64 families) were located thirty-five miles north of Camp Supply on Buffalo Creek. Big Mouth's group of 65 families was hunting on the Cimarron thirty-three miles north of Camp Supply. Powderface had 25 families on Bluff Creek, and Left Hand had 30 families on a branch of Buffalo Creek. Bird Chief had 70 families hunting on the Cimarron. Keith Poisal (an American married to an Arapaho woman) remained at the agency with 9 families. There also was a small band of Plains Apache, numbering 120 people, affiliated with the Arapahos and Cheyennes at this time.[4]

Decisions that affected the band were made by a headman in consultation with the heads of extended families and important soldiers. Headmen were respected individuals who had both significant economic means and adequate oratorical ability to retain followers. The core of a man's following consisted of kinsmen, but individuals had kinsmen in several bands; thus, a headman had to keep even his own relatives satisfied. An illustrious war record, including successful horse raids, also gave a headman an advantage, for he could lend horses to other men and support several wives to process the products of the hunt and organize other women's work along these lines. Less affluent families relied on invitations from women from prosperous families to help with work or to come as guests and, in the process, receive food.

Although most subsistence came from the hunt, government employees at the agency issued supplies of flour and other food, as prescribed by treaty. Prior to 1876 the food was issued to the band in bulk, and the headman supervised the distribution. In 1876, the agent issued ration cards to families, and each week the woman responsible for the household would present the card to receive the family's food. Rations distributed at the agency included flour, bacon (which was used as fat for cooking), and sugar and coffee, which had become regarded as necessities, according to Agent Darlington. Sugar and coffee were luxuries when first introduced in the 1840s and 1850s, but by the 1870s they possibly helped to relieve hunger pangs when the hunt was poor. The headman received the band's share of the annual issue

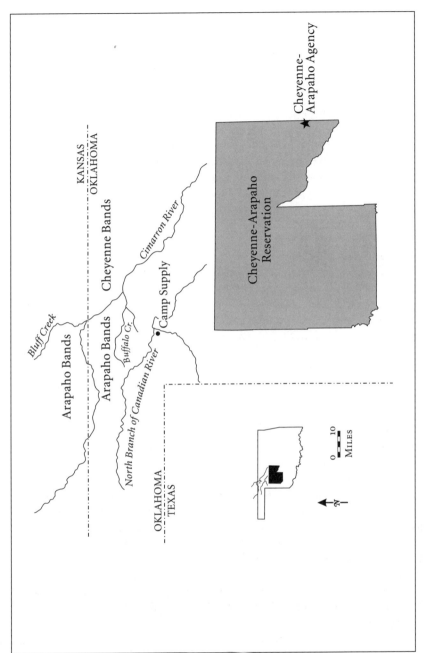

2. Cheyenne and Arapaho Hunting Bands, 1873.

of supplies (as provided for by treaty or congressional appropriation), according to the number of families he represented. The supplies that were issued as an "annuity" included clothing, several different kinds of cloth, blankets, needles, knives, axes, kettles, and pans. The band's allotted beeves (which were sometimes issued to supplement the buffalo obtained from the hunt) also were given to the headman. Cattle were issued "on the hoof" when the bands returned to the agency for the late spring and summer months. If food was plentiful, the hide and choice pieces were used; if not, the entire beef was processed and used. The men in the band chased and shot the cattle; the headman supervised the butchering and distribution, and he received the necessary ammunition from the Indian agent to distribute to the men. It was the headman's duty to disburse these resources fairly to the various extended families in the band and to provide for the "poorer class." In short, individuals felt some pressure to cooperate with the headman in giving labor and in other matters as long as he was viewed as fair-minded. Those who were disgruntled might move to another band, but some did not always have the means to move.[5]

Men's soldier organizations—Cheyenne societies and Arapaho age-graded lodges—maintained order and organized collective work (including ceremonial work). Arapaho soldier organizations, or lodges, were led by seven elderly religious leaders who had earned their position by attaining ritual knowledge in apprenticeship and by enduring a series of sacrifices or ordeals. Arapahos viewed progression through the series of lodges as the acquisition of a series of degrees of knowledge, each more important than the last. The lodges were age-graded so that most men joined the first lodge as teenagers and progressively were initiated into the entire series as they aged. Each lodge had leaders (called elder brothers) selected for prowess in battle in their younger years and for feats or accomplishments in the supernatural realm in their advanced years. When being initiated into a lodge, the novice (and his wife) received instruction from a man and his wife (called grandparents) who previously had been initiated. Thus, there was an age-based hierarchy of leaders who were responsible for directing the activities of the lodges. One of the men's lodges (generally the Staff or Spear Lodge) would be assigned policing duties during a hunt or would be ordered to execute a decision reached by headmen and chiefs in council. Under the supervision of high-ranking ritual leaders, actions of the soldiers and headmen had the force of supernatural sanction, and, since the lodge organizations were age-based, they drew together in cooperative activity men of a certain age range from all the bands. During the Sacrifice Lodge (also known as the Sun Dance), each lodge had an important role in the ceremony, which was the most important communal Arapaho religious ritual.

One Arapaho who experienced the sanctions of the lodge men during the hunting season was Little Left Hand. He described to anthropologist Truman Michelson what happened when he violated the orders of the Spearmen during the 1870s. The

8

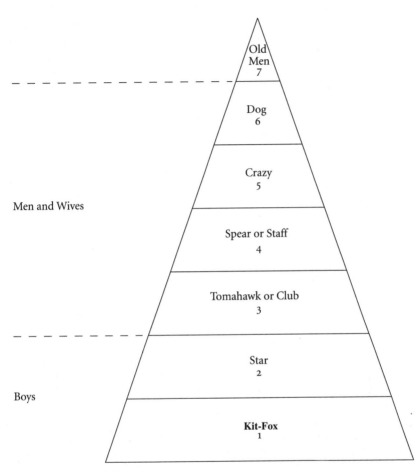

Directors   Seven Old Men
(and wives)

Old
Men
7

Dog
6

Crazy
5

Men and Wives

Spear or Staff
4

Tomahawk or Club
3

Star
2

Boys

Kit-Fox
1

1. Arapaho Age-Graded Lodges.

Spearmen, who numbered about fifty at the time, had the camp criers announce the rules for the hunt. They were "so rough in their treatment to the violators that they were feared by all other bands or societies." In disregard of the plan formulated for a buffalo chase by the Spearmen, Little Left Hand went after two heifers by himself. He told Michelson, "They immediately attacked me, cutting up the hides of my trophies, and cutting up my saddle to pieces so I can't pack the meat to the camp." As the armed men approached him, he called to them that he gave himself up and that he was resigned to being beaten to death or shot. Because he submitted to them, they did not attack his person.

The Arapaho lodge men directed camp movements and, in coordination with the intermediary chiefs who dealt with federal representatives, prevented war parties and disgruntled young men from leaving the agency. They also went on horse-stealing expeditions, guarded Arapaho herds from raids, and protected the agency from Caddo, Wichita, Pawnee, Kaw, Osage, and even Northern Cheyenne warriors. Lodge men also pursued Americans who stole Arapaho horses or sold illegal whiskey. They acted on orders of an Arapaho council of headmen and intermediary chiefs and were supervised by the leaders of the lodges, with leaders of the higher-ranking lodges supervising the men of the junior lodges. Agent John Miles noted that Arapaho soldiers would not take orders from him.[6]

Records from the agency reflect the extensive role that lodge men played in social control. When the Arapahos had their Sacrifice Lodge in 1873, agency employee John Williams noted that "their soldiers had decided that they should move in one body to the agency" and that all the bands traveled together. Lodge men also policed the movements of individuals year-round. Young men were eager to go out to encounter enemy warriors, but the federal government tried to discourage such expeditions, for war parties might encounter settlers or troops, and trouble might ensue. War chiefs, that is, high-ranking lodge leaders, tried to lead such expeditions, but if federal officials learned of an impending expedition, these chiefs took responsibility for bringing war parties back to the agency. Thus, in 1871 a war party of young Arapahos on its way to fight Utes was turned back at the direction of two war chiefs. And, in 1873 Yellow Bear sent a band of soldiers after a large war party, and they brought back thirty-seven of the fifty-one young men. The fourteen who escaped attacked some Poncas; subsequently, Yellow Bear and other war chiefs forced them to surrender themselves to the agent.[7]

During the troubles with the Northern Cheyennes and Arapahos in 1874 and 1875, the Southern Arapaho lodge men assumed responsibility for preventing young men from going north to join the hostiles. A small party of young Arapaho men left in June 1874, and a council was called in which the intermediary chiefs and leaders of the lodges decided to send a party of the lodge men in pursuit; they forced them back to the agency. In 1875 Wolf Chief led a party of Arapaho soldiers after some young Arapahos who fled north with some stolen horses. In 1874 when most of the Cheyennes, as well as Kiowa and Comanche warriors, were considered hostile, Arapaho intermediary chiefs guaranteed the safety of agency personnel, and Arapaho lodge men stood guard night and day.[8]

In contrast to the Arapaho lodges, Cheyenne societies were oriented more exclusively to military accomplishments, although they too had important policing roles during the cooperative hunt and at religious ceremonies attended by all the bands. The Southern Cheyennes had five societies, the membership of which was by invitation. A young man often joined the society of his father or a male kinsman. A man could resign from one society and join another. These societies ideally were to cooperate in camp activity, but they also were rivals. Men from different bands could belong to the Fox, Elkhorn Scraper (or Coyote), Shield, and Bowstring societies, but the Dog Society membership came from one band. Associated with each society were four unmarried girls, who could cook for or otherwise provide assistance to the society. Each society also had four military or war chiefs, chosen for their bravery. Each society had members of all ages, although when a man became elderly, he generally retired. When a member retired, he chose a successor; when a member died, the whole membership chose his successor. War chiefs also could be removed by the membership of their society, and members exerted social pressure to hold in check the ambitions or aggressive inclinations of these war chiefs, who were formidable military leaders.[9]

Because membership in Cheyenne societies to a large extent was based on kin ties, the soldier organization was less effective than the Arapaho lodge organization in unifying and persuading men from all the bands to cooperate. These societies were assigned policing duties but were more independent of chiefs or religious leaders than were Arapaho lodges. The societies' leaders (war or soldier chiefs) had no permanent, overarching authority structure except during the Cheyenne Medicine Lodge (also known as the Sun Dance), when the leaders of the ritual ideally directed the societies. The Cheyenne societies were at times competitive or in conflict, as were the bands. And the Northern Cheyennes, who occupied the reservation during the 1870s, refused to accept the authority of the Southern Cheyennes. This conflict contrasted with the acceptance of Southern Arapaho leadership in the lodge organization by the several Northern Arapaho families who settled on the reservation in Oklahoma. The Southern Cheyenne soldiers went on expeditions against enemy groups in 1873, and the intermediary chiefs were less successful in curtailing their activities than were the Arapaho chiefs. When a large Cheyenne war party went out against the Utes in 1871, the cavalry had to pursue them and force their return. While in the Arapaho case only the occasional small group of young warriors defied the orders of the lodge organization, in some instances Cheyenne soldiers confronted entire bands who would not obey their orders. In 1874, Cheyenne soldiers attacked intermediary (and council) chief Whirlwind when he kept members of his band at the agency instead of joining the hostile bands. Cheyenne families who tired of fighting and wished to return to the agency slipped back surreptitiously, leaving behind their tepees and household goods. Whether the majority of the bands favored peace or war, there were always dissenting bands that could not be controlled by the soldiers.[10]

The Cheyenne and Arapaho Sun Dances were ceremonies that drew together all the bands and soldiers, both socially and spiritually. Although their two ceremonies differed in some details, for both the Cheyenne and Arapaho peoples the Sun Dance was a ritual of mutually reinforcing communal and individual prayer. Through acts of sacrifice (of property and of the body through suffering) and through the dramatization of creation—the creation of the world; acts of culture heroes or mythological beings; successes (for example, battle exploits) that conveyed the idea of supernatural assistance; the renewal of animal, plant, and human life; fertility; and personal transformation or rebirth (as in a change in life direction)—life renewal was symbolically expressed and, in its expression, potentially achieved during the ceremony. The Sun Dance required cooperation, gift giving, and sharing between males and females, individuals, and families. Leaders were individually recognized, and societies played essential roles during the ceremony, so that the ritual reinforced political organization and provided a vehicle for individuals to pursue personal ambition. In the camp, which symbolized a circle in all its symbolic dimensions—the universe, regeneration of life, social unity—all families contributed food to the ceremony that was blessed or made to carry a sacred quality and then consumed communally so as to provide supernatural protection to those who partook of it. Participation in some capacity—whether by making a vow to fast and undergo other forms of suffering in order to obtain supernatural aid, by instructing those who were sacrificing, or by providing various kinds of support to the participants—was central to the individual's sense of well-being and of his or her perceived potential for success in life. In addition, the Cheyenne tribal medicine bundle, the Arrows, was refurbished and renewed on a regular basis, which also symbolized and helped ensure unity and perpetuation of the Cheyenne people. Cheyennes camped together, and the soldier organization helped the Arrow priest and his associates keep order while the rites were being conducted. Sticks representing all the Cheyennes were brought into the Arrow Lodge and received a blessing in the ceremony. The tribal bundle of the Arapahos, the Sacred Pipe, was kept by the Northern Arapahos in Wyoming, but the Southern Arapahos had in their keeping a set of stones that represented the Pipe and that were the focus of ceremonies, of which little is known.[11]

Band Organization, 1877–91

By 1876 Agent Miles was convinced that he needed to find a new means of subsistence for the Arapahos and Cheyennes because the extinction of the buffalo was fast approaching. An indication of this was the steady decline in the number of robes sold to traders: seventeen thousand in the winter of 1872–73 and thirty-five hundred in that of 1875–76; in 1877 only seven thousand robes were obtained. The 1876 figure was influenced by the fact that large numbers of horses died in an epidemic that winter, which adversely affected the hunt, as the buffalo were found only in small bunches in the 1870s and hunters needed fast mounts to be successful. In 1878 the hunt was also very poor. Agency employee J. A. Covington reported that the buffalo had left the region, driven out by prairie fires and American professional hunters. Only men wealthy in horses could travel far and wide enough to obtain buffalo. In 1879 the winter hunt was a failure, and it was clear that subsistence could no longer be obtained primarily from the hunt. These problems were aggravated by the arrival of over nine hundred Northern Cheyennes in August 1877. These Cheyennes had decided to avoid clashes with the army north of the Platte River by moving to the reservation in Indian Territory. Other Northern Cheyennes subsequently followed.[12]

In an effort to help the situation, Agent Miles apparently overcounted Cheyenne and Arapaho population to try to obtain more beef and rations. And Arapaho and Cheyenne women helped support their families by tanning buffalo and cow hides, given to them by the traders. The traders would pay for the work with flour, bacon, sugar, and coffee. But Miles knew he had a crisis on his hands.[13]

In 1876 Miles proposed to the Indian Office that wagons and harnesses be furnished to the Cheyennes and Arapahos and that their wagon freight trains be hired to haul supplies to the agency from Wichita, Kansas. The bands also were encouraged to disperse throughout the reservation where they could establish farms. The hunting bands made a transition to freighting and agriculture but retained their social organization. Individuals still depended on their fellow band members and their headmen, and they continued to accept as legitimate the authority of headmen and soldiers.

In 1877 forty wagons were purchased and issued to bands. Twenty of these went to Arapaho bands. Large Arapaho bands, such as Yellow Bear's and Powderface's, received two wagons. Miles placed one or more wagons with each band so that each would have a means of obtaining some income. In 1879 fifty-five more freighting wagons were distributed. The band members used their own horses, and the headman, who was the official owner of the wagon and owned many horses, represented his band in dealings with the agent and the Wichita supply companies (with the assistance of an agency employee who accompanied the freight trains to Wichita). When a band had made enough trips to pay for the wagon, the headman was paid in cash, albeit less than American freighters were paid for freighting supplies. Miles also had to struggle against opposition from American freighters and others who objected to Cheyennes and Arapahos having the opportunity to freight.[14]

Arapahos and Cheyennes embraced freighting, so more wagons were purchased each year. By 1881 they were transporting from Kansas all their supplies and much of the supplies for Fort Reno and the agency traders. In June 1882 there were over three hundred wagons. Miles reported that headmen who acquired more than one wagon furnished wagons and horses to younger kinsmen and served as the leader of a train of wagons. In November 1882 the train of Arapaho headman Left Hand had six wagons, in August 1886, ten wagons. Several bands joined together to form a large train. An Arapaho train in August 1882 consisted of twenty-six wagons, a Cheyenne train, fifty-seven wagons. The men worked together to cut hay for their teams. And there were other opportunities for group work projects, such as woodcutting.[15]

The hunting bands dispersed throughout the reservation. In May 1877, agency employee Ben Clark reported the locations of the largest camps of Cheyenne bands. Three miles from the agency up the North Canadian River were Whirlwind's 52 families. Up the river two miles from Whirlwind was Stone Calf's camp of 18 families. Two miles farther up was Little Robe's large band, consisting of 179 families. Sand Hill's band of 20 families was twenty-three miles farther up the river. Wolf Face's 32 families were one mile east of the agency, and Big Horse's 20 families were one mile northeast of the agency. Clark also located the Arapaho bands: Powderface had 59 families thirteen miles southwest of the agency on the South Canadian River. Big Mouth's band of 28 families was twelve miles southwest of the agency on the South Canadian River, and Tall Bear's 22 families were one-half mile southwest of Big Mouth's band. Cut Finger had 14 families near Tall Bear, twelve miles southwest of the agency. Bird Chief's 30 families settled near Cheyenne bands fifteen miles up the North Canadian River. Left Hand's band of 23 families was twenty-two miles up the North Canadian at Raven Springs (on the north edge of the present town of Geary). Farther up the river, forty-five miles from the agency, was Yellow Bear's band of 28 families, and nearby were Little Raven's 22 families. Below the agency, five miles down the North Canadian River, were Old Horse's 20 families, and seven miles farther downriver were Row of Lodges's 16 families.[16]

In 1880, Little Raven and his brother Heap of Bears, headmen of one of the main Arapaho bands, the Bad Faces, had a camp of 9 families settled near their brother-in-law Yellow Bear, who led 19 families. They were camped about fifty miles from the agency along the North Canadian River for about five miles, Yellow Bear settling just below Little Raven and his brother. These headmen attracted other families. Sitting Bull (later known as Scabby Bull, when his brother, the Ghost Dance leader, took the name Sitting Bull), who led 10 families, settled there, and his band, along with the other two, formed the core of the Arapaho settlement that became Cantonment District. Two of Yellow Bear's sisters had married Little Raven. Scabby Bull had married two of Heap of Bear's daughters. All the Arapahos who subsequently settled in Cantonment District were either kinsmen or affines of Little Raven, Heap of Bears, Yellow Bear, and Sitting Bull (or Scabby Bull). Scabby Bull was the headman of a band, the core of which was himself, his five brothers, and his brother-in-law (married to his two sisters).

Left Hand, also of the Bad Faces band, developed his own following, and it was this group that moved to the vicinity of Raven Springs and became known as Left Hand's band. Left Hand's following comprised his grown sons, a brother, Chimeo or Wolf Hair, and the sons of his sister Hairy Face (Mrs. Old Sun)—White Eyed Antelope and Black Lodge—as well as Hawkan, Lone Lodge, and Medicine Grass, who were husbands of Mrs. Old Sun's daughters. In addition, people from the Blackfeet band, of which Row of Lodges was the most prominent headman, married into Left Hand's band and into Medicine Grass's family. Medicine Grass's brother White Owl also camped with this band.

The band of Cheyenne headmen Little Bear (1842–1917) and Little Chief (1839–1922), who were co-parents-in-law, camped about twelve miles upriver from the agency. Their band encompassed several important soldiers who were consanguines or married to women in the band: Different Tails, Red Cloud, Bull Elk, Black Kettle, Burnt All Over, Man on a Cloud, Buffalo Chips, and Coyote. Little Bear and Little Chief were the intermediary chiefs of this band during the reservation years. Women in the band also married American men Austin Todd and William Frass as well as Mack Haag, whose father was an American employed at Fort Reno. Thus, over time the so-called mixed-blood Cheyenne community came to be very prominent at Twelve Mile Point, or Calumet. ("Mixed blood" was a cultural, rather than biological, category that did not include people with non-Indian ancestry who lived in the other bands.)

The band of Red Moon (1812–1901) settled on the Upper Washita at the time of allotment. Red Moon was allied with several important headmen and soldiers, most of whom were his affines. Red Moon, Wolf Hair, and Turtle Following Wife were parents-in-law. Red Moon's son Heap of Crows and Elk River were parents-in-law and brothers-in-law to White Shield and his brothers White Eagle, White Hawk, and Chunky Finger Nails. Most of the other men in this band were affinal relations of White Shield, who became headman when Red Moon died.[17]

In winter the large camps dispersed, divided into smaller groups, and went to warmer quarters in the timber. They used willows, tied together and placed on end in a circle around a camp, to make a windbreak. In May many bands began moving toward the agency for supplies. Some amalgamated and stayed in a large camp of several hundred tepees in the Canadian River valley near the agency.[18]

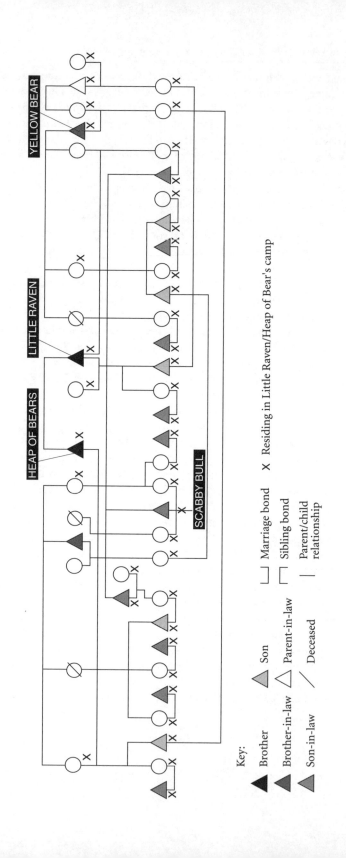

HEAP OF BEARS LITTLE RAVEN YELLOW BEAR

SCABBY BULL

Key:

▲ Brother   ◄ Son   △ Parent-in-law   ⊔ Marriage bond   ✗ Residing in Little Raven/Heap of Bear's camp

◄ Brother-in-law   ◄ Deceased   ⊓ Sibling bond

◄ Son-in-law   / Deceased | Parent/child relationship

2. The Adult Core Members of the Little Raven and Heap of Bears Band and Its Affinal Ties to the Yellow Bear and Scabby Bull Bands, ca. 1880. *Top row*: Behind (wife of Heap of Bears and sister of Red Woman, Bull Going Down, and Singing Woman), Red Woman (wife of Heap of Bears and sister of Behind, Bull Going Down, and Singing Woman), Big Nose (wife of Bull Going Down), Bull Going Down (brother of Behind, Red Woman, and Singing Woman), Wind (wife of Heap of Bears), Singing Woman (wife of Heap of Bears and sister of Behind, Red Woman, and Bull Going Down), Heap of Bears (brother of Little Raven), Yellow Hair (wife of Little Raven), Little Raven, Short Woman (wife of Little Raven and sister of Good Woman, Beaver Woman, and Yellow Bear), Good Woman (wife of Little Raven and sister of Short Woman, Beaver Woman, and Yellow Bear), Beaver Woman (wife of Little Raven and sister of Short Woman, Good Woman, and Yellow Bear), Yellow Bear (brother of Short Woman, Good Woman, and Beaver Woman), Big Head (wife of Yellow Bear and sister of Fire), Fire (brother of Big Head and husband of Bucket), Bucket. *Bottom row*: Black Wolf (husband of Walking Straight), Walking Straight (daughter of Behind and Heap of Bears), Knocking Face (husband of Night Killer and son of Behind and Heap of Bears), Owl (wife of Bear Robe and daughter of Red Woman and Heap of Bears), Bear Robe, All Killer (wife of Yellow Eyes and daughter of Red Woman and Heap of Bears), Yellow Eyes, Coal of Fire (husband of Snake Woman and son of Red Woman and Heap of Bears), Snake Woman (daughter of Arrow and Flying Woman), Arrow (brother of Scabby Bull), Flying Woman (wife of Arrow), Killing Ahead (wife of Theok Raven and daughter of Big Nose and Bull Going Down), Good Looking (wife of Scabby Bull and daughter of Wind and Heap of Bears), Scabby Bull, Traveler (wife of Scabby Bull and daughter of Singing Woman and Heap of Bears), Going Back (wife of Francis Lee and daughter of Singing Woman and Heap of Bears), Francis Lee, Ice (husband of Singing Woman), Singing Woman (wife of Ice and daughter of Yellow Hair and Little Raven), Deaf (husband of Singing in Water and son of Yellow Hair and Little Raven), Theok (husband of Sitting Woman), Sitting Woman (daughter of Short Woman and Little Raven), Theok Raven (husband of Killing Ahead and son of Good Woman and Little Raven), Anna (wife of White Shirt and daughter of Good Woman and Little Raven), White Shirt, Little Raven Jr. (husband of Bear Woman and son of Good Woman and Little Raven), Bear Woman, Old Man Tabor (husband of Curley and "brother" of Scabby Bull and Arrow), Curley (daughter of Beaver Woman and Little Raven), Night Killer (daughter of Yellow Bear and Big Head and wife of Knocking Face), Singing in Water (daughter of Fire and Bucket and wife of Deaf). This chart is intended as an illustration of band alliance and is not a complete genealogy of these families.

In 1886 Indian agent J. M. Lee established farming districts in the areas occupied by the large bands. The policy was to station a government employee (known as a government farmer) in each district to encourage farming. In 1887 there were about twenty-three hundred Cheyennes, including Cloud Chief's band, camped within three miles of the agency headquarters, or agency farming district. Twelve Mile, or Calumet, District, which began twelve miles northwest of the agency, included Cheyenne camps and, higher up the North Canadian, Arapaho camps.

Both Cheyenne and Arapaho camps were located in Bent's District, about twenty miles northwest of the agency—Left Hand's band of Arapahos camped in this district. In Cantonment District were several Cheyenne bands and the Arapaho bands led by Yellow Bear, Little Raven, and Scabby Bull. The Seger Colony District was fifty miles southwest of the agency; there a camp of Arapahos and a camp of Cheyennes had settled about ten miles apart from each other.[19]

Even before their association with the government farmers, as the bands established winter and summer camps along the river ways, they began to cultivate crops on a small scale. Gardens might be neglected when camps were moved, but families returned to harvest and replant. The work was cooperative; women worked alongside men. The agent reported in 1876 that a Cheyenne band and an Arapaho band near the agency each planted some corn, potatoes, melons, and other produce. Some who could not get a plow or hoe used their axes, sticks of wood, and their hands to prepare the ground, plant, and cultivate. The Arapahos up the North Canadian also broke ground and planted corn, vegetables, and melons. In 1878 Agent Miles reported that the Arapahos raised probably four times the crops that the Cheyennes raised. Since Cheyennes and Arapahos lacked tools and sufficient quantities of seeds, the small gardens were impressive. In the summer of 1878, the post commander at Fort Reno, J. K. Mizner, issued plows to many Cheyennes and Arapahos. In 1883 there were forty-eight Cheyenne farms and forty-four Arapaho farms. The bands farmed under the authority of their headmen. Left Hand's farm was forty acres; Big Mouth's, thirty; Powderface's, twelve. The government agents issued farming equipment, such as cultivators, to the headmen, who lent or shared the equipment with the members of their bands, and the produce was shared. The missionary to the Cantonment Cheyennes, Rodolphe Petter, observed, for example, that one stack of hay was owned by several Indians.[20]

Headmen tried to accumulate cattle, which could be used to supplement the agency beef. Young men herded for the headman and otherwise assisted him and shared in the meat distribution when cows were butchered. Powderface told President Ulysses Grant, when he went to Washington as a delegate in 1873, that the government should provide a few cattle "for principal men, not all men." Thus, cattle could be used to reinforce the headman's authority. In 1876 the agent reported that Powderface had bought cattle, paying for them with robes and horses; the Cheyenne headmen White Antelope and Sand Hill received cattle from the army as compensation for horses that the army had seized. In July 1877 the government issued 325 cattle, divided equally among forty "freighting teams" (bands). When American cattlemen grazed their stock on or moved stock across the reservation illegally, headmen negotiated or demanded tolls paid in the form of a few head of cattle. By 1878 the Arapahos had 2,185 horses, 73 mules, and 186 cattle; the Cheyenne had 2,595 horses, 206 mules, and 162 cattle. Americans married to Cheyenne or

Arapaho women also had cattle, and so did some men who were the progeny of American men and Cheyenne or Arapaho women. For example, the Bent brothers (whose father was the trader William Bent) owned 450 cattle.[21]

In 1880, Arapaho headmen Powderface, Left Hand, Yellow Bear, Curley, Little Raven, his brother Heap of Bears, and Cheyennes White Shield and Big Horse had cattle herds that the agent considered to be of good size and quality due to the use of superior bulls. Arapahos owned proportionately more stock than the Cheyennes, and the size of their herds was increasing at a greater rate, for they held their cattle in larger herds than the Cheyennes—several owners kept their cattle together but branded them individually, and some bands used one brand for all the members' stock. They used the cattle not only as a regular source of meat but also—as they formerly used ponies—as gifts or payment in rituals or as part of marital gift exchanges. In subsequent years, the accumulation of cattle continued until reservation grazing lands were leased to cattlemen in 1883, which resulted in the decline of the Arapaho and Cheyenne herds.[22]

Headmen tried to retain followers by distributing the supplies issued to them by the agency. The supplies, rations, and beeves issued by the government helped compensate for the diminished hunting. Beeves were issued "on the hoof" to the headmen of the bands. One beef was allotted per thirty-one people (a "beef band") in 1878, although the Northern Cheyennes insisted on receiving their cattle in one herd for the Cheyenne soldier organization to distribute. The cattle were put on the scale and inspected in groups of ten. When the cattle were released, the headman's representatives pursued an animal on horseback and shot it. The ammunition used to shoot the beef also was issued to the head of the beef band. Sometimes there was a discussion of the distribution among the band members present. In 1888 a three months' allocation of beeves was issued to heads of beef bands, who were responsible for managing the herd and distributing the meat. Most bands had more than thirty-one people, and some did not quite have sixty-two. In actuality the beef policy meant that bands did not get the amount of meat to which they were entitled. In 1878 the agent wrote that "Indians divide their food among each other." This helped to mitigate shortages in some bands.[23]

After 1877 the issue of beef on the hoof assumed special importance in the headman's effort to reinforce his authority, for the government began to issue other supplies to representatives of households rather than through band headmen. Although the headmen complained, in 1877 the annual supplies of cloth and household items began to be issued to women who represented families. Rations of flour, coffee, and other food also were distributed thus. The newly arrived Northern Cheyennes were so upset by this procedure in 1877 that their soldiers compelled the women to pour the issue back into one pile for them to distribute. When the intermediary chiefs and the headmen negotiated a leasing arrangement with cattlemen in 1883, the payment ("grass money") was made to the representative of each household rather than to the headmen; but, these payments (about six dollars per capita, paid twice yearly) lasted only two years.[24]

The soldier organizations continued to be important to social control after 1876. In 1878 Agent Miles organized the Indian police. They duplicated some soldier duties on occasion but did not replace the soldiers' importance. Police tried to prevent horse theft and, along with Cheyenne soldiers, Cheyenne police (some of whom were also soldiers) escorted hunting parties. In fact, Agent D. B. Dyer, Miles's successor in 1884, complained that the police would not "fight their own" but concentrated on catching drunken white men or "quelling small fusses of little consequence where orphans or men with few friends are involved." Among the Cheyenne, the soldier organizations ideally were supposed to execute the policies of councils of leaders selected as council chiefs (not all of whom were intermediary chiefs). As the soldier Big Man put it in 1882, it was a soldier's duty to enforce chiefs' decisions. But the bands were not always in agreement, and not all soldiers were compliant at all times. Agent Miles reported that in 1880 the soldier element had to be convinced to comply with council policy; thus, he thought it a good idea to take two young men who represented the soldier element along with chiefs on a delegation to Washington. And in 1890, when Little Big Jake, headman and council chief at Seger Colony, directed his soldiers to take some horses from the Arapahos, the men refused.[25]

Cheyenne soldiers did compel the camps to attend the annual Sun Dance ceremonies. As the *Cheyenne Transformer* described it in 1882, "Dog Soldiers were out Tuesday killing dogs, ripping tepees and gathering in the tribe for a Medicine dance. The tepees are ripped and torn down in case the owner refuses to take it down and move to the medicine camp." In 1885 Cloud Chief was among those apparently too slow to move to the Sun Dance camp, and the soldiers cut down his tepee and shot his dogs and chickens. And they occasionally used force against Cheyennes who were not conforming to the wishes of the majority. In 1884 Pawnee Man was prevented from farming in an area unacceptable to other Cheyennes; soldiers threatened to kill his horses. The army hired many of the soldiers as scouts at Fort Reno, Fort Sill, and Camp Supply, in part to try to channel their energies into tasks more acceptable to the federal government. As scouts they were able to use their income and other benefits to maintain or augment their influence in the camps. Sixty-three Cheyenne scouts were at Fort Reno and twenty at Camp Supply in 1890; thirty-seven Arapaho scouts were at Fort Reno.[26]

The Arapaho soldier organization also was responsible for policing the annual Sun Dance. And they carried out policies formulated by the chiefs and headmen. For example, the Arapahos decided to cooperate with the federal government's efforts to establish boarding schools on the reservation. Young people who attended boarding school nonetheless were expected to conform to Arapaho custom when in the camps. In one case, a young man who had returned from Halstead, a Mennonite school off the reservation in Kansas, was warned either to conform or to expect his horses to be shot. Arapaho lodge men filled police positions; for example, lodge men Henry Sage and Bull Thunder were police in Cantonment District. In this way, the lodge men's authority was reinforced, and they were able to subvert many of the agents' directives.[27]

The band was the major unit of socioeconomic organization, and ceremonies—particularly the Sun Dance and the Cheyenne Arrow ceremony—worked to create ties between bands. The religious symbolism, the giving away of property between people of different bands, the ritual acts that required the cooperation of people from different bands, and the cooperative activities that made large camps possible all helped to impress on individuals their dependence on the wider group.

Intermediary Leadership: 1869–91

Arapahos and Cheyennes and American officials and settlers all recognized certain individuals as political intermediaries, or chiefs. These chiefs tried to influence the actions of Americans in ways that would be beneficial to their people. The headman could represent the consensus of adults in his band, but federal officials expected to deal with leaders who could represent the tribe or several bands. Intermediary chiefs, as I refer to them, served in this capacity. They were headmen and soldiers (that is, Cheyenne society members or Arapaho lodge men—some of whom might be war chiefs) who conferred with other headmen, soldier organization leaders, and (in the case of Cheyenne intermediaries) the chiefs society (or council chiefs) and then met with federal officials to express their constituents' consensus. In the 1870s, the Arapahos and Cheyennes needed to maintain good relations with federal officials, at both the national and local levels, because they were anxious about retaining rights to a land base, securing adequate provisions in view of the disappearance of game, and obtaining protection from the army from attacks by American settlers or troops. In the 1880s preventing American trespass and settlement on the reservation was a priority.

The periodic outbreaks of hostilities in the 1870s between Americans and groups of Cheyenne, Kiowa, and Comanche warriors made the position of Arapaho and many Cheyenne bands precarious. When Northern Cheyennes arrived in 1877 and 1879, and during the escape of some in 1878, as well as through 1879 when they continued to be a problem for the agent, these Cheyennes were a threat to the government's plans. In the face of the troubles with "hostile" Indians, the U.S. government needed the cooperation and assistance of Southern Arapahos and Cheyennes during this period. In return, the government provided provisions and protections to leaders who convinced them of friendly intent. These leaders were recognized by the United States and native peoples alike as intermediaries who in some circumstances could speak for some bands. Intermediary chiefs dealt with local agents Brinton Darlington, John Miles, and their successors, and some of the chiefs went to Washington D C as delegates to represent their peoples' interests to officials there.[28]

Such chiefs acted only to express the consensus of the people they represented, and they were chosen and maintained their positions on the basis of performance, a performance that was periodically reevaluated. Arapaho chiefs had an easier time than Cheyennes did in retaining the support of their people, in large part because of the supernatural underpinnings of the lodge system. Arapaho intermediary chiefs all were lodge men. Also, in addition to having a more segmentary political organization than the Arapaho, the Cheyennes arrived on the reservation with deep-seated differences between bands, for example in their attitude toward dealings with the federal government. Moreover, the Cheyenne chiefs society was a leadership organization composed of individuals who might consider it their right to challenge the credentials of an intermediary chief, even one from their own ranks.

The chiefs society, also known as the "council of forty-four," served as a model of tribal government taught to the Cheyennes long ago by supernatural means. In its ideal form the tribe consisted of ten bands, and four men were chosen from each to be council chiefs. In addition, four older, experienced men served as head chiefs. Every few years the men could resign or be replaced. A man might choose a successor, but other chiefs should concur. The chiefs were to promote peace and care for other Cheyennes. They were to follow public opinion in making public policy for the soldier groups to enforce. Ideally, a man should not be a leader in a soldier society and a council chief simultaneously. Over time, as some bands were absorbed by others and people separated from large bands to form independent bands, the distribution of the chiefs among the bands changed.[29]

In the 1870s the Arapaho intermediary chiefs were Little Raven, Spotted Wolf, Yellow Bear, Tall Bear, Powderface, Bird Chief, Left Hand, and Big Mouth. Little Raven, born about 1809, was the main spokesperson and a high-ranking ritual authority. Identified by federal officials as head chief of the Southern Arapahos since the late 1850s, he was signatory to the Treaties of 1861, 1865, and 1867. Spotted Wolf, born about 1809, was one of the four intermediary chiefs who signed the Treaty of 1865, and he signed the Treaty of 1867. Yellow Bear was born about 1822, and Tall Bear, about 1825. Yellow Bear was the highest-ranking warrior in the lodge organization in the 1860s, and he signed the Treaty of 1867, as did Tall Bear. The other four men were born in the 1830s. All but Little Raven, Tall Bear (who was also a high-ranking ritual authority), and Left Hand died in the 1880s. Little Raven died early in 1890. Additional intermediary chiefs in the 1880s were Sitting Bull (or Scabby Bull), White Buffalo, Black Wolf (Heap of Bear's son-in-law), White Eyed

Antelope, Row of Lodges, White Snake (Spotted Wolf's son), and Bird Chief's son, also named Bird Chief.

Cheyenne intermediary chiefs in the 1870s included Big Jake, Little Robe, Stone Calf, Gray Beard, White Horse, Whirlwind, and White Shield (from the Cantonment area), all of whom died in the 1880s except Whirlwind, who died in 1891. All were council chiefs, and Little Robe, White Horse, and Whirlwind had signed the Treaty of 1867. In the 1880s, additional Cheyenne intermediary chiefs were Big Horse, Cloud Chief, Little Chief, Old Crow, Wolf Face, Wolf Chief, Red Wolf, and White Antelope.[30]

These chiefs came to the agency frequently to report on conditions and to reassure officials, including army officers. Chiefs offered protection to agency and army personnel on occasion. In 1870 Little Raven reassured officials at Fort Sill, who were anxious about attacks from "hostile" Indians, that he would protect all the Americans on the north fork of the Canadian River. At the Cheyenne-Arapaho agency, when there were quarrels between Arapahos and American employees, the agent could rely on Little Raven to pressure young men to avoid confrontations. In 1872 Little Raven gave the scouts from Camp Supply an escort of lodge men, "as he did not think it safe for them without it." These chiefs took responsibility for maintaining the peace. When the departure of an Arapaho war party alarmed the agent, Powderface and Left Hand expressed regret, and Spotted Wolf sent his son with other Arapaho lodge men to bring them back. Cheyenne chiefs expressed regret to the agent when some young Cheyenne men killed four surveyors on the Cimarron River. In 1872 Arapaho intermediary chiefs impressed a peace commission from Washington with their cooperative spirit and their guarantee to protect the agency. In 1874 Powderface and Left Hand assigned twenty-five warriors to guard Agent Miles during the troubles with Cheyennes who had left the agency. When Miles arranged to lease reservation lands to cattlemen in 1883, some Cheyennes threatened to prevent the grazing leases from being acted upon. Little Raven told army officers that he tried to "reason with" them, in order to reassure the army that there was no need to send troops.[31]

The government also relied on intermediary chiefs to approve official transactions, such as changes in the allocation of appropriations. In 1873 four Arapaho and four Cheyenne intermediary chiefs' consent was solicited to use money from the annuity clothing fund to purchase more rations for the tribes. The consent of the intermediary chiefs was sought in 1882 when Agent Miles proposed to lease reservation grazing lands to cattlemen.[32]

The chiefs also attempted to demonstrate commitment to agency programs, particularly farming, ranching, and the boarding schools. In this way they reassured the agent and helped him impress his superiors in Washington. Agent Miles praised the farming efforts of Big Mouth, Spotted Wolf, and Tall Bear and some of the headmen in 1872 and 1873. Big Mouth's daughter Lump Nose was married to an American, James Morrison, who was an experienced farmer and rancher and who gave Big Mouth some assistance with his garden, but many other chiefs farmed collectively on a smaller scale. The agents were particularly proud of Powderface, who promised to encourage cattle raising. By 1880 he owned 107 head of cattle. In 1874 Agent Miles reported that Powderface and Left Hand had placed forty-two Arapaho children in the mission school operated by Mennonites on the reservation. Among the children were Little Raven's daughter, Left Hand's son, and Yellow Bear's daughters. When children were wanted for Carlisle Indian Industrial School in Pennsylvania, Arapaho intermediary chiefs Little Raven, Left Hand, Yellow Bear and Cheyenne intermediary chiefs White Shield, Wolf Face, Bob Tail, and Big Horse sent at least one of their children. In 1876 the agent noted that Little Raven, Spotted Wolf, Left Hand, Bird Chief, Yellow Bear, Tall Bear, and Powderface had made significant achievements in farming and that Left Hand and the Cheyenne chief White Shield had helped organize an expanded Mennonite mission school. In 1884, when Chilocco Indian School opened in Kansas, Arapaho chief Left Hand and Cheyenne chief Lone Horse escorted thirty-four Cheyenne and twelve Arapaho children to the school. That same year Arapaho lodge men were directed to make sure that the Arapaho school at the agency was fully enrolled. Stone Calf and Little Robe sent children to school in 1886.[33]

Farming, cattle raising, and school attendance were featured themes in the speeches that intermediary chiefs gave in the presence of officials during this era. At the Okmulgee council of Oklahoma tribes in 1875, Big Mouth first told the federal representatives that he was committed to peace: "My brother Cheyennes were in trouble, and I tried to get them down here and get them out of it." Then he spoke about his commitment to the "civilization" policy: "I want the Superintendent to tell the President that the Arapahos want another school. I was among the first to send my children to school, and some of my children can read and write. . . . When I sleep or am awake, I am always thinking about my new farming operations, and what good corn I will raise. . . . I think this country [Indian Territory] ought to belong entirely to the Indians and have no lines drawn." Yellow Bear also stressed his support for schools and farms: "When I get back home I am going to have my children put in school. I will find good land, good water, and good timber, somewhere up and down the North Fork River, and there make my home. . . . I will buy cattle, hogs and chickens." Tall Bear and Left Hand gave similar statements. The main Cheyenne intermediary, White Shield, promised only peaceful relations on this occasion. But in an interview with the agent that same year, Whirlwind, one of the most influential intermediary chiefs, promised to put Cheyenne children in school. At a council with Agent Miles in 1882, where intermediary chiefs tried to prevent the Rock Island railroad from crossing the reservation, Left Hand pointed out that Arapahos had put more children in school, just as the Indian Office in Washington had requested them to do, and that, if the railroad came, freighting by team would be undermined. He stressed: "tell me where I am to have employment." When the Arapaho and Cheyenne chiefs were trying to influence the appointment of an agent for the reservation in 1888, they argued that they had regressed in civilization since the agent they favored had been relieved of duty. In meetings in Washington in 1891, the Cheyenne delegate Wolf Robe stressed that his people were farming, and he linked their progress in agriculture to the cession payment the delegation was trying to secure for the tribes.[34]

Intermediary chiefs helped the civilization efforts in other ways. At the agent's request in 1873, Powderface and Big Mouth testified against whiskey peddlers before a grand jury. Earlier, Bird Chief gave dramatic evidence of his support of Miles's policy: when a whiskey trader came to his camp in the winter of 1874–75 to trade, he "mounted the wagon, rolled a full barrel of whisky on the ground, knocked the heads in, and 'confiscated' such other valuables as they could find, and sent the whisky peddlers to the Kansas line—'poor.'" Powderface made it a point to attend the Mennonites' Sunday School when he visited the agency. And, in 1891, Scabby Bull's brother, Sitting Bull, the Arapaho leader of the new religion known as the Ghost Dance, who in a few years' time became an intermediary chief himself, welcomed the Mennonite missionaries at Cantonment District and told them he believed that they all had the same God and that he would encourage Arapaho children to study the Bible. Another important headman, Row of Lodges, portrayed the Ghost Dance to the agent in a way designed to minimize the fears of government officials, who suspected that the Ghost Dance movement had a militant objective. He said that they prayed to the Great Spirit to make themselves a better people and "to teach them the ways of the White man." When the agents came to regard houses as an important indication of the Arapahos' and Cheyennes' commitment to civilization, many of the intermediary chiefs had houses built (although they used them mostly for storage and continued to live in tepees or tents). At a large Cheyenne camp on the Washita River in 1882, agency employee John Seger was invited into the tepee where the men were meeting. Chiefs White Shield, Little Robe, Red Moon, and Stone Calf "settled themselves for a talk, which was carried on exclusively by the chiefs—the young men paying striking attention. They talked about their past, present and future, and wound up their talk by counseling the young men not to do anything to conflict with the wishes of the Agent or the government."[35]

In return for their participation in the government's civilization program, the chiefs hoped to obtain public support from federal officials and to influence officials' actions on matters of importance to the tribes. Delegations were viewed by the Arapahos and Cheyennes as a primary means of influencing officials. Arapaho delegates Little Raven, Powderface, and Bird Chief and Cheyennes Little Robe and Stone Calf met with the commissioner of Indian affairs in 1871 and visited eastern cities, urging the government to comply with treaties. A 1872 delegation was made up of lesser Arapaho chiefs or headmen and was given instructions by Little Raven, who was unable to go. The delegation in November 1873 was a large one: seventeen delegates with two interpreters. Among the chiefs were Arapahos Yellow Bear and Powderface and Cheyennes Stone Calf, Little Robe, Whirlwind, White Horse, White Shield, and Pawnee. The delegates urged the federal government to prevent buffalo hunters and whiskey peddlers from trespassing on the reservation, and they secured promises to that effect. The delegates also urged the government to provide their people with cattle and to assign each tribe separate reserved lands. All the chiefs requested horses, revolvers, and special clothing (a "Washington suit") to demonstrate the high regard in which they were held by the government. Without these gifts they believed that their people would ridicule them. They received horses, special clothing, and documents that supported their claim to exclusive occupancy of the reservation.

In September 1880 Agent Miles took a delegation to meet with the secretary of the interior and others. In Washington Little Raven, Yellow Bear, Left Hand, and Cheyenne delegates Big Horse and Bob Tail expressed anxiety about protecting the reservation boundaries. There was a delegation in 1884 as well: Arapahos Powderface, Left Hand, White Eyed Antelope, Row of Lodges, and White Buffalo (and two others) and Cheyennes Cloud Chief, Old Crow, Whirlwind, Red Wolf, Big Crow, and Jake (and one other). They sought to have the cattlemen who were leasing reservation land better supervised, for the Cheyennes and Arapahos were losing their stock to these and other outsiders who now had access to the reservation.

In 1891, shortly after federal officials negotiated a cession of the larger part of the reservation, a delegation consisting of Row of Lodges, Black Wolf, Left Hand, Black Coyote, and Scabby Bull representing the Arapahos and Cheyenne delegates Cloud Chief, Little Chief, Wolf Robe, and Little Bear went to see the Indian Office officials to persuade them to keep the negotiators' promise to make the second payment for the ceded lands in cash rather than in supplies. These chiefs knew they had to procure benefits for their people or their reputations would suffer. Cloud Chief said, "If I should fail in getting this $250,000, those other people will laugh at me, because I have been helping the government, and if it does not do this favor to me they will mock me. My people are poor and when I came to the depot to get on the cars there were hundreds of them following me and hoping I would succeed." Left Hand concurred. The delegates also were anxious for the government to fulfill its promise to present the intermediary chiefs who supported the cession with medals and suits of clothing—military frock coats of dark blue cloth lined with satin.[36]

The intermediary chiefs, like the headmen, worked to build consensus among the people. Arapaho chiefs did not take positions counter to those of the headmen and lodge men in their bands. Two incidents illustrate this dramatically. In 1875 a party of Northern Arapahos came into contact with some troops from Fort Hays and Fort Wallace in Kansas, and the troops provoked a confrontation. The Arapahos fled toward a large Southern Arapaho hunting camp and took refuge there. When troops from Camp Supply pursued them to the camp and asked the intermediary chiefs there to deliver the refugees to them, Powderface, Left Hand, and Bird Chief said they would hold a council and use their influence to persuade their people to agree to surrender their guests; but they reported to the army that they had failed. "The chiefs did all they could but the majority of the village was opposed to them so they were powerless," noted officer E. M. Hayes. The chiefs did not want to create dissention in the camp so they dropped the matter. Later, the camp decided to send the visitors back north.

In another incident in 1876, the son of the agency physician was killed, and two young Arapahos were accused. Following the wishes of band members, the intermediary chiefs withheld from the agent information on the two youths' whereabouts. For six months the boys were able to remain in the Arapaho camps undetected. The chiefs also sent the troops to camps where they knew the young men were not staying, in an effort to protect them. Finally, when he realized that the chiefs were not cooperating, the agent arranged for troops to take Powderface, Bird Chief, Big Mouth, Tall Bear, and Cut Finger into temporary custody; after this, the youths were surrendered by the camp. The identification of the two was by a Cheyenne intermediary chief, Little Robe, and an African American man married to a Cheyenne, the latter of whom received an advertised reward of three hundred dollars. Little Robe was threatened by Arapahos, who accused him of lying. Later, the boys' relatives assembled a large amount of property in an effort to obtain their release. Only one was set free; the other eventually was sent to a prison, where he died.

If an intermediary chief did not deliver the benefits his people expected, they might remove themselves from his camp and join another or decline to follow his advice. Thus, when Big Jake, Whirlwind, Red Moon, White Shield, and Old Crow refused to agree to accept a payment for the cession of 1891, many of their followers disregarded their counsel and accepted payment.[37]

Retaining one's authority as an intermediary chief was more uncertain among the Cheyennes than among the Arapahos, for Cheyennes did not have a unanimous view of who was entitled to the office of intermediary chief. In 1873 Ben Clark, who was married to a Cheyenne woman, reported that the Cheyennes "have had a great time making and throwing away [council] chiefs, but Little Robe and Gray Beard are still on the top shelf." Council chiefs who were replaced still might be recognized as chiefs by federal officials and by some of their followers. And, when there was a disagreement, those on one side might challenge the chieftainship credentials of those on the other. George Bent said Whirlwind was influential and trusted, a "real and hereditary chief" whose father and father's brother and father's father's brother were chiefs previously. He complained that Little Chief, Little Bear, Wolf Robe, and Wolf Face were 4 among 140 war chiefs who were not entitled to be spokespeople: "In council, war chiefs and tribe meet and head [council] chief makes a speech and passes a pipe among war chiefs and, if a majority of war chiefs smoke, the proposition is adopted." Officials in Washington were sent competing lists of chiefs from time to time, particularly during times of intratribal conflict. Agent Lee noted that when the reservation grazing lands were leased in 1883, there were two Cheyenne factions, divided over whether to lease the land. One of the intermediary chiefs who signed the lease agreements was characterized by one who opposed the leases as a man "who calls himself" a Cheyenne chief but who really was a Sioux Indian, not entitled to the status of chief.

The Arapaho political leadership had virtually unanimous support, buttressed as they were by the ritual organization. High-ranking lodge men held positions as Indian police, helping to withhold information from government officials. For example, in Cantonment District, Henry Sage, a "son" of Scabby Bull, and Bull Thunder, an affine of Little Raven, were both lodge men and police. In the 1880s, Little Raven was the highest-ranking ritual authority among the Arapahos, presiding over all their ceremonials until he died in 1890.[38]

The only occasion during which Arapaho intermediary chiefs were challenged was during the cession negotiations in 1891, when the federal government pressed the tribes to cede their reservation. Left Hand finally agreed to a price for the land that was obviously too low. He felt that it was impossible to sway the commissioners and that, from his perspective as a Ghost Dance devotee, the problems of the Arapahos would be resolved shortly, when prophesies of the disappearance of the dominant American society were fulfilled. But several scouts present at the council walked out, in an obvious rebuke. Left Hand remarked in shock that they had turned away from him for the first time since he became a chief.[39]

The interest in the Ghost Dance was encouraged by deteriorating economic conditions after the large losses in stock that accompanied the leasing of reservation range and by an associated increase in illness and mortality. The new religion offered the Cheyennes and Arapahos some hope. In the new world promised by the messiah Wovoka, the Americans would be removed and the former good life would be restored. Deceased relatives would be reunited with the living (which was of particular importance to women, who had become devotees in large numbers in response to the extraordinarily high child mortality rate at the time). When the Jerome Commission first met with the Cheyennes and Arapahos in 1890 to begin negotiating for a cession, the new world was but two years away, and the government's opposition to the Ghost Dance was perceived by many to be a sign that the movement was feared by officials. At the Jerome councils, Arapahos came into public disagreement in council for the first time. Cheyenne intermediary chiefs threatened each other with violence, and those who supported the cession demanded that dissenters be dismissed from government employment (for example, as scouts or police).[40]

In the 1870s and 1880s, the extended family and the band were the most important socioeconomic units. Individuals depended on these kinsmen for their livelihood and contributed to the support of their kinsmen in turn. They generally conformed to group consensus within the band, followed the orders of soldiers, and were influenced by the pressure headmen could exert. After the allotment of land to individuals in 1892, these socioeconomic ties persisted but began to become more tenuous, and leaders had a more difficult time generating consensus.

The Allotment Era, 1892–1902

In 1891 the Cheyenne and Arapaho Tribes were pressured into agreeing to accept land in severalty and to sell the unallotted reservation land for approximately forty cents an acre, much less than the actual worth. Each individual living at the time the lands were surveyed and assigned received 160 acres, the title to which was to be held in trust by the federal government for twenty-five years so that the land would be inalienable and not subject to local taxation. A total of 529,682 acres was allotted to 2,151 Cheyennes and 1,144 Arapahos. After this, approximately 3.5 million acres of the unallotted land were opened to settlement by American citizens, who flooded onto the former reservation area and soon outnumbered the Arapahos and Cheyennes ten to one. The tribes also received a cash settlement, part of which was subsequently paid per capita in two installments. The remainder (the "million dollar trust fund," as it was called) was deposited in the U.S. Treasury, and the interest was distributed in per capita payments in successive years.

Allotment precipitated a number of changes, including the further deterioration of the Cheyenne and Arapaho economy and the beginning of a general and gradual erosion of authority and intrafamilial cooperation that was to fully emerge after 1902. Because of the loss of their reservation lands, the Cheyennes and Arapahos lost the means of supporting themselves adequately. They also were completely vulnerable to the predations of desperate and antagonistic Americans. The more vulnerable the Cheyennes and Arapahos became, the more extensive the federal government's supervisory powers became, and, thus, they were increasingly subjected to repression of their familial, political, and religious institutions.

With the introduction of a regular source of cash income paid to individuals, cooperation between kinsmen began to be undermined, though never completely.

Although households continued to contribute to and receive support from the band, income from the rental of a few of the allotments to Americans was paid to some individuals, which gave them a small measure of independence. The agents began to try to make census records, particularly of nuclear families, thereby imposing Western ideas about family.[41]

The agents insisted that intermediary chiefs help mediate disputes over property and, in doing so, support the inheritance regulations imposed by the federal government. In 1891 Left Hand and White Eyed Antelope, two important Arapaho intermediary chiefs, met with the descendants of an Arapaho at the agent's request. The chiefs' task was to explain the new inheritance regulations. Agent Charles Ashley reported that "the chiefs talked quietly to the parties interested . . . with the advisability to be friendly with everybody and to love each other as heretofore," notwithstanding the disposal of property. This proved to be increasingly difficult.[42]

Socioeconomic Organization: Bands, Headmen, and Soldiers

Arapahos and Cheyennes selected individual allotments to create clusters that corresponded to bands. The heads of bands worked to get their members' allotments in one body, near water. The allotted lands were along partly timbered streams, covering nearly the entire valleys of the Canadian and Washita Rivers and forming almost a solid body of Indian lands for eighty miles along the Canadian. Thus the Arapaho and Cheyenne peoples could continue to live in camps and, they hoped, receive some protection from the surrounding Americans. Moreover, during droughts they needed to come together in very large camps at points where there was sufficient water, for the small streams would dry up. On the Washita River northwest of Seger Colony were several Cheyenne allotment clusters with a combined population of about three hundred. At Seger Colony, which had been made a subagency, was a band of Arapahos and Little Big Jake's band of Cheyennes, numbering about two hundred. North of Seger Colony along Deer Creek were the allotments of Cheyennes led by headman Prairie Chief. At Cantonment, which also had been made a subagency, were four Cheyenne camps along the river, two near where the military camp of Cantonment had been in the 1870s. In 1895 the largest camp was composed of nine extended families. Seven miles south of the old military camp was the largest of the Arapaho camps, which comprised nineteen families. Cantonment had two farming subdistricts and a population between six and seven hundred. The main Cheyenne-Arapaho agency, also known as Darlington, supervised several bands located along the north and south branches of the Canadian River. About twenty-five miles northwest of the agency there were Cheyenne camps and two Arapaho camps of considerable size. The Arapaho headman Gun had a camp there, and Left Hand had a very large camp. The Cheyennes and Arapahos here numbered about 350. Thirty miles west of the agency, there were about 200 Arapahos and Cheyennes, including Whirlwind's band. On the South Canadian a few miles southwest of Darlington were about 200, mostly Arapahos, including Lumpmouth's band. There were almost 300 Cheyennes living near the agency headquarters itself. These people included Cloud Chief's band and, twelve miles northwest of Darlington, Coyote's band. North of the agency were about 100 Cheyennes. [43]

Settlement pattern was fairly mobile, but bands camped in one vicinity in the winter and also had a summer camp site, perhaps shared with other bands. Sometimes large bands subdivided to tend crops or engage in other economic activities in the summer. Groups of individuals would often leave the camp in the morning, work in cornfields or other places during the day, then return at night. Families continued to live in tepees or tents; those few headmen who had houses used them for storage. In Bent's District, where Left Hand lived, there were fifteen houses in 1897 and seventeen at Seger Colony. There were some houses in the agency district, as well, but elsewhere houses were rare. One Cheyenne band on Salt Creek in Bent's District had about eight extended families in eight tepees among the trees near a spring. The headman Magpie lived in a wall tent, with six-foot-high sides made of boards and an earth floor. According to the Baptist missionary in the area, he had tables, chairs, and couches for beds. [44]

The opening of the reservation brought extremely difficult times for the Cheyennes and Arapahos. A major problem was theft by their American neighbors, and, while any Indian infringement on the property or rights of Americans was severely punished, American infractions were ignored. Juries—on which Indians could not serve—simply would not convict Americans of crimes against Indians. The U.S. district attorney in Oklahoma did not give priority to redressing this problem. Some of the settlers stole cattle, timber (which they shipped off the reservation to markets elsewhere), and even, by breaking into homes, household goods as well as agricultural tools. They broke down fences so that Indian stock would trespass on settler land and thereby make the Indian owner liable for damages. Settlers who leased Indian land not infrequently failed to pay the amount due; there was no effective redress. Traders were in the habit of taking Indian property as a mortgage against debt and thereby securing large profits when the debt was not paid on time. The agent admitted that the American settlers considered the Arapahos and Cheyennes "legitimate prey" and that Indians could farm as well as the settlers: the Indians could not provide for themselves for lack of equal protection and equal opportunity, not energy and skill. [45]

Compounding the difficulties of the Cheyenne and Arapaho peoples was that after allotment the government gradually reduced support for their subsistence and agricultural development. The loss of land through the cession made it impossible for all the Arapahos and Cheyennes to graze cattle in large numbers. The arrival

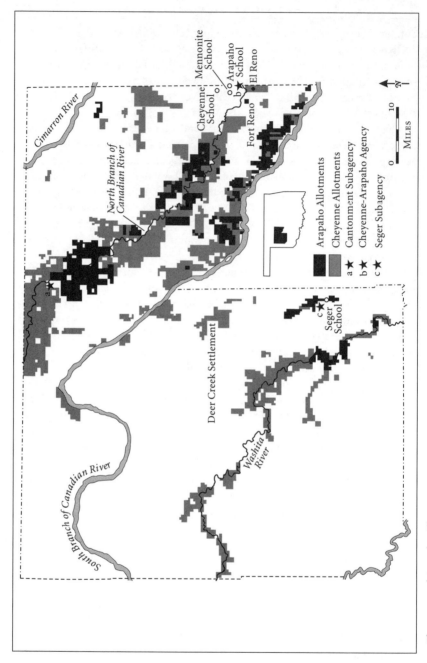

3. Cheyenne and Arapaho Allotments, 1892.

of the railroad on the reservation greatly reduced the opportunities for freighting, and the Indian scouts were disbanded. The government gradually discontinued the annual issue of supplies, including clothing and tools. Rations also were gradually withheld from all but the elderly and the disabled after 1901, and in 1896 beef began to be issued "on the block" (that is, already butchered and subdivided) rather than on the hoof, a change that also meant that the hides would be withheld and therefore could not be sold or used to make moccasins and other items. [46]

In the face of these setbacks, band members continued to share their food and to work cooperatively. A. E. Woodson, agent from 1893 to 1899, and his successor, George Stouch, are clear on this point. Woodson noted that "all eatables" were common property. Stouch discovered that those not entitled to beef issue received a share from those who were. After the implementation of the beef-on-the-block policy, band headmen vigorously and sometimes successfully pressed the agent to give them the entrails and the hides, which they could distribute in much the same way as they had formerly distributed the beef on the hoof. Several bands still had cattle herds, though huge numbers of cattle continued to be stolen. Young men of the band herded the animals, and the headman supervised the butchering and distribution. The headmen's large fields also were worked by members of their bands, and the food produced was shared. In 1900 Stouch estimated that only about 25 percent of the allottees were cultivating their own allotments. Most farming centered on the large fields. Some headmen grew wheat for sale as well as corn.

Woodson noted in 1896 that the Cheyennes and Arapahos had organized into "companies" in the districts to assist each other in their farming operations. Often they camped and worked cooperatively cutting wood or stacking hay. Baptist missionary Mary Jayne described Cheyenne work camps in her diaries. She described Buffalo Meat's camp as the temporary home for nearly all the Cheyennes in the Kingfisher District in April 1900: young men were hunting rabbits, women playing gambling games, old men conducting sweat lodges. Middle-aged or old men often delegated work to their juniors, particularly their sons and nephews, and lent them the necessary equipment. Thus, Sage, the Arapaho policeman from Cantonment, who was part of Scabby Bull's band, furnished a horse for a young relative to go to the agency and bring back the issue cattle for the Cantonment Arapaho bands. Brothers and brothers-in-law worked together as well. Little Raven Jr. (one of Chief Little Raven's sons) had his brother-in-law White Shirt drive his freight wagon between Cantonment and the railroad depot near Darlington. Brothers Sitting Bull and Arrow, Arapahos in Cantonment District, combined their freighting outfits. And women insisted on multifamily camps, so that they could work cooperatively. In addition to their domestic duties of gathering wood, carrying water, driving teams, loading and unloading wagons, and taking down and putting up tents, women helped farm and cut hay, and they sometimes transported freight. [47]

Bands came together in large camps, usually for ceremonies, such as the Ghost Dance and associated Crow Dance and Hand Game or the Sun Dance. In these gatherings, a band would prepare a feast for visiting families from another band or from another tribe. In the camps, there were visiting and recreation, food was shared, and property was exchanged in the gift-giving ceremonies that both symbolized and reinforced social bonds between individuals and that served as prayers for the well-being of loved ones. In giving away, the donor received a blessing: men and women prepared feasts for others as part of a religious vow. For example, the mother of a Cheyenne man who returned from traveling far from the reservation gave a feast on his safe return in 1901. Both men and women owned horses and cattle that could be used as gifts. While men had more opportunity for earning wages doing work at the agency, women raised their own money by, among other things, making beaded coin purses, napkin rings, chatelaine bags, ladies belts, lamp mats, and moccasins for sale to American settlers and travelers.

Although agency officials discouraged "giveaways" and camp celebrations, the Cheyennes and Arapahos presented camp activities to appear supportive of the officials' efforts to encourage assimilation. Intermediary chiefs, acting on behalf of bands, would invite missionaries to come to the camp and preach, while the Cheyennes and Arapahos carried on their own ceremonies and games. The Fourth of July became an important occasion for gatherings of bands, who feasted and held giveaways without opposition from the agent, for they ostensibly were celebrating a national holiday. Even when the bands went to the issue station to get the annual supplies or the rations, they camped for several days, dancing and feasting each other.

Mary Jayne described the Salt Creek Cheyennes' camp celebration during Christmas week. It was held on the "last day" of Christmas, or "The Cut Off Medicine Day": under the "old men's" supervision, the crier (an announcer) read a list of cooking tasks—bread makers, coffee makers, rice cookers, and so on. Then the women came forward to volunteer their help. Three pails of corn and beans were cooking; applesauce and prunes had been cooked earlier. A long table was set up for chiefs and old men, and an oil cloth was spread on the ground for women and children. Then people began to give away property for their relatives—in memory of a deceased daughter, as a sacrifice so a sick child would recover, and so on.[48]

While there were values and institutions that supported cooperation and sharing, there also was increasing potential for individuals to prosper apart from their bands. While deprivation reinforced band cooperation and sharing in many instances, it also contributed to the desperation of individuals who increasingly found it possible to obtain some sustenance apart from the resources of the band. The annual fifteen to sixteen dollar interest payment (on the million dollar land cession fund) and wages from agency work provided some individuals and heads of household with cash. Although values of sharing and generosity prevailed, inequalities developed that could not be mediated entirely. Heads of large households collected more money than others. Land was leased for about twenty cents to one dollar an acre—the agent determined the price. But not all land was leased. During the 1890s there were few leases, but by 1902 about three-fourths of the allotted lands were leased.[49]

The individual's right to the lease income from allotted land was determined according to Euro-American notions of family and property. These changes contributed to instances in which a few individuals challenged custom and to increased conflict among relatives over access to income from land rentals. Conflict escalated between in-laws, especially when a married couple separated, or between two men who were married at different times to the same woman. They might quarrel over who would control the per capita payment of children—the father or mother, the father or stepfather. Occasionally ex-husbands fought with ex-wives or plural wives over access to children's money. Sometimes wives came into conflict with their deceased husband's siblings over his property. Often the agent intervened in family disputes over the right of use of horses or other property; he could use force to enforce his decisions. Orphans might come into conflict with older relatives over property of deceased parents. For example, in one case, the daughter of an important headman with a large farming enterprise and a large herd of cattle and horses asked the agent to seize this property from the male relative who assumed control over the headman's holdings on behalf of the band after his death. She attempted to claim it as her father's heir after she returned from boarding school. Thus, as the Cheyennes and Arapahos knew, competing views of kinship were in play and the agent might impose his views.[50]

Despite the increased opportunity for individuals to exert their independence, intratribal decisions continued to be made in councils, where most adults could participate, although women's influence was usually felt behind the scenes. One government farmer stressed to the agent (from an ethnocentric point of view) that, while it was the custom of the men to hold council, the women's views were always considered and generally prevailed: "There was never a people so under the control of women as these." Women were integral to decision making but had authority in distinct spheres; usually they expressed their views because the subject under consideration involved their realm of authority, whether in the family, in a ceremonial matter, or in other areas.

The agents' reports make it clear that Cheyennes and Arapahos held councils to decide matters such as the use of tribal funds and that a headman's followers remained with him only as long as they felt he expressed their views (or as long as he could persuade them of his). At an Arapaho and Cheyenne council held at Bridgeport in 1899 to discuss an impending delegation, each argument or proposal was publicly announced by criers, and decisions were made when a clear majority agreed. At an Arapaho council at Cantonment in 1900, where the transfer of some children from the Cantonment Boarding School to the school at Darlington was discussed at the behest of Agent Stouch, Little Raven Jr. tried unsuccessfully to persuade parents to transfer children. His brother-in-law White Shirt, a headman with a large camp, and the policeman Henry Sage also tried. Eventually, after much persuasive effort some children were transferred.[51]

Headmen continued to use the resources they controlled to attract and maintain a following. They received beef hides, as discussed earlier, and heavy farming equipment, including mowing machines and breaking plows, which they lent to others. Headmen might also use the land within the allotment cluster of their band for grazing their horse or cattle herd. In return, they were expected to be generous to the allottees who supported them.[52]

Arapaho bands congealed into district communities that camped as bands at tribal ceremonies, such as the Sun Dance. Cheyenne bands were associated but not absolutely parallel with districts. The Arapahos continued to be able to mobilize consensus; the Cheyennes continued to have occasional conflicts between bands, and, although soldiers ideally implemented policies, some groups of soldiers exerted considerable independence.

Arapaho political organization continued to be based on the lodge organization, which had religious sanction. The men's lodges had important roles in the annual Sun Dance, and young men (some of whom were boarding school alumni) were initiated into the series of lodges. The headmen Pushing Bear, Bear Feathers (Spotted Wolf's son), and Black Coyote were all leaders in the Ghost Dance ceremonies. Black Coyote also was the highest-ranking Arapaho policeman. At the Sun Dance in 1901 Black Coyote, White Buffalo, Tall Bear, Left Hand, Row of Lodges, and White Eyed Antelope all had important roles. Among the young educated participants were Grant Left Hand (Left Hand's son) and Arnold Woolworth. Policemen Hawkan and Black Man were leaders in the ceremony. The leaders of the lodge instructed the novices (the men who were going to dance in the Sun Dance to fulfill a vow) not to violate any agency regulations while they prepared for the ceremony, so as not to bring federal reprisals. In 1902 Black Coyote, White Eyed Antelope, Tall Bear, and White Buffalo provided direction during the Sun Dance. Scabby Bull had made a vow and was a dancer, as was Henry Sage and Little Raven Jr. Other participants included Bull Thunder, Left Hand, and Row of Lodges.

Because young educated men like Grant Left Hand were integrated into the lodge organization, the older men had confidence in them as interpreters and advisors. In 1899, when the tribes were attempting to get an attorney to defend their interests in a lawsuit, Left Hand persuaded a council to select "school boys" (educated, or bilingual, men) to represent them in signing a contract with the attorney. Among the three Arapahos selected were Grant Left Hand and Cleaver Warden, the latter a leader in the peyote religion that was taking hold among the Arapahos at that time.[53]

The Cheyennes had greater difficulty singling out a few spokespeople. Rather, there were many leaders of various small bands or settlements, more widely dispersed than the Arapaho bands. Federal officials capitalized on these divisions, the Cheyennes thought. Little Man commented that when they had councils with officials, "some faction is always ignored" because the agent refuses to receive them because they have been "disobedient," and "that tends to break up the council and we do not reach agreement." The soldier role still was important; for example, when his soldier duties conflicted with his position on the police force, Tall Bull resigned his job as policeman. Ideally, the soldiers worked to help the chiefs implement decisions and to make sure that the chiefs presented their council's views. The Cheyennes sent two of "the soldier element" from the Red Moon band on the 1899 delegation as well as intermediary chiefs. Young Cheyenne men put pressure on their elders to give them more formal input into decision making. At a council at Seger Colony in 1895, Little Big Jake insisted on the older men speaking first, so that the younger ones would find it difficult to express a contrary opinion. Later that year, at a large Cheyenne council at Cantonment during the annual religious ceremonies, the bands from all the districts came to consider the selection of new chiefs. Henry Roman Nose wrote his friend Richard Pratt at the Carlisle Indian Industrial School that the "old Indian chiefs have now made young men to be chiefs"—almost one hundred men were chosen.[54]

"Living Up to the Treaty": New Challenges for Intermediary Leaders

After allotment, intermediary chiefs continued to try to intercede with the agent and to take problems to Washington. In the late 1890s the intermediary chiefs represented districts. Band members, while they camped together at various times of the year, were beginning to disperse into extended family clusters. Government farmers employed by the agent were assigned districts, and there they handled leases and supervised farming activity. A few chiefs in each district gradually came to represent the interests of the district rather than the band. The most influential Arapaho intermediary chiefs in Bent's or Watonga District were Whirlwind of the Cheyennes and Left Hand and Row of Lodges of the Arapahos. There were two subdistricts in Cantonment, one for Cheyennes and one for Arapahos. Bull Thunder (one of the high-ranking religious leaders), Scabby Bull, and, by 1898, Sitting Bull were the Arapaho chiefs. White Horse was the Cheyenne chief. The intermediary chief near the agency was Cloud Chief, and Little Bear and Little Chief were intermediary chiefs from Twelve Mile District. Little Big Jake was chief of the

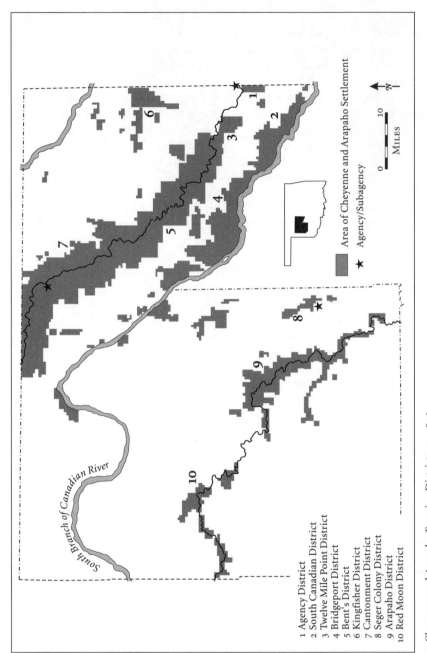

South Branch of Canadian River

1 Agency District
2 South Canadian District
3 Twelve Mile Point District
4 Bridgeport District
5 Bent's District
6 Kingfisher District
7 Cantonment District
8 Seger Colony District
9 Arapaho District
10 Red Moon District

Area of Cheyenne and Arapaho Settlement

★ Agency/Subagency

MILES
0   10

N

4. Cheyenne and Arapaho Farming Districts, ca. 1896.

Cheyennes at Seger Colony, and White Shield was chief at Red Moon District. The other farming districts were Arapaho, Kingfisher, South Canadian, and Bridgeport.

Most of the issues about which the chiefs were concerned were related to the Jerome Agreement. They pressed the federal government to make the payments agreed upon before the land was opened to settlement, and they tried to obtain the money of deceased allottees for their heirs. After the initial cash payments were made, the chiefs tried to prevent the distribution of money from the sale of the reservation lands (the principal, or trust fund, as it was called) and to pressure the government to make the interest payments on time. Another concern of the chiefs was to obtain reimbursement for the money that had been paid to a group of "attorneys" (including ex-agent Miles) out of the funds from the Jerome Agreement. The contract with these "attorneys" was fraudulent in the view of the tribes. The Arapaho and Cheyenne chiefs also raised again the issue of the political separation of the two tribes, requesting that the trust fund be divided and administered separately according to the desires of each tribe.[55]

Midway through his term, Agent Woodson attacked the leadership of the intermediary chiefs. His new policy was to ignore individuals who resisted his orders. Delegations were problematic in 1898 and 1899, for Woodson attempted to influence the selection of delegates. In fact, the principal agenda of the delegates these years was to obtain his transfer. After officials ignored their complaints about his abuse of power, the delegates met with the commissioner of Indian affairs on 30 November 1898 and portrayed Woodson as dissolute. Horse Road, a Cheyenne soldier, charged that Woodson was absent from the agency "all the time," had "sweethearts," and used liquor. Three Fingers, a Cheyenne intermediary chief, said that Woodson went down to Guthrie (a town northeast of the agency) "instead of working" and that, although he insisted that the Arapahos and Cheyennes be monogamous, he himself "goes out with other women and is under the influence of liquor." Big Bear, a Cheyenne intermediary chief, charged that Woodson tried to prevent them from dancing but that "he himself goes dancing at the school."

The 1899 delegation repeated the charge that Woodson was "not a moral man," in the words of Yellow Bear, a Cheyenne, and also accused the agent of graft. Cheyenne delegate Cohoe told the commissioner that Woodson was using the agency grounds for his personal farming enterprise, raising wheat and pasturing private stock. He also said, "The Indian Police want us to say they are employed to keep peace on the reservation and to keep whiskey out but instead they are required to act as servants for the employees." Cleaver Warden, a young Arapaho delegate selected by the chiefs to help negotiate, told the commissioner that Woodson "stands in with the storekeeper" so that an Indian is allowed to use his income only for the purchase of supplies at prices set by the trader, a silent partner of the agent. "In that way they get the drop on the Indian," he said. Warden added that "At one time the agent was financially embarrassed and when the lease money came in he took it and paid his debts with it," thus delaying the Indians' receipt of their lease money until he could replace the funds he took. He also accused Woodson of using the Arapaho and Cheyenne supplies, such as wire and seed, for his own farming enterprise. Robert Burns, a Cheyenne who was an agency employee and was interpreting for the chiefs, supported Warden's charges. The following year, Woodson was replaced by George Stouch.[56]

As they had done before allotment, intermediary chiefs continued to try to convince the federal officials that they were setting good examples in the way of farming and formal education. In describing the important intermediary chiefs in 1897, Woodson pointed out that they were leaders in stock and agriculture as well as "in council." As a delegate to Washington D C in 1895, Cloud Chief told the commissioner, "I am a chief; I work and show them by example." Education was a favorite project of Woodson, and he told the commissioner that it was necessary "to enlist the aid and interest of the chiefs and headmen in the matter of schools." He appointed three Cheyenne and three Arapaho intermediary chiefs as a board of trustees for the Cheyenne and Arapaho boarding schools: Cheyennes Cloud Chief, Little Chief, and Little Bear and Arapahos Left Hand, Row of Lodges, and Black Coyote. They visited the schools, heard complaints, and helped to recruit students and return runaways. At a council on 1 May 1893 with Agent Charles Ashley, the chiefs made an association between the treaty agreements and support of education. Little Chief, a Cheyenne, stated, "Putting the children in schools was in the treaty. I want the treaty carried out." Left Hand said that his support of the schools was "living up to the treaty." On the 1895 delegation, Left Hand and Row of Lodges told the commissioner how they encouraged education. Row of Lodges said they visited the Arapaho school to see if it was properly managed: "We have that duty to perform." He also reported that the school superintendent was of "bad character."

While they promoted the boarding schools, intermediary chiefs also attempted to convince the agents to refrain from interfering in religious ceremonies and social gatherings. In 1892, at the height of the government's concern about the Ghost Dance, Black Coyote, speaking through Jesse Bent, a bilingual Arapaho, told an official that the Ghost Dance was a replacement for the Sun Dance and that they were praying to God so that "he may teach them the white man's ways, show them how to work industriously." He suggested that Arapahos wanted to learn more about Christ and the Bible and that they were making progress toward the "true religion." In reality, the Ghost Dance helped revive and reenergize ceremonies such as the Sun Dance. Chiefs began to assume the responsibility of intervening with the agents to obtain permission to hold ceremonies. White Horse asked for a permit for

Cheyennes to have a five-day dance in 1895. Similarly, in 1901 Left Hand obtained permission for an Arapaho Sun Dance.[57]

As members of delegations, chiefs stressed that their peoples expected them to influence policy in Washington, that their authority and influence depended on it. Whirlwind so stated in 1895: "People blame me and the agent" when there were not enough supplies and when the government failed to live up to the Jerome Agreement. Symbols of the confidence in which they were held by the federal government were still important, as was their ability to convince others that they were obtaining benefits for the people through intermediary activity. The 1895 delegates asked for medals. The 1898 delegations asked for money to provide a feast for their people, medals, and special clothing so that they could "show it at home." The 1899 delegation obtained clothing and money to provide a feast.[58]

The Arapaho intermediaries presented their views through a few spokespeople and did not disagree in public. The Cheyennes continued to have conflict over the legitimacy of individual intermediaries and to present rival groups of chiefs. Disagreement over the Jerome Agreement aggravated conflicts. Some Cheyenne leaders initially refused to take allotments and refused to accept the cession payments. Chiefs who accepted the cession publicly were denied legitimacy by their rivals. This was distressing to many Cheyennes. Wolf Face, an intermediary chief, objected, blaming the agent for "allowing the Indians to pull away from each other." Chiefs were also retired or replaced. Little Big Jake, an outspoken opponent of allotment, told an agency employee in 1895 that "although at one time he was a chief," he had been "supplanted by his followers." School attendance was another issue over which there was bitter conflict. As late as 1901, some were still objecting to Cheyenne children attending school. Little Man, an important ritual leader (the Arrow Keeper), was threatened by Cheyenne chiefs with losing his position as keeper if he continued to oppose the school. When the Cheyennes were attempting to select the delegates in 1898, conflict discouraged some from participating. Although a council at which all the bands were represented agreed to hire a particular attorney to help them negotiate in Washington, those who dissented refused to support the decision and protested to officials.[59]

After allotment, the federal government required chiefs to participate in realty transactions. Determination of guardianship (that is, which adult would collect the interest payment or the lease money of a minor) was a process that involved certification by intermediary chiefs. Often the chiefs would assume guardianship of orphans themselves. Heirship, though determined by the agent, also had to be certified by two chiefs. Although it rarely happened, orphans or their kinsmen might object and protest the guardianship, and competing heirs might challenge the certifiers. Thus, federal policies made it difficult for chiefs to retain the confidence of their districts.[60]

As the intermediary chiefs became less important to federal officials in negotiations over land, chiefs increasingly assumed responsibility for facilitating the gatherings and ceremonies that were so important to the Arapahos and Cheyennes. Particularly under Agent Woodson, these events were targeted for repression. Ghost Dance ritual, the Sun Dance, peyote ritual, and the Omaha Dance (a ceremony derived from contacts with other Plains peoples), as well as large gatherings of any sort, were subject to prohibition. Visiting between districts and gift giving also were banned. Woodson used the threat of prohibition of gatherings to try to enforce other policies (such as school attendance); he would give permission for small gatherings or for gatherings that lasted a few days instead of a few weeks. He withheld rations or beef from families or districts that tried to hold gatherings without a permit. When withholding food did not produce the desired effects, Woodson demoted the Arapahos and Cheyennes who held positions assisting the government farmer in their district, accusing them of not reporting violations. The intermediary chiefs negotiated with Woodson and subsequent agents for permits to hold gatherings and for passes to travel to gatherings in other districts or to other tribes' gatherings. Gatherings, religious or otherwise, assumed a political importance. The constraints placed on them symbolized the general repression experienced by Arapahos and Cheyennes and also interfered in relationships, such as gift exchanges, that underpinned the local political order. This adversely affected the ability of Arapahos and Cheyennes to govern interpersonal relations and to motivate individuals to conform to group norms. Persistence in holding these gatherings and ceremonies, then, was an act of resistance.[61]

The Cheyennes and Arapahos initially had considerable success adapting the institutions imposed by the federal government to their own cultural understandings and social organization, for the federal agent on the reservation had only a limited ability to coerce compliance. In struggling to survive the harsh forms of exploitation that they faced, Cheyennes and Arapahos persisted in cooperating at the band level as they adopted new economic and political forms. Freighting, cattle herding, small-scale farming—all were undertaken largely on their own terms, through cooperative band or family-based labor and sharing of food. Headmen, soldiers, intermediary chiefs, and leaders in religious rituals accepted these innovations and maintained positions of authority by participating in them. New political roles, such as police and intermediary chiefs, were accommodated to preexisting norms and institutions. Intermediary chiefs did not make decisions on behalf of others; they tried to shape and articulate group decisions. Not infrequently, police ignored the agents' orders.

The Cheyennes and Arapahos were friendly to the Mennonite missionaries in the Darlington, Cantonment, Seger, Upper Washita, Kingfisher, and Watonga areas, but the missionaries had little success in getting even the converts to abandon native ceremonies. There was clearly some indigenization of the Christianity learned from the Mennonites during the 1890s. The Ghost Dance prophet and the "Jesus" spoken of by the missionaries were fused in the minds of some Cheyennes and Arapahos. In 1890 one schoolgirl wrote, "Now the Indians are talking of Jesus that he is in Wyoming or in Dakota. They say that he has a tent like the Indians, and herds of buffaloes." Often the missionaries were told that Cheyenne or Arapaho individuals attended Christian services subsequent to a dream in which a supernatural being so advised. The most popular service was the Christmas tree celebration, where gifts were distributed by the missionaries. The Christmas tree was linked with tree symbolism in native rituals, including the Sun Dance. The Cheyenne leader Little Chief, interpreted by a young bilingual Cheyenne, noted: "We must ask him [Great Father or Creator] for a new life. All of you Indian people, look at this pretty Christmas tree. It is a green cedar tree, it never seems to get old. It is a picture of our Great Father, for his life is like the cedar tree."[62]

"While You May Not Know It": Confronting Stereotypes

It was in the agents' interest to compromise with Cheyennes and Arapahos, exaggerate the degree to which they were complying, and blame their failure to comply on the Indians' "natural" deficiencies. Characterizations of these deficiencies formed the crux of a discourse that appeared in the official correspondence of federal officials and missionaries in the local and national press and in Indian imagery in general. This discourse both rationalized and buttressed the policies that worked to exploit native peoples—inadequate appropriations, low wages, below market appraisals of trust land, and discrimination in access to education, health care, and the legal system. This discourse also supported and rationalized the destruction of Cheyenne and Arapaho social and cultural institutions. In the local context, the message was that the Cheyenne and Arapaho peoples were fundamentally deficient and that federal officials, missionaries, and settlers were attempting to help them compensate for their deficiencies.

The creation of the reservation and the confinement of the Cheyennes and Arapahos to an area that did not afford them the opportunity to be self-supporting and that enabled settlers to exploit vast areas of land that had formerly been assigned by treaty to the Cheyenne and Arapaho Tribes were portrayed as means for the "preservation of peace." Consistently, written and quoted remarks referred to the Cheyennes and Arapahos as "childish" people who could not or would not be industrious workers and who "wasted" resources. Labor was "unknown to them," said the commissioner of Indian affairs in 1871, and therefore they had to be taught to cook, make garments, and so on. In 1872, the local agent noted that the Cheyennes and Arapahos had a "constitutional aversion to labor." Portrayed as government "wards," these "willful children" were consumers rather than producers in

1877. In 1884 the local agent charged that Cheyenne and Arapaho men did "literally nothing." In 1885 the agent argued that they "have no use for 4,297,771 acres of valuable land," that their "aversion to manual labor" was a defect of Indian character, and that they would not take care of their cattle. In 1893 Agent Woodson wrote that the Cheyennes and Arapahos collected in "villages where they are accustomed to idle away their time when they ought to be at home and at work. When congregated they engage in dancing, gambling, and other indolent habits." And, in 1898, "The prejudice manifested throughout the West toward the Indian is due largely to the fact that he is a consumer and not a producer." Even the editor of the *Cheyenne Transporter*, a newspaper published locally for businessmen and cattlemen, who generally was sympathetic to the Cheyennes and Arapahos (on whose goodwill the businessmen and cattlemen depended), occasionally echoed this discourse. In 1882 he commented that Agent Miles was "teaching them [the Cheyennes and Arapahos] to be self-reliant." In an 1883 article he described them as "weak and ignorant," suggesting that local "Whites" "would teach them by object lesson that what is worth doing at all is worth doing well." That same year the Mennonite missionary S. S. Haury wrote, "Indians are from childhood up encouraged to 'slug in sloth and sensual delight.' This is part of their religion." Other Mennonite missionaries described the Cheyennes and Arapahos as "in general like children who are in need of instruction and guidance in everything." They also found them to be "lazy." J. J. Kliewer commented, "Their life of idleness must be changed to a life of labor." In 1894 Rodolphe Petter described them as "indolent and slothful," and J. S. Krehbiel complained, "What will the knowledge of labor profit the Indian, as long as he is not willing to work?"[63]

After federal officials no longer feared for their safety and could use more coercive means to enforce policies, Cheyenne and Arapaho leaders were castigated as dictators who opposed progress. Woodson characterized the chiefs in 1895 as assuming "an air of censorship and control . . . so that the younger and more intelligent Indians have no opportunity to be heard." He described the chiefs as "always growling and wanting more." Several agents suggested that the chiefs took more than their share of food and goods. In 1897, the agent argued that "tribal government" was a "heavy handicap to the individual who strives to acquire independence" and to the "progress of these Indians."[64]

The federal government's controls over people and resources consistently were portrayed as "humane" and generous "Christian efforts." The agency programs were described as the "Great White Road," the goal of which was to make the Cheyennes and Arapahos "self-supporting." The president was a "Great Father" and a "friend" to the Cheyenne and Arapaho peoples. The *Cheyenne Transporter* argued that the government boarding schools "elevated" girls by training them to be more than "hewers-of-wood and drawers-of-water." In 1885 the agent justified repressive policies by proclaiming, "It is our duty to relieve the suffering" by forcing Cheyennes and Arapahos to obey the dictates of the Office of Indian Affairs (later known as the Bureau of Indian Affairs). Missionary Haury supported the policies of breaking up "tribal communities" and separating individual families from bands; he insisted that the missionaries were trying to "elevate the Indians." Agent Woodson justified the particularly harsh measures he took—withholding rations and wages, for example—and promoted leasing land to settlers and controlling the money received by Cheyennes and Arapahos for these leases by telling the commissioner that the Cheyennes and Arapahos were "greatly dependent on their agent" and on the aid of "a generous government" and that they were "not competent to make intelligent use of their money." He thought they needed "an object lesson" from "energetic and industrious white neighbors." He wrote, "Like children, they succumb when a will power greater than their own is exercised."[65]

The Cheyennes and Arapahos were aware of this discourse, for the writings of agents, the sermons of missionaries, and newspaper stories were interpreted to them, at first by English-speaking spouses and, by the 1880s, by several children and youths who were bilingual and literate. Intermediary chiefs (and others whose words were not so frequently recorded) refuted this discourse directly, but of equal significance are the more indirect kinds of challenges that indicate that Cheyennes and Arapahos refused to abandon the band organization and the religious rituals on which they relied while attempting to appear cooperative with the dominant society.

There is a clear element of pose in the way that Cheyennes and Arapahos characterized the innovations in their lives during this period. New economic ventures that provided vehicles for intraband cooperation and support for the headman role were cast as commitments to civilization. Thus, chiefs conspicuously pointed to their peaceful intent, their accomplishments as farmers, and their support of schools and missions. Yet, while missionaries were welcomed into the Arapaho camps generally and to many Cheyenne camps, participation in native religious ceremonies continued unabated. As Baptist missionary Mary Jayne complained, native ceremonies might be postponed until the missionaries were out of hearing but not abandoned. Mennonite missionaries reported to their superiors that the Arapahos tried to keep the Sun Dance "secret from the agent." In characterizing the Ghost Dance as a means to learning "the ways of the White man," Row of Lodges and Jesse Bent clearly were using their understanding of the fears of officials (of Ghost Dance militancy) to obtain more favorable treatment for their people. While houses were in demand, the tepee was not abandoned as the family's place of abode. Dances could be held without fear of reprisals if they were portrayed as Fourth of July celebrations or as bring-the-children-to-school gatherings. Many of the children who were brought to boarding school were orphans who, although incorporated into the families of their relatives, had fewer advocates in the camps to oppose their being taken away. Chiefs who sent children to these schools, and particularly to Carlisle, could use the occasion of visits to children (ostensibly to promote education) to visit officials in Washington and elsewhere and to try to influence policy. Most of these children were reintegrated into the band organization when they returned.[66]

When Cheyenne and Arapaho chiefs directly challenged officials, they often did so by appropriating elements of the dominant ideology. For example, in the delegates' attempt to counter Agent Woodson's disparaging description of Cheyennes and Arapahos, they turned his own discourse against him: Woodson was lazy, neglected his work, was fiscally imprudent, and fell short of the ideals of monogamy and sobriety. He spent idle hours dancing while trying to prevent the Cheyennes and Arapahos from having dances. This same tactic was used in regard to local boarding school superintendents and even to missionary Haury, who was caught in an adulterous relationship.

Cheyenne and Arapaho chiefs gave voice to a critique of the dominant discourse that makes clear they were aware of the lack of fit between their lived experience and the expressed ideals of civilization with their associated claims of material and spiritual improvement. Delegates insisted that the reservation had not promoted peace because Americans continued to trespass. They refuted the idea that government representatives were capable of managing their money and their resources, pointing out that these same officials did not protect Cheyenne and Arapaho property or secure fair prices for leases. Arrow complained to the Mennonites that settlers were "robbing them of their land, their freedom, and their children." As they saw it, the promotion of individualism was a device to defraud the Cheyennes and Arapahos; the tribal organization offered protection to individuals. Thus, the Cheyennes and Arapahos chose allotments close together so that the settlers could not live in close proximity to them. The chiefs consistently argued that their labor was exploited—both in that adults were paid less than non-Indians for the same work and that schoolchildren were forced to work for non-Indians with little compensation. Chiefs charged that girls became "hewers" and "drawers" for the white government employees. The delegates attributed the decline in livestock to theft by settlers, not to indolence on the part of their people. As for Christianity, Cheyennes and Arapahos recognized the disparity between Christian ideals and actual behavior. As one Cheyenne told Reverend Petter, "When you come I will call the White people of our neighborhood together, so that you may tell them of God too; I believe they know less of Him than we do, because they are doing so many bad things, and are trying to teach us that which is bad too." Left Hand made these remarks in 1901: "We old Indians have our God, and while you may not know it, it is the same God as yours. We love to worship him as well as our white brothers do, though our methods of worship widely differ. . . . Among white people you will find many different ways of worshiping, and many varied beliefs concerning the hereafter, and they are all tolerated. . . . Why should we not be allowed to worship God in our own way?" Even the schoolchildren, subject to close supervision and pressure to accept American views of the world, knew the reality of their circumstances. Walter Road Traveler, an Arapaho pupil, wrote: "We are compelled to talk only English but most don't want to leave the Indian language."[67]

The delegates always framed their comments in the context of the treaty relationship between the tribes and the federal government. In doing so, they refuted the notion that the Cheyennes and Arapahos were the recipients of charity or beneficence. Thus, Little Raven had argued that the Treaty of 1867 guaranteed agricultural support and that federal representatives, not the Cheyennes and Arapahos, were ineffective producers. Support of boarding schools was always cast as a symbol of the treaty relationship that bound both native and American peoples, not as a commitment to a rejection of tribal life or an admission that the Cheyennes and Arapahos were backward. By keeping their part of the bargain, the chiefs hoped that the United States would fulfill the promises that the tribes believed had been made.

2
"They Are Trying to Make Us Stingy"
THE LAND SALE ERA, 1903–27

Rodolphe Petter, the Mennonite missionary to the Cantonment Cheyennes, observed firsthand the social consequences of the economic, political, and ritual constraints confronting the Arapahos and Cheyennes: "They say everything is against them and have many complaints, accuse one another, and get angry with one another." He added, "This unrest and dissatisfaction we delight to see, knowing that it may cause them to despair in themselves and lead them to acceptance of Christ." Petter was witness to the implementation of federal policies that stripped the Cheyennes and Arapahos of their lands and property and that contributed to a host of social problems. His remarks, made at the time settlers were moving onto the ceded reservation, also illustrate the tone of the discourse used by federal officials, missionaries, and local settlers to characterize the plight of native peoples—namely, that the remedy for their problems lay in their conformity to American expectations (in Petter's terms, "conversion to Christianity"). Petter also alludes to the "unrest" or overt social conflict that developed as a consequence of the federal directives and that intensified as the twentieth century wore on. The unrest he speaks of became escalated many times over after Congress passed the Dead Indian Land Act on 27 May 1902, for although in 1891 the Cheyennes and Arapahos were promised that their allotments would remain in trust for twenty-five years, this 1902 legislation allowed for the sale of the lands of allottees after they died. Thus began the loss to the tribes of their land base. Subsequently, through the Burke Act of 1906, the federal government encouraged allottees to obtain a fee patent on their land so that it could be taxed or sold; this escalated the loss of Cheyenne and Arapaho land. By 1928 about 63 percent of the land had been sold.[1]

Available, inexpensive land attracted thousands of new settlers, whose activities undercut the economic position of the native population. The proximity of Euro-American and African American settlers also exposed the Cheyennes and Arapahos to frequent face-to-face contact and to a discourse about "the Indian" that appeared, among other places, in local newspapers. This Indian imagery, largely demeaning, challenged the Cheyenne and Arapaho communities' way of life as well as factored in the choices Cheyennes and Arapahos made in interpreting and responding to the opportunities and restrictions of their new circumstances. For leaders, representing the interests and the image of their constituents was a difficult task, but a task still assumed by chiefs.

This chapter begins with a description of the implementation of the legislation and policies facilitating the loss of Cheyenne and Arapaho lands, then explores two central questions. What were the social consequences of these new policies? And, if there was resistance to the policies, what forms did Cheyenne and Arapaho resistance take, and is there evidence of resistance to the rationalizing ideology as well as to the efforts to divest them of their lands, to deny them access to their income from their lands, and to Americanize them generally?

Indian Land Policy and Its Social Consequences

The loss of the allotted lands, along with federal policies that ostensibly promoted the assimilation of Cheyenne and Arapaho individuals into mainstream society, encouraged economic individualism because cooperative agricultural ventures became less feasible. Moreover, the new legislation had the effect of creating economic differentials, particularly in the ownership of land and in income. Such differentials and the trend toward economic individualism helped create the unrest that Reverend Petter described.

After the reservation was opened in April 1892, 25,000 American citizens flooded onto the reservation and established land claims where Indians had not taken allotments. Small towns were established at that time or just prior to the opening. After 1902 there was more land available, more settlers came, and the town populations swelled. In 1889 El Reno and Kingfisher opened. The town of Watonga opened in 1892 and by 1902 had a population of about 1,000. In 1899 Geary, near the Arapahos and Cheyennes in Watonga District, had a population of 300; in 1902, 2,650. Amid the allotments in Cantonment District, Eagle City opened with a population of 2,000 in 1902. To the southwest, Clinton opened in 1903. And Canton opened with less than 600 in 1905.

Townspeople and other settlers aggressively pursued the "business" of the Arapahos and Cheyennes by giving them credit and accepting mortgages on their property and by other financial dealings that worked to defraud them of their property, money, and land. After the passage of the Burke Act, federal officials could classify individuals as "competent" and thereby remove the trust restrictions on allotted land. Then the land would be subject to local taxation or be available for sale. Speculators, sometimes aided by agency officials, targeted "competent" individuals and purchased their land, often for less than market value. The superintendents at Darlington, Cantonment, and Colony agencies followed instructions from Washington stating that the Cheyennes' and Arapahos' income from land leasing and sales could be paid to them only in small, monthly amounts. In this way, they were dependent on credit and made vulnerable to local entrepreneurs, who charged usurious rates of interest and purchased Cheyenne and Arapaho property at prices far below market value. As the fortunes of many citizens of Oklahoma were made, those of the Cheyennes and Arapahos declined.[2]

The reduction of the Cheyenne and Arapaho land base resulted in subsistence farming and group work parties becoming less feasible. Families tried to retain at best a part of one member's allotment as a homeplace. The household grew smaller, though often comprising three generations, and increasingly over time the large camps formed around ceremonial obligations and holidays for several days at a time rather than for several weeks or months. Wage work took on more importance than subsistence farming. Jobs were available in seasonal farm work, railroad labor, road repair, and, for women, domestic service as well as farm work. The agency began using funds earmarked for rations to hire men to work on agency projects. By the 1920s, there was insufficient land for individuals to make an adequate living from cooperative agricultural efforts with the other families in their district (map 5 shows the extent of the loss of land in the Canton Arapaho community). Instead, most individuals hired out to neighbors (usually small settler family farms) either seasonally or on a fairly regular basis. In fact, the main source of family income came to be the leasing and sale of Indian lands to local settlers and businessmen.

Reliance on wage work and the sale and leasing of land made for unequal access to the cash with which to purchase farm machinery, clothing, and other desired goods. Until after the passage of the Burke Act in 1906, everyone still received two interest payments from the million dollar trust fund. The Dead Indian Land Act permitted individuals who inherited land to sell it; and since some individuals inherited more land than others, the potential for economic differentials was great. People born after 1892 owned no land unless they inherited some. By 1907 and thereafter, there was a great deal of heirship land that could potentially be sold, so the amount of cash involved was considerable. For example, in the Darlington District in December 1902, 454 of the 1,144 Arapaho and 685 of the 2,141 Cheyenne allotments belonged to deceased allottees. In a conference with the superintendent of the Darlington agency, the Arapaho chief Hail tried to explain the social repercussions of the federal policies regarding trust land and income: "One gets the use of the money while the other one suffers."[3]

Individual income from trust property (referred to as Individual Indian Money, or IIM) ranged from very little to thousands of dollars. For example, for the years 1912, 1917, 1922, and 1927, 25 percent of the Arapaho households in Canton District had high incomes from rentals and sales of land. Another 25 percent had almost no such income. In 1912, annual income of the upper 25 percent ranged from $836 to $2,966; in 1917 (as land sales escalated), from $1,616 to $6,573; in 1922, from $2,456 to $7,224; in 1927 (when most of the land had been sold), from $562 to $6,513. During these years, the income of the lower 25 percent ranged from zero to $175 in 1912 and from zero to $1 in 1927.[4]

The more prosperous families clearly had a higher standard of living than most. Jess Rowlodge's father, Row of Lodges, was a headman and an intermediary chief who was relatively prosperous by Arapaho standards. As Mr. Rowlodge recalled,

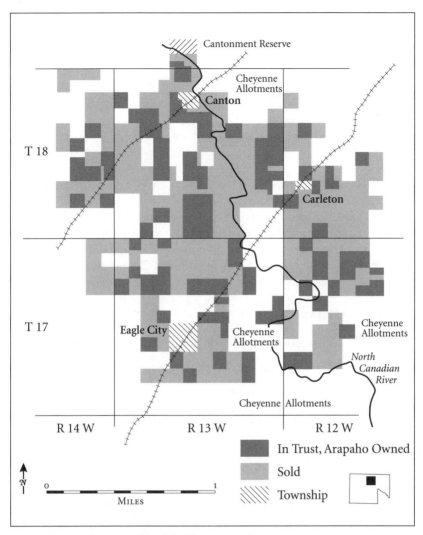

Cantonment Reserve

Cheyenne
Allotments

Canton

Carleton

T 18

T 17

Eagle City

Cheyenne
Allotments

Cheyenne
Allotments

North
Canadian
River

Cheyenne Allotments

R 14 W   R 13 W   R 12 W

In Trust, Arapaho Owned

Sold

Township

0   1
MILES

N

5. Arapaho Lands in Trust and Lands Sold, Canton, 1928.

for a few years after the reservation was opened, the settlers were greatly dependent on Indian farmers: "They'd come over and buy their garden stuff, you know, chickens. And borrow plows to mark off their land. . . . My dad had about a two-acre garden—potatoes, corn, onions, radishes, and a lot of things. . . . They'd come any time of day and have their sack, and get corn, potatoes, mostly, and onions. . . . They paid a good price for them. . . . And that fall when they started getting their corn and pumpkins these White folks would come over in wagons and buy pumpkins and chickens, and maybe a pig or two." On the other hand, Myrtle Lincoln's parents were deceased, and she was cared for first by a widowed "grandmother," then by her "uncle" (her mother's "sister's" husband): "It was hard, way back. I know I was raised pitiful by old people. Half the time I was barefooted—didn't have no shoes. And when I got to the age where I could take care of myself, why, I tried to furnish my clothes. When I went to school I was better off [because of the meals and clothing furnished by the school]." She married a young man of little means and spent her married life living in a tent in a large camp during the winter and various places where her husband could get work in the fields during the summer.[5]

The economic disparities became even more extreme after the Burke Act because individuals could acquire large sums of money through land sale and could receive their pro-rata share of the trust fund. In 1917 a Competency Board, comprised of BIA officials, visited every Cheyenne and Arapaho adult and made a determination as to that individual's "competency." In general, young men in their twenties were found to be competent, and approval was given for the issue of a patent-in-fee title to their land. This approval was given over the objections of individuals who did not want a fee patent. In a few cases, young men judged noncompetent, but who expressed the desire for fee patents, received them. Usually, married and single women were declared noncompetent; the effect of this classification of married women was to allow them to retain some land for a homeplace in the likely event that their husband's land was sold. Elderly people were also classified as noncompetent. What seems clear from the commission's journal is that educational background was not a factor in the assessment of an individual's competency. Of course, all individuals in their twenties would have attended at least a few years of school by 1917.

In the case of one Arapaho family, a widower with two children, the father had deeded 80 acres to his children and had leased his other 80 acres, which provided one hundred dollars in annual income. He had attended the government boarding school for five years, and he was farming "a little corn." He was deemed noncompetent by the commission, but as he expressed a desire for a fee patent, he was issued one. In 1923, the superintendent reported that this man had sold 80 acres and was leasing the remaining 80, having given up farming. He and his second wife had three children and were living in a tent. In another case in 1917, an unmarried Arapaho man owned 160 acres and was heir to another 160 acres. He leased his land for pasture for forty-five dollars a year and owned a three-room house on his heirship land. He had attended the government boarding school for five years, studied three years at Haskell Institute in Kansas, and worked as a carpenter at the government boarding school. He was declared competent and, despite his objections, given a patent-in-fee. In 1922, the superintendent reported that the man was married with three children, had no home, and had "nothing to work with." In 1925 he and his family lived on a relative's land: "They have no home, he having received a patent in fee for his land and disposed of it."[6]

Household surveys done by the B I A during the 1920s reveal how disparities in landownership over time created widely diverging lifestyles. The 1922–23 survey among the Cheyennes and Arapahos at Cantonment subagency identified 60 percent of the families living in a house on their own land and 6 percent who were residing with another family and contributing income to the support of the host family. All these families were headed by elderly persons with an allotment or inherited allotments, or both (usually from children, siblings, or spouses), that produced income. Young people—either too young to have received an allotment or deemed competent and pressured into selling their allotments—by and large were either living with parents and helping them farm or living with parents and working for wages. A few were heir to enough property to have a homeplace, and 10 percent were without land or funds, camping on a headman's land and working for wages when they could find a job.

Detailed descriptions of these households identified property and stock, condition of the house, and economic activity of family members. Two cases from the 1925 survey will serve as examples of families in good economic straits. One prosperous family by Cantonment standards consisted of a middle-aged Arapaho man, his wife and five children, and his elderly father, who had substantial income. They lived in a new four-room house. On this homeplace there also were a one-room bungalow, cement cellar, barn, chicken house, pump and windmill, and granary. The family owned two horses, six ponies and colts, a cow, and twenty-four chickens, and they had an orchard of peach, pear, and apricot trees, plus thirty blackberry bushes and thirteen grape bushes. They also had considerable farming equipment: a wagon, a set of harness, a walking plow, a lister, a hay rake, a harrow, a cultivator, a corn sled, a riding plow, and a John Deere tractor. They cultivated 30 acres and also owned a new Ford car and had an old Ford in reserve. Another family, headed by an elderly Arapaho, consisted of this man, his wife, his adult son and his wife, and two children in boarding school. On a 320-acre place, they had a four-room house with a porch, barn, six horses, eight ponies and colts, hogs,

chickens, and two cows. They owned three sets of harness, one wagon, one grain binder, one harrow, one buggy, and a Ford car.

"On the way down" the scale was a middle-aged Arapaho man and his wife, who in 1917 owned 160 acres, which they leased for two hundred dollars annually, and a two-room house. Over his objections, the husband was declared competent and given a fee patent on the land. In 1925 he and his wife reportedly had a three-room house with a cement cellar, a barn, a granary, a well, and an orchard with plum and peach trees and grape bushes. They owned two horses, two ponies, ten chickens, one wagon, one set of harness, and a Ford car. But Superintendent E. J. Bost noted that the man had sold his fee-patented land and purchased the 80 acres they were on and that the family was about to lose the land because it was heavily mortgaged. He wrote: "I do not know any way for him to get money to pay off the mortgage."

Three cases from the 1925 survey will serve to illustrate the circumstances of families with little or no land. The superintendent reported that one Cheyenne couple at Cantonment had been allowed by a former superintendent to sell their own allotments and all their inherited interests in other allotments. "They now have nothing. They have no home. They live in a tent on his sister's land. He works some at day labor." Of another Cheyenne he noted that he and his wife had no land. The family lived with the husband's grandparents and relied on "the old folk's income." Of another Cheyenne couple he wrote that "he and his wife have no land. They sometimes pitch their tent on the land of some of their kin folks." A Carlisle alumnus, the wife received a patent-in-fee for her land and sold it.[7]

In coping with their deteriorating circumstances, Arapahos and Cheyennes did continue to draw on well-established traditions of sharing and cooperation. Thus, in 1903 George Stouch, whose office now carried the title of superintendent rather than agent, noted that the Arapahos and Cheyennes tended to work in "gangs," doing agricultural and construction work for wages just as they had in earlier times when they helped each other farm their own lands. After group work parties were phased out, people continued to share food, whether grown on family farms or purchased. As Superintendent Charles Shell, who replaced Stouch at Darlington, explained, as far as food was concerned, "they divide to the last scrap." Even the Arapaho family portrayed as on the way down was observed by the superintendent on the day of his visit butchering a calf to sponsor a feast to which they had invited other families. Nonetheless, cash became increasingly important in the lives of Cheyennes and Arapahos, and consumer goods were less shared or less widely shared than food. Sharing increasingly took place in the context of ceremonial gatherings.[8]

The disparities resulting from income differentials made for interpersonal conflict. For example, elderly people who had large land holdings often lived with the family of a son or daughter and made large contributions to the family income. As a result, it was sometimes the case that other relatives, even other children, became resentful and embittered toward the recipients of the elderly relative's largess. There especially was conflict over who would inherit from deceased allottees. As the economic position of the Arapahos and Cheyennes worsened over time, individuals struggled all the more to obtain access to funds through heirship.

Sometime after an allottee died, the Indian Office appointed an examiner of inheritance, who held a hearing to determine the allottee's heirs. Proceeding from a Western point of view, the examiner gave the marital tie more emphasis than the Cheyennes and Arapahos did, and he viewed lineal relatives to be more important than collateral ones. In identifying kin, the examiner disregarded mutual support and association and allowed male and female children to inherit equally from their parents. Interested parties had to provide witnesses to support their claims of relationship. Public confrontation and conflict in matters of inheritance were the consequences. This conflict over heirship challenged notions about the reciprocal obligations and underlying value system of kin relations and led to disputes between Arapahos and between Cheyennes over whether a particular birth was legitimate, over paternity, over whether a kinship relationship should be biologically or sociologically defined, and over the nature of proper social rights and obligations between kin. Moreover, the credibility of witnesses and claimants was challenged, and the ability of claimants to press their cases depended to a large extent on their access to funds to pay witnesses. Headmen and chiefs who were claimants or witnesses had their credibility, and therefore their authority, challenged. Intermediary chiefs who went to Washington as delegates in 1912 viewed the social repercussions of heirship problems to be significant enough to bring it to the attention of the commissioner of Indian affairs.[9]

Many disputes revolved around whether a marriage had been legitimate and therefore whether paternity was established. Some of these cases show that some Cheyennes and Arapahos were beginning to argue that biological paternity should take precedence over sociological paternity; others insisted on continuing the native, sociological definition. Examiners generally accepted Indian custom marriages in lieu of church or courthouse ceremonies, at least if the marriages had occurred before the early twentieth century.

Typical of cases in which the legitimacy of a birth was questioned was the Polly Red Horse hearing. Polly was a student at the government boarding school at Darlington in 1895. She and Chokecherry's son Rider had a sexual relationship when they were both adolescents at the school, and Polly gave birth to a baby, naming Rider as the baby's father. Polly and members of her family testified that there was an Indian custom marriage in 1896 between the two parents after the birth of the baby. From the Cheyenne or Arapaho perspective, an Indian custom marriage was legitimized by an exchange of gifts and a formal feast involving the families of the bride and groom. Polly and Rider lived together, and, until his death in 1898, Rider contributed to the support of Polly and the child. There was a hearing to determine Rider's heirs in 1914. Chokecherry and her daughter, who were Rider's heirs if he died unmarried without legal issue, testified that Polly and Rider were never married—that Rider "only visited" Polly (that is, that no gift exchange and feast had taken place)—and therefore that the child was not Rider's. Polly and her family members testified that the Indian custom marriage took place and that Rider acknowledged his child. Each side paid witnesses to testify on their behalf. The examiner determined that Polly's case was the more credible.

In another case in 1914, a woman named Martha claimed to be the biological daughter, and thus the heir, of Jack Strong. Sam Strong also claimed to be the heir, denying that Martha's mother, Plum, was ever married to his brother Jack or that Jack treated Martha as a father treats a daughter. Sam's witnesses testified that Plum had had sexual relations with a number of the Indian scouts at Fort Reno in the 1880s, that she "did not have the reputation of being a virtuous woman." One witness, a former scout who occupied the same tepee at the fort as Jack, said that Jack did not bring Plum into the tepee. Plum testified that she and Jack were married "privately" but never lived together openly and that when she became pregnant he told her to leave the fort and go where she could be taken care of until she gave birth. Her daughter Martha testified that she visited Jack before he died and that he "acknowledged" her as his child. It was decided that Plum was never married to Jack; without a formal and public exchange of gifts between families, her relations with him were not legitimate and her child could not inherit. The testimony about Plum's reputation was a likely factor in the examiner's assessment. In both the Polly Red Horse and Plum cases, there was considerable resentment and ill will on the part of the parties concerned.

In the Small Ear hearing in 1915, Small Ear's mother's brother Otter claimed to be Small Ear's sole heir. Oto challenged Otter, claiming to be Small Ear's biological father and therefore his sole heir, as Small Ear's mother, Pretty Girl, and his siblings had died. Oto stated that he and Small Ear's mother "started living together" but that they were not married according to "the custom of the Indians." Oto was married to Sparrow at the time. He testified that he left Pretty Girl two months before Small Ear was born, but subsequently was visited by the boy when he got older, and that they "acknowledged" each other. One of Oto's relatives testified that her mother was the midwife at Small Ear's birth and that Pretty Girl said Oto was the child's father. Otter testified that Pretty Girl was married by Indian custom to Flying and that they had a daughter. After Flying died, she did not remarry but had another child, Small Ear; Otter stated that he did not know who Small Ear's father was. After Pretty Girl died, her brother Hawk took her two children and raised them. Otter pointed to Oto's failure to treat Small Ear as a father treats a son. He stated that Oto never claimed to be the boy's father until the heirship hearing and, in an effort to discredit Oto, that "the witnesses I have brought in to testify I do not expect to pay them anything for testifying, but I do not know whether Oto expects to pay his witnesses or not. One of the witnesses who testified for me told me yesterday that Oto told him if he would testify for him that he would pay this witness any price he wished." In this case, since Oto had acknowledged that he had not married Pretty Girl by Indian custom, the examiner ruled that he could not claim to be his legal father and therefore could not inherit.

The examiner's decisions were not consistent, however. In the Red Bear case heard in 1915, there was a disagreement about whether there had been a legal (that is, Indian custom) marriage, and the examiner ruled that there had been a marriage, so John Blade, the disputed son of Magpie, inherited Magpie's land, instead of Magpie's brother Red Bear. Red Bear's witness, Chief White Shirt, testified that Blade's mother was Short Woman: "Magpie and I were great friends. I heard that Magpie and Short Woman were married. Magpie told me he had two wives, Short Woman and Blue and that the agent, Mr. White, had sent for him to come to the agency. . . . I think he had been keeping Short Woman only about a week when someone reported it to the agent and he, the agent, sent for Magpie and told him to give up Short Woman, and Short Woman left Magpie's tepee the same day he returned from the agency. Magpie stated that the agent told him if he did not give up one of these women, he would be sent to the pen. . . . Short Woman went to live with Coming Back, a woman who lived near Bridgeport; this was in September. She came back to Sitting Bull's place the following July and I heard that Blade was born the following December. The Indians called it a night baby [illegitimate]." Relatives of John Blade testified that he was born while Magpie and Short Woman were living together. Superintendent Byron White indicated that he had been informed in 1904 that an Indian midwife who was with Short Woman when Blade was born said that Short Woman claimed at the time the child was born that Blade was the child of a man named White Feather on the South Canadian. According to the superintendent's information, Blade was born five months after Short Woman and Magpie began to live together, and Magpie never treated Blade as his own child. Paul Willis, a witness, stated that at times Magpie had, in his presence, acknowledged Blade as his son and at other times denied him and that members of the tribe generally believed that Blade was the son of Magpie. The superintendent at Canton District disliked Red Bear, whom he considered a troublemaker. This may have been a factor in the examiner's ruling against Red Bear despite the questions surrounding John Blade's birth.

In the White Otter heirship case in 1914, two of White Otter's daughters challenged the right of a third, Little Woman, to inherit, claiming that White Otter had not fathered Little Woman. Little Woman's mother was Osage Woman, who testified that she and White Otter were married, then due to the jealousy of his other wives separated, but that he continued visiting her. She stated that Little Woman was born after the separation but White Otter drew Little Woman's interest money twice a year. White Otter's two daughters and their witnesses claimed that, while White Otter did "visit" Osage Woman, Little Woman had been fathered by another man. The midwife who testified for Little Woman said that the night Little Woman was born White Otter "took her in his arms." The midwife was interpreted at the hearing by Little Woman's husband, and her sisters accused him of interpreting incorrectly. The examiner found Osage Woman credible, and Little Woman inherited. In this case, the fact that White Otter collected Little Woman's interest money helped her case.

In the Gatherer case, heard in 1926, Bird Chief Jr. and his siblings claimed that they had the same father as Gatherer and therefore were heir to her property, as she died with no husband and no living children. However, Joe Red Sky and his siblings also claimed to be siblings of Gatherer, who should be among her heirs. Bird Chief Jr. and his siblings claimed that they and Gatherer had the same parents, Bird Chief and Play Rags. Red Sky claimed that Gatherer's mother was Play Rags but that her biological father was Big Horse and that Big Horse was his father also. It seems that Play Rags was one of Bird Chief's three wives. She gave birth to Bird Chief Jr., then separated from Bird Chief and married Big Horse. While living with Big Horse she gave birth to Gatherer. Subsequently, she went back to Bird Chief, taking her daughter Gatherer with her. One of Red Sky's elderly witnesses, under questioning from the examiner, explained that "A good many Indians say that Gatherer was the daughter of Big Horse and some say she was a daughter of Bird Chief. I do not know." Red Sky and his siblings testified that Bird Chief Jr. assured them that they would not be left out: Bird Chief Jr. denied that he had so promised. These accusations of Red Sky were especially significant because Bird Chief Jr. was an important headman and intermediary chief, and doubts about his honesty or generosity worked to undermine his authority. Another elderly witness testified that a member of Bird Chief Jr.'s party had told him not to testify, presumably because his testimony included the statement that after Play Rags returned to Bird Chief he "outcasted" the child of Big Horse. Others said that Gatherer continued to live in Bird Chief's camp after the death of her mother.

In the Weasel case, Indian Office records showed that Weasel acknowledged Ward Weasel as his son in the 1914 heirship case of his wife's mother. At a 1926 hearing to determine Weasel's heirs, Weasel's brother Legging denied that Ward was the son of Weasel and argued in essence that biological paternity should take precedence over sociological paternity: "Kills Enemy, who died before allotments, was his mother. I think Crowman was his father. . . . They were separated [when Ward was born]." Weasel married Kills Enemy after Ward was born, according to

Beef Issue at Cheyenne-Arapaho Agency, Darlington, 1889. The cattle were released from the corral and run down and shot by men on horseback. Photo by William S. Prettyman, Lollar Collection, Courtesy of Archives and Manuscripts Division of the Oklahoma Historical Society (neg. no. 11043).

Camp of Chief Left Hand on the Canadian River, 1893. In the camp there were ten tepees, protected by brush wind screens, and several wagons. Courtesy of Western History Collections, University of Oklahoma Library.

William Pulling with Cheyenne and Arapaho Police, Cantonment SubAgency, ca. 1890. Pulling, the issue clerk in charge at Cantonment, and his wife are seated. Dan Tucker, an Arapaho alumnus of Carlisle Indian Industrial School who interpreted for Pulling, is between them. The Cheyenne police are on the left and the Arapaho police on the right. Photographer C. C. Stotz, Courtesy of Mennonite Library and Archives, North Newton, Kansas.

Cheyenne and Arapaho Scouts at Fort Reno, 14 August 1890. These scouts were in Company A (Indian scouts) in Troop C of the Fifth Cavalry. Washee (Arapaho) is sixth from left, and Tall Red Bird (Cheyenne) is seventh from left. The photograph was probably taken at the scouts' camp near the fort. Courtesy of Western History Collections, University of Oklahoma Library.

Yellow Bear and Daughter, 1880. Yellow Bear was visiting his daughter Minnie, a student at Carlisle Indian Industrial School, who is dressed in the clothing issued by the school. At the same time, Little Raven and Left Hand were visiting their children. Courtesy of National Anthropological Archives, Smithsonian Institution (photo no. 36,728).

Delegation of 1871. The delegates were visiting eastern cities to confer with government officials, who wanted to impress these delegates with the necessity of remaining peaceful. This photograph was taken in New York City in June 1871. Seated, *left to right*: Little Raven (Arapaho), Bird Chief (Arapaho), Little Robe (Cheyenne), Buffalo Good (Wichita). Accompanying the delegation were, *left to right*, Edmund Guerrier, Cheyenne and Arapaho interpreter; Mahlon Stubbs, Indian agent for the Kaws; John Smith, Cheyenne interpreter; Phillip McCusker, Wichita interpreter. Courtesy of National Anthropological Archives, Smithsonian Institution (photo no. 179b).

Cheyenne and Arapaho Delegation, Washington DC, 1891. Standing, *left to right*: Row of Lodges (Arapaho), Black Wolf (Arapaho), Jesse Bent (Arapaho, interpreter), Captain D. L. Wright (Indian Office official), Leonard Tyler (Cheyenne, interpreter), Kish Hawkins (Cheyenne, interpreter), Benjamin Beveridge (local businessman). Seated, *left to right*: Scabby Bull (Arapaho), Black Coyote (Arapaho), Mrs. Left Hand (Arapaho), Left Hand (Arapaho), Cloud Chief (Cheyenne), Little Chief (Cheyenne), Wolf Robe (Cheyenne), Little Bear (Cheyenne). Photo by C. M. Bell, Washington DC, Courtesy of Archives and Manuscripts Division of the Oklahoma Historical Society (neg. no. 9471).

Little Raven Jr. Giving Away a Pony at the Arapaho Sun Dance, 1901. The gift, given on the sixth day of the ceremony, was a prayer-sacrifice for his daughter's health. Photographer George Dorsey, Courtesy of National Anthropological Archives, Smithsonian Institution (photo no. T10135).

Cheyenne and Arapaho School Boys Laying Brick, 1900. These students at Seger Boarding School are helping the masons work on the hospital building being constructed at Seger agency. Boys spent more than half of their time doing manual labor at the school. Courtesy of National Archives (photo no. 75-SE-38A).

Bird Chief Sr. and His Wife, Woman Going Ahead, at Their Home Place, 1923. Bird Chief Sr.'s one-room house was on his allotment in Twelve Mile District. The photograph documents the superintendent's visit during an "industrial survey." Bird Chief Sr. had a barn for eight horses, hay, and grain; two ponies; a wagon and set of harness; a well; and a windmill. In his report, the superintendent does not mention the tepee behind the house, which was important to Bird Chief Sr.'s role as an Arapaho chief. He provided a place for people to camp or to meet, and he was a ceremonial leader. In this photograph, Bird Chief Sr. was sixty-seven years old. Woman Going Ahead, forty-six years of age, was a co-wife until the death of her older sister in 1913. Bird Chief Sr., regarded by the agency officials as a supporter of the civilization program, was not prosecuted for having two wives. Courtesy of the National Archives (Industrial Survey Report, 1922–23, Entry 762).

Reverend Robert Hamilton Baptizing the Wife of Chief Howling Wolf (Cheyenne), Kingfisher Creek, 1905. Photo by Fred S. Barde, Barde Collection, Courtesy of Archives and Manuscripts Division of the Oklahoma Historical Society (Neg. no. 3631.2).

Indian Parade at Cordell, Oklahoma, on the Fourth of July, 1910. Cordell was a few miles south of Clinton and west of Seger Agency. Photo by Davis West Side Studio, R. R. Hornbeck Collection, Courtesy of Archives and Manuscripts Division of the Oklahoma Historical Society (Neg. no. 8822).

Cheyenne Delegates, Washington DC, 1911. Standing: John Otterby (interpreter). Seated, *left to right*: Thunderbull, Prairie Chief, Wolf Chief, Big Back. Courtesy of National Anthropological Archives, Smithsonian Institution (Photo no. 355a).

Arapaho Delegates, Washington DC, 1911. Standing, *left to right*: Sage, Bird Chief Sr., Jess Rowlodge (interpreter). Seated, *left to right*: Arnold Woolworth, Bird Chief Jr., Washee, Sun Road. Courtesy of National Anthropological Archives, Smithsonian Institution (Photo no. 179a).

Hammon Camp, 1953. This was the home of Frank and Christine Starr. They are using tar paper to keep out the wind. Many Cheyennes moved to Chief White Shield's allotment when their lands flooded; this settlement became known as Hammon Camp. Photo by Robert H. Wood, Robert H. Wood Collection, Courtesy of Archives and Manuscripts Division of the Oklahoma Historical Society (20685.356.53.50).

Giveaway at Watonga Powwow, 1947. The woman on the left is receiving a gift of dress goods from the woman on the right. Several horses were given away at this powwow. Photo by Pierre Tartoue, Tartoue Neg. Collection, Courtesy of Archives and Manuscripts Division of the Oklahoma Historical Society (20912.5.92).

Seiling Women's Club, 1954. These Cheyenne women are refinishing an old lyre-backed chair, which took second prize at the county fair. The government extension agent, Robert H. Wood, organized these clubs to encourage self-improvement and training in leadership. Photo by Robert H. Wood, Robert H. Wood Collection, Courtesy of Archives and Manuscripts Division of the Oklahoma Historical Society (20685.356.52.145).

Cheyenne-Arapaho Business Committee, 1962. Business committee members met with BIA officials at Concho. The Cheyenne and Arapaho men wearing war bonnets are chiefs. BIA officials received war bonnets as gifts. Standing, *left to right*: Dave Williams, Ralph Goodman, John Sleeper, Eugene Woolworth, Herman Haury, Woodrow Wilson, Walter Roe Hamilton, Jim Fire, Eugene Black Bear. Seated, *left to right*: Ralph Little Raven, assistant commissioner of Indian affairs John Old Crow, Sam Buffalo, commissioner of Indian affairs Phileo Nash, Lavern Woolworth, BIA official (unknown), Fred Hoffman, Ed Burns. Photo by Bill Wyrick.

Legging, and Weasel "raised him [Ward] and treated him like he was one of his own children." Ward testified that he and Weasel had lived together ever since he could remember until he married. When Weasel's last wife died he came to live on Ward's place, where he stayed for ten years until he died. Ward stated, "Weasel told me that my mother had been married first to Crowman, a cousin of Weasel, that my mother and Crowman separated, and he married her, and seven months after they were married I was born. . . . Weasel was my father." Because Weasel (the sociological father of Ward) had acknowledged him as his son on record, Ward Weasel was declared his heir.

In the Susie Many Sky case, the issue was not legitimacy or paternity but rather what constituted a close kinship relationship. A hearing was held in 1915 to determine Susie Many Sky's heirs. She was the daughter of Falling and Kettle Woman. After her parents died, her father's brother Chief White Eyed Antelope came for her and took her (along with her property, consisting of three ponies) to his camp, where he and his family took care of her. White Eyed Antelope considered her as a daughter and sought to inherit after her death in 1893. But Falling had another wife, besides Kettle Woman, who had not wished to care for Susie after her mother died, and this woman had children who sought to inherit Susie's estate as her half-siblings. They claimed that, since White Eyed Antelope was not Susie's biological father, he should not inherit. The examiner ruled in their favor on the grounds that the half-siblings of Susie were closer relatives biologically than her father's brother.

There also were many cases in which an elderly parent signed a will leaving his or her estate to one relative, such as a son, and excluded other relatives, such as other sons and daughters. The hearings to determine heirship in these cases involved one set of relatives claiming that the elderly person had been pressured or tricked into signing or that the elderly person was mentally incapacitated, while another set of relatives argued that the beneficiaries were family members who actually took care of the elderly person and that the will validated that relationship. The ill will generated in these cases persisted for generations. The Lame Deer case is an example. Lame Deer had a son and a daughter. He revised his will in 1926, leaving all his property to his daughter's daughter, June. His son Lewis protested: "When I was staying with my father during the summer of 1926, I heard June ask Lame Deer on two different occasions to made a will and give her the south eighty acres of his land. He had already made a will giving her the north eighty. He afterwards made the will but I was not staying there at the time he executed the will. . . . I was at the house the day before he died and I was making my home with him there. . . . He said that June and the others were not paying any attention to him when he was sick and they would go away and leave him." The examiner asked Lewis if he thought June "influenced" Lame Deer to change the will. Lewis replied, "I think she talked to him so much that she influenced him to do it." Here, the claimants also are making a case, which the examiner is not prepared to recognize, that legitimate (socially activated) kinship required care and attention. Lewis cast doubt on June, and she portrayed him as absent much of the time. The examiner, however, ruled that Lame Deer was of sound mind, and the will was approved.

An extreme example of a dispute over a will involved an accusation that the deceased had been forced by threat of violence to will her property to a particular individual. Kiowa Woman made a will in 1928 just prior to her death, in which she bequeathed her property to her husband, Frank Storm, excluding her brothers, Ralph and Tom. The brothers both testified that she had been threatened by her husband. Tom told the examiner, "I went to the home of Frank Storm to take a load of wood and a wagon obstructed the driveway so I would not be able to get in. I managed to get in and unloaded my wood. Then I went in the house but nobody was home. I went into the rooms where my sisters, Kiowa Woman and Willow [who died before Kiowa Woman], slept and the bedclothes had been disarranged as if they had left in a hurry. I knew something was wrong. I then went to Canton to look for them but couldn't find them. When I passed the house of White Man, an Arapaho man, somebody waved at me and I went in his house. There I found my sisters. I was told that Frank had threatened to kill Kiowa Woman if she didn't make a will to him. . . . Kiowa Woman told me that if she destroyed this will that she was afraid that her husband Frank would leave her and not care for her any more."

Heirship matters produced accusations of corruption on a regular basis. In 1903 Mrs. Eagle complained that the individual who was selected by the agent to act on behalf of the other heirs to an allotment was leasing the land and keeping all the income for himself instead of dividing it with the other heirs. W. D. Goodwin, the examiner of inheritance in 1914, noted that "The Indians here have a habit of charging each other a considerable sum for their services as disinterested witnesses in the cases." He reported that such payments "affected the outcome." In 1915, a chief was accused by one witness of trying to testify falsely in an heirship case: "When he saw Minnie Cooper coming in the office he patted me on the shoulder and said, 'do you see that girl?', and pointed to Minnie. I said yes, and Chief _____ then said, 'that is my own daughter. She is a poor girl and I would like to see her get a share in the estate of White Deer [whom the girl was claiming as her father] because she needs the money.'" Another witness testified, "Chief _____ came to my home and said that if the heirs to the estate of White Deer would pay him fifty dollars he would come to the office and swear that he was the father of Minnie Cooper [thereby making her ineligible to inherit]." Chiefs were among those sought as witnesses and thus were vulnerable to suspicions of corruption. When they were paid for witnessing in these cases, they could be viewed as profiting from dealings with constituents rather than as providing for followers in a chiefly manner.

In another case, Lewis Hawk claimed that he had been defrauded of an inheritance by Jeff Stevens. Lewis claimed to have been adopted as a son by Chases Enemy and her husband, Lodge. Lodge was his uncle, and, because Lewis's father died when he was six years old, "he was given" to Lodge and his wife, "adopted by them in accordance with Indian custom," and lived with them until Chases Enemy died in 1922. Jeff was Lewis's uncle and Chases Enemy's brother. According to Lewis Hawk and his witnesses, Jeff informed Lewis that it would not be necessary for him to appear at an heirship hearing, as Jeff, a bilingual graduate of a boarding school who was employed at the agency, would act for him and protect his interest as an adopted son of both deceased allottees. Lewis subsequently learned that Jeff had testified that his own son Adam had been adopted by Chases Enemy (who had no children of her own) and that Adam had inherited both estates. Lewis stated that he confronted Jeff Stevens and threatened to report the affair to the superintendent but that Jeff promised, if Lewis would not discredit him before the Indian Office, he would have the property transferred to him. Jeff paid "various sums of money" to Lewis Hawk for several years but never transferred the property, despite Lewis's "trust and confidence in his uncle." When Jeff inherited the property from his son Adam, Lewis filed a protest, but he did not prevail, for the examiner ruled that too much time had passed since the original heirship hearing.

In these probate hearings Cheyennes and Arapahos contested Euro-American ideas about kinship as well as federal inheritance regulations. While a biological relationship or marriage ceremony often took precedence in the view of the federal officials, many Cheyenne and Arapaho claimants argued that the nature of the social bond was paramount. From these parties' perspective, the person who took responsibility and cared for a child should inherit the child's property. Or adult siblings who lived in the same camp as their deceased brother or sister should be able to claim the property of their adult sibling. Individuals who actually cared for each other and cooperated as members of the same household or camp were considered close relatives whether they were related biologically or not or whether there was a legal will or not. Those who actually lived with an individual were considered more closely related than relatives who had little contact with, or who did not contribute to the support of, a relative. The issue of the nature of the social relationship between parties was the crux of the heirship matter for many Cheyennes and Arapahos. Thus, Little Woman's "father" was the man in whose household she lived; this man, as head of household, collected her interest payments when she was a child. Gatherer's case hinged upon where she lived—in whose camp she received support. Weasel not only raised Ward, but Ward cared for him in his old age. Susie Many Sky was rejected by her father's second wife after her mother died; she was cared for by her father's brothers. What kind of support did Lame Bull receive from his son and granddaughter? Who actually gave Kiowa Woman more support: her brothers who brought her firewood and checked on her well-being or her husband? In all these cases Cheyennes and Arapahos protested a biological interpretation of kinship. While the examiner looked for legal transactions in agency records (for example, who had collected interest payments, who had been declared a kinsman in another probate case, or who was named as heir in a will), many Arapahos and Cheyennes persisted in arguing for a definition of close kinship based on behavior.

The examiner gave the spousal relationship considerably more weight than consanguineal ties. In contrast, Cheyennes and Arapahos gave the latter more weight; in fact, it was the custom for spouses to receive property from the deceased only at the behest of the deceased male relatives, who would be praised for generosity to the surviving spouse and who were expected to support widows and their children in any case. Goodwill and mutual aid of affines were based on reciprocal gift giving. Disputes over property threatened reciprocity between affines. But even in cases where siblings disputed a spouse's claim (as in the Kiowa Woman case), the parties framed their argument in terms of degree of support provided the deceased during his or her lifetime.[10]

It is also clear from these cases that there were competing discourses of kinship. Individuals could, and some did, take advantage of the view of kinship and inheritance put forth in federal policy and regulation and, in making a case based on biological paternity or spousal tie, might benefit personally from the imposition of federal regulations. Some took advantage of the opportunity to present a signed will and testament to the examiner. That examiners were not consistent in their rulings, that bilingual individuals might influence the examiner, or that an examiner might be biased against a troublemaker all encouraged individuals to dispute the claims of others to social bonds of kinship even though such claims were rooted in Cheyenne and Arapaho understandings of kinship. What these disputes did was to provoke the ill will and suspicion that Reverend Petter believed encouraged the Cheyennes and Arapahos to lose confidence in themselves, their leaders, and their community. Accusations of selfishness, of using income to gain advantages over others, and of dishonesty may have distracted some Cheyennes and Arapahos from commitment to cooperative economic, political, and ritual efforts. Nonetheless, community cooperation continued into the 1920s, primarily in the camps or ceremonial gatherings, where households came together periodically throughout the year.

Confronting Assimilation Pressures

Federal agents placed high priority on ending camp life and gift giving as well as on encouraging hard work and fiscal responsibility. Cheyennes and Arapahos doggedly persisted in perpetuating camp life, including the associated features of sharing food and exchanging gifts. Camp life was both dependent on and the main occasion for sharing and gift giving and, as such, served as an alternative or a counterpoint to the individualism encouraged by the wider society. Thus, cooperative economic activity became associated with ceremonial camps or gatherings rather than with making a living, as in earlier times.

The Politics of Camp Life

Large camps, comprised of families from several districts, congealed during American holidays and major native religious ceremonies. In addition, there were smaller permanent camps scattered among the allotments and managed by headmen. The headmen's camps allowed individuals who owned no land, or who had leased their land, to live in tents on an allotment with several other families.

Headmen often attracted people to their allotment (or to a family member's allotment), where they instigated or participated with others in sharing both tasks and food, and they also played an important role in the holiday camps or religious ceremonies that served as the focal point of Cheyenne and Arapaho life. People camped around those headmen who were relatively prosperous by local standards, in particular, those who had land sufficient for a camp. Bird Chief Sr. had a camp for Arapahos, and Coyote had a Cheyenne camp at Calumet. There were camps on the Red Man and Scabby Bull allotments in the Canton District. Several of the Cheyenne headmen, including Mower at Canton and Red Bird at Hammon, attempted to have houses built for band members in a village to be located on the headman's allotment. Headmen often took the responsibility for caring for sick and elderly individuals who lived in their camps. Older men in the camps would enlist younger men to work on their farms. In the 1920s, after most families had moved to allotments and erected houses, the headmen took responsibility for raising funds and providing labor to build council halls, where meetings and dances were held. One was built at Carleton in the Canton District, and one was built in the Geary District for Arapahos. The Cheyennes had one at Longdale and one at Fonda in the Canton District.[11]

Cheyennes and Arapahos camped for religious ceremonies, including the Arapaho and the Cheyenne Sun Dances, Arapaho men's lodges, the Cheyenne Arrow Renewal, and hand games (associated with the Ghost Dance, which lost support after the turn of the century). In addition, peyote ritual and Christian meetings attracted people to camps, although they were smaller than the Sun Dance or holiday camps that drew most Arapahos and Cheyennes. Feasting and gift exchange occurred at all these camps.

The superintendents made note of Cheyenne and Arapaho Sun Dances in 1903 and subsequent years. The ceremonies drew most of the tribal members, who camped for weeks in late summer while they prepared for the ceremony, participated, and had social interactions and activities after the religious ceremony. Sun

Dance symbolism in the twentieth century expressed the unity of the people in several ways: the circular camp, the exchange of food and property, and communal acts of prayer. Food and property given to others served as a religious sacrifice that brought the donor supernatural attention and support. Superintendent W. W. Scott commented that the food eaten at the end of the 1918 Arapaho ceremony was blessed by ritual leaders before it was distributed through the camp. The sharing of food and property also reaffirmed social bonds and was encouraged by supernatural and political sanction. In the exchange, individuals were recognized as "kin" and at the same time expanded their network of relatives. Families helped each other participate, and the men's societies were called upon to make sacrifices of property and to provide cooperative labor. Scott noted that the man who vowed to sponsor the dance called upon his lodge for help. This help could not be refused easily—only on penalty of a fine or other forfeit. At the Arapaho Sun Dance in 1923, Young Bull, who vowed to sponsor the ceremony that year, took a pipe to all three districts and presented it to the men there. In smoking with him, they committed themselves to help him with the ceremony. He also collected donations as he traveled from camp to camp, the donors' gifts expressing their support of Young Bull, his family and friends, and the event itself.[12]

While these gatherings encouraged social unity, they were not entirely free of conflict. For example, in the 1923 Arapaho Sun Dance, one of the individuals who had custody of a key ritual object used in the ceremony demanded an exorbitant amount of cash from the sponsor of the ceremony before the ritual object could be used. The ceremony was delayed while Arapahos struggled to collect money; prior to this, gifts of dress goods or a horse or perhaps a small amount of cash was an appropriate gift from the sponsor to the custodian of the object. In 1918 there were two Cheyenne Sun Dances, due to disagreements among Cheyenne leaders. That same year Cheyennes in the Clinton area had two Christmas camps, one for those who embraced the Mennonite church and the other for those who followed peyote ritual.[13]

The men's societies actively recruited during the early twentieth century. Their duties increasingly were confined to the ceremonial context, for example, participation in the annual Sun Dance. But the bonds between members of the same society obligated them to mutual aid and cooperation. In the case of the Arapahos, men in the junior lodges deferred to the men in the senior lodges, and the senior men conferred honors on some of the young men, which also worked to encourage deference. In 1903 the Arapahos initiated the Star society members into the Tomahawk Lodge at a huge camp, where up to fourteen hundred Arapahos and some visitors from other tribes were present. At this time, the Kit-Fox society members were initiated into the Star society. The man who had vowed to sponsor this lodge had tried to renege on his promise, but the leaders of the lodges pressured him to continue. This was a religious event, where the people all prayed for social harmony and good health. Three of the Star men did not undergo initiation into the Tomahawk or Club Lodge and thereafter were unable to play important roles in the other dances. Honors, or degrees, were awarded to several of the new Tomahawk men. In 1906 the Arapahos held a Crazy Lodge, where the Darlington, Colony, and Canton Districts each had a section in the Arapaho camp circle. The Spear Lodge members were initiated into the Crazy Lodge, and their families helped the individual who vowed to sponsor the ceremony. As the honors were awarded, the dancers' relatives held giveaways. In 1911 the Arapahos initiated the Tomahawk men into the Spear Lodge. The Cheyennes also were holding society initiations during the early years of the century; they referred to the society leaders as "headsmen."[14]

The missionaries encouraged Arapahos and Cheyennes to attend their sermons by sponsoring camps and helping to facilitate the travel of families to camps. Missionaries allowed families to leave property at the mission while they traveled, so that their belongings would not be stolen by American neighbors. The Mennonite and Baptist missions also distributed clothing, food, and other supplies, which helped to mitigate the poverty of Cheyennes and Arapahos. Several headmen and intermediary chiefs encouraged the work of the missionaries in large part for these reasons; in fact, several participated in both native and Christian rituals. In 1906, Hail, the Arapaho headman and a chief, promised to "become Christian" when he cultivated the assistance of Baptist missionaries. At the same time, he was an important ritual leader in the Arapaho lodges. In 1907, Chief Left Hand had a major role in the Arapaho Sun Dance—he enacted his war exploits during a phase of the ceremony—and he relied on Arapaho "medicine" (aid from his spirit helpers) to maintain his and his family's health. Bird Chief Jr. held a high position as one of the directors in the Arapaho lodges. Both Left Hand and Bird Chief Jr. told the Baptists they would convert but "keep their medicine." The Arapaho Sun Dance often was held on the Left Hand allotment, which became Grant Left Hand's place of residence after the death of his father in 1911. Grant also invited the Baptists to hold camp meetings there.[15]

After the Sun Dance, people made preparations to move to a large camp for a gathering during Thanksgiving week, where there were social dances (including the Omaha Dance) and other activities. Then, in December and January people camped again for the Christmas dance. Later in the year, they camped again for Easter and, a few months later, perhaps a Fourth of July celebration. The Arapaho districts took turns hosting these social gatherings for Arapahos from other districts, and Cheyenne districts hosted each other as well. The host district would present gifts and provide a feast for the visitors. This reciprocal exchange worked to maintain group identity and to reinforce political consensus and social mores among Arapahos and Cheyennes. Members of a district worked cooperatively and pooled resources in their capacity as hosts.[16]

Fairs organized cooperatively by Cheyennes and Arapahos were popular for a time. Here the people could camp and engage in dancing, games, and horse racing (and gambling). The first Cheyenne-Arapaho fair was held in Weatherford in 1910, and in September 1911 one was held in Watonga. The tribes' fairs in 1912 and 1913 impressed the superintendent as "old time" and not "progressive," and he therefore withheld permission and support in 1914.[17]

Every week there were peyote rituals in all the districts. The Arapaho and Cheyenne rituals differed in some respects, which allowed leaders to perpetuate their authority in a tribal context. These ceremonies attracted a camp where people from the same or different districts stayed for a week or more. The communal feast at the end of the ceremony, sponsored by a supplicant, worked symbolically to reaffirm and promote social harmony and cooperation among the families present. In 1919, in the face of considerable opposition from local and federal officials, several Cheyenne men, who were leaders in the peyote religion, organized as the Native American Church and obtained a state charter.[18]

While Indian resistance to attempts to quash native ceremonial and camp activity was not always so overt, the superintendents at the three agencies made it clear that they were unable to prevent camp life, despite their emphasis on the development of homeplaces on individual allotments. Superintendent Scott admitted that sharing, particularly of food, and gift giving in ceremonial contexts and the dances that were part of camp ritual continued in spite of his efforts to prevent them. Ceremonies such as peyote rituals or peyote feasts were held in secret so that he could not easily suppress them. Scott admitted that the Indian police could not be counted on to stop religious rituals or recreational activity (such as gambling) in the camps and that he could do nothing to eradicate peyote because he could not get Indians to testify against each other. Scott's successor, L. S. Bonnin, who served as superintendent of the Darlington agency from 1920 to 1928, admitted that he was unwilling to try to eradicate peyote ritual or even to shorten the week-long Arapaho Sun Dance: it would create "discord, dissatisfaction and a rebellious spirit." He also noted that although he had tried to start an "outing" system, whereby schoolchildren would be placed in settlers' homes to work, "the boys refused to stay."[19]

Cheyennes and Arapahos tried to subvert federal policies not only by defiance where possible but also by pose, that is, by appearing to cooperate with the superintendents in order to forestall punishment or to benefit in some way. During Scott's and Bonnin's administrations, agency personnel routinely inspected Cheyenne and Arapaho homes to monitor such things as cleanliness, amount of farming activity and property owned, and size of household. Families often kept "show" rooms (to satisfy standards of cleanliness) for the agency personnel to inspect, while they actually lived in tents. Individuals might lease the house on their allotments and move their tents to a camp. Individuals also attempted to subvert the superintendents' control over the money in their IIM accounts by applying to use funds for a purpose that the superintendent would approve (such as the purchase of farm machinery or material to build a house), then use the funds in a different manner or illegally sell the property and use the cash as they wished. Missionary G. Phelps noted how one Cheyenne circumvented the superintendent's policy on distribution of IIM money: Burnt All Over was to direct the 1909 Cheyenne Sun Dance and needed at least one thousand dollars for the expenses of a feast. He had inherited his brother's allotment, which could be sold "if he could think of a plausible story to tell the agent [superintendent]." He first tried to bribe the government interpreter, then, with the assistance of a bilingual relative, told the superintendent he wanted to start farming. He got two thousand dollars, which he used for the expenses of the ceremony. Scott also suspected his Indian employees of shirking or sabotage on occasion—breaking machinery, killing time, being careless with stock—which might have prolonged their term of hire.[20]

Arapaho and Cheyenne leaders cooperated with the superintendents' efforts to demonstrate the agency's progress in the BIA's civilization program by referring to the religious ceremonies by names other than "Sun Dance." By using the name "Willow" or "Sage" Dance they deflected criticism that the ritual was primitive or barbaric, for the Sun Dance was associated with torture or "sun worship" in the view of many federal officials. During World War I, the Arapahos and Cheyennes presented their religious ceremonies as events designed to support the war effort, that is, as patriotic events. In 1918 when the superintendent gave the Arapahos their permit for the Sun Dance, he referred to them as "very enthusiastic Red Cross workers" and reported that they raised $167.47 at the dance for Indian soldiers overseas.[21]

One of the participants in the effort to obtain patriotic status for the Sun Dance was Jess Rowlodge. From his perspective, the connection with the Red Cross was a deliberate strategy to subvert attempts of federal officials to prevent the Arapahos from holding the ceremony: "One year—1917—during this first World War, the Arapahos—a man by the name of Charlie Campbell—was going to make a Sun Dance. . . . So the older chiefs, Hail and Cut Finger and those older chiefs went to the agency at Concho [formerly known as Darlington] and asked to have a Sun Dance the usual month—August. The superintendent said, 'No, we don't allow no Indian ceremony. In fact, no Indian doings during this war.' So they got turned down." Letters to officials in Washington, including the president's office, produced the same result. The chiefs presented the problem to Mr. Rowlodge, who previously had gone with a delegation to Washington: "Now, what I'm going to do? My mind was refreshing. I had visited the National Red Cross in Washington. . . .

Well, I thought about that. . . . I wrote a telegram to the National Red Cross in Washington D C of what we were trying to—the Arapaho Sun Dance that year— to raise money for the boys that's already in the army." Approval from the Red Cross allowed the Sun Dance to be held. Mr. Rowlodge remarked on his success, "My statement in that telegram was that the purpose of this old time Arapaho Sun Dance was to donate money by different social organizations. And the gate receipts to give, to send to the National Red Cross for the boys of the Cheyenne-Arapaho tribe for their cigarettes and all those things. And we raised three hundred and forty-four dollars during that Sun Dance. So I run over the president of the United States that time!"[22]

The missionaries, like the superintendents, made compromises in trying to convert Cheyennes and Arapahos to Christianity. The Mennonites admitted that, although they were successful in attracting crowds to their camp meetings, Cheyennes and Arapahos held intertribal gift-giving ceremonies and other camp activities there.[23]

The Cheyennes and Arapahos were not the only subversives faced by the superintendents attempting to prevent camp life. Settlers also aided its perpetuation because they found Indian camps beneficial to the local economy. The *Carrier Pigeon* (published at the Darlington agency) printed many stories in the early part of the century about these camps: in 1911 displays of "primitive Indian life" at the local town fairs were thought by Oklahomans to be "well worth watching," as was the "parade of Indian chiefs, dressed in complete costumes of barbaric Indian splendor." Sham battles, gift-giving ceremonies, and soldier dances were featured as well. Towns in western Oklahoma provided campgrounds and provisions to Cheyennes and Arapahos who would camp at town celebrations (particularly during the Fourth of July or a fair) and perform. These "entertainments" drew people from other areas of the state and from Kansas, which increased the profits of local merchants. At all the large camps settlers set up concession stands, merchants increased their sales of food and property (used in gift giving), and settlers sometimes charged Cheyennes and Arapahos for the return of stray stock during the duration of the camps.[24]

Camp life offered public validation of ideals of cooperation and generosity and was clearly emotionally satisfying for Cheyennes and Arapahos, who obtained support from others, opportunities to earn prestige, and a religious means to realize their hopes. Public discourse in the camps discouraged conflict and personal gain at the expense of others and thus served as a counterpoint to the more private heirship hearings. The camps also were the setting for councils of chiefs and other prominent men who met to discuss the history of their relations with the United States and their strategies for dealing with federal officials.

Intermediary Leadership

Intermediary chiefs continued to be spokespeople for the Cheyennes and Arapahos after 1903, working to hold the attention of federal officials and, at the same time, to inspire the confidence of their constituents. The treaties provided the chiefs with a sacred charter in their dealings with the federal government and with their own people as they tried to protect the land base of the Cheyennes and Arapahos and to retain services and aid they believed the government had promised them. Disappointed in these objectives, they eventually pursued a court claim against the federal government for treaty violations. Chiefs also were associated with Cheyenne and Arapaho ceremonial life. As well as helping to organize and sponsor rituals, they took responsibility for protecting religious freedoms. The chiefs faced great obstacles during this time because federal officials had less need of their assistance than in reservation days and began in the 1920s to press for an end to intermediary chieftainship.

In representing their communities, or districts, chiefs dealt with the local agency superintendents and with officials in Washington D C with whom they corresponded or with whom they visited on periodic delegations to Washington. At the local level, chiefs both pressured the superintendents to be responsive to the Cheyenne and Arapaho communities and tried to help them with some aspects of their job. When W. W. Scott replaced William Freer as superintendent at Darlington in 1914, Cheyenne and Arapaho chiefs met with him to reaffirm their responsibility. The Arapaho chief Young Bear said, "You help us and we will help you." Cheyenne chief Coyote Robe said, "We are going to watch you and the minute you go wrong we are going to make report." The Arapaho chief Middleman was more persuasive in tone: "If you help us we will stand by you and never forget you." In fact, chiefs did assist the superintendents, largely to engender their cooperation on other occasions. For example, Middleman dealt with the government farmer in his district in 1907, then conveyed the man's advice and instructions to his people. Cheyenne chiefs were often less subtle: in 1907 Chief Cloud Chief insisted that "whatever the Agents wish to do for the good of the Indians, first they always call a meeting with the leaders and if the leaders give their consent to the agent, then the agent goes ahead." Chiefs primarily were concerned with events in their own districts. In 1911 the government farmer in the Greenfield subdistrict of Darlington reported that he relied on the Arapaho chief Hail and the Cheyenne chief Soft Belly to help him with his job. In 1912 Arapaho chiefs Cut Finger and Cut Nose protested to the superintendent on behalf of their subdistrict that the government farmer's assistant was not familiar with the community.[25]

Intermediary chiefs were influential with the superintendents in large part because the superintendents perceived most chiefs as progressive. Superintendent Charles Shell appointed chiefs to visit the boarding schools to encourage children to attend regularly and to apply themselves to their studies. The chiefs also could consult school personnel about school conditions. For example, in 1907 Shell appointed Chiefs Hail, Cut Finger, Sage, and Bird Chief Jr. to visit the Arapaho Boarding School. In 1907 the superintendent wrote to the commissioner, recognizing outstanding Indian farmers at the agency fair: the Arapahos named were Chiefs Hail, Sage, Cut Nose, Bird Chief Jr., and Cut Finger. In 1910 the Arapaho chief Black Coyote was recognized as an outstanding farmer. In 1912 in the Calumet subdistrict of Darlington, the superintendent recognized the Arapaho chief Bird Chief Jr. and the Cheyenne chief Coyote as good farmers; in the Bridgeport subdistrict, Arapaho chiefs Sage and Cut Finger were recognized as well as Cheyenne chief White Spoon. In 1913 Chief Roman Nose Thunder, a Cheyenne from Canton, was similarly recognized. When a delegation of Arapahos and Cheyennes met with the commissioner in 1915, the Arapaho delegate Bringing Good remarked that he encouraged young people to get an education and to attend school and that he was farming, "sweating and working hard." In the 1917 delegation's meeting with the commissioner, Cut Finger made a point of saying that he "was the first one to stand out and fight against the liquor traffic in our reservation, because the commissioner requested" the chiefs to discourage it. Another delegate, Grant Left Hand, said that the chiefs used their influence to encourage children in school. In 1922 the Cheyenne chief Yellow Hawk tried to influence the commissioner by telling him that Cheyenne men were farming and their children were in school.[26]

Chiefs had to reassure their constituents that they were influential with federal officials without overstepping their authority as spokespeople. When they met with officials they insisted on receiving gifts that symbolized to the home community that they were held in high regard by the president and, thus, that they could potentially influence federal policy. In this way, they hoped to mobilize support at home. For example, in 1915 the delegates asked for presidential medals so that, as the Arapaho delegate Lime said, the medals could "show to the tribe and . . . will represent that they have brought these matters before the [commissioner of Indian affairs]." The chiefs consistently affirmed that their role was to articulate consensus. Chiefs took into consideration the views of women as well as men and felt a special responsibility to represent to officials the needs of poor and debilitated individuals. For example, one Arapaho woman confidently told the superintendent in 1925 that she could count on the chiefs to express her concerns to officials: referring to the chiefs, she wrote, "I will see that they make a complaint to the commissioner of Indian affairs about the two Indian women cooks at Cantonment School. My children complain." Arapaho chiefs spoke with one voice. Cheyenne chiefs, on the other hand, continued to come in conflict with one another on occasion, but each attempted to articulate the consensus of his own district.[27]

The chiefs viewed their positions as sanctioned by the treaty relationship that existed between the Cheyennes and Arapahos and the federal government. When they went as delegates to meet officials in Washington, they presented their case—for protecting the land base, retaining boarding schools, or protecting religious freedom, for example—in the context of treaty rights. They viewed themselves as successors of earlier generations of chiefs, often alluding to their descent from a signatory or to promises made to the "old chiefs" whom they succeeded. When Cloud Chief petitioned the commissioner in 1907 to extend the trust status of Indian lands, he insisted that "the treaty is to run twenty-five years"—the Jerome Agreement of 1891 (which they considered a treaty) guaranteed that allotted lands would be inalienable for at least twenty-five years. Chiefs believed that they had been verbally assured by the commissioners at the agreement council in 1891 that the lands would be in trust at least fifty years. There also was a belief locally that "treaty" commissioners promised that the agency reserves and Fort Reno would revert to the Cheyenne and Arapaho peoples when the federal government ceased to use them on the Indians' behalf. When Cheyenne and Arapaho chiefs petitioned the commissioner of Indian affairs to allow them to send delegates to Washington in 1911, the Arapaho chiefs Bird Chief Jr., Circle Left Hand (Left Hand's son), Black Coyote, Black Bear, Red Wolf, Arnold Woolworth, Sage, Warpath, Young Bear, Middleman, and Big Nose stressed that they had the backing of the "old chiefs" White Eyed Antelope and Left Hand, even though these two chiefs had retired. In 1914 the Arapaho chief Hail explained, "I have taken the place of those chiefs that have passed away." The Cheyenne chief Three Fingers remarked to the superintendent in 1914, "We younger men were made chiefs in the stead of those older who signed the cession [Jerome Agreement]." In other words, each new generation of chiefs succeeded an earlier generation. This succession was set in motion at the Treaty of 1851.[28]

The Cheyennes and Arapahos requested permission to send a delegation almost every year, and they obtained approval in 1908, 1909, 1911, 1912, 1915, 1917, 1918, 1920, 1924, and 1926. Usually the delegates paid their own expenses. The 1908 delegates left for Washington determined to convince officials of the need to retain Indian land in trust. They understood that the Dead Indian Land Act was a threat to their land base, and they viewed this legislation as a violation of the Jerome Agreement. As they understood the agreement, they had received a guarantee that the allotted lands all were to remain in Indian ownership. They protested the injustice of this "treaty violation" to the commissioner. Cloud Chief remarked, "By selling to you I give wealth to the people who live in the state of Oklahoma." In return, as he understood it, their "treaty" was to run twenty-five years and then "a new contract is to be made for Indians." Some participants in the Jerome council believed that they had been promised fifty-year trust patents on the allotments. Thus, the delegates understood the sale of the allotments of deceased allottees to settlers to be a treaty violation. The Burke Act of 1906 made it possible for the secretary of the interior (on the advice of local officials) to declare allottees competent to have their land in fee patent, making the land taxable and allowing the allottee to sell his or her land. In 1908 Congress established measures to allow some noncompetent allottees to sell their land. The members of the 1908 delegation protested this new policy, but to no avail. All the subsequent delegations focused on trying to obtain a guarantee that the trust status of allotments in general would be extended beyond twenty-five years (that is, beyond 1917). When President Woodrow Wilson extended the trust status for ten years (until 1928), the delegations subsequent to 1917 pressed for a further extension, which they received in 1927. Delegations were adamant that the Cheyenne-Arapaho land base was all-important, necessary to their survival as a people and necessary to the survival of Cheyenne and Arapaho communities.[29]

Congress passed legislation in 1907 that provided for the distribution of the Cheyenne-Arapaho million dollar trust fund, that is, the remainder of the money the Cheyennes and Arapahos received when they ceded the reservation. Individuals deemed competent could apply for their pro-rata shares (about $350) as well as for a fee patent to their land. Thus, the 1907 legislation threatened the trust fund as well as the Cheyenne-Arapaho land base. Every delegation tried to persuade the Indian Office to stop distributing the pro-rata shares and to stop issuing fee patent title to allotments, for a group of young landless and impoverished individuals had emerged as a result of the new policy. Despite the protests of the 1917 delegation, the commissioner appointed a competency commission to interview Arapahos and Cheyennes to determine how many were competent. This commission provided a means of coercing individuals to forfeit the protections of trust status and resulted in the further loss of Cheyenne-Arapaho resources and the creation of more landless individuals.[30]

Another concern of the chiefs was the status of the agency reserves at Darlington, Canton, Colony, Red Moon, and Fort Reno. Americans coveted these lands as well as the allotments. When the federal government sold part of the Darlington reserve in 1910, including the Arapaho Boarding School, the chiefs protested vigorously. When their protests were ignored, some demanded that the proceeds of the sale be distributed per capita. Instead, the federal government used the money to make repairs on the Cheyenne Boarding School, which then became the Cheyenne-Arapaho School (known later as Concho School). In 1912 there was an unsuccessful effort on the part of Americans to obtain some of the land at Cantonment reserve. From the chiefs' perspective, by the "treaty" the Cheyennes and Arapahos were guaranteed title to the reserves if the lands ceased being used for the support of the Arapahos and Cheyennes.[31]

The money from the rental and sale of allotments was deposited in the IIM account of the landowner or landowners (in the case of inherited lands). The superintendent oversaw the I I M accounts, allowing only a small monthly expenditure (usually ten dollars) regardless of the size of the account. Individuals could make an appeal to the superintendent if they wanted to make a large purchase. If the superintendent agreed that the expenditure was practical (for example, a house, farm equipment, or a medical bill), he might allow a larger monthly withdrawal. This was a great frustration to the Arapahos and Cheyennes, and the delegations protested the practice. In 1911 Arapaho delegate Arnold Woolworth remarked to the commissioner, "We have all become debtors to the class of traders." What he meant was that since ten dollars per month was inadequate, in order to subsist, Arapahos and Cheyennes had to mortgage their property to tradespeople to obtain credit in order to buy provisions. The trader could foreclose, taking an expensive buggy, for example, as payment on a grocery bill of a few dollars. Farm equipment, livestock, family heirlooms, and other property were forfeit to the local businessmen. Meanwhile the I I M funds drew low interest in local banks, so that the money was useful primarily to the banks. In 1920 the monthly allowance was twenty-five dollars, which also was inadequate, and the delegates continued to protest.[32]

All the delegations pleaded with federal officials for help in putting a stop to the rampant fraud and mismanagement that was impoverishing them and creating the social conflict so disturbing to the Cheyennes and Arapahos. The 1909 delegation informed the commissioner that local federal officials appraised Indian lands below market value. Delegations complained that decisions made in matters of competency and inheritance were culturally inappropriate. Delegations protested the fact that local non-Indians not only took mortgages on Indian property worth far more than the amounts of credit given but also stole Indian property outright. In 1926 the delegation, aware of oil development elsewhere, complained that the government, as trustee of their lands, should take initiative in getting oil companies interested in Arapaho and Cheyenne lands.[33]

The delegations also expressed their people's fears that the federal government would abandon the boarding schools and agencies, leaving the Arapahos and Cheyennes more vulnerable to their non-Indian neighbors and less able to improve their circumstances. In 1911, Arapaho delegate Bird Chief Jr. tried to convince government officials to pay more attention to the boarding school. In his speech he attempted to evoke sympathy for the children there, whom he portrayed as having to "sleep in sheds, barns and under the roof and they are affected by exposure and weather." Delegates pointed out that Indian children were not welcome in the public schools and, in addition, that parents did not have the funds to outfit them for public school. In 1919, as the government began to demand that parents who had been declared competent as a result of the Burke Act be required to pay tuition for their children at the boarding school, Cheyenne delegate Little Hand protested, "This would appear to be the beginning of the end of the U.S. school for Indian children." Arapahos and Cheyennes regarded the boarding schools as a treaty right. Cheyenne delegate Yellow Hawk said in 1920 that "the old chiefs" obtained the schools.[34]

Chiefs petitioned and the delegations also pressed for assistance in pursuing a claim against the federal government for violating treaties and for the fraud involved in the 1891 Jerome Agreement. They wanted permission to hire an attorney to prepare their claims, and in 1923 a contract with an attorney was signed.[35]

Chieftainship clearly was associated with the ceremonial realm, and chiefs were intermediaries at the local level in the efforts of the Cheyennes and Arapahos to prevent the suppression of ceremonial activities. Perhaps it seemed strange to the superintendent in 1914 when Bird Chief Jr. said that the chiefs believed "God is helping us" to speak the truth and that they hoped there would be "results." But Bird Chief Jr. and the other intermediary chiefs were important ritual leaders who could obtain supernatural intervention on behalf of their communities. The delegates, when in Washington, always made an argument for religious freedom. The 1912 delegation obtained approval from the commissioner for the Willow Dance (Sun Dance) and the "gift dance." The chiefs took it as their duty to regularly petition the superintendents for permits to hold the ceremonies, and the permits were given during the 1920s. In addition to obtaining permits, the chiefs assumed the responsibility for collecting money and other items to sponsor gatherings and took a prominent role in the secular rituals. Cheyenne and Arapaho oral tradition about the treaty councils stressed that the treaty commissioners and the Cheyenne and Arapaho chiefs smoked a pipe, passing it in a circle from man to man. In this, they derived supernatural sanction of the agreement between the parties. The smoke mediated between the human and supernatural participants, drawing them all into the circle and binding the human participants to their word. Chiefs in the early twentieth century took on their predecessors' sacred obligations and expected (or hoped) that federal officials would do the same.[36]

Most of the Arapaho intermediary chiefs were participants in the men's lodges. The Arapaho intermediary chiefs during the twentieth century were born in the late 1850s and early 1860s. They were elderly men who were among the highest-ranking lodge men. They were ranked just below the Old Men, or highest priests (some of whom had been initiated into the Dog Lodge but had not gone through a formal initiation into the highest lodge). Circle Left Hand, son of Left Hand, served on the 1908 and 1909 delegations. He had been initiated into the Crazy Lodge in 1906; he died in 1910. Other 1909 delegates, Arnold Woolworth, Little Raven Jr., and Cleaver Warden, also were in the men's lodge organization, lower in rank than Circle. The delegates Sage and Bird Chief Jr. were Crazy Lodge members. Crazy Lodge membership carried with it curative powers, and these lodge men were greatly respected by Arapahos for their access to supernatural powers. The 1911 delegation consisted of Sage and the lower-ranked Bird Chief Jr. and Big Belly—all Crazy Lodge members—and three other lodge men of lower rank, including Arnold Woolworth. The 1915 Canton delegation was led by Rabbit Run, a member of the Crazy Lodge and a Sun Dance leader, and the Darlington delegates included Hail, Big Nose, and Bird Chief Sr. (another son of Bird Chief), Crazy Lodge members who outranked the Crazy Lodge men initiated in 1906, including Bird Chief Jr. The 1917 delegation included Hail, Cut Nose, Bird Chief Sr., and Sage—senior Crazy Lodge members—and Bird Chief Jr. as well as several lodge men who had not reached the Crazy Lodge. The 1920 delegation from Darlington agency included three Crazy Lodge men—Chiefs Big Nose, Young Bear, and Medicine Grass—and three junior men from Canton. In 1926 all the delegates (including Young Bear and Medicine Grass) were lodge men and one, Chief Ute, was the highest ritual authority in the Sun Dance as well as a member of the Crazy Lodge. The Cheyenne intermediary chiefs included council chiefs and Sun Dance leaders. The Cheyenne Arrow Keeper, Little Man, was a member of the 1909, 1915, and 1917 delegations.[37]

The chiefs' difficulties in obtaining permission for delegations reflect the declining interest of federal officials in dealing with spokespeople for Cheyennes and Arapahos, a disinterest largely the product of the erosion of the land base. Negotiations over land sales centered on individual allottees, not tribal land. Moreover, by the second decade of the century, the Indian Office was actively attempting to replace chieftainship with representative democracy, that is, with elected leaders who took "progressive" positions in support of federal assimilationist policies. In 1910 Superintendent Dickens suggested that younger men be encouraged to assume leadership positions. He suggested to the "chiefs and headmen" that each farming district elect two committeemen to organize the upcoming fair, one "old, influential" man and one young, "progressive" man. Nonetheless, the committeemen selected were chiefs and other influential men, not the younger leaders Dickens hoped for. Young men who had positions requiring formal education, such as that of assistant government farmer, had difficulty exerting authority. The superintendent at Darlington in 1915 reported that Indian men did not accept instruction from the Indian assistant farmer because they felt they knew as much as he did. However, there were young, bilingual men who worked with the chiefs as interpreters or as advisors on the treaty claim, and in these activities was the beginning of an eventual partnership between the chiefs and several younger, formally educated men. In 1921 Superintendent L. S. Bonnin tried to organize a "general council" of elected representatives from the three agencies. Young, bilingual men were selected for this council, but it was never active and disbanded in 1922, as the young men faced opposition from their communities.[38]

When the 1920 delegation arrived in Washington, the delegates reportedly were "in full Indian garb." Cheyenne delegate White Wolf presented the commissioner with a peace pipe and tobacco pouch. Cheyenne delegate Yellow Hawk also presented a pipe, and Arapaho delegate Lime presented an Indian coat to Commissioner Cato Sells. Sells reflected on the gifts by commenting about the donors, "These Indians represent nature in all its beauty and integrity." The local superintendent, however, advised the commissioner that the delegates' presentation of themselves and their gifts were calculated to elicit sympathy in an era when Sells was promoting the issuance of competency certificates. The superintendent complained that the younger men were becoming adept in using "so-called chiefs" as "instruments and tools" in order to get sympathy. In fact, Cheyennes and Arapahos were aware of the prevailing Indian imagery and not adverse to making use of it, particularly the romantic images, in political contexts. They also were prepared to reject this imagery, in the context of both federal and local settler discourse.[39]

The Cheyenne and Arapaho Critique

Ideology about Indian character and society was central to the federal discourse surrounding assimilation policy. Aware of the ideology, Cheyennes and Arapahos confronted and challenged it where they could. In rationalizing policies that served local settler interests, federal officials demeaned Indian character. The character traits emphasized were laziness, improvidence, and a childish dependence on ceremony and tradition. Federal policies of supervision, direction, and punishment and reward were rationalized as necessary in view of such character deficiencies. Thus, they believed Indian land should be leased or sold cheaply because Indians were not using it industriously and efficiently, and settler farmers would improve the land so that eventually Cheyennes and Arapahos could farm it successfully. Rations should be stopped so that Indians would have to provide for themselves and therefore develop the ability to work. Strict controls over Indians' access to the money from the lease and sale of their lands were necessary because Indians could not manage their money wisely. Indians should not receive protection from discrimination because contact and competition with settlers ultimately would expose Indians to civilizing influences. Over time, as federal policies were changed, there were subtle modifications in the discourse. The emphasis on laziness lessened when sales replaced leasing in importance. Leases had been encouraged in order to provide Cheyennes and Arapahos with an opportunity to learn good work habits by watching; when land sale was promoted, the Indian farmer benefited, federal officials argued, because he would have money to extend his farming operations. The emphasis on improvidence rationalized tight control over IIM accounts, but once the land base and income thereof shrank, officials stressed that the Indian needed to assume greater responsibility for financial management. The annual narrative reports of the local superintendents contain the discourse, which was repeated in circulars and general instructions to agency employees, including Cheyennes and Arapahos.

In Washington the commissioner of Indian affairs in 1904 defended the policy of restricting the distribution of the proceeds of sales of allotted lands to small monthly allowances: the Indian was "incapable of saving or caring for his money." But only two years later, the Burke Act, which allowed for the identification of competent Indians to which fee patents were issued, would allow for "an intelligent and self-dependent Indian" to obtain "relief from the shackles of wardship."[40]

Local superintendents expressed similar views. John Seger was superintendent of Seger (one of the three Cheyenne-Arapaho agencies), where 607 Cheyennes and 139 Arapahos resided. He insisted on the need to protect Indians from their improvident nature: the Indian lacked the ability to "look ahead and think reasonably." Seger promoted the sale of inherited lands: "In selling this inherited land the Indian will get experience in the way of handling money; he will have the opportunity to see how easily it slips away from him, and when it is all gone he will be a wiser if not a better man." In 1904, Seger insisted that the Cheyennes and Arapahos had "too much money to spend that they do not have to work for." The fact that low monthly allowances necessitated the Cheyennes' and Arapahos' going into debt to merchants (buying on credit, often providing property as security for the loan) and that merchants charged usurious interest was discounted by Seger: "It will be seen that these Indians have a large revenue; if they would use it judiciously they could support themselves comfortably. These Indians use their money so extravagantly they soon use it up and have to run into debt, which causes them to pay high prices for what they buy." George Stouch, the superintendent at Darlington agency, where 794 Cheyennes and 557 Arapahos were located, agreed, noting that a major cause of poverty was the "propensity of the Indians to borrow money." Stouch justified his policy of assisting only some of the Cheyennes and Arapahos with their farming efforts by explaining that he restricted aid to "deserving" individuals. Byron White, superintendent at Cantonment agency, where 558 Cheyennes and 239 Arapahos were located, noted that Indian lands should be leased until Indians could accumulate enough money from land sales to buy the equipment they would need to farm. He indicated that he tried to get Indians to take as much rental as possible in improvements instead of cash.[41]

As land sales increased during the next few years, Cheyenne and Arapaho poverty increased. Local superintendents attributed this economic decline to laziness or poor work habits. William Freer, Darlington superintendent from 1910 to 1912, summarized Cheyenne-Arapaho deficiencies thus: "The chief problem met in the efforts to induce Indians to do more farming are their habit of traveling about, their aversion to work and their too great willingness to depend on their funds arising from lease rentals, etc. for their support." He also noted that an additional factor was the "too frequent gatherings of the Indians for their ceremonial and other dances, their too long sojourn at these gatherings, the unwillingness of families to live by themselves away from their friends and acquaintances." He affirmed that the lack of success on the economic front was due to Indians lacking in the "essentials of character." In his 1912 report Freer wrote, "The Indians seem unable to resist the temptation to attend such gatherings. I heard of one case where an Indian who attempts some farming and who is reasonably industrious, was cutting alfalfa hay in his field when he heard of a proposed gathering and of the proposed attendance of his neighbors. He immediately stopped his work, unhitched his team, returned to the house and within a few hours the family set out in their camping outfit for the gathering in question, where they remained so long that the value of the crop depreciated materially." The superintendent also took responsibility for publishing an agency newspaper, the *Carrier Pigeon*. This publication included items on each farming district, particularly news of visits, sickness, births, deaths, and, most prominently, activities of the "progressive" individuals—those with "neat" farms and homes, "nice gardens," and crops in the field. In descriptions of district activity, the newspaper portrayed individuals in demeaning terms. One article, for example, stated that a man "once thought to be the laziest Indian in my district, is now at work." Another man, whose son's birth was announced, was admonished, "We hope that he will not neglect cultivating his corn on this account." In Darlington District, the newspaper reported, "Our Indians do too much moving about and engage in too many gatherings from July to October and November, inclusive. Due to this failing, many of them do not put up hay in sufficient quantities to winter their stock satisfactorily." The prevailing view was that those Indians with the best character were "individuals of the old type" (whose numbers decreased each successive year). Freer encouraged the leasing of Indian lands despite low rentals because lessees placed "improvements" on the lands. He extended "favors" to "industrious" Indians and withheld them from "idle" ones. [42]

W. W. Scott, Darlington superintendent from 1913 to 1919, wrote in the same vein. In 1914 he noted, "Like all Indians the Cheyennes and Arapahos are improvident in the use of money." Scott noted that when the Indian "shows industry, authority is secured to turn over to him reasonable amounts of his money to spend at his own discretion." He characterized Cheyenne and Arapaho participation in dances as making "a show of themselves." Dances were "very mild imitations of the wild orgies of the past." They "overdo" it, he wrote. Superintendent Scott was especially critical of the neglect of the home. He wrote in 1919: "Every visit to an Indian home is understood to be an inspection." On the discrimination faced by Indians, Freer and Scott disagreed. Freer noted that the settlers were prejudiced against Indians; Scott maintained that they were "unusually free from race prejudice" and insisted that Indians would face no race prejudice if placed in public schools. Freer thought that the Indians needed the protection of having their lands in trust: "We consider it an indication of competency on the part of an Indian not to request a fee patent to his allotment." Scott wrote: "These Indians should be given a patent in fee for their land, all money due them, and their names stricken from the rolls"— he thought that they could support themselves by farming the lands remaining to them. Scott had a "liberal policy" on releasing i i m funds to individuals. He also recommended that a doctor no longer be provided for the Indians by the federal government.

Why the different emphases in the reports of Freer and Scott? During Scott's term, the federal government was reducing its appropriations for the support of the Cheyenne and Arapaho peoples and was encouraging an increase in land sales through the provisions of the Burke Act. In 1917, the commissioner of Indian affairs sent a commission to review the competency of every Cheyenne and Arapaho allottee; those declared competent would have the title of their land put in fee status, and thereby it would be taxable by local authorities and the individual owner would be encouraged to sell land. Scott's characterizations of the Cheyenne and Arapaho peoples worked to rationalize the policies that encouraged the land sales and the reduced appropriations. The commissioner of Indian affairs also facilitated the dissipation of the trust fund by encouraging individuals to apply for their pro-rata shares of the funds remaining in the U.S. Treasury. In 1916, 637 of the 1,253 tribal members had withdrawn their pro-rata shares; in 1920, 404 allotments were in trust and 194 were in fee patent. Lands in fee status were rapidly sold.[43]

Scott's successor, L. S. Bonnin, continued Scott's interest in pointing out that Indians were deficient in home management and personal grooming and argued for more supervision and contact with non-Indians. In 1921 he reported that he ordered the Indians to use sheets, to not spit on the floor, to bathe often, and to not share chewing gum or not chew it in public—"refined people do not do it." He also maintained home inspections. Bonnin's survey of households included comments on the character of individual Cheyennes and Arapahos. Those who had little inherited land and property were described as lazy. Those who were well-off in inherited land and property were described as progressive. Thus, one couple with "no home" and "no funds" "live around among the Arapahos for whom the husband works some. Also he works for white farmers whenever he can get work and *feels like working*" (italics mine). Similarly, in the case of another couple, the wife received no allotment and the husband obtained a patent-in-fee for his and subsequently sold the land: "They have no home and no funds." The husband, a veteran of World War I, "works at some day labor and interpreting for non-English-speaking Arapahos *whenever he has to* for something to eat" (italics mine). In contrast, another man, who had been declared noncompetent in 1917 and who still owned land and a house, was "the most progressive Indian of this jurisdiction."

He cultivated about thirty-five acres of his own and his wife's allotment. The superintendent does not make the connection between having land in trust status and being able to support a family when he characterizes the above individuals. Similarly, he refers to a prosperous young Cheyenne farmer thus: "He has large land interests. He did not have an allotment of his own, but is the sole heir to two allotments and has a half interest in several others. He has several thousand dollars in Liberty bonds and about four thousand in cash." The man and his wife lived in her parents' house, and he farmed, raising twenty-eight loads of milo maize, one hundred bushels of corn, and ten tons of hay.[44]

Although the chiefs were generally acknowledged as legitimate spokespeople for their districts, as the government became less interested in promoting farming and more interested in destroying the Cheyenne-Arapaho land base and trust fund, the superintendents' characterizations of these leaders increasingly turned negative. Superintendent Scott reported, "We teach the Indians that one man is as good as another. That any of them can come to the office and transact business for himself more successfully than through a 'chief.' The result is that the younger and more progressive element is rapidly gaining the ascendency." He challenged the chiefs' right to represent the views of others and implied that chieftainship was elitist. Scott advised the commissioner that to undermine the chiefs was to "lessen tribal control" and economic cooperation among Cheyennes and Arapahos.[45]

The chiefs disputed this characterization. We have seen that chiefs who went as delegates to Washington also directly opposed government policies on leasing, land sale, distribution of IIM money, religious repression, competency classifications, and social integration with settler society. They also directly challenged federal officials' discourse about Indians. In 1909 the delegates made it clear that they knew enough about local economy to recognize that they were being cheated in land transactions and that the agency officials were not protecting their interests. Chief Mower argued, "When the Indian comes to sell his land, very often his land is undervalued, about half what the value of the land is in the same community. Although some white people are getting $6,000 and $8,000 for their land right beside the land belonging to Indians, the Indian's land is selling at from $1,000 to $3,000. We want our land to be appraised at its market value. Also, while white people are getting from $200 to $300 for their leases, we are getting from $50 to $150 for the same or better land."

The characterization of laziness and improvidence was addressed by delegates in 1911. Arnold Woolworth challenged the idea that leasing improved Indian lands and helped them acquire the means to farm: "These land grafters . . . lease all these lands and do not work it themselves but sub-lease it to some poor farmer . . . and in that way make more money. . . . The consequences are that he . . . lets it run into cockle berries." He also challenged the wisdom of the IIM restrictions: "I am honest and try to be honest in the payment of my accounts but since the lease money has been . . . paid in the form it has been we all have to become debtors to the class of traders who accommodate us" and lose the property we mortgage. The restrictions on I I M money were challenged by Arapaho chief Middleman in 1915: "Young men handicapped by lack of money—*so called lazy,* [the superintendent] want them to work on farms on nothing. All want to make good living, but want some one to show us—give us money to start" (italics mine). He was arguing that the government employee who was supposed to assist with farming efforts was incompetent and that small monthly allowances were not adequate to purchase equipment to farm successfully. Chief Fighting Bull added, "White farmers have all equipment—we have money on deposit but cannot get it." In 1926 Chief Crooked Nose argued that Indians should be allowed to purchase an automobile if there were adequate funds in their I I M accounts: "They would save [money]. After working the horses in the field all day they don't like to drive them around in the evening."

The competency policy was challenged by the 1909 delegation. Chief Mower insisted, "We do not want to be blamed for non-progressiveness. . . . We want the Indian Office to hold our trust funds here as tight as it can. We want the restrictions tightened instead of removed, because . . . speculators take the money from us; we are not able to cope with such people." He also recommended that an Indian court be allowed to determine competency, not outsiders. The heirship policy was challenged by the 1912 delegation. Chief Old Crow remarked that older Indians should make heirship decisions: "It has happened several times that property, both land and personal, has not gone to the right persons." In 1914 the chiefs protested the competency categorizations again: Chief Big Nose argued, "We are not the prosperous people that the government thinks we are."[46]

Not only did delegates disassociate camps and gatherings from lack of industry, but they occasionally challenged the officials' characterization of their ceremonies as fundamentally different from those of the settlers. As Red Bird told the commissioner in 1911, "Sometimes I feel that they will prohibit me from having these celebrations and gatherings, and since I have come here to this country [Washington] I notice that the white man has different ways of amusing himself, as the theater and moving pictures." Chief Mower told the commissioner of Indian affairs in 1922, "There is other work which God has given us as Indians. . . . I have special reference to our dances." In other words, ceremonial "work" was a valued contribution to the support of the society.[47]

Delegates also challenged the idea that Indians would be "civilized" by contact with settler neighbors. The threat to put Indian children in public schools and withdraw government support from the local boarding school provoked Chief Hail to argue: "Mr. Scott encourage us to send our children to the public schools. There are some Indians who have tried that, and we find out that it don't work, and we want to put all our children back to the boarding school." Assistant Commissioner H. B. Meritt countered, "We want to . . . develop the Indians to a higher civilization, and it is our wish that the Indians . . . learn to work and become progressive the same as white men. . . . We want the Indian children to get in contact with the white children and to get the benefit of their civilization." Bird Chief Sr. remarked in response, "Now in regard to the public schools of our state. Compare the white children and the Indian children. They look on one another—one is the black sheep." In 1920 Lime argued, "We can't send them to the public schools because the white people don't want them to go there." In 1926 Lime reiterated, "We find that in public schools our children come in contact with the fast, forward movements of life and do not as a rule get the attention that they are entitled to and do not learn to assert their rights. Or, in other words, they are usually kept back and are considered as inferior and all the white children are considered superior and so it is impressed in the minds of our children."[48]

The delegates rejected the idea that the discourse in the official correspondence was accurate and made that point to the commissioner. Arnold Woolworth said, "It is all right and proper work of looking into the conditions of the Cheyenne and Arapaho tribe of Indians . . . but it would be more justifiable . . . [if you were to] go there in person and consult with every Indian on the lands . . . and that information is better than to step into the office and see a letter from the farmer and base your opinion on that." Chief Tobacco challenged the entire rationale for the civilization program, arguing that the federal government should live up to its treaty obligations and that when the Cheyennes and Arapahos ceded the lands in 1891 they thought they would have their allotments in trust status for fifty years. In any case, they argued, fee patents should not be given before the end of the twenty-five-year trust period written into the Jerome Agreement. Assistant Commissioner Meritt responded, "We are living in a new time. . . . We are living in the time of the telephone, the flying machine, and the telegraph, and we cannot expect to revert to the old days. . . . It is the duty of the Indians to . . . get out of their minds the question of the . . . old time." Tobacco replied, "I was thinking of the early days, before the white people discovered America. I wonder if that history has been done away with?"[49]

The delegates also rejected the characterization of native leadership put forth by local superintendents, for example, that they were elitist and dictatorial. In 1914, when Arapaho chiefs requested permission to send a delegation, they reported that they "gathered in council" to send "unanimous sentiments and wishes." Members of the 1917 delegation made the same point. Hail began his speech by saying that he was "requested by my people." Cut Finger said, "My people have sent me here to state certain facts to you." The other delegates made similar statements. White Wolf, a Cheyenne member of the 1920 delegation, stated: "I am not here personally but through my people." Medicine Grass, an Arapaho delegate in 1926, stressed that he was "directed as a delegate"; his fellow delegate Henry Little Bird remarked that he was "acting on the instructions of" his people.[50]

Cheyenne and Arapaho individuals who never went on delegations also confronted and challenged federal policies, although the record of these confrontations is not as well preserved as the transcripts of the delegates' councils with officials. On the general policy of economic individualism, one Cheyenne man's views appeared in a local newspaper and stand as a general critique: "They are trying to make us stingy and so mad over the money. White people has got mad houses full of people that craves money but I never want to see a mad Indian over money." On another occasion, John Seger related an incident when he was in conflict with Cheyennes and Arapahos over a permit for the Sun Dance: "I told the Indians that all . . . who wore a blanket and had paint on their faces could have a 'Sun Dance.' On looking over the crowd of 150 persons it was found that only three had paint on their faces and only three were wearing blankets. . . . They said, however, they thought the line was drawn too close. I then told them that I was willing to let all the Indians have a 'Sun Dance' who had their scalp locks braided. Seven of these were found. . . . The subject was dropped with a laugh, some Indians remarking, however, that they liked to get together once in a while and visit their friends and have a good time, even if they did not wear a blanket and have their faces painted." Seger was oblivious to the import of gatherings for the Cheyennes and Arapahos during these years, just as the Cheyenne man's challenge to federal policies was ignored by officials.[51]

Characterizations of Indian character appeared not only in the discourse of federal officials but in the local print media as well. Were there parallel themes that worked to rationalize the exploitation of Cheyennes and Arapahos by their settler neighbors? Newspapers began to be published in Canton, Geary, Calumet, and other towns amid or adjacent to allotment clusters soon after these towns were opened. These papers reflected the popular attitudes of Euro-Americans toward African American and Indian American peoples. These views were given public expression in courts, schools, state and county politics as well as the media. Cheyennes and Arapahos were aware of the media presentation of Indian imagery, and some subscribed to local newspapers and most read them, at times using the newspapers as a vehicle to address this imagery.

Canton's newspaper was the *Canadian Valley Record* (later renamed the *Canton Record*). Canton, established in 1905, was a small town with a few businesses, which at first were operated out of tents: a general store, hardware store, grocery, bank, law office, feedyard, newspaper, and saloons. The population was only about 650 by 1909. Canton's early settler population had a high percentage of first-generation European migrants and was predominantly Republican. Calumet was an even smaller town, whose non-Indian population was only 429 as late as 1917. Although Calumet was predominantly Democratic, the newspaper there, the *Calumet Chieftain,* and it seems the general populace, was less virulently hostile to minorities than was the Geary populace. There were several mixed-blood Cheyenne and Arapaho families that settled in this area and involved themselves in the local community affairs of the non-Indians there. Geary was established in 1898 and by 1902 had a population of 2,500. In 1902 Geary had ten groceries, four hardware stores, four lumberyards, three pool rooms, seven saloons, four feed stores, three blacksmiths, five restaurants, three harness shops, three meat markets, a bottling works, two dry goods stores, two general merchandise stores, two furniture stores, four liveries, two cotton gins, four hotels, one flour mill, four elevators, two brickyards, two banks, six churches, six lawyers, seven doctors, and two newspapers. The Geary population was solidly Democratic, and there was a sizable segment of the community who were ex-Confederate soldiers or other immigrants from the southern United States. African American immigrants also moved to the Geary area.[52]

During the early twentieth century, there were a number of general themes in the local newspapers' coverage of the native population. Most of the references in the Canton and Calumet newspapers were to local Cheyennes and Arapahos rather than to other groups in Oklahoma and elsewhere. The Geary newspapers paid less attention to the local native population. Local Indians were presented as harmless, childish people. Many of the stories, especially in the Canton newspaper, concerned their usefulness as entertainers who drew business to the area. Their value as entertainers lay in their representations of the "olden days." Indians received treatment that would not be appropriate for Euro-Americans, and this treatment was reported as humorous anecdotes. It is also clear from the media coverage that Canton and Calumet residents associated with Cheyennes and Arapahos in social contexts more than did Geary residents. Canton and Calumet newspapers mentioned individuals more frequently and characterized them more positively than was done in the *Geary Bulletin* and the *Geary Journal.* Positive mention of Cheyenne and Arapaho individuals consisted of praise for agricultural or property-oriented activity (for example, having a house built). In all these newspapers, there was a sharp contrast between the coverage given Native Americans and that given African Americans. While Native Americans might be ridiculed, African Americans were vilified.

In all the newspapers mentioned above, local Indians were portrayed as childish and somewhat ridiculous. Consider the *Canadian Valley Record.* In a 1905 item, the editor commented that a townsman discussing a political matter struck "the attitude of an Arapaho brave addressing his followers just previous to a melon-stealing expedition." In a 1906 story about an incident in Canton entitled "Indians and Booze," the editor told of how two "white men" watched a particular individual, who was intoxicated, walk into a building in town, followed him, and forcibly removed him from the building: "The Indian struck at his captor, as the latter thought, with a knife. Charlie landed once and Mr. Indian hit the street 'all spraddled out' . . . but . . . he was unhurt." They searched him for weapons and found none. Then Charlie "picked up a piece of thin board and literally 'spanked' the red man." Later, they saw him and asked if he was lost. "He said no; but his tepee was." In a 1926 story about the early days in Canton (when merchants in Kansas were competitors), the editor recalled that there was much drunkenness, that "the Indians celebrated with newly-made Kansas friends." And their "friends cut the pigtails from the heads of the drunk Indians and carried them away as souvenirs." The publication also sporadically made reference to the general laziness of most Indians. For example, in a 1912 story, the editor tells of an Indian who was hauling wood during one of the stormiest days of this winter and was asked, "Why don't you haul your wood on good days and not haul in a storm?" His answer was: "On good days I have no time to haul wood." In a 1927 story about a meeting of superintendents from the seven western Oklahoma Indian agencies, the editor comments that they discussed how to make Indians "a real asset to the counties and communities they live in, which many of them are not at the present time."[53]

The *Calumet Chieftain* published the following item in 1911: "An Indian was told one time that feathers made a nice soft bed, so he decided to try it. In consequence, he got himself one lone feather and after sleeping all night on it, he decided the 'white man heap much liar. Feather bed no good.'" The editor stated in a 1912 issue: "Indians in a few years will be on an equal footing with their white brethren." Indicative of the laziness theme, a 1915 story reported, "Almost all the Indians have good gardens this year. Mr. Tardy [government agricultural worker] has kept after them pretty close."[54]

The *Geary Bulletin* quoted Black Coyote, one of the most prominent Arapahos in the Calumet area, as purportedly saying in February 1902, "heap big rain this week," thereby ridiculing not only Black Coyote but also native ritual life by characterizing it as "rain dancing." Similarly, the Arapaho Sun Dance was described as "a mammoth frost" in a 1908 story. When two Arapaho men were arrested for public drunkenness in July 1903, the editor described the incident thus: "Ollie had to use force in taking them and is now carrying his arm in a sling. Use a club next time, Ollie." The editor also had this comment on Indian work habits in an August 1903 story about federal protections for Indians: "Those who know the Indian best know that lots of money has been wasted on him. Uncle Sam should put 'poor Lo' to work for his daily bread, and then he wouldn't want to spend all his rental money for 'fire-water.'" (Stories often referred to Indians as "Poor Lo," from a line in a popular poem written by Alexander Pope). In a 1907 issue, the editor made this satirical comment on federal policy: "Heap Big Indian! Me No Work! Squaw Do Heap Work!"[55]

Stories about Indians from other parts of Oklahoma also portrayed them as harmless, childish, and unjustly wealthy. In a 1924 *Canton Record* story originally printed in *Leslie's Weekly,* an issue of beef to the Ponca is described as a "savage fete," where excitement was as "great as at their ghost and war dances" and where there was "wild, weird chanting." In a story reprinted in 1926, Yaqui dances are characterized as "weird-looking" and exhibiting "semi barbaric music" and "mystic chanting." These events are portrayed as primitive but not dangerous. In another 1926 story about the exploitation of the Osage, they are described as having "untutored minds" because the oil royalties they received resulted in their being victimized by non-Indians. The *Calumet Chieftain* referred to the Osage as having a "protracted picnic" with their money in 1909. The *Geary Bulletin* referred to the "passing" of "Poor Lo" as "decreed" when the Dead Indian Land Act was passed in 1902. Resistance to federal Indian policy in Oklahoma was largely confined to a group of Creeks under the leadership of Crazy Snake, whom the *Geary Bulletin* described as an "armed revolutionist" in 1902. In a 1903 story, the Osage were described as "the richest people on earth." In 1910, the *Geary Journal* editor referred to Indians in Oklahoma thus: "Lo, the Rich Indian."[56]

In contrast to the patronizing tone of stories about local and nonlocal Indians, the stories reprinted in the Canton and Calumet papers about African Americans in other parts of Oklahoma stressed the violent nature of African Americans and the legitimacy of violence used against them. Almost weekly in the Canton newspaper and frequently in the *Calumet Chieftain,* there were stories about violent crimes reportedly committed by African Americans and the almost routine lynchings that followed. The terms "negro" and "nigger" were used in reference to African Americans. The Geary newspapers expressed overtly hostile sentiments toward the local African American population as well. In 1902 the editor of a Geary newspaper reportedly commented that he "wouldn't shake hands with colored." In retaliation, according to the *Geary Bulletin,* the "colored people of Blaine county" decided not to shop in Geary if the businessmen did not renounce the editor's statement. An African American man subsequently assaulted the editor, and thereafter a story appeared that maintained that "colored people are nice to trade with," don't "push themselves onto white people socially," and "do not contend that they are our equals socially." The *Geary Bulletin* continued to regard African Americans as a threat in Geary, attacking their support for the Republican Party in 1906: "These coons had better bring a 'laetle' out."[57]

The Canton newspaper was more circumspect about local African Americans. In two 1911 stories, reporting that a Negro killed a white man in Watonga, the editor also noted that there were "law abiding colored people in Watonga." When a Ku

Klux Klan organization bent on attacking "negros and foreigners" became active in Blaine County in the 1920s, opposition materialized, and the editor reported on the opposition's activity. Comparatively, the Native American population in Blaine and Canadian Counties was not regarded as dangerous. In 1905 an Arapaho man and a Euro-American neighbor had a violent confrontation in which both were killed. The editor of the Canton newspaper pointed out that the "white man" was trespassing and had made himself "obnoxious to the Indian." The incident was referred to as a "mutual killing." During the early twentieth century, there were two other incidents reported in the local newspapers of an Indian assaulting a white man, one in the Calumet area and one in Geary. In both cases, the Indian was arrested and fined but not harmed physically. When the African American was compared to the Native American, as in this 1908 item, the former was portrayed as potentially dangerous and the latter as naive: "Poor Lo has got the negro crowded close for first place in affection for a ripe watermelon. The Indian will have them if he has to buy 'em and the negro will get his if he has to—ah hush."[58]

All the aforementioned newspapers commented on native religion. The significance of Cheyenne and Arapaho ceremonies and of camp life escaped the understanding of the settlers, but the Cheyennes and Arapahos often were described as "good entertainers," who could be counted upon to draw crowds to witness "olden time" performances. As historical relics, they were useful. Their images in nineteenth-century garb were used in advertisements in the Canton newspaper. The Fourth of July celebrations were major occasions when towns competed to attract Indian camps with dances, horse races, parades, sham battles, and "traditional" performances. Businessmen provided beef and other provisions to persuade Cheyennes and Arapahos to attend and perform at the celebrations, and the *Canadian Valley Record* editor encouraged non-Indians to attend. In a 1911 story, the editor commented that the "Indian dance" was "certainly worth going to." Later he added that visitors from Chicago had come to see the Indians "in their native wilds, and secure Indian relics." In a 1921 story, the editor noted that a large crowd of whites and Indians had come to Cantonment to the celebration there to observe Indians dancing in "costumes of the olden times." In a 1924 story, he commented that the Fourth of July celebration at Cantonment was "something worth coming many miles to see" with the "full blood Indians dressed in native Indian costume." In 1926 he wrote that the Cheyenne Sun Dance camp at Cantonment was "in the customary horse-shape figure as in the days of old" and that the "camp is alive with the spirit of the old west." He described the ceremony as a "reenactment," where "rapidly diminishing members of the old generation" told stories.[59]

The Calumet newspaper also presented the camp ritual life as a relic of the past, doomed to extinction. In a September 1911 story, the Cheyenne and Arapaho fair was described as "a representation of old time Indian life, manners, customs, with games and dancing. . . . The entertainment will be interesting and instructive." The Arapaho Sun Dance in August of that year was referred to as a "fiesta." The activities at the 1912 fair were described thus: "mounted Indian warriors, dressed in the regalia of old time Indian warfare [engaging in a sham battle]"; "a wild and picturesque spear and scalp dance," where the dancers would "reproduce a scene of primitive savagery now seldom witnessed." In a 1915 story, the fair was referred to as "a source of curiosity."[60]

The *Geary Bulletin* took a more hostile stance toward dances and fairs. In a 1902 story, the editor remarked that whites who went to the dance near Geary would "see a gang of old Indian bucks act the fool." In an item later that year, he added this description of events at the dance: "a few of said 'noble red men' hopping up and down and yelling 'ki yi, ki yi' and keeping step to the soul-inspiring sound 'tum, tum, tum, tum' made by the medicine man." The next year the Sun Dance was described as a "barbarous," "fanatical frenzy" with features of "madness, mutilation, physical ruin, and death." In later years, the ceremonies largely were ignored by the *Geary Bulletin*.[61]

While the majority of the Cheyennes and Arapahos were described as useful to the Canton community only in their role as historical relics, a few individuals were singled out and praised for productive activity, such as those who were doing road work, farming, building houses, and attaining formal education. The newspapers mentioned Cheyenne and Arapaho individuals from time to time, and for some years there were "Indian columns." Individuals regarded as progressive received the most attention; the nonprogressive ones generally were mentioned only when they died. In a 1907 story, the editor singled out a young Cheyenne man who had written him: the letter was "a pretty good letter for one of our Indians"— written in a better hand than that of most local non-Indians, the editor thought. Indian or white Canton men who served in World War I were mentioned in praiseworthy terms. Deaths, births, marriages, and visits to the newspaper office and to out-of-state locations were reported. Sporting events, including horse racing, in which Cheyennes and Arapahos excelled, also were reported in the Canton newspaper. In the *Calumet Chieftain*, the individuals mentioned during the first and second decades of the century generally were from one of the mixed-blood families, that is, descendants of white men (who had been agency employees or soldiers at Fort Reno) and Cheyenne or Arapaho women. One mixed-blood youth was often singled out for athletic prowess: "the star Indian pitcher" in 1909. Both baseball and basketball were popular, and the towns organized teams. The best Indian athletes played on these teams, and the towns played teams from the agency boarding schools. The Cheyennes and Arapahos at Canton had their own team during some years. Productive activity also was mentioned in the *Calumet Chieftain*: an Arapaho man, who was farming, was described in 1915 as a man who is an "exceptionally bright Indian and [who] looks out after No. One." The Geary newspapers had fewer references to individuals, and most of these were items about drunken Indians, but the editor did mention the marriage of a boarding school graduate in 1903, "a bright looking and well educated" girl. [62]

By and large local editors avoided acknowledging the forms of exploitation to which settlers subjugated the Cheyennes and Arapahos. Editors in Canton and Calumet did acknowledge, though very infrequently, that Canton and Calumet benefited economically from the presence of the Arapahos and Cheyennes, who were important consumers, who had title to inexpensive land that drew farmers to the area to settle, who attracted tourists and people from other towns to support local businesses, and whose ceremonies offered opportunities for merchants to run concessions. In a 1925 story, the *Canton Record* editor noted that the monthly payroll at Cantonment was from $11,000 to $35,000, second only to the payroll at the nearby gypsum company ($50,000). He also noted that Indians spent over $30,000 in the area from their rentals. The exploitation of Indians was noted only in connection with Watonga residents, whom the editor criticized in 1909 as "land grafters." The editor at the *Calumet Chieftain* noted in 1903 that the Cheyennes and Arapahos spent about $3,000 a month in Calumet, income essential to the town merchants. He wrote in 1910: "The road northwest of town is being worked by the Indians. . . . They are doing fine work and have twenty men and ten teams. In fact, they are showing the 'pale faces' how to 'do things.' " There was no mention of the ways in which settlers profited from the vulnerability of Cheyennes and Arapahos. Superintendent Bonnin turned a blind eye to the exploitation as well, noting that settlers wanted Indian business and Indian land, if not social intermingling: "in a business way there is complete cordiality." And in 1927 he wrote: "The business men of the different towns covet the Indians' business and naturally solicit their trade, and they can not afford to be unfair with them because there is too much competition," and ownership of automobiles allows at least some Indians to travel to where better prices can be obtained. (Automobiles were one of the "extravagant" purchases that control of I I M accounts was designed to prevent.) [63]

The Geary newspapers portrayed the Cheyennes and Arapahos as parasitic members of the community. In 1902, in urging the passage of the legislation that promoted the sale of deceased allottees' lands, the *Geary Bulletin* argued that "Dead Indian Land" retards the development of Oklahoma. In later years, Geary editors pressed for the abolishment of the trust status of all Indian land. The editor of the *Geary Journal* wrote in 1909 that it was "a great pity that every acre of Indian land can't be sold to the white settler. . . . The noble (?) Red man is certainly a wart on civilization for he neither lives on, cultivates nor improves his land, pays no taxes, never works the roads, and in fact does nothing to uplift himself or uphold the community in which he lives." [64]

The visibility of Cheyennes and Arapahos as groups and as individuals in local newspaper stories decreased gradually until the second decade of the century, when the examiner of inheritance began to hold frequent hearings to resolve a backlog of cases. Federal agents released income from land sale only in small amounts each month or in large amounts for a specific purpose that promoted productivity or improved property. The superintendent might approve the purchase of farm equipment, stock, and materials for house building. Newspaper coverage of individuals' activity increased as Cheyennes and Arapahos obtained cash, with most of the published references drawing attention to house building and so on. These activities employed local non-Indians and improved business in the towns. In the *Calumet Chieftain,* an Indian column was published under various names from 1913 to 1919: "C & A Agency," "Indian Mission News," "Indian Items," "Indian Inklings" (the heading of which featured a dancing Indian male wearing a feathered bonnet and carrying a spear and tomahawk), and "Among the Indians." These columns praised Cheyenne and Arapaho individuals who sold land and purchased property from merchants.

Beginning in 1921, the column "Indian News" appeared in the *Canton Record.* Unlike the columns in the *Calumet Chieftain,* this feature was written by a member of the native community. The column appeared almost weekly in the newspaper and reported births, deaths, marriages, and the health status of Cheyennes and Arapahos (mostly Arapahos, as the columnist was Arapaho). The most significant material, however, was about the native community's activities—this information provides a window into the efforts of Arapahos and Cheyennes to perpetuate communal economic activity and cooperation. The columnist routinely reported about joint farming endeavors or cooperative work parties when they occurred. Sponsored feasts—in which the household on an allotment butchered stock and invited other families to a feast, often financed by an elderly member of the household— were frequently mentioned. Many of these feasts were described as "Indian weddings"—that is, an exchange of property between relatives of the bride and groom. The columnist noted visits between families of different districts, an item parallel to the numerous mention of visiting in local news columns written by settlers about the settler community. Of course, the visits involved camping with other families. That the bilingual columnist wrote about these activities for the local newspaper, in cooperation with members of the native community, indicates that the resistance to assimilation policies was widespread and involved more than chiefs confronting federal officials.

Not only did the reported activities serve as a counterpoint to federal discourse arguing that assimilationist policies were beneficial to those willing to work. The columns also satirized or tweaked the federal officials and the settler community generally. Nicknames sometimes were used as a kind of in-joke, as was the title "chief" in connection with young individuals who actually were not regarded as chiefs. Arapahos and Cheyennes had the custom of changing their names to reflect new experiences or statuses. Individuals were referred to by new names translated into English. Arapahos or Cheyennes could identify the individuals but non-Indians could not, unless they knew the individuals intimately. These nicknames, Indian names, and titles worked to satirize white imagery. Code phrases were used to communicate about peyote meetings, virtually under the nose of the non-Indian officials, who subscribed to the newspaper. Similarly, one of the Arapaho community leaders, active in sponsoring feasts and dances well into the 1930s, was quoted by the editor in a 1924 item as remarking that Indians must "give up the customs of their forefathers."[65]

Sometimes the correspondent made pointed remarks critiquing or satirizing the behavior of particular local Cantonites and agency personnel. In a 1922 column, he commented, "There are a quite a few white people did not like they Indians children in Public Schools. What you know about it." In an item later that year, he reported that the agent and the government farmer soon would visit Indian homes in the Canton District: "Farmer and Agent are the visitors, so look out Indians." The federal policy was to discourage though not forbid dancing in the 1920s. One Arapaho ritual leader regularly directed these dances, and in a November 1922 item the correspondent reported that "Heap of Crows made it rain" (a play on the newspaper stories that often characterized Indian ceremonies as "rain dances") and that the "Indian Farmer visited the dance and says hope to have another dance." The government farmer was so piqued that he insisted that the editor print a disclaimer.[66]

In 1928 Cheyenne and Arapaho local communities still had a sense of group identity and still challenged the dominant ideology about Indian character in the ways open to them. In the years to come, the land base continued to shrink and the communities and the chiefs faced new challenges. While the use of the term "chief" in "Indian News" served as a critique on the inability of settlers to understand the native society in their midst, it can also be argued that the somewhat cavalier use of the term, even in jest, reflected the beginning of a loss of respect for the ability of intermediary chiefs to help the native community deal with economic problems, although in camp rituals, chiefs continued to perform respected roles.

3
Toward a New Deal
TRANSFORMATIONS IN COMMUNITY AND GOVERNMENT, 1928–76

In the spring of 1933 five elderly Arapaho chiefs traveled to the agency office at Concho to talk to Superintendent L. S. Bonnin. Little Raven Jr. had made the seventy-mile trip from Canton to urge the superintendent to persuade the commissioner of Indian affairs to support an extension of the trust status of Cheyenne and Arapaho lands beyond 1937. Bonnin refused to discuss the matter, insisting that only the elected representatives of a tribal council he organized in 1928 would be heard. Shocked, Little Raven Jr. exclaimed, "Am I a Chief?" Bonnin replied that he was but an honorary chief and could not expect to speak to officials on his people's behalf. This incident highlights the attitude of the federal bureaucracy toward native leadership at the time, an attitude that helped transform Cheyenne and Arapaho political organization. The federal attack on chieftainship and other Cheyenne and Arapaho political traditions at once spurred native leaders to resist as much as they could the imposition of Western political values and encouraged them to adopt political innovations. In 1928 the Cheyenne and Arapaho General Council was established, and the Cheyenne-Arapaho Business Committee organized in 1937 under the auspices of the Thomas-Rogers Act (or the Oklahoma Indian Welfare Act). In the mid-1950s, the Cheyennes and Arapahos received a judgment for the United States' violation of the 1851 treaty. Through all these changes, leaders persisted in pursuing legal claims on behalf of their tribes, insisted on the relevance of chieftainship in the polity, and criticized the federal government's performance as trustee for Cheyenne and Arapaho lands. At the same time, the sentiment of Cheyennes and Arapahos in the prewar years was to make political changes that could accommodate both the traditions of chieftainship and the ambitions and concerns of young people whose economic future was especially precarious. By involving younger men in councils, the Cheyennes and Arapahos also addressed the criticisms of the BIA. The new political institutions that emerged after 1928 occurred in a social context in which Cheyennes and Arapahos also challenged an ideology promoted by the wider society, that Indians were poor because of their own deficiencies and that Westernization of their political traditions offered an opportunity to progress.[1]

World War II led to a significant exodus from the local communities, as Cheyennes and Arapahos worked in the war industry or fought as members of the armed services. After the war, the federal relocation program encouraged the trend of out-migration, and intertribal ceremonies became more popular. The local, rural community's control of political and ritual life began to weaken. In this new social context, the Cheyenne and Arapaho peoples realized the long-held goal of winning their claim against the United States for the violation of the 1851 treaty. The tribal membership increased dramatically after 1955 by the addition of individuals deemed eligible to share in the award. In this "claim era" Cheyennes and Arapahos began to challenge the business committee and the concept of tribe. In 1975 this challenge culminated in the revision of the 1937 constitution that had been accepted at the time the Cheyennes and Arapahos agreed to reorganize in conjunction with the Thomas-Rogers Act. And, concomitantly, the post–Self-Determination Act tribal government was born. This chapter first considers the social consequences of out-migration for the rural communities, then discusses the struggle of the Cheyennes and Arapahos to preserve political traditions and counter the way they were characterized by the wider society during the New Deal era. The third section of the chapter focuses on how the 1955 claim award led to a grass-roots movement to change these traditions.

Community and Its Transformations, 1928–76

In the 1930s Cheyennes and Arapahos found themselves impoverished, with their land base largely gone. Civilian Conservation Corps camps provided an irregular source of income for many, who worked together in "Indian camps." In 1939 only seventy families still worked at farming their own land, and 68 percent of the allotted lands were no longer owned by Cheyennes and Arapahos. Some of the remaining allotments had as many as 150 heirs. The rural communities continued to suffer during the war as the United States withdrew funding from the BIA. Adverse weather conditions resulted in crop losses from which Indian farmers could not recover, and more and more land was sold. By 1949 most of the Cheyennes and Arapahos were living in what officials described as deplorable conditions in "shack camps or tent settlements" near towns. The few Cheyenne and Arapaho farms that remained had less than half the average acreage of non-Indians. Rehabilitation projects established on the tribal reserves by the federal government had fared no better than the family farms, and several of the families there subleased to non-Indians. Local organizations, aided by agricultural extension workers who encouraged gardens and tried to teach such skills as canning, offered some social support for those still living on allotments. In 1952 the extension agent reported that only about one-fourth of the families had gardens and that families moved frequently, accepting hospitality from others when their supplies ran out. By the 1950s, few Cheyennes and Arapahos still farmed. After World War II high prices for equipment and low agricultural prices forced most to sell or lease their land. Only forty-three families were farming in 1953, and, of that number, twelve were "successful," according to federal officials. That year the median family income was between $1,000 and $1,200. Almost half of the families relied on welfare and lived in multiple family households. The remainder were described as "self-supporting" on "seriously deficient budgets."[2]

After the United States entered World War II, several hundred Cheyennes and Arapahos joined the armed services. Many families left the rural communities to work in defense plants in nearby states. Their return to the communities in significant numbers after the war helped transform ceremonial life and also had political repercussions. Veterans expected leadership positions and needed nonagricultural jobs. But jobs in rural western Oklahoma were hard to come by. Many families did not return after the war. In 1947, 35 percent of the 3,528 Cheyennes and Arapahos resided away from the agency. In the mid-1950s, when the federal government began to encourage relocation from rural or reservation communities to urban areas, Cheyenne and Arapaho families again left Oklahoma for Wichita and Dallas, and many relocated to Oklahoma City.[3]

Before the war, Cheyenne and Arapaho ritual life was centered in the home districts until the annual Cheyenne and Arapaho Sun Dances, when people from all the districts congregated. Community halls and camps that formed around these buildings drew people in the districts together for hand games, feasts, and social dances. These gatherings required the cooperation of senior family members in the districts and often were organized by chiefs, most of whom had recognition for their support of ceremonies more than for their intermediary political roles. In fact, after the 1930s those chosen to replace the "old chiefs" might be referred to in the local communities as "honor chiefs." Holiday dances—Christmas, New Year, and Easter, in particular—served as opportunities for districts to entertain each other. Veterans of World War I played a key role in organizing many of the dances, especially those held on Armistice Day or Flag Day. In these contexts, families might distribute gifts to honor a family member. The giveaway tradition expressed and reinforced values of generosity and sharing and continued to be associated with prayer, that is, with making a sacrifice that could bring favorable attention from the Creator.[4]

During World War II, soldier dances to honor and support Cheyennes and Arapahos serving in the armed services became a community preoccupation. World War I veterans played prominent roles here also, but the chief organizers were the women of the War Mothers organizations in the local districts. Several of these women composed honor songs for these ceremonies. Symbolism associated with war exploits helped spark new interest in the Cheyenne soldier society and chiefs rituals as well. For example, a "Fox Clan song" was sung in honor of two servicemen in a 1951 ceremony. Veterans were inducted into these organizations, and Arapaho veterans were selected in later decades for Arapaho chief positions. During the Korean War, these ceremonies to honor soldiers continued. They were sponsored by the soldier's family but held in the local community hall. In 1950 the Forty-Fifth Club was organized by mothers of Cheyenne and Arapaho soldiers mobilized into the Forty-Fifth Infantry Division. The club gave soldiers "warriors' honors." Many Cheyennes and Arapahos made a career out of the military and, after they retired, returned to the Cheyenne-Arapaho area, where they became involved in chiefs' and societies' activities.[5]

In the 1950s, district communities continued to sponsor dances, but the trend of individuals' families sponsoring a dance for them—a birthday dance or other honor dance—gained ground. The powwow also became increasingly important. Dances referred to as "powwows" were held in the late 1940s, often with the assistance of local towns that hoped to use the "Indian Dance" to attract business. Gradually these events became managed exclusively by Cheyennes and Arapahos. They were held in towns and attracted people from a number of tribes, who came for contest dancing and to see the variety of outfits and dances, to hear the different kinds of songs, and to visit. A local committee made up of people from several districts organized the powwows. Families held giveaways on these occasions.[6]

The powwow became a vehicle for individuals and families who had left the local communities to maintain or reestablish ties with their home communities or the Cheyenne-Arapaho community. Sometimes in the early years dances were referred to as "homecomings." These gatherings also offered people still in the districts an opportunity to revitalize dances and associated customs, although powwow committees usually had some members who did not live in the local district. Communities held benefit dances to raise money for their powwows. Benefit dances also were held for individuals (for example, a soldier returning to duty) or organizations (for example, the Native American Church). Between 1958 and 1962, the head staff tradition became institutionalized. Individuals and groups were invited to help the powwow committee organize and support a powwow. These head staff positions were the emcee, head singer (or head drummer), and head man and head lady dancers. The selection of a powwow princess also became institutionalized. Gradually, more positions were added: head little boy dancer, head little girl dancer, and co-hosts (groups such as clubs or veterans' organizations). Individuals and their families could fulfill their obligations by attending the powwow but might offer additional help and involve their relatives in more long-term support for the powwow. Thus, people not living in the local communities might serve on the head staff for a powwow. Honor ceremonies for individuals were incorporated into the powwow as "specials" (which included a giveaway by the family or the honoree). Annual powwows began to be held in Colony, Clinton, Canton, and other communities on a fairly regular basis.[7]

The powwow also became an arena for the expression of self-determination and pride in Cheyenne and Arapaho heritage. The prominent role of veterans and the associated American flag, the focus on the war dance (derived from the older Omaha Dance), giveaway ceremonies (into which the powwow princess and head staff were integrated when as individuals they were honored), and the feast (or "feed" or "dinner") all combined elements of ceremonial life of prior eras with post–World War II interests or developments. The powwow clearly was viewed as a ceremony that helped promote social cooperation and attract a blessing from the Creator. The Cheyenne-Arapaho columnist in the *Watonga Republican* characterized the powwow season thus: "long summer of fellowship, friendships renewed and the spirit of the drum." In their powwows Cheyennes and Arapahos distanced themselves from the imagery of Indians as relics and presented their communities to the public on their own terms. Although some of the romantic imagery of the town celebrations involved portrayals of "traditional" life and Indian princesses, the meaning of powwow symbolism, appropriated or not, emanated from the contemporary experiences of Cheyennes and Arapahos.[8]

The struggle to regain the Fort Reno lands figured in the ceremonial life of the Cheyennes and Arapahos in the 1930s and after. They held gatherings there to affirm their rights to the land even when the army still occupied the site. The El Reno powwow in the 1950s took form in the context of the Cheyennes' and Arapahos' conflict with the town of El Reno, which objected to the tribes' recovery of Fort Reno and was attempting to enlist Cheyenne and Arapaho performers in a tourist-oriented powwow. In this context, the Cheyenne and Arapaho Business Committee opposed cooperating with the city on the organization of the powwow. In addition, there were speeches made by Cheyennes and Arapahos during the powwows that praised the Cheyenne and Arapaho way of life and contrasted it favorably with the life ways of the surrounding non-Indian community. Settlers who were regarded as helpful to Cheyennes and Arapahos might be singled out for praise, as in the case of J. M. Haigler, for whom the Canton Arapahos named their Barefoot Powwow; as one spokesperson said, Haigler "never turned an Indian way from his door without some sort of aid."[9]

While the participation in powwow activity grew, the Sun Dance ceremony remained important to many families. The Arapaho Sun Dance was last held at Cantonment in 1938, where a Northern Arapaho ritual leader presided. After 1938, several Arapahos went to Wyoming to participate in the Sun Dances there. The Cheyennes had a Sun Dance and Arrow Renewal ceremony on a regular basis, holding the rituals near Canton until 1974, when rival groups of ritual leaders came into conflict. In 1974 and 1975 the ceremonies were held in the Watonga area. At the 1974 Arrow Renewal, there were about one hundred camps. At that time initiation ceremonies were held for the Dog, Kit, Hoof Rattler (Elk), and Bowstring societies. Arapahos ceased to initiate men into the lodges; the last lodge ceremony was the Tomahawk Lodge, held in Canton in 1931. There also was a brief revival of the Star

Lodge, but it was secularized and functioned largely as a powwow organization sponsored by Arapaho chiefs. Sun Dance participation had for some time bridged differences between peyote devotees and Christians, for Cheyenne society members had responsibilities in the Sun Dance regardless of their association with peyotism or Christian churches, and Arapahos viewed the Sun Dance as noncompetitive with peyote and Christianity, although there might be friction between some peyote and Christian families.[10]

Because peyotism faced opposition from the state of Oklahoma, supporters of this religion cooperated to resist persecution. Distinct Cheyenne and Arapaho forms of the ceremony had developed, and each group sent its own representatives to Native American Church conventions. Peyotism allowed an individual more flexibility in ways of worshiping, and it involved a less onerous and expensive apprenticeship than the Sun Dance organization. There was a fusion of native and Christian elements that greatly assisted individuals through life crises, and prayer meetings took place frequently. Congregations formed in cities, such as Dallas, where Cheyennes and Arapahos had migrated, and local prayer meetings gradually involved both Cheyennes and Arapahos as well as the occasional person from another tribe. Thus, peyotism accommodated the more urban lifestyle of many Cheyennes and Arapahos. During the Vietnam War, meetings were held frequently for soldiers.[11]

Christian congregations led by native preachers and with strong women's organizations developed and enabled Cheyennes and Arapahos to separate themselves from a repressive missionary tradition. Christians and peyotists (participation in these faiths was not necessarily mutually exclusive) were drawn together in powwow activity, which drew everyone's participation because of the broad-based values and political interests it served.

The chieftainship positions were held by men who participated in peyotism or Christianity (or both) as well as in the Sun Dance. Cheyenne chiefs had duties connected with the Sun Dance, although they did not necessarily participate as directors or votives. Prior to 1928 the chiefs were elderly men who were prominent in their districts; many were considered experts on treaties, and some of these served on the business committee. The chief position had to be earned by years of good works and by giving economic assistance to others. A new chief was chosen by the sitting chiefs, who considered a man's character carefully before appointing him. Before World War II only a few men were chosen to replace deceased chiefs. About 1920, Arapahos chose as chiefs Dave Meat and Wilbur Tabor, both born in the 1880s and both successful farmers who, with their wives' help, could help needy families. Ralph Goodman and George Rearing Bull were among the few chosen by the Cheyenne chiefs. Several veterans of World War I were selected later; in 1945 Dan Blackhorse, for example, was chosen by Arapaho chiefs. These five men were major supporters of community activities in their rural districts. In the 1950s several others were chosen.[12]

In the 1960s, in the midst of a movement to revive traditional activity, many men were selected as chiefs, and this pattern continued into the early 1970s. Selections included middle-aged and younger men. Most were employed full-time in the wider economic sector or were retired and drawing pensions. Many lived outside the local rural communities, which reflected the increase in the urban sector of the Cheyenne and Arapaho population. Often the selections were proposed by the individual's female relatives, who appealed to the sitting chiefs and promised full support from family members. At about this time, some people began to express the idea that chieftainship was hereditary, for example, that a son should succeed his father or grandfather. Elderly people were skeptical of many of these selections: those chosen had not earned the position and lacked the ability or inclination to help the local communities. Although Cheyenne chiefs were expected to be present for certain of the Sun Dance rituals, not all were. During the 1960s two Cheyennes selected were Lawrence Hart, a retired Air Force officer and Mennonite minister in Clinton, and Sam Buffalo of Seiling, a fairly prosperous farmer and Native American Church official. Arapahos selected Willie Hail of El Reno, a veteran who retired from a job at Tinker Air Force Base and a participant in the American Indian Exposition, and Clarence Tall Bull, a decorated World War II and Korean War veteran, who lived and worked in the Oklahoma City area. Participation in community activities and, by the late 1960s and 1970s, support for native religion were viewed as important qualities for chieftainship. In short, the intermediary leadership (or business committee) role and the chieftainship role had become compartmentalized by the 1970s.[13]

"We Are Not Slaves or Children": Treaty and Tribe, 1928–55

Although the Cheyenne and Arapaho chiefs had succeeded in getting the trust status of allotted land extended from 1927 to 1937, the federal government continued to promote the detribalization policy by exerting pressure to force the Cheyenne and Arapaho peoples to accept Western social institutions and abandon tribal customs. Officials particularly set about undermining the chieftainship tradition whereby local communities authorized chiefs to articulate their views to officials. The poverty of Cheyennes and Arapahos worsened during the Depression, compounded locally by a drought. Still, as before, federal officials attributed poverty to character deficiencies on the part of the Indians. World War II brought a withdrawing of federal resources from Indian communities, as attention shifted to the war effort. For elderly people, most of whom had land from which they drew income, and those few younger people who had retained some inherited land, the economic problems of the community adversely affected their ability to collect rent from their leases.

Landless young people particularly struggled, trying to find work in a depressed economy in which Indians were socially marginal.

At the suggestion of Superintendent L. S. Bonnin, a General Council was organized in 1928, to which local rural districts elected representatives. The intent of the BIA was that the General Council would replace chieftainship. After John Collier became commissioner of Indian affairs, the Cheyennes and Arapahos elected representatives to a business committee, which was recognized by the BIA and dealt with as a tribal government, acting on behalf of the members of the two tribes. During the years when the General Council represented the tribes and during the time when the tribes were pressured to organize a business committee under the Thomas-Rogers Act, the issue that particularly engaged both federal and tribal officials was that of chieftainship.

The General Council and the Thomas-Rogers Act, 1928–37

On 6 January 1928, Cheyenne and Arapaho men organized the General Council in response to suggestions from Superintendent Bonnin. At the time, the tribes' effort to file claims against the United States for treaty violations was stalled. Their requests for permission to send delegations to Washington to obtain the commissioner's support for hiring an attorney and obtaining Congress's consent to file claims had been refused. The feeling among Cheyenne and Arapaho leaders was that if they agreed to form an elective body, these leaders would be more successful at moving the claims forward than the chiefs, whom the federal government disparaged.[14]

On May 5 the participants in the General Council met and agreed to make the organization permanent. The following year they worked on a constitution and bylaws with Bonnin's help, and the council approved it on 25 May 1929. Officers (president, vice president, and secretary) would serve two years, and local communities would each elect four delegates. By custom, two delegates were "old chiefs" and two were young, "educated" men, according to federal officials. The Cheyennes had eight communities: Calumet, Kingfisher, Watonga, Canton, Longdale, Weatherford, Clinton, and Hammon. Later, in 1932, Canton and Longdale combined for the purpose of electing councilmen. The Arapahos had six communities: Calumet, Geary, Greenfield, Canton, Carleton, and Colony. Later, in 1934, Geary and Calumet combined. A majority of the districts had to be represented in order for a quorum to be established. The council rotated the meeting place among the communities, and local businessmen donated dinner when the council met in their town. The few members who had automobiles picked up the others and drove them to the meetings. Other than mileage expenses for the drivers, the councilmembers received no compensation.[15]

Delegates chosen by the General Council went to Washington in March 1928 to try to secure permission to retain their attorney, who had already begun working on their claims as well as those of the Northern Cheyennes and Arapahos. The bilingual delegates, Cheyennes Alfred Wilson and Robert Burns and Arapahos Arnold Woolworth and Jess Rowlodge, needed the Indian Office's approval of the attorney's contract and of their efforts to get Congress to extend the deadline for filing claims.[16]

The General Council continued to try to send annual delegations to pursue the claims and to work on other concerns, but they frequently met with resistance from the Indian Office. Consistently, the council chose delegations that contained both old chiefs and young, educated, bilingual men. This combination was viewed as promising in terms of dealing successfully with the bureaucracy in Washington. The older men knew the history of the treaties, and the younger men could communicate effectively and comprehend the legislative process and legal contracts. But the Indian Office wanted to limit the size of the delegations and to discourage the selection of non-English-speaking delegates.

In 1931 the General Council obtained permission from the commissioner to send four delegates to Washington to discuss the attorney contract. In February, Chiefs Turkey Legs and White Shirt went with Alfred Wilson and Jess Rowlodge, after other Cheyennes and Arapahos donated money toward their expenses. Both Wilson and Rowlodge had made a study of claim matters. The delegates succeeded in getting a contract with an attorney. Councilmembers Chief White Shirt from Canton and Chief Little Bird and Henry Rowlodge (a Carlisle alumnus) from Geary signed the contract for the Arapahos. For the Cheyennes, Chief Turkey Legs from Watonga, Chief Kias from Clinton, and Philip Cook, a bilingual man from Kingfisher, signed. Another delegation, authorized in June 1932, consisted of only two councilmembers, Jess Rowlodge and Alfred Wilson, after the Indian Office rejected a larger number. The two delegates urged action on the claim, expansion of the Concho school to include grades higher than the ninth, collection of outstanding rents on Indian land, and protection from taxation of Indian trust land. Although the council wanted to send a delegation again in 1933, the commissioner refused to allow it.[17]

It is clear that the organization of the General Council was viewed by Cheyenne and Arapaho leaders as a means to attain influence with the officials in Washington, given these officials' hostility to chieftainship. Arapaho Chief White Shirt did not hesitate to describe himself as a chief who was *also* a "member of the chair and table council," which he contrasted with the earlier councils of men who had met at gatherings to discuss the tribe's well-being and sat on the ground in a circle. White Shirt stated that the men's rationale for organizing the council was to seek legislation to allow the pursuit of claims: "the government ought to see we are teaching ourselves many new ways and thereby assisting the commissioner and his staff in many ways, especially through these councils, . . . and that he, our commissioner, ought to see or recommend that we get this money [to pursue claims] as we want it; if not, I think Congress will help us."[18]

Although the constitution, which Bonnin had taken part in drafting, provided for the election of representatives to council office and for decision making by majority vote, both of which were new kinds of political processes, these procedures were implemented in a way that the superintendent had not anticipated. Majority voting was tempered by customs of civility that deterred speakers from directly contradicting or criticizing others, and individuals were reluctant to appear too prominent. Sometimes those who had held an office declined to serve again so that the position would rotate, and the group resisted delegating any authority to the president to make decisions independently of the council. Remarks were carefully translated into English, Arapaho, and Cheyenne.

The presidents of the council (successively, John Block, John Fletcher, and Mack Haag) were Cheyennes whose fathers were non-Indian, but there is no evidence that "traditional" people generally opposed the General Council. Chiefs, Cheyenne headsmen, Arapaho lodge members, Native American Church members, and elderly as well as young men all served on the council. All the important Arapaho chiefs were councilmembers: Little Raven and White Shirt from the Canton area and Ute, Sage, and Little Bird from the Geary area. Cheyenne chiefs from all the Cheyenne communities had council positions, for example, Turkey Legs from the Watonga area, Jacob All Runner from the Thomas area, Elk River from Hammon, Kias from Clinton, and Magpie from the Canton area. There were far more Cheyenne than Arapaho chiefs, however, so not all of the Cheyenne chiefs were on the council, which occasionally led to bad feeling. When the young secretary, Jess Rowlodge, was criticized by some tribal members for accepting reelection, both Arapaho and Cheyenne chiefs spoke on his behalf, stressing his knowledge about claims and the financial sacrifices he had made on behalf of the pursuit of the tribes' claims. Generally, all the districts were represented at the meetings, which were held several times a year. Women participated in the local district meetings and apparently could vote, although none served on the General Council.[19]

Cheyenne and Arapaho leaders insisted on including both chiefs and the young bilingual men favored by the BIA on the council and on delegations. Cheyenne men who submitted a petition to Commissioner C. H. Rhoads in 1931 wrote, "It is nothing but right and fair to our people to have on all committees at least as many chiefs and head men as there are of the younger men. That would satisfy all." In a 1930 council meeting, Chief Red Bird Black from Canton argued for the importance of including men who were "informed correctly like our young men are informing us today." In selecting delegates in 1932, Henry Rowlodge expressed the council's consensus: for each tribe to choose a "well informed educated young man that is also a good interpreter, one old chief, and the third man a middle age, head man or leader who can understand both [either Cheyenne or Arapaho and English]." Significantly, to be qualified as a representative, these leaders stressed, a man must be able to speak and understand his native language; thus, those raised by a non-Indian father and unable to demonstrate their loyalty to and cultural understanding of the Indian community by and large were not supported for council positions.[20]

A reading of the minutes of council meetings shows that the representatives from the local communities confronted and critiqued the ways Cheyennes and Arapahos were represented by federal officials. Superintendent Bonnin consistently linked improvements in living standards to a commitment to individualism. He said, "The most important place from which Indians can and should expect help . . . is from themselves." They should "struggle just a little bit harder to make a living," for most were "too dependent on the government." Ironically, and to the disgust of the council, this superintendent urged that non-Indian lessees who were in arrears be given extensions on payments. Commissioner Rhoads was sure that the elective General Council would be superior to the "older form of council which was not representative, as the so-called chiefs were not selected by the tribe." Superintendent Bonnin insisted that the views of people in the local communities could not be factored into council decisions: constituents "naturally" "can not keep in close touch," so representatives should think for themselves. As for delegations, Bonnin was adamant that only "educated" men should make the trip to Washington.

But Cheyenne and Arapaho leaders publicly disagreed with these views, arguing that the treaty relationship was the basis for improving conditions and that chieftainship, as part of the treaty relationship, was a valid form of political representation. These leaders viewed themselves as acting in the best interests of their tribe, a corporate property-owning entity whose existence preceded them and would succeed them. They viewed their role as supernaturally sanctioned at the time the treaties were made. They were skeptical that the federal government would act in their best interests; it was the duty of chiefs and their helpers to lobby the federal government. Councilmembers talked at length about their role, as they saw it. Ben Buffalo stated, "We are moving into the right direction slowly for our children and the old people's good." Helping children and elderly people was part of a man's religious duty, especially if he had a leadership position. Cleaver Warden agreed: "This council was organized for our best interests of our future generations." He insisted that his father told him that "the Government promised [by treaty and thus with supernatural sanction] to always help Indians; he wants to see that promise made to his father fulfilled." Chief Little Face, referring to the delegates' sacred duty to the people, commented that the delegates should "try hard and think of [that is, pray for] the people who will stay awake in their homes at night listening for good news." Cheyennes and Arapahos viewed chieftainship as relevant to the tribes' interests, even though most recognized that compromise was necessary in terms of involving young men with different kinds of background in council activity. Jess Rowlodge insisted, "Without the old chiefs and headmen, the council could not function very well." As for the rejection of the council's choice of delegates, which included chiefs, Chief Kias told the superintendent, "We will re-adopt the resolution [to send certain delegates] even if the Commissioner of Indian Affairs has seen fit by his limited knowledge of our affairs to object to our reasonable request." He continued, "We know the conditions of our people." Woolworth, a chief and former scout, said, "We have some old chiefs, leaders, while they may not be educated, they are deep and logical thinkers." Thus, Woolworth countered the idea that a councilmember or delegate should have a formal education. Little Bird agreed, saying that he "knew what he was doing when he was a chief"; he asked the superintendent if he was still a chief, and the superintendent told him it was an honorary position. Little Bird threatened to see an attorney. The Arapaho delegates viewed their responsibility to be to other Arapahos, as did the Cheyenne delegates to other Cheyennes, for each tribe's representatives had signed treaties separately. As Cheyenne Chief Turkey Legs explained, they would work "as two tribes." And Woolworth said, "Let us be equal representatives in all."

Although the superintendent insisted that the federal government would act in the best interest of the Cheyennes and Arapahos, council representatives publicly disagreed with him. Chief Little Raven said that the patent-in-fee Indians are not capable of taking care of themselves and should be protected "just the same as the 'so-called' incompetent Indians" (here he reflects on federal officials' use of the term "so-called chiefs"). Local newspapers had help from federal officials, the councilmembers thought, in promoting the idea that Indians were wealthy and did not need all their land. Sage said, "Talk was common among white people that the Cheyenne and Arapaho Indians were all 'well-to-do,' but that belief was wrong and not true." When the superintendent assured the council that the federal government would protect Indians that needed protection, the councilmembers challenged him. Woolworth said, "Look back a few years when we had hundreds of thousands to our credit, most of which has been spent on our now abolished reservations [schools and agencies] which buildings are now rotting or wasting away. Think of old Darlington [agency] that sold almost for nothing and we know nothing about it in time." Jess Rowlodge referred to the refusal of permission for a delegation: "If the council is recognized as an organization of any power or effect and the government wants us to learn to be self-reliant as Indians, here and now is the time to prove our rights." Wilson said, "We can not sit here and let the Indian Office think for us. . . . Our future generations depend on our duties in a fruitful way. If we are of any power as a council, we should be represented in person by our delegates. We do not want to be as our seven chiefs were treated in the Agreement of 1890, when the claim to pay attorney fees was slipped in by fraud." Chief Kias noted, "We had lots of land once, now it is just a memory that hurts us." Chief Little Face said, "The Commissioner of Indian Affairs handles our money for us. We never use much of it directly ourselves; he is used to handling it for us anyway he wants to but it does not benefit us much as Indians. White men that work for him get more help than we get; they get new cars, good houses to live in but we remain poor at our poor homes. Our children get hungry and wear old torn clothes. These things we want our delegates to talk about for us up there." John Heap of Birds argued, "It seems the Cheyenne and Arapaho tribes have been doing their business by force against the dictators of the Indian Office, so I think we can do it again." Chief Turkey Legs maintained, "This council is nothing the way the commissioner seems to look at it. We are not slaves, or children, as far as expressing our own conditions are concerned."[21]

The ability of the council to retain community support depended in large part on the extent to which they could influence federal policy. Early in 1931, Dan Black-horse, an Arapaho representative from Canton, remarked that the people in Canton were interested in the work of the General Council but were "sometimes disappointed" with the results of their efforts. A group of elderly Arapaho chiefs went to see Superintendent Bonnin in November 1932 to express their worry that the most recent delegation did not get guarantees of economic aid, that the issue of the extension of the trust status of the Cheyenne and Arapaho lands (due to expire in 1937) had not been resolved, and that there were no loans for economic development. They also expressed fears that the government would "turn loose" people who had patent-in-fee status land. Again in March 1933, Arapaho chiefs Ute, Sage, Little Bird, Little Raven, and White Shirt met with the superintendent on these problems. Economic survival for Cheyennes and Arapahos now was dependent on cash income, and individual wage work or income from landownership (allotments or shares therein) had replaced the communal sharing organized by chiefs in the past. Chief Sage realized how these conditions contributed to the organization of the council on which he then served, stating that he knew he was not an "active chief" anymore, that "money is the important thing now."[22]

The beginning of the Depression sent Oklahoma into an economic decline, and a drought from 1934 to 1936 compounded the problem. The farmers leasing Cheyenne and Arapaho lands could not make their lease payments, which deprived the Indian landowners of income. Arapahos and Cheyennes who owned land could not afford the equipment necessary to farm it; and, they could not obtain loans from local banks, as they could not put up trust land as collateral. At the same time, the federal government was reducing services. Desperate for aid, the hopes of Cheyennes and Arapahos were raised after John Collier became commissioner of Indian affairs in 1934.

Collier took office in 1934, appointed by President F. D. Roosevelt, whose New Deal policies were designed to counter the effects of the Depression. The New Deal for Indians was described as "self-determination," although in practice much of the program was imposed on native communities. Collier intended a radical change of federal Indian policy. He proposed that the land base for Indians be increased, reservation economies developed, native culture and language encouraged, and tribal governments given real responsibility and authority. At the same time, the federal government, in an effort to counter the social and economic problems of the Depression, instituted work and other programs that eventually brought new opportunities to Oklahoma native communities as well as to reservations.

In Oklahoma, the general population did not embrace the proposal to increase Indian landownership and reverse the longstanding trend of land loss. Senator Elmer Thomas worked against including Oklahoma tribes in Collier's Indian Reorganization Act (or the Wheeler-Howard Act), which was the legislation passed in 1934 designed to put Collier's policies into effect. Instead, Thomas worked on revisions that culminated in the Thomas-Rogers Act (or Oklahoma Indian Welfare Act), passed in 1936. All this activity generated renewed interest in the General Council among Cheyennes and Arapahos.

After Collier took office, he instituted a series of meetings with tribal officials from throughout the United States to explain his new approach and to try to generate support for the passage of the legislation. Few Cheyennes and Arapahos actually understood the proposed legislation, and they were fearful that it would result in the further loss of their lands. Collier was proposing to buy allotments and put the land into trust for the tribes rather than for individuals. This struck Cheyennes and Arapahos as a ploy to force the few remaining landowners to give up their land. Collier and his staff met with General Council delegates in Oklahoma City on 8 February 1934, after they had been briefed on his proposals on 3 February. The council selected Chief Kias and John Fletcher (Cheyennes) and Chief White Shirt and Dan Blackhorse (Arapahos) to attend Collier's address. Chief Turkey Legs and John Otterby, a Cheyenne headsman, also went, though not as official delegates. The delegates used the opportunity to mention their claims to Collier, and they obtained his consent for a delegation that spring to check on the progress of the claims. The General Council met 17 February to discuss Collier's plan but took no action. Although much of what Collier said was looked upon favorably, they still feared that they would lose land and even be removed from their homeland altogether. However, hopes were raised for the extension of the trust status of allotments, and the young, landless men, who had not been allotted or who had sold their allotted lands, hoped that they would benefit from the new policy.[23]

One of the most encouraging developments to come out of the talks and corre-spondence with Collier and his staff was the possibility that the reserves (the lands retained by the federal government for agencies and boarding schools at the time of allotment) would be used to settle landless families on farms and that the Cheyenne and Arapaho Tribes would regain joint title to these lands. Elderly Arapaho and Cheyenne leaders were adamant that the government had agreed to return these reserves to the tribes when they were no longer being used for agencies and schools. The reserves at Colony (Seger), Canton, Hammon (Red Moon), some of the land at Concho, and Fort Reno (no longer being used for troops) were all viewed by the tribes to be rightfully theirs as a result of the Jerome Agreement. These lands were being leased out to non-Indians by the federal government, the proceeds being used to help pay the Concho agency's expenses. The size of the land involved was 2,445 acres at Colony; 154 acres at Clinton; 1,280 acres at Hammon; 3,020 acres at Canton; 5,200 acres at Concho; and the acreage on the Fort Reno military reserve. In 1934, out of the original 528,789 acres there were only 172,000 acres of allotted land still in Indian ownership, 130,000 of which were in heirship status (and, therefore, likely to be sold).[24]

Thomas's bill had most of the features of the Wheeler-Howard Act, or Indian Reorganization Act, which was prepared by Collier's staff. Thomas met with the Cheyenne and Arapaho General Council to explain the bill and solicit their sup-port. He linked the success of their claims to acceptance of the Thomas-Rogers Act, and as he was chair of the Indian Affairs Committee in the Senate, his support was vital to the tribes. The bill had many attractive features, aside from the fact that they stood to gain support for the pursuit of their claims against the United States: educational loans, land acquisition, extension of the trust status of Indian land, and preferential hiring in civil service positions. But still the General Council was suspicious, and they did not vote to support the bill in their 8 December 1934 meet-ing. By 1935, Collier personally was urging the General Council to cooperate with Thomas. Superintendent Charles Berry, along with other agency superintendents in Oklahoma, advised Thomas to make revisions in the bill to satisfy the tribes: insistence on the security of their title to trust land, the retention of heirship regu-lations, and economic corporations to encourage business development.[25]

Despite Collier's assurances that he favored self-governance, in April 1935 he authorized only a two-man delegation rather than the delegation of six (including elderly chiefs) that the General Council requested. Subsequently, Jess Rowlodge and John Fletcher were elected by the council, and they attended the Senate hear-ings on the bill. In meetings with officials, they expressed general support for the bill, and Collier's staff reassured them that benefits would be forthcoming—for example, that the Concho school would be improved. The delegation also worked on persuading Collier to support their effort to gain an extension of time in which to file their claims. In 1936 Jess Rowlodge and John Otterby went as delegates to try to accelerate action on the claims.[26]

The council began to feel that their suspicions were well founded when they learned that a move was afoot in Congress to transfer the Colony lands and buildings to the local public school district. The General Council protested, arguing that title to the reserve should pass to the tribes. They decided to try to forestall the loss of title by agreeing in 1935, in a fifteen-to-eleven vote, to lease thirty-one acres to the school district for a five-year period if the remainder of the land was used to establish farms for landless Arapaho and Cheyenne families.[27]

Between 1934 and 1936, federal officials applied pressure on the Cheyennes and Arapahos to reduce the size of the General Council. In December 1934 Superintendent Berry suggested that the council would work more efficiently if they elected a smaller group, a "business committee," to act as a kind of executive for the council. In this way, he thought, decisions could be reached without taking the time to listen to numerous speeches, all of which had to be translated. He suggested a committee of twelve, with the president of the council to assume responsibility for choosing applicants for various kinds of aid and for leasing tribal lands without the superintendent's approval.[28]

But the council was reluctant to agree to Berry's plan, reiterating the same objections made during the establishment of the General Council earlier. Involving a large group avoided rivalries, and dissention and bitterness would follow from a few councilmen making decisions about the lives of other Cheyennes and Arapahos, they argued. Although many of the chiefs could not speak English fluently, their participation was necessary for broad community support. In short, despite pressure from Washington, the council did not accept the idea of an executive committee making decisions for others. Chief Kias said, "Let the districts consider the thing." In the districts, the community members customarily met and discussed the issues of the day, old and young, men and women. For example, at Geary, when the Wheeler-Howard Act was discussed on 8 February 1934, two elderly women, both landowners, spoke against it. In another instance, White Rabbit, a Cheyenne, remarked at a 3 February 1934 council meeting, "I don't think there is any use asking the councilmen as to how they might answer the [Wheeler-Howard Act] proposal which is before them. I think that we all [should] go back home and ask them women folks." In fact, a large number of landowners were elderly women.[29]

Clearly, the Cheyennes and Arapahos were not ready to give up the institution of chieftainship and depend altogether on bilingual, younger spokespeople. For example, when delegates were selected to go to Washington, one Cheyenne councilmember, John Otterby, complained to Berry in a letter written in March 1935, "A young Educated Element are trying to deprive us older people from our Trible [sic] authority." He said that the council was created by a few "mix bloods" and

Superintendent Bonnin and that, while the Arapahos were satisfied with the council and "some of their old chiefs" were delegates, the Cheyenne "chiefs and Headmen" were not. He maintained that peyotists among the Cheyennes dominated the council; he described himself as "a [Christian] Church member." Apparently Otterby's peers on the council responded by electing him as the Cheyenne delegate to Washington in May 1936. The Arapahos responded through two of their chiefs, Ute and Woolworth, by suggesting in December 1935 that the council reorganize so that there would be twelve Arapaho members and twelve Cheyenne members, giving the Arapahos more leverage. Otterby's views aside, Cheyenne Chief Kias proposed in 1936 that the Cheyenne chiefs select four chiefs and the Arapahos select four to serve on the council as permanent delegates. He stated that "we older Indians look forward to the young educated element for guidance." Kias engineered a compromise, allowing for a formal role for the elderly chiefs while creating opportunities for younger men. The council supported his proposal thirty-three to zero.

The Indian Bureau continued to press for a smaller council, however. Berry suggested in 1936 that each of the eleven districts elect one spokesperson. Apparently a compromise constitutional amendment was developed; in this, the council would have one representative from each of the districts (eight Arapaho, eight Cheyenne) plus four Arapaho and four Cheyenne chiefs at large. But Reorganization was to wait until 1937.[30]

In 1937 the Indian Bureau increased the pressure on the tribes to reorganize under the provisions of the Thomas-Rogers Act. At a meeting on 19 March, Cheyenne and Arapaho councilmembers still had reservations. Henry Rowlodge asked, "Do we have to organize whether we want to [or not]? Suppose we don't organize? You know the old and young do not agree." Elderly Woolworth argued that their focus should be on pursuing the claims and that reorganization would not help them in that area. John Fletcher also pointed out that "the old Indians are difficult [to persuade]. They don't trust the younger element." Collier's representatives informed the council that economic assistance would not be forthcoming if the tribes did not reorganize. For younger men, loans and other forms of assistance were essential; landowning older people worried about the security of their land tenure. Some of the old chiefs, especially among the Cheyennes, feared that, if more power were given to an elected council, it would increase the influence of "mixed breeds" (in Calumet). James Curry, a government official, in a letter from 28 April to the commissioner of Indian affairs discussed the establishment of credit associations with some Cheyennes, reporting that one man "didn't seem to care one way or the other [about Reorganization]. All he wants is money to buy a couple of milk cows." Finally, in May Collier refused permission for a delegation to come to Washington to work on the claims. That month, the council agreed unanimously to work with bureau officials on a draft of a constitution. On 19 June a public meeting was held to discuss this constitution and hear suggestions from the tribal members.[31]

After a few minor revisions, the secretary of the interior approved the constitution and bylaws of the Cheyenne-Arapaho Tribes of Oklahoma on 25 August 1937 and steps were taken for a ratification vote. The constitution's preamble mentioned that one purpose of the business committee would be to look after claims and treaty relations. The business committee also was to act on credit applications and land acquisition. The constitution also established criteria for membership—a person had to be listed on the 1936 roll or be a child of such a person. If only one parent was Cheyenne or Arapaho, and the other was non-Indian, the business committee reserved the right to vote on the applicant. The secretary of the interior reserved the right to review membership rules. The business committee was to have fourteen Cheyenne members and fourteen Arapaho members. For the Cheyennes, chiefs and headmen were to appoint one of their number as a representative from each of the seven districts. Each district would also have one popularly elected representative. Arapahos were to have three representatives from Greenfield, four from Canton, three from Colony, and four from Geary. The constitution specified that some of the Arapaho representatives "may be chiefs." The term of the representatives was to be two years, and an individual did not have to live in a district to represent it. The quorum was to be half of each tribe's representatives.[32]

On 18 September 1937, with the expectation that support for the claims and economic rehabilitation funds would be forthcoming, the tribes voted on the proposed constitution. Many elderly and young Cheyennes and Arapahos compromised and agreed to work together toward their goals. The constitution won majority support in three Arapaho and four Cheyenne districts: Geary, Greenfield, Colony, Watonga, Kingfisher, Calumet, and Thomas. In five districts, a majority voted against its adoption. The final tally was 542 for and 417 against; out of 1,784 eligible voters, 962 voted—a little over half. Subsequent to the adoption of the constitution, candidates were nominated for the business committee. In Canton, the Arapaho chiefs Little Raven and White Shirt did not run (both were dead by 1939, so poor health may have discouraged their participation). Several Arapaho chiefs were elected in Geary, Greenfield, and Colony Districts, which had produced majority votes for the new constitution. Cheyenne chiefs met on 4 November to make their selections. The first business committee meeting was held on 13 December 1937, attended by the winning candidates, who were to serve from 1938 to 1939. Ed Burns, a Cheyenne headsman, was elected chair, and Bird White Bear, an Arapaho, was elected vice-chair. Subsequently, it became the custom to alternate the chairmanship between tribes. The new members requested $2,500 of tribal funds to pay committee expenses, including per diem. Superintendent Berry urged them to start working on accepting a charter of incorporation.[33]

The Cheyennes and Arapahos accepted Reorganization but clearly felt pressured to do so by their economic circumstances. Federal officials presented Reorganization as self-determination and argued the advantages of a small representative government for the Cheyennes and Arapahos as one people, but native leaders countered these characterizations, insisting on their treaty history as the proper model for government. In presenting the initial plan for Reorganization, Collier stressed to Cheyenne and Arapaho leaders that the new form of organization was suitable for them if they were "equipped" to exercise "powers of self-government." He insisted that the "Bill does not force upon the Indians anything" and that "no cut-and-dried formula of organization or procedure is imposed by the Bill." Senator Thomas insisted that his revisions of the Indian Reorganization Act were best for native people in Oklahoma, for "you Indians have made progress" by ceding the reservation lands and turning away from tribalism: "What is good for the white folks is good for you and what is good for you is good for the white folks." Thomas pressured Superintendent Berry to get the tribal council membership reduced in size in order to facilitate his getting their support for his own reorganization bill, the Oklahoma Indian Welfare Act. Subsequently, Superintendent Berry argued to the tribal council that they were "not able to accomplish much business" because they insisted on involving local leaders from all the rural districts, translating the long speeches of elderly chiefs, and otherwise adhering to tradition. When the Cheyenne and Arapaho leaders began to work on a constitution for the reorganized government, Berry pressured them to organize as "the Cheyenne-Arapaho Tribe" and referred to the combined peoples as "your tribe." B I A officials also wanted to reduce the enrollment of the Cheyenne-Arapaho Tribe by requiring a minimum "blood degree." "It seems logical," Berry wrote, that anyone less than "one-fourth Indian blood" "should not be considered an Indian at all." When presented with these arguments, Cheyenne and Arapaho leaders directly challenged the statements and views of federal officials.[34]

In response to Collier's initial proposals, councilmember and chief Alfred Wilson remarked, "I think that the Commissioner should ask the Indians to lay a proposition before him instead of him laying a proposition before the Indians to consider." Three years later, councilmen still were skeptical about whether a "new deal" existed for native leaders: Chief Kias complained, "When we get together, the first thing we hear, 'You are not to talk of other things [depart from the meeting's agenda]. . . . We can't speak our thoughts. This must be a white man's council." As in pre–New Deal times, chiefs particularly warned Cheyennes and Arapahos not to believe federal policies to be in their best interest; as one put it, they "treat us like horses [that is, drive us]. . . . The white man is not really our friend." They were clear on why they agreed to Reorganization—to get access to government funds and to pursue treaty claims. Cheyenne and Arapaho leaders, supported by their constituents in the rural communities, continued to insist that by treaty right chieftainship was a legitimate form of governance and that their method of holding council and their chiefs' participation would permit good management of tribal affairs. Cheyenne councilman John Fletcher expressed consensus when he insisted that chieftainship "history" had "a sacred origin." The desire to have old and young representatives on the council, the compromise developed by the council in response to B I A pressures and economic cleavages within Cheyenne and Arapaho communities, was validated by that treaty history. As Jess Rowlodge explained, the chiefs needed "young men to read for them. Way back to Medicine Lodge Treaty they had some one to aid, read and learn for them." Cheyenne chief William Goodsell urged, "Young men, chiefs and head men, let us cooperate as one body. . . . We as chiefs are unable to present our need to the Superintendent." A representative of the Calumet Cheyenne community, the home district of most of the Cheyenne councilmen who were descended from American settlers, also urged the council to resist pressure to alter the compensation of the council: "For the sake of harmony . . . let the tribal committee, as now composed, be allowed to stand, as an elective body, now reorganized by most of the old chiefs and head men." The business committee, then, became the main vehicle for Cheyennes and Arapahos to realize their goals.[35]

"Looking for Money Power": The Business Committee, 1938–55

The 1938–39 business committee became disillusioned very early in their tenure when they realized that they could not meet all the expectations of their constituents (see table 1). When committeeman Chief Elk River spoke in a June 1938 meeting, he noted that people were dissatisfied because they saw no benefits from Reorganization and that they were "blaming the committee." A general council, attended by people from all the districts, was held on 5 October 1938. Continuing the custom of a gathering held on Labor Day, there was a feed, or "feast," a dance, and, in addition, in the afternoon a meeting in which committee members gave reports and heard comments. People complained about inadequate medical care, the failure of the government to provide credit and more land, little progress on the claim, and, especially, new regulations on the disbursement of individuals' income from leases and land sales. The new policy was to disburse small amounts monthly and to stop advance payments and purchase orders. The changes would make it more difficult for people to subsist. They would have to go into debt to storekeepers to obtain supplies.[36]

The business committee members were particularly incensed that they continued to have difficulty sending delegations to Washington. In April 1938 the commissioner refused to support a delegation. The committee kept insisting, and, finally, in August 1939 Jess Rowlodge, Theodore Haury, Ed Burns, and John Otterby went

Table 1

Cheyenne-Arapaho Business Committee Membership, 1938–41

1938–39 (1st)

Cheyenne	Arapaho
Ed Burns	Anita Washee// Philip Watan
Albert Short Teeth	Wilbur Tabor// Charles Woolworth
Phillip Cook// Sampson Lamebull	Sage
DeForest Antelope	Henry Rowlodge
Big Medicine	Otis Bates
John Heap of Birds	Ralph Little Raven
Alfred Wilson	Robert Sankey
Guy Heap of Birds	Bill Williams
Henry Elk River	Theodore Haury
Ernest Goss	Oscar Birdshead
Kish Hawkins	Ute
John Greany	Scott Harrison
Herbert Walker	John Blackman
Ida Chapman// David Fan Man	Bird White Bear

1940–41 (2nd)

Cheyenne	Arapaho
Sampson Lamebull	Philip Watan
DeForest Antelope	Otis Bates
Alfred Wilson	Charles Woolworth
Ernest Goss	Theodore Haury
Kish Hawkins	John Blackman
Herbert Walker	Jess Rowlodge
David Fan Man	John Levi
George Rearing Bull	Walter Fire
Richard Boynton	Charlie Cedartree
Frank D. Bushy // Clarence Shepard	Matthew Hail
Baldwin Twins	Dan Blackhorse
Flynn Goose	Thomas Lee
Albert Hoffman	Ben Red Buffalo Jr.
Joseph Washa	Luther Bringing Good

KEY: // Resigned

to Washington, where they obtained a new contract with an attorney and lobbied for a jurisdictional bill from Congress that would allow them to present a case to the Court of Claims. Delegates also appealed to the Indian Bureau for more help in alleviating poverty.[37]

Committee members and other leaders complained that the Indian Bureau routinely disregarded their wishes in matters relating to the hiring of government employees and to the leasing of allotted lands. Committee members also insisted that tribal government lacked adequate financial resources. As Saul Birdshead put it in a June 1938 meeting he attended as a visitor, the business committee needed to have "money power." But money power was a double-edged sword. Funds for economic recovery and development were inadequate, so when the committee made decisions about how their resources were to be used, those left out were resentful. The availability of rehabilitation money from the federal government raised people's expectations, but only a few could actually be assisted.

Constituents often were unwilling to accept the committee's decisions, especially if they were denied assistance. In a September 1938 meeting, committee member Chief Philip Cook warned the committee that the people in their districts should be consulted to make sure they approved of committee actions: "The Committee thinks it is the boss and it is not. If you take up this [rehabilitation fund] matter so that it will be satisfactory to the tribes, there will be no trouble. If you do not take it up with the tribes, there will be rumors against the committee once again." People in the districts wanted community halls built or repaired, homes built and repaired, farming equipment, and relief payments or relief work. In response to their constituents, the committee designated rehabilitation funds for the construction of community halls in the districts. The federal government permitted families to settle on the Colony reserve lands, allowing the committee to choose the applicants who were to settle there.[38]

The second business committee (1940–41) continued to try to convince the federal government to transfer title to the Red Moon and Canton reserves to the tribes. At the committee's annual meeting in October 1940, attended by about one thousand Cheyennes and Arapahos, a resolution was introduced to that effect in front of several Indian Bureau officials anxious to win the tribes' acceptance of a charter. Tribal leaders had long held that by treaty the reserves should have been returned to the tribes after the agencies closed there. Indian farms could be established on these lands. Moreover, if the tribes had title, the money from leasing land would go to them rather than to the federal government.[39]

In August 1940, with Indian Bureau support, the committee began discussing amending the constitution to reduce the size of the committee in order to cut down on expenses. In August 1941 seven Cheyenne and seven Arapaho members were selected from the committee membership to draft a constitutional amendment to reduce the number of representatives and to determine their manner of selection. In October, at the annual meeting, only four hundred Cheyennes and Arapahos were in attendance, but a standing vote was taken, and the group accepted the amendment virtually unanimously. In the amendment, chiefs were not given special representation; all representatives were to be chosen by popular vote. The secretary of the interior approved this draft in December, and the amendment was ratified by the tribes on 4 February 1942. The vote was 193 to 161 to approve the amendment.[40]

A fourteen-member business committee was elected in April 1942 and took office in May. This committee and subsequent ones from 1944 to 1955 focused on approving leases and assignments on tribally owned land and on approving land sales and loan applications (see table 2). The business committees, always short of funds, struggled to obtain higher fees on leases, to pursue the tribes' claims against the federal government, and to recover former reservation lands still controlled by the federal government, including lands at Concho agency and the Fort Reno reserve. Tribal resources were augmented in 1942 when Congress restored title to the Red Moon (Hammon) and Cantonment reserves to the tribes and, again in 1946, when Colony reserve was restored. Farming and grazing rental of these lands went into the tribal account to be used for rehabilitation funding and tribal government expenses. The business committee budgeted the money. The committees never gave up on acquiring the Fort Reno reserve. After the army vacated it in 1949, they sent delegation after delegation to Washington and offered testimony in congressional hearings on the issue. They hoped to establish a cattle enterprise on these lands, which would have been a much needed boost to the economy and would have been modeled after the Arapahoe Ranch in Wyoming. Citizens of El Reno actively opposed the tribes' recovery of these lands, hoping to profit by the continued presence of the federal government or by the eventual sale of the land. The effort to recover damages for treaty violations was bolstered by the creation of the Indian Claims Commission in 1946, created by Congress to resolve the longstanding grievances of native peoples over treaty violations and other problems. Without funds to finance the litigation, the committee's task was formidable. In 1948 they hired a new attorney, William Payne, who they hoped would be more aggressive than the former one and who agreed to take their case on a 10 percent contingency fee basis. In 1955 a delegation of Jess Rowlodge, Woodrow Wilson (Alfred's son), and Fred Bushyhead represented the tribes in a meeting with Northern Arapaho and Cheyenne representatives, all jointly pursuing their claim over the violation of the 1851 treaty.[41]

In 1948 the tribes were offered a loan program, from which they borrowed $200,000 to lend to individual farm operators or to students. Problems with delinquency began soon after the start of the programs. Small-scale crop production

Table 2

Cheyenne-Arapaho Business Committee Membership, 1942–55

1942–43 (3rd)

Cheyenne	Arapaho
DeForest Antelope	Otis Bates
David Fan Man	Theodore Haury
Richard Boynton Sr.	Jess Rowlodge
Joseph Washa	John Levi
Henry Elk River	Walter Fire
John Heap of Birds	Dan Blackhorse
Ralph Goodman	Henry Rowlodge

1944–45 (4th)

Cheyenne	Arapaho
Joseph Washa	Otis Bates
Henry Elk River	Jess Rowlodge
Ralph Goodman	John Levi// George Levi
Fred Bushyhead	Walter Fire// Saul Birdshead
Peter Birdchief Jr.	Dan Blackhorse
Ben Osage	Charles Loneman
Woodson Shortman	Tom Rouse //Luther Bringing Good

1946–47 (5th)

Cheyenne	Arapaho
Joseph Washa	Otis Bates
Henry Elk River	Jess Rowlodge
Ralph Goodman	George Levi
Peter Birdchief Jr.	Saul Birdshead
Ben Osage	Dan Blackhorse
Woodson Shortman	Charles Loneman Sr.
Richard Boynton Sr.	Luther Bringing Good

1948–49 (6th)

Cheyenne	Arapaho
Joseph Washa	Jess Rowlodge
Ralph Goodman // (Unfilled)	George Levi
Ben Osage// Sam Buffalo	Saul Birdshead
Woodson Shortman	Charles Loneman Sr.
Fred Bushyhead	Luther Bringing Good
William Albert Hamilton	Thomas Lee
Fred Standing Water	William Sutton

1950–51 (7th)

Cheyenne	Arapaho
Sam Buffalo	Jess Rowlodge
Fred Bushyhead	George Levi// (Unfilled)
Albert Hoffman	Charles Loneman Sr.
Woodrow Wilson	Dan Blackhorse
Joseph Yellow Eyes/ Fred Roman Nose	Philip Watan
Oliver Roman Nose	Ben Little Raven
Sullivan Miller	Dave Williams// Walter Fire

1952–53 (8th)

Cheyenne	Arapaho
Sam Buffalo	Jess Rowlodge
Woodrow Wilson	Dan Blackhorse
Oliver Roman Nose	Ben Little Raven
Kish Hawkins/ Fred Bushyhead	Walter Fire
Joe Antelope	James Fire
Henry Whiteshield	Herman Haury
Charles Wicks	Gus Yellow Hair

1954–55 (9th)

Cheyenne	Arapaho
Sam Buffalo	Jess Rowlodge
Woodrow Wilson	Ben Little Raven
Oliver Roman Nose	Walter Fire
Fred Bushyhead	James Fire
Joe Antelope	Gus Yellowhair
Raymond Buffalomeat	Saul Birdshead
Amos Hawk	Philip Watan

KEY: // Resigned   / Died

---

in an area subject to drought was very risky, and the committee was reluctant to foreclose on clients. Before the program was terminated, tribal funds were used to retire some of the debt. The rehabilitation projects on the reserves suffered the same kinds of problems. Although in 1936 President Roosevelt had agreed to extend the trust status of Cheyenne and Arapaho land to 1962, individually owned acreage continued to decline, in part because the state of Oklahoma required families to sell their lands before receiving welfare payments and partly because loan clients often sold their land to pay off their loans. By 1953 only forty-three Cheyenne and

Arapaho families were still farming. The BIA was promoting the relocation of families to more urban areas in the 1950s, and career military service also drew both men and women from the rural districts.[42]

A major blow to the tribes was the consolidation of Concho agency with other agencies in western Oklahoma at Anadarko in 1947, which resulted in a reduced staff. An economy measure for the federal government, the cutbacks caused hardship for the Cheyennes and Arapahos. It became much more difficult for the BIA to manage rentals and sales in a timely fashion with this reduction in service. Local Indian clinics closed, and the Cheyennes and Arapahos were told to go to Anadarko. In addition, educational assistance was dealt a blow when the federal government cut funding to public schools that enrolled Cheyennes and Arapahos. The Concho Boarding School was scheduled to be closed, and the criteria for admission were narrowed. School attendance fell sharply, for Cheyenne and Arapaho families could not afford the books and other supplies their children needed in public school. Discrimination also discouraged attendance. The committee managed to convince authorities not to close the Concho school, but juniors and seniors were bused into El Reno, and thereafter attendance declined. Due in part to pressure from the Oklahoma tribes and their allies, Concho agency was reopened in 1948 with reduced staff. Threatened with the termination of federal protections in the 1950s, the business committees protested through delegations and correspondence. BIA officials concluded that the tribes were not ready for termination.[43]

The business committee members realized soon after the first committee took office that the promise of self-determination (in hiring, leasing, and land policy in general) would not be easily realized. Their constitutional government allowed only limited authority, and the financial base of the tribal government was inadequate. The business committee's constituents felt as much disillusionment as the committee members did, even refusing to consider adopting a charter of incorporation, as the BIA insisted they do. Although some BIA officials privately admitted that the available loan and land-buying programs did not allow for the Cheyennes and Arapahos to make a living on their land, federal officials publicly attributed the economic decline of the Cheyennes and Arapahos to Indian character deficiencies. Business committees protested, maneuvered, and pressured officials in an effort to achieve their goals; they also repudiated the characterizations of Indians and the officials' claims that federal directives had led to efficient and generous programs.[44]

When the business committee pressured Superintendent Guy Hobgood to accept their recommendations for hiring employees and other matters, he indicated in a December 1938 meeting that Cheyennes and Arapahos could not make wise decisions. For example, he said parents could not provide useful input on school employees, for "they would probably . . . make a poor selection." Committee member Clarence Shepard, when this topic was discussed with Hobgood again in 1941, countered that Hobgood "might think people didn't know what they were doing but the Indians knew." When committee members spoke to the need for relief from widespread poverty, Hobgood replied that Cheyennes and Arapahos were "not spending their money wisely"; therefore, he would pay out I I M money only in small monthly payments. A committee member pointed out that only about one-third of the people received lease income and that they shared with the others to prevent them from starving. John Fletcher charged that Indians who criticized government policy were put on "the black list" and were discriminated against by federal employees. In response to the business committee's effort to regain the lands at Cantonment and Hammon, Hobgood stated in 1941 that, if Congress "thought the tribes would use the land to establish farm units" (rather than leasing it for "unearned income"), they would approve the transfer.

At the general meeting of the tribes in October 1941, Assistant Commissioner William Zimmerman addressed the crowd, commenting on the character of business committee members when he remarked that a smaller business committee would be an improvement, for "a smaller committee is usually composed of more active members who do more real work." Running through B I A commentary about dealing with the tribal government was the suggestion that lack of industry led to poverty. Committee member Jess Rowlodge countered this view in that same general council meeting, remarking that the Cheyennes and Arapahos were discouraged because B I A credit regulations were too rigid and funded too few clients. John Fletcher remarked that the "reorganization program" had failed.

The kinds of exploitation and discrimination that prevented Cheyennes and Arapahos from making a living in Oklahoma and that the business committee pressured the B I A to address were not addressed, the Thomas-Rogers Act notwithstanding. Committee members pointed out that allottees did not receive market value for the land they leased, and they insisted that tribal lands should be advertised for competitive bidding when not leased by tribal members. Committee chair Richard Boynton sarcastically wrote to the Indian Bureau on 20 April 1946, stressing that without competitive bidding local non-Indians obtained Indian land very cheaply: "We the Indian did not know we were in the poor farm business to care for and give the white farmer a place to live and further give him the preference right [the right to continue to lease land that the lessee was currently farming] and security of livelihood during his natural life." Eventually, the Indian Bureau did require competitive bidding. Business committee members objected to the loss of facilities for health care, the loss of federal support for education, the reduction of B I A staff, the lack of progress on the Fort Reno claim, job discrimination, and the fact that poverty was forcing the Cheyennes and Arapahos to sell their land—all these problems were cast in terms of treaty rights. As committeeman Frank Bushy said, "Once upon a time Indians owned this country, lived all over, and they were at peace. After the white government came around and told them they were going to be protected as long as the grass is growing and the rivers run. . . . What kind of protection are they getting!" The local non-Indian community, as they did in the first half of the century, also characterized Cheyennes and Arapahos as less than fully contributing members of society. Visiting the business committee meeting in May 1948, a politician from the Canton area, working to develop the Canton Reclamation Project and to secure Indian cooperation, said: "The Indian gets a free ride, otherwise, if the Poor Lo does not want to participate," they can sell their land.[45]

In the 1950s, as the business committees struggled on behalf of the Cheyennes and Arapahos to prevent the termination of federal protections and services, they refuted local non-Indian and federal characterizations of Cheyennes and Arapahos as a people with ample resources who were poor because of their own deficiencies and whose programs should be terminated for their own good. One official reported that the Cheyennes and Arapahos (whom he described as insecure and irresponsible, not up to the "realities of life," "primitive," and "incompetent") expected the "rights of citizenship" but were unwilling to "assume all of the responsibilities that go with" it. And, "they find it difficult to resist the beckoning of the pow-wows and other native rites." Social discrimination, or racial prejudice, was discounted as not based on reality but rather as something that Cheyennes and Arapahos *felt* and that allowed them to discourage themselves: "a feeling of this type on the part of the Indians does constitute a hardship" in efforts to find a job. Local non-Indians were referred to in this report as "the normal citizenry." Much of the blame was attributed to the business committee, which "assumed but little of the responsibility for tribal welfare and self-government." Local opposition to the recovery of Fort Reno centered in part on the belief that undeserving Indians would "get rich," as one senator put it. Oklahoma A & M University was competing with the tribes for the land and presented its plan for a research station as a benefit to the tribes. Committee member Fred Bushyhead challenged the university: I have "lived here quite a while" and have "yet to see A & M College promote something where the Indian was included." Similarly, El Reno citizens who opposed the restoration of Fort Reno to the tribes were portrayed as a community that only pretended to be friendly to the Cheyennes and Arapahos. Committee member Jess Rowlodge insisted that, even though the B I A indicated that termination was inevitable, the Cheyennes and Arapahos were "not ready to be turned loose." Committee members publicly challenged the information federal officials used to promote termination. Otis Bates in a 1951 meeting charged that officials from Washington consulted the local chamber of commerce rather than inspecting Indian homes to "see actual conditions." Rowlodge commented that, if confronted with actual living conditions, "the government would be ashamed, and the state would be ashamed."

The view of the B I A, publicly expressed as well as put in official correspondence, was that the economic decline of the Cheyenne and Arapaho people was due to their inability to be "business-like," as a B I A representative put it in a business committee meeting in March 1953. Business committee members expressed their outrage at these characterizations. Committee member Walter Fire insisted: B I A officials "tell us what to do," forcing us to "act under limitations." These limitations included the closing down of boarding schools and the withdrawal of support for Indian students in public schools. The Indian students "had two strikes against them before they start." In a November 1952 business committee meeting Cheyenne constituent John Fletcher agreed with committeemen that "prejudice still exists" and that Indians are unable to get jobs and receive higher education. He stated that B I A employees who should be responsible trustees "ride in good cars," "don't look after Indians' affairs," and were incompetent in their assigned jobs: "one [government] farmer was sent here from Arkansas who didn't know the difference from maize to kaffir corn—that's the kind of people we get." As for the lack of a businesslike approach, in 1953 committee member Oliver Roman Nose confronted the official who made this accusation and insisted that the B I A was as responsible for bad loans as the business committee, because the B I A had approved all financial transactions. Fred Bushyhead pointed out that when the loan program was started they were assured that a client would be supported "all the way" in view of the problems that confronted farmers, particularly during times of drought. Foreclosure, he argued, was inappropriate. Committee members consistently pointed to constraints in the form of "regulations as set by the Washington office" and "new laws" passed by Congress without consultation with Indians as the major reasons why the Cheyennes and Arapahos were in economic decline. Walter Fire remarked, "We were [told by the B I A at the time of organization under the Thomas-Rogers Act] to help landless Indians and [the loan program] was thrown open to all the tribe for anyone who wanted to set themselves up." In this way, Fire argued, the tribes could "prove to the Government that we are going to make these lands productive" (in other words, to meet the conditions for the recovery of the tribal reserves). The B I A urged the business committee in 1954 to take legal action against loan clients, which amounted to pressure on the client to sell his land; instead, the business committee used some tribal income to make a payment to the federal government, preventing loss of land and financial ruin for the Cheyenne and Arapaho farmers who had struggled through three years of drought. Committeeman Saul Birdshead portrayed the B I A's attitude about the outstanding loans as another attempt to "squeeze" money out of the Indians.[46]

Constituents were disappointed that the promise of the Thomas-Rogers Act went unrealized but generally did not blame business committeemen personally. One committeeman, John Heap of Birds, speaking on behalf of his Thomas District in 1939, reported that his constituents opposed the B I A's disregard for the business committee's urgings that a change in the scheduling of lease payments not be made: "they say if the committee can't do anything, that we dissolve this committee." Frustrated, he said people in his district were saying that the business committee "haven't got the power," that they "were just merely put there, just by courtesy of the Indian Office." Jess Rowlodge, meeting with BIA officials in 1946, also attributed the Cheyennes' and Arapahos' lack of interest in tribal government to cynicism: "I am sorry to say there seems to be some feeling of disappointment. They [the BIA] seem to start something with the Indians, then leave them. . . . They are discouraged." People in the rural districts generally felt that, although the business committee had not been able to significantly improve living conditions, the committee was the only hope for improvement. Business committee members generally were respected senior members of families in the districts; often they were chiefs. These older men used the forums provided by business committee and general tribal meetings to air before federal officials the complaints of their districts and to persist in demanding treaty rights, as prior generations had done.

The political activity of most Cheyennes and Arapahos was at the district level. Thirty Cheyennes served on the business committee during the period 1942–55, and several were chiefs and headsmen (for example, Sampson Lamebull, George Rearing Bull, Baldwin Twins, Ralph Goodman, DeForest Antelope, Kish Hawkins, Herbert Walker, John Heap of Birds, Alfred Wilson, Philip Cook, and Henry Elk River). The average age declined as old chiefs were replaced with middle-aged men. In the 1950s there was continuity in some districts, as experienced men won reelection (in Canton, Clinton, Calumet, and Thomas), but much turnover took place in Hammon, Watonga, and Kingfisher. Among Arapahos, twenty-two men served on the committee during the period 1942–55. Few were chiefs (there were only thirteen chiefs still living in 1938, and these were not all replaced at death), and they were largely middle-aged. There was little turnover in the Arapaho districts. In the early 1950s, there was more turnover generally but still a stable leadership, considered well versed in treaty matters. After 1941, Arapaho chiefs who served were Dan Blackhorse and Theodore Haury.[47]

Local districts sent resolutions and petitions to the business committee, which were then formalized, and minutes from business committee meetings often were read at district meetings. For example, in January 1939, Geary District protested a change in lease payment policy; instead of issuing large payments several times a year, the superintendent made small monthly payments and discontinued advance payments. The district residents demanded their "right as an organized tribe to have a voice in our affairs"; "if not, then our organization means nothing and we here recommend that it be dissolved." The business committee members polled their districts on important questions. When federal officials refused to fund delegations to Washington, people in the local districts donated money to fund the delegations. Cheyenne chiefs and headsmen directly involved themselves in committee business. Individual chiefs (including the Arrow Keeper Baldwin Twins) attended meetings from time to time, giving speeches in support of committee goals, such as the return of Fort Reno. Chiefs sent petitions to the business committee, which formalized the requests as resolutions. Occasionally, they sent a representative along with the business committee delegates to Washington, and the business committee occasionally sent chiefs as representatives to intertribal meetings.[48]

Constituents' disillusionment is reflected in the election tallies. For example, 959 voted on whether to accept the constitution. In the 1937 business committee election the number of Cheyennes voting in Hammon, Thomas, and Watonga was, respectively, 80, 60, and 100, compared to 87, 76, and 99 who voted on the constitution. In the 1951 business committee election, 40 voted in Hammon, 20 in Thomas, and 26 in Watonga. In Colony District 65 Arapahos voted in the 1937 election; 21 voted in the 1951 election. A BIA report in 1953 concluded that about 30 percent of the eligible voters (1,985) participated in the 1951 election.[49]

In the mid-1950s, during the implementation of the federal termination program, there began to be some public expression of dissatisfaction with tribal government and suggestions that individualism offered the better course. There also were mumblings from some constituents that, unlike leaders in the chieftainship tradition of former times, business committee members might benefit personally from service on the committee while their constituents received few benefits. The per diem issue served as a lightning rod for the criticism. In 1940, committee members received three dollars per meeting when there were adequate funds. In actuality, months went by without members receiving per diem. Transportation and food expenses had to be covered by per diem; for men traveling from Canton or Hammon, for example, the per diem did not cover expenses. Per diem was paid for attending committee meetings, which were held monthly, and for occasional special meetings to make decisions on rehabilitation applicants. In 1946 the per diem was raised to four dollars; in 1948, to six dollars; in 1952, to eight dollars. In these times, a day laborer made about seventy-five cents an hour (about ninety dollars a month). The committee's policy in 1945 was to use no more than 15 percent of the farming and 5 percent of the pasture lease money for committee expenses. In 1946, they raised the percentages to 40 and 10 percent. In 1948, the committee budgeted $10,430 for rehabilitation projects and $1,003 for the committee expenses, which included per diem, office supplies, elections, and delegation and claim expenses. In 1953 the committee budgeted $7,385 for a burial fund to enable people to borrow money to pay the costs of funerals. That same year $5,000 was budgeted for committee expenses.

But the tribes' income was not sufficient to finance the committee's programs. The tribes' attorney, William Payne, worked to secure an oil lease on the Colony reserve lands, which would bring in more money. In talking about her father's service on the business committee, one woman from Geary recalled, "He paid half to the person who gave him a ride into town and then bought bread and meat. That's all he got out of it." Generally, business committee members were as destitute as their constituents. One of the officers was described in 1954 as a recipient of public assistance, drawing $81 a month and leasing land for $275 annually; 332 out of 711 families received public assistance at the time, and the median family income was $1,000 to $1,199. In addition to per diem, some committee members, who were trying to farm, received loans. There also were accusations that some committee members took money from loan and rehabilitation clients in return for favorable action on their requests. Once when a committeeman used some tribal funds for an unauthorized purpose, the business committee decided not to prosecute him but rather "to help him" and to "forgive" him, in the words of two committee members. They thought rehabilitation was the proper course to take in a society where people thought of each other as "relations" and where people needed to stick together in order to survive.[50]

Aware of criticism, business committee members defended themselves and their mission publicly. Jess Rowlodge, who was a long-term member of the committee and who had represented the Arapahos in Washington on treaty matters several times, stressed that building a tribally owned land base was crucial to Cheyenne and Arapaho interests and that he was worried constituents might not "appreciate having land in tribal title." At the general meeting in 1951, commenting on a constituent's statement that there were complaints about the widespread poverty, committee member Walter Fire stressed that the committee was doing their best to help. Another member, Fred Bushyhead, expressed frustration with "personal attacks." At this time there were Cheyennes and Arapahos working and residing in towns outside the local rural districts who were interested in running for election to the business committee, which some committeemen found troubling because they viewed such individuals as "outsiders," that is, no longer members of rural communities. In 1951 outsiders wrote officials in Washington while the business committee delegation was there attempting to persuade Congress to relinquish title to the Fort Reno lands. The correspondents claimed that Cheyennes and Arapahos wanted money for the land, not the land itself. Business committee members expressed alarm, urging the B I A officials not to be influenced by individuals who "don't speak for the tribe." One of these individuals began to attack the competence of committee members. Sam Dicke, a Cheyenne businessman living in El Reno who referred to himself as a "Full-Blood," had received various kinds of assistance from the committee over the years, but in 1953 he promoted the termination of federal protections and the per capita distribution of tribal assets. He told the secretary of the interior: "I realize our people will be much better off if they were not under government supervision. . . . Let our Indians come out of this backward-ness, timidness, . . . and learn to work steadily and improve themselves. . . . I realized the only way to be happy was to get away from my folks." He accused the business committee delegates of "under-world activities." The commissioner reassured Mr. Dicke about tribal finances, but he and others continued to criticize the committee members.[51]

When the tribes began receiving mineral payments from Colony reserve (from oil leases negotiated by attorney Payne), criticism escalated about how the funds (forty thousand dollars in 1954) should be used: the options were to help preserve the land base, help farming families, help the most needy, or distribute it per capita. An Oklahoma City resident and World War I veteran, Alfred Whiteman, objected to the loan program, referring to the committee as "dictatorial." Whiteman's parents were Arapaho chief White Shirt and Anna Little Raven, and his wife was Cheyenne. He had supported himself with salaried positions at the agency and, later, at Tinker Air Force Base near Oklahoma City. In a February 1954 committee meeting he argued that money from oil leases should be distributed per capita, not used for rehabilitation or legal assistance in pressing claims: "It is tribes' money; it is not the chairman's money, it is not the council's [business committee's money]." He opposed helping Cheyenne and Arapaho farmers and insisted that the business committee take a "business-like" approach: "Make the loan client dig any way to pay it back." At the annual tribal council meeting in October 1954, Whiteman presented a petition with more than one hundred signatures, which he said demanded the dissolution of the committee: the "Indians wanted a change." Sam Dicke criticized the committee for not accepting his suggestions and stated that he wanted "new people" on the committee. Arapaho chief Dan Blackhorse spoke in support of the committee's accomplishments, and Jess Rowlodge reported on the delegation's work against termination legislation. Cheyenne headsman John Fletcher, former committee member and delegate to Washington, recounted the accomplishments of the committee and stated that he "had no apologies" to make and that he had "done his duty." Charles Wicks, a World War I veteran, warned those present that if the business committee were abandoned, the Cheyennes and Arapahos "might just as well disband." Arapaho tribal member Oscar Birdshead concurred: "What would become of the people if the organization [business committee] was dissolved?" Also speaking for retaining the business committee was Arrow Keeper Baldwin Twins and Cheyenne chief All Runner, who told the council that if the business committee was dissolved, "everything would stop." All Runner said he had heard rumors but wanted people "to go along in a good way"; perhaps some committeemen could "retire for awhile and later come back but [don't] throw each other away." He and others proposed resolving the contention in the next election, when new members could be chosen to replace incumbents. In December the business committee decided to forward Whiteman's petition to the B I A.[52]

In a business committee meeting held in June 1955 the regional director of the B I A, W. J. Pitman, said that the wording of the petition was unclear but that, if clarified, a referendum could be called on changing the tribal government. There followed a long discussion, with many visitors to the meeting participating. Whiteman said his complaints centered on "questionable" bank withdrawals but that he trusted the B I A's supervision. When he was criticized by a chief for making his attacks on the committee personal, Whiteman responded that he was "born a leader" (the exchange reflecting tension between the idea that chieftainship was based on conduct and the newer view that chieftainship was inherited). Much of the support for the petition was from veterans of World War II, who wanted a larger role in tribal affairs. One veteran, Joe Pedro, said that he supported the business committee form of government and urged people to make their feelings known in the next election. Others advocated a new definition of "tribe," one that viewed the tribe as a collection of individuals entitled to an equal share of whatever income the tribes possessed so that each individual could look after himself, unhampered by others. Theodore Cutnose spoke in favor of dispensing tribal income in per capita payments. Sam Dicke stated that the business committee was not "systematical," not "smart people"—echoing, it seems, B I A characterizations of Cheyenne and Arapaho leadership. Many others expressed support for the committee, and committee members defended their activities. Committee member Woodrow Wilson noted that the expenses of the delegates were supervised by the attorney and defended his work on the committee, commenting that if he had "done wrong" he would like to be informed about it. Some Cheyennes objected to what they saw as an Arapaho attempt to unduly influence tribal government by circulating the petition. Chief Blackhorse underscored that "the Arapahos try to work together," admonishing Whiteman, who "should have come to the chiefs [traditionally peacemakers] and told them what he was doing." At the end of the day, the business committee voted to bring the petition before the next annual meeting of the tribes.

In the annual tribal council meeting in October 1955, Rowlodge spoke about the origin of the committee, noting that "it was adopted by the chiefs and headmen," and asked Whiteman to explain what he would substitute in its place. Elderly Cheyenne chiefs argued against disbanding the committee, and headsman John Fletcher appealed to the people: "Think of our sons." He maintained that a federally recognized tribal organization was necessary for the well-being of the Cheyenne and Arapaho peoples and for the continued existence of the people beyond those living then. Apparently, community leaders had come to a consensus on the issue before the meeting. Otis Bates, seconded by Rowlodge, moved that a vote be taken. Ten voted to dissolve the business committee government; thirty-five were opposed.[53]

The election for the 1956–57 committee produced two new members. For the Arapahos, four of the incumbents were replaced, but two of those elected had served previously. The new members were Alfred Whiteman and Joe Pedro, who was at least thirty years younger than the other members. For the Cheyennes, three incumbents were reelected, and the four new members all had served previously. One of these died in office and was replaced in 1956 by Sam Dicke. More significant change was to follow, for the 3 November 1955 headline in the *El Reno American* was "Cheyenne-Arapahos Win Great Victory—$25 Million Is Involved." The Indian Claims Commission had ruled that the federal government did violate its treaties with the tribes. The expectation of the distribution of the monetary award not only affected the outcome of the 1955 business committee election, but it was to produce far-reaching repercussions in the years to come.[54]

The "Outsiders": The Claim and the New Constitution, 1956–76

After 1955 the business committee came under more scrutiny, for the events of those years precipitated coverage in the local and regional media. Woodrow Wilson's words were prophetic when he called the committee meeting to order in January 1956: "This is a thankless task and will have a lot of complaints." Criticism of the business committees centered on their handling of financial matters stemming from the recovery of lands on Concho reserve and the settlement of the valuation issue regarding the claim. With reference to the latter, the court had ruled that the Cheyenne and Arapaho Tribes were due a settlement for the lands taken in Colorado, Kansas, Wyoming, and Nebraska; however, they would have to prove the value of the land before they could receive a settlement. Controversies over tribal income led to and were reflected in a dramatic increase in turnover on the business committees. Moreover, a greater number of members did not live in the rural districts and had employment outside the local community.[55]

The tenth through the twelfth business committees (1956–61) continued to pursue the longstanding committee goals of obtaining oil leases on tribal lands, restoring Concho agency services, advertising tribal farming and grazing leases for the highest bid, obtaining assistance for education, and administering rehabilitation funds to assist Cheyennes and Arapahos who wished to stay in rural communities within the boundaries of the former reservation (see table 3). For these purposes, as well as to obtain 3,900 surplus acres on Concho reserve and to obtain a valuation of 1851 treaty lands favorable to the tribes, the committee, at the urging of their attorney in Washington, sent delegations to Washington almost on an annual basis. In 1956 and 1957, delegations went to meet with Northern Cheyenne and Arapaho leaders, where an agreement was reached for the wealthier northern tribes to pay for the appraisal of the lands involved in the claim. The tribes in Oklahoma were to reimburse the northern tribes after settlement. The appraisal was necessary to counter the federal government's own appraisal, which the tribes viewed as too low. The Justice Department proposed four cents an acre; the tribes, eighty cents. In 1958 another delegation continued negotiations, and a delegation attended the hearings in Washington, where a settlement was reached. When the Indian Claims Commission awarded the Cheyenne and Arapaho tribes $23.5 million in 1961 in compensation for treaty violations, about half of this was designated for Southern Cheyennes and Arapahos, once they established the exact amount due them in future court proceedings.[56]

The lands on Concho reserve had been declared surplus after the boarding school there was scaled back. National farm organizations, fearful of competition, had protested the agricultural programs at Indian schools, and, in response, the government closed the school's agricultural operations and declared the farming and grazing lands surplus in 1956. In September 1960, after Congress approved the necessary legislation, President D. D. Eisenhower transferred title to 3,900 acres to the tribes, but in fee simple rather than trust status. This meant that the tribes would have to pay tax on the lands to the local county government.[57]

The year 1961 marked the first time that the business committee was sued by tribal members. In March, Sam Dicke and Theodore Cutnose filed a lawsuit in U.S. district court against the business committee, which was leasing the tribes' Concho lands to a local non-Indian farmer. Dicke complained that the committee was dominated by Woodrow Wilson, John Fletcher, and the tribal attorney, William Payne, and that they refused to give a satisfactory accounting of the lease money. The committee and their attorney filed a motion to dismiss the case on jurisdictional grounds. In April, Cheyennes Gilbert Payne and James Holland also filed suit over the Concho lands to force the sale of the land (worth $400,000) and the per capita distribution of the proceeds. Although these suits were dismissed, due to the refusal of the federal government to support the cases, the local newspapers gave the suits coverage and, along with rumors about misuse of tribal funds, generated suspicion of the committee. Some members of the committee were suspected of taking under-the-table payments from the lessee on Concho lands in return for generous terms on the lease. This lessee, who had a network of Cheyenne and Arapaho friends and "clients" whom he regularly helped with donations for community activities and personal financial difficulties, was also selected as an honorary Arapaho chief. Such patron-client relationships between lessors and lessees had been quite common since allotment.[58]

The committee's operational budget, which included the money from the Concho lease, also was a source of resentment among some tribal members, and the suspicions of a few spread through rumor to others with less direct knowledge

Table 3

Cheyenne-Arapaho Business Committee Membership, 1956–76

1956–57 (10th)

Cheyenne	*Arapaho*
Sam Buffalo	Jess Rowlodge
Woodrow Wilson	Walter Fire/ Saul Birdshead
Raymond Buffalomeat/ William Tall Bird Jr.	James Fire
John Fletcher	Otis Bates/ Ralph Little Raven
Albert Hoffman	Herman Haury
George Rearing Bull	Joe Pedro
Richard Boynton Sr./ Sam Dicke	Alfred Whiteman

1958–59 (11th)

Cheyenne	*Arapaho*
Sam Buffalo	Saul Birdshead
Woodrow Wilson	Herman Haury
William Tall Bird Jr.	Joe Pedro
John Fletcher	Alfred Whiteman
Fred Bushyhead	Dan Blackhorse
Joe Antelope	John Sleeper
Denny Old Crow	Glen Lumpmouth

1960–61 (12th)

Cheyenne	*Arapaho*
Sam Buffalo	Saul Birdshead
Woodrow Wilson	Herman Haury
William Tall Bird Jr.	Joe Pedro
John Fletcher	Alfred Whiteman
Fred Hoffman	Glen Lumpmouth
Compton Boynton	James Fire
John Burgess	John Pedro

1962–63 (13th)

Cheyenne	*Arapaho*
Sam Buffalo	Herman Haury
Woodrow Wilson	James Fire
Fred Hoffman	John Sleeper
Walter Roe Hamilton	Eugene Woolworth
Ed Burns	Dave Williams
Eugene Blackbear	Ralph Little Raven
Ralph Goodman	Lavern Woolworth

1964–65 (14th)

Cheyenne	Arapaho
Woodrow Wilson	Herman Haury
Fred Hoffman	Ralph Little Raven
Harry White Horse	Joe Pedro// John Sleeper
Fred Bushyhead	Tom Levi// Eugene Woolworth
Guy Hicks	Wendell Whiteman
Albert Hamilton	Clarence Tallbull
William Albert Hamilton	Willie Hail

1966–67 (15th)

Cheyenne	Arapaho
Woodrow Wilson/ Leslie Hawk	Eugene Woolworth// Willie Hail
Sam Buffalo	Alfred Whiteman Jr.
Ralph Beard	Edward Woolworth
George Swallow	Lillian Pratt Toahty
Henrietta Whiteman	Floyd Sankey**
Lawrence Hart	John Washee Jr.**
Howard Goodbear	Juanita Learned**

1968–69 (16th)

Cheyenne	Arapaho
Sam Buffalo	Alfred Whiteman Jr.
Ralph Beard	Floyd Sankey
Howard Goodbear	John Washee Jr.
Leslie Hawk	Clinton Youngbear
Thomas Blind Woman	Pauline Blind Harjo
Ed Burns	Betty Bailey
William Fletcher	John Washee Sr.

1970–71 (17th)

Cheyenne	Arapaho
Ed Burns	Alfred Whiteman Jr.// Clarence Tallbull
Guy Hicks Sr.	John Washee Sr.
John Antelope Jr.	Steve Birdshead// Clinton Youngbear
Leonard Yellow Eagle	John Sleeper
Alvin Hart	Juanita Learned
Norma Clark	Willie Hail
Tim Nibs// Gilbert Curtis	William Charles Hamilton

1972–73 (18th)

Cheyenne	Arapaho
Alvin Hart	Clarence Tallbull
Howard Goodbear	John Washee Sr.
Sam Buffalo	Clinton Youngbear
George Hawkins	John Sleeper
Alfrich Heap of Birds	William Charles Hamilton// Virgil Franklin
Moses Starr Jr.	Patrick Spotted Wolf
Woodson Whitebird	Arthur Sutton

1974–75 (19th) (election delayed, remained in office until 1976)

Cheyenne	Arapaho
Howard Goodbear	Clarence Tallbull// (Unfilled)
Alfrich Heap of Birds	Clinton Youngbear
Moses Starr Jr.	Patrick Spotted Wolf
Ralph Beard	Arthur Sutton
Fred Hoffman	Virgil Franklin
Max Watan	George Sutton
Thomas Blind Woman/ Gilbert Tasso Jr.	Rutherford Loneman

KEY: // Resigned   / Died   **Seated after a court-ordered new election

---

of the committee's activity. From 1956 to 1961, the committee's operating budget (for the expenses of transacting tribal government business) increased, as did the per diem rate. This was made possible not only by the Concho lease but also by mineral leases on tribal land. In 1958 the operating budget was $16,248; in 1961, $19,882. Per diem went from eight dollars per monthly meeting in 1956–59 to fifteen dollars in 1961. During this time the committee made grants in amounts of several hundred dollars to powwow groups and leaders of native religious organizations, including one to "The Cheyenne Chiefs and Headsmen" to travel to Montana with the "Sacred Arrows." Alfred Whiteman continued to criticize committee procedures with regard to elections, for committee members supervised the process, and he pointed to potential conflict of interest when some committee members participated as clients in the rehabilitation programs. Other committeemen and tribal members thought that a farming background and residence in the rural communities were good preparation and experience for committee service. Whiteman also called for audits, implying that there were financial irregularities.[59]

With regard to the criticisms and the critics themselves, the committee attempted to respond by delegating responsibility for some tribal business. They chose Whiteman as chair of the rehabilitation committee and selected him for delegations. They selected election judges who were not committee members. And they gave the responsibility for the enrollment of tribal members (in anticipation of the claim payment) to Joe Pedro and accepted his design for the official tribal seal, which combined symbols of peyote, Christianity, and native religion.

The need to prepare an official roll of Cheyennes and Arapahos entitled to receive a share of the claim judgment funds also preoccupied the business committee. In 1956 the committee chose some of their number to work with Pedro on a plan for enrolling Arapahos and Cheyennes born after the last official roll of 1936. The advisability of requiring a minimum degree or amount of Cheyenne and Arapaho ancestry was discussed, and the committee anticipated a flood of applications from people who were enrolled in other tribes or who had disassociated themselves from the Cheyenne-Arapaho community. An initial roll, based on the 1936 roll, was prepared in 1957 and, with clerical assistance paid for out of the committee's operating budget, updated in subsequent years. In November 1959 the tribes voted 505 to 126 to hold a referendum to amend the constitution to require one-fourth Cheyenne-Arapaho blood and to allow the enrollment of persons not on the 1936 roll. There were 1,211 eligible voters; the vote was 468 to 148 for the amendment to require a minimum blood degree. The business committee passed an ordinance in 1961 to prevent those who had accepted claim payments from other tribes from transferring to the Cheyenne-Arapaho roll. By 1967, just prior to the Judgment Fund payment, the enrolled tribal membership had jumped from 3,528 in 1953 to 5,323. Up to 50 percent of the membership lived outside the boundaries of the former reservation.[60]

In the wake of the conflict over the leasing of the Concho lands and other matters, the election for the thirteenth committee (1962–63) resulted in significant turnover. All three of the incumbent representatives from Geary were defeated. Of the new members, two had not previously served on the committee. Among the Cheyennes, there were four new members, two of whom had not served previously on the committee.

The years between 1962 and 1968, when the claim money was finally paid, were marked by increased rancor and more broadly based participation in tribal government. During these years (the tenure of the thirteenth through the sixteenth committees), conflict centered around the use of the Judgment Funds and the kind of experience desirable for service on the business committee.

The thirteenth committee (1962–63) sent a six-member delegation to Washington in 1962 and eight members in 1963 to lobby Congress for appropriation of a monetary settlement of the claim favorable to the tribes and for the conveyance of the Concho lands from fee simple to trust status. They were not successful, and the expense of such a large delegation resulted in public criticism from constituents.

The election for the fourteenth committee resulted in the replacement of five Cheyennes; four of the new members had never served on the committee. Five Arapahos were replaced, and four of them had not served previously on the committee.[61]

The fourteenth committee (1964–65) sent a delegation (financed largely by the lessee of the Concho lands) to lobby for the recovery of the Fort Reno lands. The cost of the delegation received criticism, as did the committee's practice of paying its members per diem for tasks other than attending committee meetings. One member of the fourteenth committee was pressured into resigning for misappropriating some funds (apparently $127), and the committee as a whole was labeled irresponsible by the B I A area director for failing to pay the taxes due on the Concho lands. These problems—publicly aired in local newspapers—contributed to general dissatisfaction with the committee and reluctance to allow the committee to manage programmed Judgment Funds. The 1965 delegation also participated in arriving at a settlement of the claim in the amount of fifteen million dollars (more than the government's initial offer). Congress appropriated these funds in October 1965, and they were put in the U.S. Treasury to draw interest while the B I A and the tribes began to try to work out a plan for the distribution of the funds. The Indian Bureau insisted to the committee that the funds be programmed, that is, distributed for specific purposes—family allowances, educational assistance, and so on. The sentiment among many tribal members, however, was for immediate distribution of all the money per capita. This controversy exploded into a series of public meetings of tribal members in which individuals, who for the most part lived outside the rural districts and referred to themselves as outsiders, harangued and insulted business committee members and challenged the role of the committee altogether. The debate over the Judgment Fund distribution spilled over into the election for the members of the fifteenth business committee.

In November 1965, as the votes were being tallied publicly, a group of about twenty-five individuals in the audience challenged the committee's management of the election. This group, the C and A Club (otherwise known as the Ripcats, because the outspoken members were women), set the agenda for tribal politics for the next few years, an agenda that featured the distribution of 100 percent of the Judgment Fund in per capita payments. At the November meeting, C and A Club members argued that ballot boxes had been left unlocked and that absentee ballots were filled out by others than those to whom the ballots were addressed. The committee member who was supervising the count decided to continue the tabulation, and he advised the protesters to file a complaint. The *Daily Oklahoman* reported that at that point there was "an angry outcry from the spectators." Every suggestion made by the committeemen as to how the problem could be resolved was "shouted down." The ten committeemen present voted to call for a B I A investigation, and when this did not satisfy the protesters, the committee voted five to four to void the election. In a December 1965 meeting, the committee decided to hold another election that month. In the election for the fifteenth committee (1966–67), twelve incumbents were defeated; seven of the new members had the backing of the C and A Club, whose chairperson and spokesperson, Emma Archer, was a woman of Cheyenne and non-Indian ancestry who lived in El Reno and whose spouse was non-Indian. In the Arapaho Canton District, where Clarence Tallbull, Dave Williams, and James Fire had won, the C and A Club's candidate, Juanita Learned, an army veteran who lived in Oklahoma City and whose spouse was non-Indian, challenged the election results, arguing that her write-in votes were not counted. It took a year to resolve the case in court.[62]

Learned filed suit in federal district court obtaining an injunction against seating the Canton delegates. Thus, the Arapahos began the year with four representatives. This federal court sent the case to state district court. The business committee opted not to file a brief, believing that the court did not have jurisdiction, but when the court ruled in Learned's favor, a new election was held in Canton, and Learned and two others were voted into office. Both the Learned case and the C and A Club's success in obtaining a new election helped make the business committee more vulnerable to attack by tribal members.[63]

The fifteenth business committee membership represented a departure from committee makeup in past years. One Cheyenne and two Arapaho women (including Juanita Learned) were elected—the first women to sit on the committee, with the exception of a brief period in 1938 when a Cheyenne woman was elected. In the years that followed, women were elected often. Moreover, members of the fifteenth committee lived in urban areas outside the districts that they represented; nine were employed at either universities, businesses, or federal installations, and two had pensions during their tenure on the committee. The only ones who did not fit this pattern were elderly Sam Buffalo, who farmed in the Cheyenne Canton area; elderly Woodrow Wilson from Thomas (who died in office); and Floyd Sankey, a young man who lived in the Arapaho Canton District. There were two Cheyenne and two Arapaho chiefs (recently selected), and the committee included seven members who were veterans of the armed services. The fifteenth committee also broke with tradition by electing Cheyennes for both the chair and vice-chair position. The new members arrived at the committee meeting place in January 1966 and, according to the *El Reno American,* "demanded" that they be sworn in.[64]

The central project of the fifteenth committee was to see to it that Congress passed legislation to provide for the distribution of the claim funds. In a tribal meeting held in May 1966, those present voted 287 to 25 for the distribution of 100 percent of the funds in per capita payments. But BIA officials told the business committee that they would oppose per capita distribution of the entire award. Through negotiations the committee began to consider placing part of the funds in trusts for specific purposes. An education trust fund was a possible use for the claim monies, but it was opposed by C and A Club members. Business committee members were particularly interested in encouraging tribal members to further their education—in fact, they had increased the size of the tribally funded scholarship program. At the annual meeting in October 1966, Emma Archer moved that the fund be distributed per capita, with the provision that minors' funds be withheld except for specific programs until the age of twenty-one. This motion passed 121 to 7. The C and A Club tried to intimidate committeemen who spoke on behalf of some programming of the funds, insisting that each member vote publicly on Archer's motion. In April 1967 the committee supported the Archer motion by a vote of ten to one. Archer stated that programs would not benefit tribal members who lived outside the former boundaries of the reservation and that, therefore, the club opposed programs. Working with their attorney, Jap Blankenship (Payne's successor), the committee negotiated with Congress on legislation that in the end provided for a $500,000 Education Trust Fund, a Minor's Trust Fund, and the per capita distribution of the remainder.[65]

Another interest of the fifteenth committee was the Concho lease. They refused to renew the five-year lease, arguing that the lessee would be paying $13,464, which was less than market value, an estimated $43,500. An additional project was the recovery of 120 acres of surplus land around the Indian hospital at Clinton. The committee initiated legislation and went to Washington several times to lobby for the transfer of this land and the Concho acreage to the tribes in trust status, and they also attempted negotiations on the disputed Fort Reno lands. The committee worked with the federal government to establish Headstart, Neighborhood Youth Corps, and Upward Bound—new federal War on Poverty programs for job training and education.[66]

Dissatisfaction with this committee grew, however, to the point that there was great turnover in the next election. One of the committee members recalls, "The B I A had asked us to make up a program to use the fund. 'We can't give it all out per capita,' they said. We had to submit a proposal. That's where the hassle was. I thought we should proceed that way, and all members thought that. The outside [tribal] members thought different. . . . We proposed we should follow the procedures outlined by the government. We were out! There was all new business committee in." The committee also faced criticism about their expenditure of most of the tribal income on business committee operating expenses (including expenses for the claim) and about the size of the delegation that negotiated the claim settlement. The operating budget was $66,141, and although per diem remained at fifteen dollars, the committee instituted a policy of paying expense money in addition to the per diem. The committee gave grants to Cheyenne religious leaders for the Arrow Worship and the Sun Dance, to a Southern Arapaho participant in the Northern Arapaho Sun Dance, and to the local communities for dances. In the November 1967 election, there were forty-five candidates. Three of the Cheyenne and four of the Arapaho incumbents were not reelected. On the next committee, seven members lived outside the rural communities they represented.[67]

The Judgment Fund payment was made in 1968, soon after the sixteenth committee took office. Adults received $2,325. Subsequent to another general council vote, a business committee delegation had protested the establishment of the Minor's Trust Fund, but to no avail. Complaints about the Minor's Trust Fund continued, and, during the eighteenth committee's tenure, the age was lowered from twenty-one to eighteen in an agreement with Congress. The sixteenth (1968–69), seventeenth (1970–71), eighteenth (1972–73), and nineteenth (1974–76) committees focused on applying for federal War on Poverty programs. A Community Health Representative (c h r) program began in 1967, and a housing authority was established in 1969. By 1974, 150 homes had been built. The business committees worked on getting tribally owned lands declared eligible for projects funded by the Economic Development Act (e d a) of 1965. The nineteenth committee obtained e d a funds to begin developing a recreational site at Canton reserve (where a lake had been created by a federal water project) and hired a business manager. The eighteenth committee began negotiating to buy 160 acres of allotted land near Watonga that was eventually purchased by the nineteenth committee. The Fort Reno recovery continued to receive attention from the committees.[68]

Conflict continued over the authority of the committee, with a small group organized in 1970 working toward revising the constitution to facilitate the recall of committee members by constituents and to drastically limit what the committee could do without calling a public meeting to obtain tribal members' consent. Pressure for the per capita distribution of tribal assets continued. Two of the three Cheyennes who were most involved with the revision effort lived in the Oklahoma City vicinity. Misappropriation of tribal funds by two members of the sixteenth committee and an ongoing problem with paying the taxes due on the Concho lands gave support to the pressure for constitutional revisions, as did the fact that the nineteenth committee's operating budget was $116,000 and that the committee raised their per diem to twenty dollars.[69]

The committee selected to work on revising the constitution received complaints about problems and proposals for remedies from Cheyennes and Arapahos: "Nothing in the revised document was arbitrary. Everything was justified by the specific complaints," recalled one member of the constitution committee. Another member commented, "We knew a lot was weak. People sent suggestions from all districts. . . . It was a handful [of people] in every district that caused all the commotion." The committee made preliminary recommendations about how to give "the people" "full authority" over the committee, after consulting the tribal attorney about the wording of the new constitution. At a meeting in October 1970 a vote of approval was obtained, seventy-nine to one. In 1971 a business committee delegation went to Washington to try to expedite a referendum on the revisions and to discuss the reduction of the age for trust termination in the Judgment Fund. The eighteenth committee continued to press the secretary of the interior to call a referendum vote.[70]

The secretary of the interior approved the revised constitution on 3 April 1974, but shortly afterward the B I A discovered an error in the text and there was a delay in calling the referendum. The referendum finally was held 9 April 1975; it passed 480 to 226 in what was described as a light turnout. The new constitution specified a reduced committee size—four Cheyenne and four Arapaho representatives—and limits on per diem and travel, all in order to cut operational costs. There was a provision for recalls. At a meeting of at least seventy-five tribal members, the participants could approve the budget, leases, attorney contracts, and expenditures of tribal funds over fifteen thousand dollars. An election board was to be elected at the October meeting of tribal members. Business committee members could not serve on the election board. Elections were to be held by mail, not at polling places. During the term of the nineteenth committee, meetings often were occasions for small groups of individuals to protest. These occasions became very raucous, which led many people to stay away. In 1975 two attempts to hold a general council failed for lack of a quorum of seventy-five.[71]

In the fall the election board began to prepare for the election of a new committee, with some representatives to be elected for three years and some for one so that the terms would be staggered, as the new constitution required. In October 1975 the election had to be canceled when an error was discovered in the description of electoral district boundaries. The twentieth committee was not actually seated until 1977. There were a series of meetings of people who wanted to revert to the 1937 constitution, but the B I A insisted that any changes would have to be made by amending the new constitution. In the election of November 1976 all the incumbents were replaced by new representatives. All but four of these representatives refused to attend the last meeting of the nineteenth committee, where the chair suggested they might make a "smooth transition."[72]

In the post–claim era, federal discourse about Indians and native leaders showed continuity. In these times, however, the Cheyennes and Arapahos did not respond with one voice. Instead, divergent views of the relationship between tribe and individual and between committeemen and constituents emerged. This divergence developed in and from a transformed social context. By the 1960s the Civil Rights movement and the War on Poverty brought new ideas about politics and new social institutions—all of which came into play in Cheyenne-Arapaho country. Despite these national trends and their local expression, the B I A persisted in attributing Cheyenne and Arapaho poverty to character deficiencies and to incompetence and corruption on the part of native leaders. This image was reinforced by the local media, which had resumed publishing stories about the Cheyennes and Arapahos when it was clear that cash from the claim settlement would be spent locally.

In the late 1960s and early 1970s, federal policy shifted toward giving tribal governments more authority, particularly in the operation of programs. The business committees embraced the idea of self-determination (as they had tried to do in the late 1930s) but were disappointed. In 1975 funds for one of the programs did not fully materialize, and, as a result, the program operated in deficit. The B I A blamed the committee for bad management. Similarly, the county home extension service had a low opinion of Cheyenne and Arapaho abilities. In 1966, an agent developed a program to show Indian women a better way to wash dishes. Despite the Civil Rights movement, local towns continued to ban African Americans from parks and some schools and continued to withhold from Cheyennes and Arapahos the respect they routinely gave non-Indian citizens. Particularly galling was the mascot of the local high school in El Reno, in which many Cheyennes and Arapahos felt unwelcome; "Big Blue," or "The Chief," was an Indian mannequin in a war bonnet and breechcloth, carrying a tomahawk and painted blue, standing in a comic pose. The high school team was the "Tribe"; teams at El Reno Junior College were "Chieftains."[73]

As for media portrayals of the Cheyennes and Arapahos, the raucous meetings over the distribution of the Judgment Fund and the litigation involving the business committee made the front page of the *El Reno American*. In a story entitled "Indians Hit Warpath, Ask Shakeup in Cheyenne-Arapaho Council," tribal finances were said to be mismanaged and committee members to have held office too long. When the Concho lands were recovered, the headline read "Tribes Given County Land"— the implication being that the Cheyennes and Arapahos were a burden on the local economy and that they did not have to earn their own way. The *Daily Oklahoman* picked up on the disruptive conflict over the 1965 election, reporting on election "irregularities": there was an "angry outcry," and when a suggestion was made about how to resolve the issue, the spectators "shouted this down." The election judges were Christian ministers who, the *Daily Oklahoman* reported, walked out of the meeting rather than be a part of the proceedings. In a 1966 story the *El Reno American* reported that the business committee had its "integrity questioned" by a tribal member and editorialized that the Cheyenne-Arapaho Tribe would "need help from somewhere in handling tribal functions" and that the "political situation in the Cheyenne-Arapaho Indian Tribe is making state politics look like a Sunday school election" (a dubious conclusion, perhaps). In 1974 the *Watonga Republican* began extensive coverage of Cheyenne and Arapaho tribal government. A 1974 tribal council meeting was described as "less than a harmonious encounter between members of the tribe and the councilmen." And in 1975, a business committee member reportedly "drew jeers" when he tried to explain how personal contacts with federal officials helped the committee pursue tribal interests.[74]

The business committees tried to counter B I A paternalism, particularly in the 1970s. When the B I A rejected the committee's choice for a superintendent to be assigned to Concho agency (which had been restored after 1957 and had grown in staff due to the increase in oil and gas leases), Patrick Spotted Wolf, a member of the business committee, questioned whether committee actions "mean anything," that is, whether the promise of more authority was a reality or not. When the B I A withheld approval of the tribes' plan for the claim distribution, committeeman Chief Guy Hicks, who was arguing for regular payments over a period of years rather than one payout, remarked sarcastically, "You think the government would let us work out this good deal for ourselves?" The financial problems of programs were in large part the fault of the federal bureaucracy, committee members argued. One of the most serious financial problems of the committee was the payment of tax due on the tribes' Concho land in fee title. When the B I A failed to file a tax report, the tribes were charged a penalty; committeemen were able to insist that the B I A was responsible for paying the penalty. And despite the practice of B I A officials to refer to these Native Americans as the Cheyenne-Arapaho Tribe, the committee's letterhead read "Cheyenne and Arapaho Indian Tribes of Oklahoma."[75]

At first the media portrayals did not go unchallenged. Joe Pedro began to write a column for the *Watonga Republican* in 1965. It was short-lived, but, using his Indian name Red Wolf as a byline, he determined to write "provocative news coverage in the field of Indian affairs." Rather than allowing the negative portrayals to go unchallenged, he wanted to bring news to the "A B C people" (Americans Before Columbus) to improve public relations: "My people have suffered at the hands of the press. Too often we read only the bad news. . . . Let us share with you what the best of my brothers have." Aware of the demeaning Indian imagery in use in western Oklahoma, in his next column he offered this example of Indian humor:

> The Cowboy, in a saloon, was passing the time of day with this singer and in comes the Indian. Singer says H O W. Chief says H O W. Singer: How, Chief! H O W. Singer: H O W chief. H O W. Cowboy, wishing to join in, said, "I didn't know ya knew how to talk Indin." Replied the singer, "It's all in a way of knowing H O W." She whispered in a low voice, "Whacha doin' in town, Cheefee?" The old Indian said, "Me come town, me sue railroad for crossing my land, me sue whiteman for getting my land, me sue this bad place for selling young bucks bad fire water." The singer asked, "What are you a S I O U X I N D I A N?"

Here, the stereotypical Indian greeting is ridiculed, as is the use of the term "chief," the association of broken English with native people, and the genre of the American Western in which native people were stereotyped as the naive but loyal sidekick or the savage. The resentment over land loss and over the exploitation of native people, including the use of alcohol to defraud native people of property, is highlighted. And the "old Indian" in the account is presented as assertively pressing his rights.[76]

When an official of the newly organized Oklahomans for Indian Opportunity visited Canton in July 1966 and talked with some native people about how to address the social and economic problems in the area, he was challenged: "What are you trying to do, civilize us? . . . We're not civilized. We have to pick cotton for eighty-five cents an hour. We'll never be civilized as long as we have to work like that." The speaker was expressing resentment of the implication that Indians needed to improve their skills in order to be more prosperous and giving voice to the Cheyennes' and Arapahos' realization that they were being taken advantage of by the non-Indian society that prospered from the exploitation of native people.[77]

There was still support for the intermediary tradition as carried on by the business committee and for the view that the tribe had an existence beyond that of its individual members at any particular point in time and that the tribal community should take responsibility for the well-being of all the members of the community, by supporting the weak through generosity of the strong and by providing for future generations. Proponents of this view generally were elderly Cheyennes and Arapahos and many of their younger relatives who lived in the rural communities and had memories of how men were apprenticed to or instructed by intermediary chiefs of the pre–Oklahoma Indian Welfare Act (o i w a) era. Jess Rowlodge's work for this tradition was acknowledged when he was invited to accompany the delegation to Washington to resolve claim issues. Fred Hoffman, one member of the delegation, tells this story: "The attorney got us together. He started questioning the eight of us. We appeared the next day before three judges. Our expert witness was Jess. That guy was sharp. He said, 'Judge, I want to know one thing. Indians used to get a flag when they made a treaty. Do we get the flag on the top of the capitol?' The judge said, 'No, they disallowed that.' I told Payne I forgot a resolution. I went to get it during recess and while they were at lunch I took the flag from its stand in the room and put it in the attorney's briefcase, wrapped it up small." Thus, the delegation affirmed the treaty relationship. Land recovery, viewed as central to the treaty relationship, was important in Cheyenne and Arapaho memories, as were the values of cooperation and mutual respect and respect for "the life of service" to the people that longtime committee members, such as Woodrow Wilson, gave. Arapahos recognized Jess Rowlodge's service by acknowledging him as an Arapaho chief in his old age.[78]

In his column, Joe Pedro wrote, "For the sake of our future and the little children placed in our care we must act in the best interest of all." Some individuals who returned to the rural community, having been influenced by the Civil Rights movement and hoping to improve conditions for people in the rural communities, also advocated tribal unity, although they may have disapproved of the old councilmen. One returned veteran, with a salaried position in one of the local towns, when interviewed in 1968, stressed that Cheyennes and Arapahos should "organize as a group of Indian people . . . not as an individual. We're not going to get nothing as individuals. Indians [who do not understand tribalism] can't see the difference between tribal business and personal business." And, on the trouble over the 1965 election, Pedro wrote, "Let us close ranks as one and set our house in order for the new year." The following year, he bemoaned that "in-fighting and bitterness and hatred" were "messing up the good waters of unity." Here he uses a Christian and peyote ritual symbol, holy water, to remind his community that there were supernatural sanctions against doing harm to others. Such views still were being expressed in the tribal council of 1974, when the Cheyenne religious leader chairing the meeting urged the people there to "submit problems in a business-like manner and avoid personal conflict." At the following year's tribal council meeting a Cheyenne participant noted that it was a "historic Cheyenne observation" that periods of "calamity" result from incidents of "misconduct": "There is something we are doing wrong—we have lost a lot of Cheyenne people among us and now it's time for us to take a look at ourselves and we had better." Cheyenne and Arapaho chiefs (several of whom served on the business committee) appealed for unity, urged using the tribal land reserves to help the most needy, and criticized the historic efforts of the B I A to undermine chieftainship. This viewpoint was represented by a group that attempted to have the new constitution revoked because it undermined the land recovery effort.[79]

The public expression of hostility to tribalism and its proponents also was deeply disturbing to the people in the rural communities. One long-term committee member, commenting on the behavior of the outsider candidates for the committee, complained that although members of the fifteenth committee had "achievement through school," "that don't count for nothing as long as they don't have the background." These "young high school smarties" lacked "tribal historical background" and had not been trained by the older business committee members. They did not understand that the 1937 constitution, because it was approved by "the old people" and the chiefs, deserved respect. This constitution, he argued, also has "stood in the courts that has recovered their claims. . . . So there's no joke about this constitution. There's nothing to be ridiculed. This business committee that came on two years ago [fifteenth] tried to make a joke out of it." He explained that the outsider group attempted to bring the tribal electoral process more in line with the surrounding non-Indian society's practices. For example, candidates "filed themselves" (nominated themselves), whereas the practice in the local communities had been for the community to meet and agree on candidates, then send those names to the business committee: that way they elected a committee "that had good background, tribal historical background." These candidates would have the "backing of relatives and friends" who would help the person carry out his "obligations." Without these controls, the process was abused, he maintained. In the 1967 election, he charged that at least two candidates bought alcohol for individuals in return for their vote.[80]

Rural people were suspicious of some of the nonresident group who attended tribal meetings. One C and A Club member (whose grandfather was a non-Indian) whom I interviewed recalled, "An old man said, 'She's a White woman—she has no business here.'" She remembered that critics also remarked, "That woman she's telling you wrong. They got good watches and big cars and come here and make us look bad." But the nonresident, outsider group was able to capitalize on people's suspicions of financial gain on the part of the committee. As one club member told it, "We dug up dirt and let people know. . . . We made remarks about the business committee: 'Do you want to eat beans while the business committee is in Washington eating steaks?' We was real nasty." Club members appealed to resentment of the federal government: "We told them, 'You are becoming like everyone else, an American like everyone else. Eventually, the government won't be able to tell you what to do.'" Some of the club members also took advantage of their contacts in non-Indian society: "Because I am half white and have a white spouse, I got the Oklahoma [City] Times interested that there was trouble at Concho. And I called the U.S. Marshall. We got by by using that tactic." The lawsuits and the successful effort to change electoral procedures and nullify an election shocked many in the rural communities. One litigant recalled, "I got an attorney and sued. People said I couldn't do anything but I proved to them I could." One C and A Club member put it this way, "They said we couldn't stop them. We stopped that election. . . . The business committee were so against what we had done. We just stood up to them."[81]

During the 1960s and early 1970s, young people born after World War II, with no firsthand memories of the earlier political traditions and with experience outside the rural area—particularly in the armed services, universities, or the American Indian Movement—were comfortable using the political behaviors that were widespread in the United States. As one of the young people who participated in tribal politics in the 1970s explained to me somewhat ruefully:

People were getting more involved, attending tribal council meetings. It used to be just old people would go, forties on up. They were the ones to do all the business for the tribe. . . . They were still under the influence of "Be Quiet and Don't Say Nothing." Until younger ones started looking at it: "Hey, we're being taken." Older ones would tell younger, "They're trying to do business, don't say nothing to them." In the late 1960s, people started finding out they could do something, have a sayso about tribal government. Because non-Indians outside were protesting, it took effect on the Indians. . . . That's when people started coming out [to Concho from urban areas] and talking to people, presenting arguments. This undermined the respect. [82]

The broader-based participation of constituents expressed itself in contention over the use of the Judgment Fund, over the adoption of a new constitution, and, at a deeper level, over the relationship between tribe and individual, leader and constituent. Many, led by people from the nonresident or outsider group, held the view that the tribe was merely a collection of individuals and that the interests of the individual took precedence over collective interests or concern for weaker members. The push for per capita distribution of tribal resources gave expression to this view. Native leaders, and the rural tradition they attempted to promote, were challenged when they appeared to thwart individual interest, and the challenge took the form of the appropriation of the non-Indian discourse about the limitations of native leaders.

Proponents of the new constitution wanted to reorganize tribal government to allow for the distribution of oil and gas money in per capita payments. Thus, in tribal council meetings, they moved to budget money from mineral income on tribal land for per capita payments. They proposed revising the constitution so that any large expenditure would need tribal council approval. Spokespersons for this view questioned the limitation of program participation to those living below the poverty line, questioning why some tribal members should receive more help than others. Similarly, business committee members were criticized for accepting per diem, and disapproval of programs was linked to the view that only "tribal employees" benefited from the War on Poverty programs, that is, that those who were employed by businesses or institutions other than the tribe did not receive an equal share of tribal resources. In this view, a return to the "old" constitution "would give our checkbooks to the business committee." [83]

Those living outside the local communities were the most prominent in criticizing the ability of the "old business committee" (many of whom were elderly leaders from the rural districts and long-term advocates for filing the claim against the federal government). One of the themes in C and A Club members' oral accounts of the late 1960s and early 1970s era is that the old business committee and the local, rural communities in general were backward. One club member describes his participation thus: "We who worked for a living wanted to be able to spend it as we wanted. We formed the C and A Club. These [local Indian] people had no idea of how to have an election, do politician things. . . . At that time the Indian was reticent, did not express themselves. I went to business committee meetings— and they are supposed to handle business—they just sat with their heads down and said nothing. . . . They just sat and listened in the tribal council. They needed that lesson [taught them by the C and A Club about how to behave politically]." Another club member, disappointed with the fifteenth committee, which the club had helped to elect, remarked: "I said, 'I've taken you as far as I can go. You have to do something for yourself. I can go no further.' Later, I went out [to a commit- tee meeting]. I was shocked. They were doing the same thing as the old business committee. You knew their minds were perfect blanks. They did not know how to conduct a meeting." Efforts made by the business committee to exercise oppor- tunities for greater self-determination were belittled or opposed by the outsider group. For example, the nineteenth committee attempted to help the tribes con- tract with the B I A to operate the boarding school at Concho. At a tribal council meeting, opponents led by the nonresident group passed a motion that the Chey- ennes and Arapahos were "not ready" (advanced enough) to operate the school. At this same time, a few tribal members were involved with the American Indian Movement, and one publicly accused the business committee of being "B I A yes- men." When advocates of the old constitution argued that that constitution had the support of the chiefs, one woman in the nonresident group charged that the chiefs who approved the constitution were "ignorant." Another insisted that em- bracing the old constitution would mean the Cheyennes and Arapahos would "go back a hundred years." Another stated publicly that the business committee should be abolished and tribal government turned back to the B I A. The comments from critics of business committee leadership were published in the local newspapers, which had a readership among many Cheyennes and Arapahos. When the new constitution passed in 1975, it largely stripped the business committee of authority to develop businesses or to buy land for the tribes and promoted the per capita distribution of tribal assets. It also abandoned district representation, reducing the size of the committee to four representatives from each tribe.[84]

Gradually, the publicized views of the outsiders began to influence people in the rural districts. This is apparent from the proceedings of tribal meetings held after 1976. While the business committees continued to have members who strongly supported land recovery and poverty programs, negative characterizations of their leadership potential, including their ability to get things done for the people, were common. Even in Pedro's column, at first dedicated to presenting a positive image, disdain for the nature of the hostile personal confrontations among committeemen and for the committeemen's abilities was expressed. In 1965 he described the new electoral process as "silly" and the election as a "mudbath": "The road between here and the prized council table is long, dirty, rough, and filthy." That year he wrote: "Poverty in its full meaning like a dead sea floods and touches the lives of eighty percent of my Indian brothers in the eight-county area of northwest Oklahoma. Tribal leaders like children play and fight over minor matters while the tribe makes the best of what life has to offer in this land of plenty. It was like offering a child candy when the government offered to settle all claims for the sum of fifteen million dollars."[85]

2
THE SELF-DETERMINATION ACT ERA, 1977–99

4
"A Reason to Fail"
DOMINANCE DISGUISED

On a hot day in Oklahoma City in July 1995, the U.S. Western District Court went into session. On trial were two ex–business committee members, both elderly grandmothers who had been leaders in their communities since the late 1960s. Viola Hatch had been a member of the American Indian Movement, an officer in the National Indian Youth Corps, and a field coordinator for Oklahomans for Indian Opportunity. More recently, she had been the twenty-seventh business committee representative for the Canton Arapahos. Juanita Learned had been a director of Oklahomans for Indian Opportunity and, subsequent to her election to the business committee under tumultuous conditions in 1966, had served on the committee three times during the late 1980s and early 1990s, representing the Geary Arapahos. She had been the chair of the twenty-seventh committee. These women, as well as the comptroller and business manager (both nonmembers of the Cheyenne and Arapaho Tribes hired by the twenty-seventh business committee), were charged with several counts of embezzlement, conversion (using funds legally obtained for an unauthorized purpose), and conspiracy. The charges against Hatch largely stemmed from alleged irregularities concerning a few business trips she made on behalf of the tribes, and Learned was charged with travel irregularities and with not repaying loans from the tribes in a timely manner. The amount of money the federal government held to have been illegally spent from program funds by Hatch was $734 and by Learned was $7,498.[1]

This was the first such prosecution in business committee history. Why did these financial transactions assume so much importance from the perspective of the federal government, which spent hundreds of thousands of dollars on a three-year investigation? What defense did Hatch and Learned make? To answer these questions, it is necessary to understand how Cheyenne and Arapaho tribal government has operated in this post–Self-Determination Act era, during which time the federal government encouraged the contracting of programs.

Federal initiatives have enabled the Cheyenne and Arapaho Tribes to develop culturally sensitive programs, provide new jobs for the community, and be a more aggressive advocate for the Cheyenne and Arapaho people. But federal supervisory institutions also have predisposed tribal government to have difficulty accomplishing self-determination goals and convincing constituents of their legitimacy and effectiveness. The federal government both approved the tribes' constitution and allowed a contracting process that seemingly violates that constitution. The U.S. government approved a legal code that is inadequate for the resolution of political conflicts in the tribal court. As trustee for the lands owned by Cheyenne and Arapaho people and by the tribes, the federal government mismanaged these assets and the income derived from them—a situation that has contributed to the tribes' reliance on federal programs to relieve widespread poverty. This chapter describes the way in which decisions are made about the use and distribution of tribal resources and outlines the structure of authority in Cheyenne and Arapaho government, first by examining the role of the tribal council, then that of the business committee and its supervision of administrative departments, programs, and business enterprises. I also explore the nature of the supervisory powers of the federal government and their impact on tribal government.

The Organization of Cheyenne-Arapaho Government

The 1975 constitution set in place a structural opposition between the tribal council and the business committee and between the business committee and the election board. The framers of the constitution intended these oppositions to operate as a checks and balances system, with the tribal council holding the balance of power. This structural opposition has been progressively intensified by the business committee's ability to contract grants and programs on behalf of the Cheyenne and Arapaho Tribes of Oklahoma, contracting authorized by the Indian Self-Determination and Educational Assistance Act of 1975. Contracting has served to shift the balance of power to the business committee. In addition, because judicial institutions that can enforce constitutional provisions and resolve conflicts have not been developed, the intended checks and balances system has gone unrealized.[2]

The Tribal Council

The constitution reads that the tribal council "shall be the governing body" of the Cheyenne and Arapaho Tribes. The term "tribal council" refers to all enrolled tribal members at least eighteen years of age. The term also refers to a meeting in which a quorum of at least seventy-five tribal members is present. And, in some contexts, in popular idiom, tribal council refers to a dissident group in opposition to the business committee, B I A, or other person or persons in positions of power.

Before 1959, the membership of the Cheyenne and Arapaho Tribes consisted of descendants of people who settled on the reservation in 1869, or soon after, in association with Cheyenne and Arapaho bands. In 1959 a constitutional amendment changed the criteria for membership, such that those persons born after 1959 had to have one-fourth degree Cheyenne and/or Arapaho blood quantum and at least one parent enrolled in the Cheyenne-Arapaho Tribes. In 1993 there were 10,173 enrolled Cheyennes and Arapahos, and by the end of 1999, almost 11,000. In 1987, 50 percent of tribal members were enrolled as full bloods (8/8 Cheyenne-Arapaho ancestry).

The 1975 constitution confers specific powers on the legally convened tribal council. First, the tribal council annually budgets money received from the leasing of tribally owned lands, including farming, grazing, and mineral leases. The budget must be approved at a tribal council meeting, and the business committee may not dispense these tribal funds in excess of those set forth in the annual budget without tribal council approval. Second, any surface lease or easement of tribal land in excess of five years must also be approved by majority vote of the tribal council. Third, the tribal council approves contracts that the tribes sign with legal counsel and, fourth, approves the filing of legal claims, including those for recovery of land. The tribal council also determines enrollment criteria for tribal membership and the boundaries of the voting districts.

The tribal council may propose amendments to the constitution and bylaws and may limit or restrict powers of the business committee by referendum vote. In a referendum, ballots are mailed to all registered voters; if at least one-third of the ballots are returned, the outcome is determined by the majority of votes. A referendum is required to sell, exchange, or mortgage tribal lands or to expend tribal monies, incur tribal indebtedness, or obligate tribal assets for a transaction amounting to more than fifteen thousand dollars.

In the October tribal council meeting of every even-numbered year, an eight-member election board is nominated and elected from the floor, and the tribal council budget includes election board expenses for per diem and mileage for the days that they do election board business. Four Arapahos are elected, two from each of the two Arapaho districts. And four Cheyennes are elected, one from each of the four Cheyenne districts. The election board handles voter registration and estab-lishes the dates, voter qualifications, and rules to govern the election of committee persons and referendum voting. The board is responsible for issuing, receiving, and tallying ballots in primary, runoff, and recall elections. The board also hears and determines the validity of challenges to registration, candidacy, or election results. Each election board, which serves for two years, makes its own rules and regula-tions in areas not specified in the constitution and elects officers. No member of the business committee or any person running for business committee office is eligible to serve on the board. The constitution requires the business committee and business manager to assist the election board.

In elections, ballots are mailed to registered voters with a blank envelope and an envelope addressed to the election board. The voter is supposed to mark the ballot and seal it in the blank envelope, then insert the blank envelope in the envelope addressed to the election board, and sign the back of the addressed envelope. Ballots remain at the U.S. post office until election day, when three members of the election board, escorted by the tribal police, retrieve the ballots and bring them to the tribal office at Concho. There, the election board checks the name on the outside of the addressed envelope against the list of voters. They open the envelopes with ballots and tabulate the votes. If no candidate receives more than 50 percent of the vote, a runoff election subsequently is held between the two candidates with the most votes.

The tribal council budget also includes a line item for the Health Advisory Board's expenses. This board is an eight-member advocacy group that works to resolve the Cheyenne-Arapaho community's complaints about health care services, primarily services provided by the I H S. They take complaints to officials of the I H S, to the tribal health director, or, occasionally, to their congressman. The two Arapaho districts each elect two board members in a community meeting. Each of the four Cheyenne districts elects a representative. The Health Advisory Board also elects officers. Members of the board receive per diem and mileage.

Each of the Arapaho districts has a community hall and a community or community hall committee. Two Cheyenne districts have four Cheyenne community hall committees between them. The tribal council budgets money from the farming and grazing funds to help these committees take care of their halls and sponsor activities in their communities. Members of the committees are elected in community meetings.

The Business Committee

The business committee is a group of elected representatives: two Arapahos from Geary-Greenfield-Colony District (hereafter Geary District); two Arapahos from Canton District; a Cheyenne from Kingfisher-El Reno-Calumet District (hereafter El Reno District); a Cheyenne from Thomas-Deer Creek-Weatherford-Clinton District (hereafter Clinton District); a Cheyenne from Hammon-Elk City District (hereafter Hammon District); and a Cheyenne from the Seiling-Watonga-Longdale District (hereafter Watonga District) (see maps 6 and 7). Absentee voting is allowed, and people living outside these official districts may choose to register or run for election in any district of their own tribe. Four committee persons are elected every four years, with two years' overlap due to staggered terms. The constitution defines eligibility criteria for business committee candidacy: a candidate must be a member of the Cheyenne and Arapaho Tribes, be at least twenty-one years of age, and never have been convicted of a felony involving dishonesty. A representative is not required to live in his or her district. There is an election in November in odd-numbered years, with usually a runoff election that follows a few weeks later in at least some of the districts; then, in January four newly elected members join four incumbents. Council persons may serve three consecutive terms; they are not eligible to serve again until two years have elapsed.

A business committee member can be removed for misconduct or neglect of duty by a majority of the committee and by recall election. The election board holds a recall election upon the business committee's receipt of a petition signed

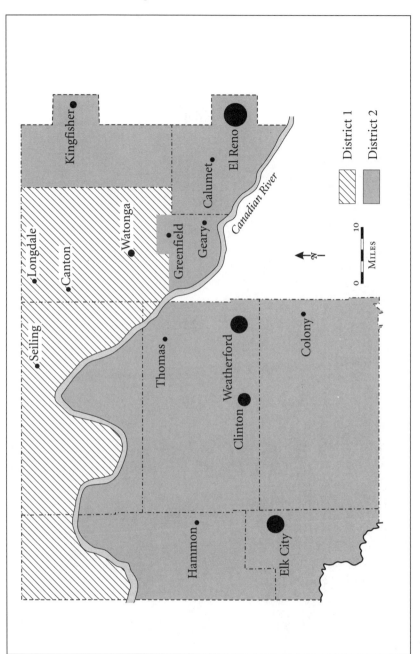

6. Arapaho Voting Districts, 1995.

District 1

District 2

Kingfisher

Longdale

Seiling

Canton

Watonga

Greenfield

Geary

Calumet

El Reno

Canadian River

Thomas

Weatherford

Clinton

Colony

Hammon

Elk City

N

0   10

MILES

7. Cheyenne Voting Districts, 1995.

by one-third of the registered voters of that member's district. As the constitution reads, "The Cheyenne-Arapaho Business Committee shall, upon receipt of a valid petition" from voters of a district requesting the recall of their representative, "direct the election board to conduct an election." Nowhere does the constitution clearly state who decides that the petition is valid. This has become a controversy that frequently has had to be resolved in court.[3]

In January of every second year, the eight committee persons elect officers—a chair, vice-chair, secretary, treasurer, and sergeant-at-arms, all of whom serve two-year terms. The chair presides over meetings, votes in case of a tie, and exercises any authority delegated to him or her by the committee members. The vice-chair calls the roll, may read the minutes of the previous meeting, and presides over meetings in the absence of the chair. The secretary certifies the accuracy of all the committee's actions, which must be pursuant to resolutions that require a majority vote after a quorum of five is established. The treasurer, according to the constitution, is custodian of all monies that come under the control of the business committee. The definition of what monies come under the control of the committee has varied from committee to committee. Disbursements of tribal funds require a business committee resolution and the signature of the treasurer and one other officer designated by the committee by resolution.

The business committee is required by the constitution to meet publicly on the first Saturday of every month. They also may have planning sessions or special meetings. In addition, they spend time in their offices at the tribal complex at Concho, where they meet with or take phone calls from constituents or otherwise work on their behalf. The business committee also is mandated to invite Cheyenne and Arapaho chiefs to address the committee at their March and September monthly meetings. Meetings proceed according to *Roberts Rules of Order.*

The constitution states that the business committee has the power to act for the tribes in all matters other than those specifically restricted to the tribal council. Much of a committee person's time is devoted to policy-making sessions and to involvement in personnel actions, such as interviewing job candidates and making decisions on the hiring and firing of approximately 165 tribal employees. According to the constitution, tribal members are to be given preference in hiring; spouses of tribal members are to be given second preference. Business committee members are directly involved in tribal enterprises and programs. The constitution provides that the business committee shall receive per diem and mileage (from tribal funds at rates set by the BIA for its employees) on the days they meet. Presumably the intent was that the funds for per diem would come from tribal lease income, the only source of tribal income at the time the constitution was drafted.

In 1993, half of the committee members' salaries was derived from an indirect cost pool based on the programs contracted and the grants received by the tribe subsequent to the adoption of the constitution. In former years indirect costs were used for a larger portion of the salaries of business committee members—in 1980, 85 percent. The salary was $18,250 in 1980; $20,000 in 1988; $35,000 in 1993. The portion of the committee members' salaries not derived from indirect costs is taken from tribal funds—in the 1990s from income from the tribal enterprises (bingo, smoke shop, and Farm and Ranch operations) and from taxes on business activity on tribal lands. The income from enterprises and taxes also was produced subsequent to the adoption of the constitution. Thus, while the constitution limits the business committee's expenditure of tribal funds, the committee (with the support of the B I A) has treated the funds from enterprises and taxes as distinct from the tribal funds (that is, income from the leases on tribal land) mentioned in the constitution. The constitution also limits business committee travel paid with tribal funds: up to two committee persons and one additional person may collect per diem and mileage for travel to represent the tribes, but business committees have designated program monies (considered distinct from tribal funds by the business committees) for business committee travel, without adhering to the constitutional limits on travel.

In order to operate the programs and enterprises, the tribes have several administrative departments and a business manager (see fig. 3). The business committee hires and supervises the business manager, who is responsible for maintaining records reflecting receipts and disbursements and for properly accounting for those expenditures. The scope of the business manager's responsibilities fluctuates, depending on administration policies. Generally, the business manager supervises the disbursement of the monies from the tribal budget based on farming and grazing lease money. He or she helps the treasurer of the business committee to report monthly on the status of these monies. He or she also may cooperate with the comptroller to oversee funds from programs, including direct and indirect costs. In addition, income from the tribes' enterprises and taxes is received and disbursed through the tribal office, and the business manager may be responsible, in cooperation with the comptroller or the treasurer of the business committee, for supervising these monies. The business manager also is responsible for supervising tribal employees. The business manager and the chair of the business committee have secretarial help.

Also hired and supervised by the business committee, the comptroller has responsibility for maintaining records reflecting receipts and disbursements and for properly accounting for federal program monies. He works with the accounting firm hired by the business committee (out of program funds) to audit program monies and with accountants from the B I A in the event they audit tribal budget funds, as they are required to do by the constitution. The comptroller heads the

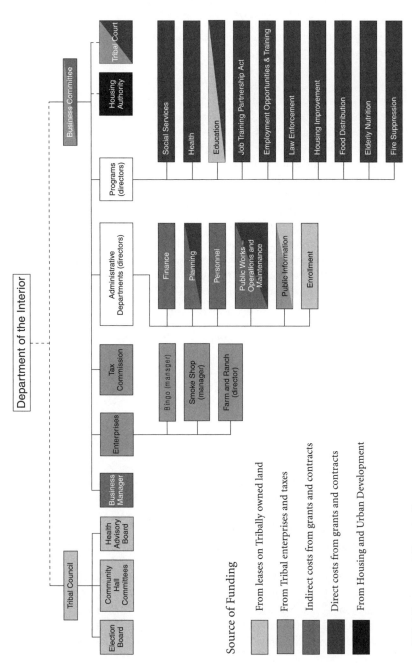

Department of the Interior

Tribal Council

Election Board
Community Hall Committees
Health Advisory Board

Business Manager

Enterprises
Tax Commission

Business Committee

Bingo (manager)
Smoke Shop (manager)
Farm and Ranch (director)

Administrative Departments (directors)

Finance
Planning
Personnel
Public Works — Operations and Maintenance
Public Information
Enrollment

Programs (directors)

Housing Authority
Tribal Court

Social Services
Health
Education
Job Training Partnership Act
Employment Opportunities & Training
Law Enforcement
Housing Improvement
Food Distribution
Elderly Nutrition
Fire Suppression

Source of Funding

From leases on Tribally owned land
From Tribal enterprises and taxes
Indirect costs from grants and contracts
Direct costs from grants and contracts
From Housing and Urban Development

3. Tribal Government Organization, 1995.

Finance Department. His responsibilities also can vary depending on administration policies.

Administrative Departments

Program funds are allocated to direct costs and to indirect costs. The indirect costs are used not only to pay business committee salaries but also to support the administrative departments supervised by the business committee. In addition to the Finance Department, the Planning, Personnel, Public Information, Enrollment, and combined Public Works and Operations and Maintenance Departments support tribal programs and enterprises.

The Planning Department is important to the tribes' effort to compete for grants, contract for programs, and plan for economic development. This department is responsible for identifying sources of funding for programs and for writing proposals. The staff of three also researches economic development options. They obtained funding to review production records and severance tax payments on tribal wells and, in cooperation with the tax commission, are investigating inaccurate reporting and underrecovery of payments. They also develop tribal ordinances and codes for law and order, taxation, gaming, hunting, fishing, and business activity on tribal lands. In addition to funding from indirect costs, the Planning Department obtains grants from time to time.

The Personnel Department is responsible for developing hiring and salary guidelines, screening applicants for tribal jobs, and providing appropriate additional training for tribal employees. This department also attempts to resolve grievances of tribal employees and works with tribal programs to find employment for tribal members.

The Public Information Office publishes a monthly newsletter that contains stories about business council activity, accomplishments of tribal members, notices of deaths, and announcements of powwows, dances, and other events of interest to Cheyennes and Arapahos. The office also tries to respond to inquiries about the tribes from the general public. In addition to receiving money from indirect costs, the Public Information Office periodically has received an allocation from the tribal council in the annual budget.

The Enrollment Office processes applications for tribal enrollment by researching the cases and making a recommendation to the business committee, which must approve applications. The office maintains a current tribal roll and prints and issues per capita checks when income from oil leases on tribal land is available for distribution. This office also administers the Minor's Trust Fund (unclaimed payments from the 1968 claim distribution, most likely belonging to tribal members who were adopted by nontribal members or moved away) and the Burial Trust Fund. When there is an application for a burial grant, the office verifies enrollment and makes direct payments of from $350 (for infants) to $1,300 (for adults) to the vendors for funerals of tribal members—from forty-three to seventy funerals annually. The staff issues Certification Degree of Indian Blood (C D I B) cards, which entitle individuals to access to Indian clinics and to some educational grants. They also issue a tribal identification card with a photo, which entitles a member to various tribal services and which is particularly useful to individuals without credit cards or a driver's license, for it can be used as identification throughout the state. The office also does genealogical research for people who contact them in order to trace Arapaho or Cheyenne ancestry. This office usually receives an annual allocation in the tribal budget; it does not receive indirect costs.

The combined Public Works and Operations and Maintenance Department operates with a director and five staff. Operations and Maintenance is responsible for the upkeep of the tribal complex, an office building of about seventeen thousand square feet. Public Works takes responsibility for other buildings and grounds on all tribal lands and, on occasion, assists individual tribal members with environmentally related projects, such as cleaning out septic tanks for a nominal fee. Public Works takes water samples from the water plant on the Concho reserve and delivers them to state labs for testing. The staff takes responsibility for road repair on the reserves at Concho, Canton, Colony, and Hammon and maintains powwow grounds on tribal reserves by mowing grass, maintaining water tanks, and checking outdoor wiring. Public Works also does the maintenance for the tribes' multipurpose center at Watonga, where there is a clinic, smoke shop, and bingo operation, and for the tribes' Headstart building at Canton. On Concho reserve, Public Works maintains a number of buildings, including those formerly used by the boarding school and the B I A agency buildings that were turned over to the tribes and that are now used to house tribal programs. The staff also is responsible for the buildings on tribal lands at Clinton, which include the Emergency Medical Service (E M S), the smoke shop (cigarettes and sundries store), and the Elderly Nutrition Center. Public Works maintains the homes that the tribes rent to individual tribal members on Concho and Colony reserves (houses that were formerly maintained by the B I A). The department also administers federal disaster relief; for example, working with the Federal Emergency Management Agency (F E M A), a staff member did estimates for flood damage to tribal members' homes in Kingfisher. And Public Works tries to work on the cleanup and fencing off of sites where the public has illegally dumped trash on trust lands. In addition to these activities, which are funded from indirect costs, Public Works has obtained grants from the Environmental Protection Agency (E P A) and the Department of Housing and Urban Development (H U D). The E P A funded a project to build an adequate lagoon system for waste disposal at Concho. The sewer system at Concho feeds into this lagoon. H U D awarded a Community Development Block Grant to the tribes to develop a new well field that will meet E P A standards for drinking water and another grant to build a facility to adequately house the E M S at Clinton. These jobs are contracted out, but tribal members work on the projects.

Each of the administrative departments has a director and, with the exception of the Public Information Office, which in 1994 was operated by one individual, a staff that varies from three to twelve persons. All the departments have difficulty obtaining the level of funding necessary to do the work required.

Programs

The business committee also supervises tribal programs. Programs consist of contracted services from federal or state agencies and grants from federal, state, or private sources. Programs are contracted from the Department of the Interior (through the B I A); the Department of Labor (D O L); the Department of Health and Human Services (through the I H S and the Administration on Aging); the Department of Agriculture; and the Department of Commerce (through the Equal Employment Opportunity Commission [E E O C] and the E P A). There also are programs obtained through the state of Oklahoma. The program budget is usually between four and five million dollars annually, with 95 percent coming from federal sources.

The programs serve Cheyenne and Arapaho tribal members and sometimes other Native Americans and non-Indians in a service area that covers from eight to eighteen counties (some programs operate in eight or nine counties and others in a wider area). The service area for most programs corresponds roughly with the 1869 executive order reservation. However, the Food Distribution program covers a ten-county area but excludes large towns (such as El Reno). Social Services accepts clients from an eleven-county area and the I H S from eighteen counties. The population eligible for participation in the programs includes almost five thousand Cheyennes and Arapahos, but the eligibility requirements vary by program. The largest amounts of funding go to programs in social services, health, education, and job training. Salaries for program employees and program-related expenses are funded by direct costs.

SOCIAL SERVICES

The Social Services director is responsible for several programs, including general assistance, a Community Services contract, an energy assistance program, a Child Care block grant, Indian Child Welfare (I C W) grants, and the Youth Shelter. The director works with nine other staff members on all but the Child Care, I C W, and Youth Shelter programs, which have additional staff. The department also is responsible for supervising the I I M accounts of minors and incapacitated adults.

The tribes' general assistance program is contracted from the B I A. Temporary monthly assistance is given to eligible tribal members until they can qualify for state and other programs. The staff refers clients to Aid to Families with Dependent Children (A F D C), the Veterans Administration, and unemployment services. A person with one-fourth degree Native American ancestry who is unemployed and actively seeking work is eligible for services. In 1993 Social Services had 287 cases of a parent or parents with children and 191 cases of single clients. Clients come from an eight-county service area. The department can assist about 75 percent of those eligible before the program depletes its funds. The staff also helped 173 clients with medical disabilities until they could qualify for state aid. The general assistance payment is $200–783 a month, depending on the size of the family. Although the payment is lower than what the client could receive from the state, tribal members feel more comfortable dealing with other tribal members. The state payments are stigmatized as welfare, and state workers sometimes are perceived as rude and insensitive to the Native American population.

The tribes' tax commission set up an emergency assistance fund, which is administered by Social Services. Grants were initially given for utilities, rent, and expenses connected with hospitalization or death of an immediate family member. The requests for money for rents and utilities were so numerous that the guidelines were changed to provide only money for hospital-connected needs up to $150 and expenses connected with a death, such as a wake, travel, or ceremonial requirements, up to $250. Recently multipurpose grants have been given again. And the department has a miscellaneous fund to help victims of natural disasters or fires and to help with temporary housing.

Social Services also administers a Community Services contract, which gives food vouchers to persons who do not qualify for the Food Distribution program. The vouchers amount to $100–200 annually, depending on household size. The Low Income Home Energy Assistance program serves about 175 clients between December and March, paying vendors for clients' gas and electricity. About 90 percent of those eligible can be helped with the funds available. Social Services administers a Child Care block grant from the Department of Health and Human Services (H H S), which pays for childcare for low income families whose head of household is employed, goes to school, or is in the Tribal Work Experience Program (T W E P). Families with children too young for Headstart or out of school for the summer are eligible. This program operates with a coordinator and a secretary.

The Social Services department also has a child protection worker whose position was contracted from the B I A. This person works with I C W and the tribal court to investigate and monitor referred cases of abuse, neglect, and abandonment. The I C W staff receives referrals from out-of-state, state, and tribal court on cases involving Cheyenne and Arapaho children. I C W works to unify parents and children or, if that is not possible, to place children with relatives or other foster families with Cheyenne and Arapaho members. I C W advises parents of their legal rights and can monitor cases where parental rights are terminated. I C W generally intervenes in out-of-state cases where parental rights are terminated and places the child locally with a Cheyenne or Arapaho foster family after transferring the case to tribal court. I C W also offers counseling to parents, foster parents, and families and makes referrals to other counseling services for parenting skills, substance abuse, and other problems.

The I C W staff emphasizes sensitivity to Cheyenne and Arapaho cultural and socioeconomic circumstances. When the state handled these cases the staff was non-Indian, and when the B I A operated the program the workers generally were Native American but not Cheyenne or Arapaho. The tribes' I C W workers are familiar with local families and communities. Foster families are paid by the state, but the tribes' I C W program sets the standards and guidelines and chooses the foster families. The tribes' I C W office pays less attention than the state did to such factors as economic resources, space, and privacy for individuals. The state guidelines limit the number of children in a home to six; the tribal I C W office does not. Access to a telephone is acceptable to I C W rather than possession of a telephone in the family's home. Unlike state guidelines, I C W does not require the family to carry insurance. Because virtually all Cheyennes and Arapahos live near the poverty line, state socioeconomic guidelines are not feasible; these guidelines also may be culturally inappropriate. I C W is understaffed, compared to state offices that handle comparable populations. There is a coordinator, caseworker, and assistant caseworker/secretary. They administer to about two hundred clients annually.

The Youth Shelter was contracted from the B I A in 1992 in response to a perceived need for services for children in homes where there was substance abuse or where children had substance abuse problems themselves. It also is designed to provide care for children in family crisis situations. Before the tribes contracted the shelter, Cheyenne and Arapaho children were eligible to enter the state's Department of Human Services (D H S) shelters in El Reno and Clinton, but there was not sufficient space to meet the need, and these shelters were not responsive to the special needs of Native American children. The shelter serves one hundred residents annually. There are seven beds and an average of nine residents per month. Children whose ages range from newborn to seventeen are accepted, as are both Indian and non-Indian children. Non-Indian children are referred to the shelter because it is licensed by the D H S. Referrals of all children come from D H S, I C W, tribal court, Cheyenne-Arapaho Law Enforcement, and sometimes from parents and relatives who are having family crises. The program seeks to provide a family environment for the children with activities that, aside from transportation to school, include general recreation and all sorts of tribal activities. The shelter has playground equipment, purchased with funds raised by a benefit basketball game. There are also a television and several kinds of games. The staff members, all certified childcare workers, include a coordinator, four houseparents, and two part-time houseparents.

HEALTH

The tribal health director is responsible for administering four programs obtained through contracts or grants from the I H S—Community Health Representative (C H R), E M S, Substance Abuse, and Health Educator. Each program has its own coordinator. The C H R program, which began in 1968–69, provides for the hiring of one or more outreach workers in each district. The outreach workers do eight to ten thousand annual home visits, organize about one hundred annual screenings and educational health fairs for the general public, and deliver medicine and provide transportation for patients who have no other means to keep doctors' appointments. The C H R program is responsible for covering a nine-county area and serves non-Indian clients as well as Native American and Cheyenne and Arapaho tribal members. Screenings are offered to the general public for hypertension, diabetes, and cholesterol. C H R clients are encouraged to attend the screening sessions, which are held throughout the service area at Indian community halls, churches, schools, bingo operations, city halls, and the tribal complex. C H Rs offer illustrated lectures and provide literature on injury prevention and first aid to Headstart workers and parent organizations. They provide information on diabetes, prenatal care, breast examination, and hypertension at health fairs held in cooperation with I H S clinics and hospitals throughout the service area. For their home visit clients, C H Rs provide counseling, check on medications, monitor blood pressure and other conditions, and check for home hazards and other potential problems. The C H R program has a coordinator, ten C H R outreach workers (some of whom are certified in A I D S and fetal alcohol syndrome counseling), one worker who drives a van through rural areas picking up clients who have medical appointments, and one dialysis transport specialist who takes dialysis patients to treatment centers and offers counseling and referral services.

The E M S operates two ambulances with a crew of eight. The crew is on call twenty-four hours a day, and the members are licensed by the state of Oklahoma. The ambulances can transport people who live near Clinton to hospitals that will admit them. Before this service, Cheyenne and Arapaho people had difficulty getting to a hospital in an emergency, for local ambulances could not always be relied on to transport them. The tribes' two ambulances cannot meet the needs of all the districts, for they cannot service an area much beyond Clinton. E M S staff also provide C P R training to tribal employees in such programs as Substance Abuse,

Youth Summer Camp, and c h r, and they are on duty at tribal events to provide first aid or emergency transport.

The Substance Abuse program operates an inpatient treatment program and offers counseling services. The Transitional Living Center handles twelve patients for eight weeks, with seventy-two openings annually. To qualify, patients have to have completed a treatment program elsewhere. The center offers counseling, therapy, and Native American cultural activities and monitors patients for six months and one year after they have completed the program. Patients are transported to a a meetings, powwows, and dances and are invited to participate in sweat lodges (a religious ritual of renewal). The center also has sponsored peyote meetings for patients in order to aid their recovery. The program offers outpatient counseling as well. A youth counselor, who serves as a liaison between the community and the program, obtains referrals from the community. This counselor also starts local chapters of various kinds of support groups, organizes teen dances in several communities, coordinates a summer camp that promotes Native American cultural activities, and, along with a family counselor, holds group counseling sessions at the treatment center. The family counselor gets referrals from i c w, the Indian clinics in El Reno and Watonga, and the hospital at Clinton. About ten families are contacted and three are accepted as clients for counseling or referral by the family counselor. Substance Abuse operates with a coordinator, a counselor supervisor, two inpatient counselors, two outpatient counselors, a cook, two attendants, a secretary, and a receptionist.

The health educator works on preventive medicine, giving talks and demonstrations on, for example, weight control and smoking. The health educator also serves as a liaison between the tribes and the health programs of the state of Oklahoma, for example, in arranging for the state to provide a mobile mammography unit for Cheyenne and Arapaho women.

EDUCATION

The education programs include Higher Education, Adult Education, Johnson O'Malley—all funded by the b i a—and the Headstart program. Higher Education, a college scholarship program, gives out each semester about 130 scholarships averaging nine hundred dollars. To be eligible a student must have a p e l l grant.

The Adult Education program pays tuition, fees, and the cost of books for about one hundred part-time students per semester who are enrolled in vocational training or career development programs. This program also administers grant funds that pay general equivalency diploma (g e d) testing fees for about fifty to one hundred clients annually. The g e d classes are held at six sites and charge no tuition. Another grant allows for the hiring of tribal members to teach classes in native language and culture. In 1993 six Cheyennes and two Arapahos were teaching very basic language classes for a few hours a week. The classes are free to the public.

The Johnson O'Malley program provides money for about fourteen hundred Indian students attending public elementary, middle, and secondary schools within tribal jurisdiction. The money (approximately one hundred dollars per student) usually is used for supplies and fees and is allocated by parent committees in each community.

The Headstart program, funded by H H S, has been operating two centers, one at Concho and one at Canton, that serve sixty-nine children. Recently, centers have opened in Hammon and Geary. Centers have classes with children from the ages of three to five from families at or near the poverty level. The center at Canton has both Indian and non-Indian children. Each center has a teacher supervisor, two teachers, two teacher's aides, and two cooks. A bus provides transportation for the children. Unlike the state Headstart programs, the tribes' program emphasizes activities that reinforce Cheyenne and Arapaho culture and language. Children play games and participate in hands-on discovery in their classroom activities, where they explore drama, reading, science, music, and nutrition. Field trips also are a part of the program. Parent involvement is stressed, so that parents and grandparents teach dances, stories, and songs; help with meals; eat meals with the children; and help with activities generally. Parents organized fund-raising projects to purchase a computer for the children in one of the centers. The goals of the tribes' parental involvement focus include encouraging the parents to continue to be active when their children enter public school.

The program offers comprehensive health services through I H S, in the case of the Indian children, and the county health department or Medicaid, in the case of non-Indian children. Nutritional education also is a focus of the program, which serves the children two meals and a snack four days a week. There is a nutritional consultant who comes to the centers and provides workshops and a newsletter for parents and staff and does nutritional assessment for the children. The program has a contract with the Child Studies Center at the University of Oklahoma to provide observation, counseling when necessary, and advice to the staff on early child development. The fifteen staff members have, or are working toward, child development associate credentials, the training for which is paid for by the program. The director has an advanced degree. Although the opening of centers at Hammon and Geary has helped, more Headstart centers are needed, for there is not sufficient space for Cheyenne and Arapaho children in the local centers operated by the non-Indian community and parents feel reluctant to send their children to these programs, which do not have a Native American focus.

The education director also is responsible for administering the tribes' Education Trust Fund, which was established with money from the judgment awarded the tribes for the violation of the 1851 treaty. This fund helps about four hundred students annually with amounts ranging from fifteen to six hundred dollars. Recipients are not required to live within the service area. High school students also are given money for fees for school expenses, and all students are given emergency grants for illness, glasses, travel to funerals, and other education-related expenses. The Education Trust Fund also gives scholarship money to college students ineligible for B I A funding and to graduate students.

JOB TRAINING

The tribes have two programs that concentrate on improving employment opportunities: the Job Training Partnership Act program (J T P A) and Employment Opportunities and Training services (E O T). The J T P A program, contracted from the Department of Labor, helps both adults and youths. The adult program is for people over the age of eighteen whose family income is below the poverty line, who have been laid off, or who lack the skills to find employment. There are four components: classroom training, work experience, community service employment, and supportive service. The classroom training option provides a stipend for individuals who enroll in a vocational training program. They are paid the minimum wage for thirty hours per week, which enables them to meet living expenses while they are training for work. Eighteen people can be funded per year. The work experience component allows for the program to pay a worker's wages for six weeks at a nonprofit organization, such as a hospital, nursing home, tribal program, or school. When an opening becomes available, clients are sent for an interview. The program encourages the employer to give their clients an opportunity to demonstrate competence while the program pays the individual's salary. Minimum wage is paid for the six-week time period, after which time the employer can negotiate a salary with the worker. J T P A helps about twenty-four clients per year with this kind of assistance. The community service employment component of the program also encourages employers at nonprofit organizations to hire Native American workers if a position is anticipated but not yet funded. The program can pay the person's wages for up to a year and a half, but usually the person goes on the payroll before this time expires. There are funds for about two positions per year. The supportive service component provides start-up money for newly employed individuals working for a nonprofit organization. Individuals can be supported with gas money, lunch money, money for uniforms, or money for tools until they receive the first paycheck or for up to six weeks. About seventy-five people apply for this kind of assistance; about forty-five people are helped annually by this program.

J T P A's summer youth program places youths between the ages of fourteen and twenty-one in short-term, temporary positions working for nonprofit organizations under adult supervision. The program's aim is to encourage good work habits and provide some income to economically disadvantaged youths. Clients are required to report to work sober and drug free and can miss no more than three working days. Projects that youths work on include painting and landscaping at schools, homes of elderly and handicapped persons, hospitals, and community halls as well as cleaning graveyards. Those who qualify include youths who left high school before graduation, individual heads of household, single and teenage parents, and handicapped youths whose families are below the poverty line. Youths are eligible every other summer until the age of twenty-one. About two hundred youth apply; only about sixty-four can be hired. The J T P A program serves the eight-county service area. Enrolled members of other tribes are eligible, but preference is given to enrolled Cheyennes and Arapahos.

The director of E O T administers four programs: Adult Vocational Training (A V T), contracted from the B I A; Job Opportunity and Basic Skills (J O B S), contracted from the state of Oklahoma's D H S; T W E P, funded by the B I A; and Tribal Employment Rights Organization (T E R O), funded by the E E O C. The director works with two other employees. A V T gives financial assistance for full-time students in trade or vocational school. The student can receive tuition as well as money for books, fees, living expenses, eyeglasses, tools, car repairs, and emergency expenses. The program serves approximately twenty clients. The J O B S program is designed to help Cheyenne-Arapaho A F D C clients become more self-sufficient. The program helps them find or maintain employment by paying for transportation and other costs associated with educational or work situations. About twenty clients are helped annually. The staff holds workshops in local communities throughout the service area where clients and tribal members in general are invited to practice job-seeking skills, through, for example, mock job interviews. T W E P provides work experience for about twenty Cheyenne and Arapaho clients who are referred by Social Services. Clients, who are general assistance recipients, are placed in schools or jobs in the local community, where they receive no salary. The program can send clients for training and give incentive pay. T E R O works to protect Cheyenne and Arapaho workers from discrimination and to try to ensure equal opportunity and fair treatment from employers. The director files about twelve complaints annually with E E O C. The E O T program also assists all its clients by helping to complete job applications and prepare resumes, soliciting work for clients, giving references, and taking messages for clients from prospective employers. The office receives job announcements from county, state, federal, and city agencies and from tribal offices.

LAW ENFORCEMENT

The Law Enforcement program was contracted from the B I A. There are nine officers, including the chief of police, and a dispatcher, all hired by the business committee. Another B I A contract provides for a criminal investigator, who works with the police force. Five reserve officers also provide assistance when needed, but the program is short-staffed. The contract funds are not sufficient to support the police force at the level needed, but the program can apply to the Cheyenne-Arapaho tax commission for occasional assistance, for example, in constructing a pistol range or replacing a police vehicle. All the officers graduate from the B I A police academy; some are certified by the state of Oklahoma as well. The business committee chair is commander-in-chief of the police force. The police officers live in their own communities—in 1993 they lived in Watonga, Geary, Hammon, Weatherford, Concho, Colony, and Canton—and are dispatched from there to where they are needed. They also provide security at community events. The police respond to calls, patrol, and serve court papers where they have jurisdiction, which is on trust land, fee patent land, and dependent Indian communities (H U D housing under the Cheyenne-Arapaho Housing Authority) where Indians are living. The police also investigate traffic accidents on trust property and roads maintained by the B I A. The criminal investigator investigates suspected crimes and works with Social Services and I C W on cases of suspected domestic abuse. He or she also does background checks on prospective foster families and applicants for tribal jobs, when so requested.

The Law Enforcement program also has a grant from the B I A for an attorney general (part of whose salary is from tribal funds), an assistant attorney general, and a public defender. These individuals work through the tribal court and are hired by the business committee. The attorney general decides if there is enough evidence to prosecute in criminal cases and argues on behalf of the tribes. But he or she also tries to make referrals in cases where treatment or social services of one sort or another would be appropriate. The public defender is assigned to criminal cases by the tribal court.

Jurisdictional questions create problems for the Law Enforcement program, for the state of Oklahoma retains jurisdiction over crimes committed by non-Indians on trust property but is reluctant to act in these cases. Tribal police lack jurisdiction over non-Indians. Some county and town law enforcement personnel are cooperative, and some are not. The F B I (with offices in Elk City and Oklahoma City) has jurisdiction over major federal crimes, including murder, rape, assault with a deadly weapon, assault with intent to kill, incest, robbery, burglary, and arson.

With tribal control of the Law Enforcement program, customary and traditional ways of handling conflict are given more emphasis than when the B I A operated the program. For example, conflict between individuals over ceremonial issues or objects is treated as a matter for ceremonial authorities, not the tribal police. And, powwow committees make the decision of whether to allow a Forty-Nine dance late at night after the conclusion of the regular program of events. Drinking to excess is the norm at a Forty-Nine dance, but, if the powwow committee gives approval, law enforcement officers may not make arrests. The program contracts for jail space with two counties, for the tribal court can sentence individuals to up to six months in jail as well as impose fines. But the tribal Law Enforcement program emphasizes getting people into various treatment programs, such as Substance Abuse, and using community service alternatives to jail. The program makes many referrals to other tribal programs designed to aid families and individuals experiencing problems with substance abuse or family crises.

OTHER PROGRAMS

The Housing Improvement program (H I P) is contracted from the B I A. Contract monies are used for home construction and repair, with the clients selected on the basis of income and need. Elderly tribal members are given priority, but all members of federally recognized tribes living within the service area are eligible. Since 1985 the work has been put out for bid to subcontractors, with tribal members, then other Native Americans, receiving preference. Before 1985, tribes had their own crews. About one new home is built annually (when it is not feasible to repair an old home), and about ten homes are remodeled—depending on available funds. The program is designed to bring housing up to state or local code requirements. There is a long waiting list, approximately eighty-five applicants in 1993. The program operates with a director and a secretary.

The Food Distribution program is contracted from the Department of Agriculture. This program distributes commodities to qualified tribal members living within the tribes' service area, about fifteen hundred people annually (about four hundred households in 1993). Foods from the main food groups—meat, grain, fruit and vegetables, fats, and dairy products—are issued.

The Elderly Nutrition program is contracted from the Administration on Aging. This program began by serving meals four times a week to elderly Cheyennes and Arapahos in Clinton and to others for a nominal charge (and by providing assistance to a group that serves meals in Geary). Meals are delivered as well as served at the senior citizens' center in Clinton and the Indian Baptist Church in Geary. Service has been extended to Concho and Hammon. Transportation is provided for the elderly, and recreation, such as bingo or craftwork, is included in the program. About thirty-five elderly people in Geary and up to one hundred in Clinton participate in the program.

The Fire Suppression program is funded by the B I A and, since its inception in 1989, has trained as firefighters ninety-five Cheyennes and Arapahos who can meet the physical qualifications and who are over the age of eighteen. The training program includes firefighting skills, fire behavior, and safety. The program sends crews of twenty to sites around the United States when they are needed to fight forest fires. They also respond to natural disasters, such as flooding.

Cheyenne-Arapaho Enterprises

The tribes have several business enterprises that have the potential to produce income as well as provide employment for tribal members. The tribes' smoke shops at Concho, Watonga, Clinton, and Canton sell cigarettes, cigars, snuff, chewing tobacco, and also various sundries, including lighters, pipes, T-shirts, and locally made beadwork. Customers may pay a lower price on tobacco products sold on trust land, for state taxes are not levied on all these products.[4] The smoke shops also have bingo games in the evening and sell pull tabs (a game of chance) throughout the day. There are ten tribal employees at the Concho shop, eleven at Clinton, five at Watonga, and five at Canton. The tribes established bingo halls in Watonga, Clinton, and Concho (which closed in 1994). Most of the customers are Cheyennes and Arapahos, who spend an average of thirty dollars a visit. The payment rate is very high, 85 to 90 percent, so the profit margin is low. These three bingo halls employ about forty-five tribal members. The bingo halls and smoke shops are not on major thoroughfares, which limits the potential for customers. The business committee appoints the managers of the smoke shops and bingo halls. In 1994 a new casino opened at Concho, replacing the smaller tribally owned bingo hall there.

The Lucky Star casino may eventually be owned by the tribes, if the business does well. It was built and is operated by a management company that specializes in gaming. The manager is a non-Indian employee of the management company. The tribes receive an annual payment from the company and receive a head tax on the patrons. If the casino business makes enough profit to reimburse the management company for the cost of the building, the tribes have the option to take over the management or to take the larger share of the profits while retaining the management firm. The casino employs about 130 tribal members, and in 1999 the profits amounted to between two and three million dollars. The business committee may try to exert pressure on the management in personnel matters, but the final decision is with the management firm. Tribal members work in all sorts of jobs—accounting, inventory, marketing, cashier, floorwalker, maintenance, food preparation. The casino offers traditional bingo, two varieties of video bingo and other games, and pull tabs. Players can win up to one million dollars. There is also a cafe and gift shop.

The Farm and Ranch operation is a diversified agricultural business that operates at a profit some years. In 1993 Farm and Ranch was dry farming 3,200 acres of tribal land at Concho: 1,200 acres in wheat, corn, and alfalfa and 2,000 acres in pasture. Cattle are raised to produce yearlings that are sold. The herd numbers eighty head. Farm and Ranch also grazes about nine hundred head of cattle for other ranchers who pay the tribes a fee. The grass on the Concho lands is native, original blue stem, never broken out. Here cattle gain one-third more weight than on other grass. The tribes also have a buffalo herd of eighteen, which grazes on fenced pasture and is fed hay grown on Farm and Ranch pasture. Some of the hay is sold, and some is used for winter feed. The buffalo are occasionally donated to tribal organizations for ceremonial purposes. Hogs are also raised in order to produce show pigs, which are sold at the age of six months.

Farm and Ranch has a director, hired by the business committee, three full-time laborers, and a secretary. They also use up to eight part-time laborers. To encourage or assist tribal members in agriculture, Farm and Ranch donates stock to Cheyenne and Arapaho youths for their FFA or 4-H Club projects when parents cannot afford to purchase them. The operation also provides technical assistance to the few tribal members who farm. The director will negotiate leases for tribal members, acting as their agent in dealing with non-Indian lessees in order to obtain the best possible terms. Farm and Ranch also helps the local communities and the tribal programs by using their heavy equipment to maintain community halls, powwow grounds, cemeteries, and driveways. Farm and Ranch is currently expanding onto other tribally owned land, which may bring more income to the tribes than if they leased the land and should provide more jobs for tribal members. Land purchase is another option.

The Tax Commission

In 1988 the tribes passed a General Revenue and Tax Act that required oil companies to pay tribes a severance tax on oil and gas extracted from tribally owned land, and the act also created a tax commission to levy and collect the taxes. The oil companies challenged the act's application to severance taxes on minerals extracted from allotments. Up until 1993, over three million dollars in taxes had been paid into escrow awaiting a final resolution of the case in the courts. In 1997 the tribes prevailed. These and other taxes are collected by the Cheyenne-Arapaho Tax Commission. A tax ordinance adopted by the Cheyenne and Arapaho Tribes prescribes that the bingo operations pay an entertainment tax (or head tax) of one dollar for each customer. The smoke shops pay a stamp tax of five cents on each pack of cigarettes sold. A tobacco tax of 15 percent of the manufacturer's price is paid on cigars, snuff, and chewing tobacco. Businesses and professional services on tribal land are required to pay a retail tax of 3 percent. The smoke shops pay the retail tax on the souvenir and other items sold, aside from the tobacco products. The commission also developed a plan to assess taxes on automobile license plates, which have been issued and taxed by the tribes since 1996. Originally, the tribal council determined allocation guidelines for the tax monies and assumed authority over allocation. In 1992 the business committee administration overrode the tribal council's instructions and began deciding how these tax commission monies should be used. Requests for funds by programs and individuals or groups are reviewed by the tax commission, which meets at least once a month, and their recommendations are forwarded to the business committee, which makes the final decisions on allocations.[5]

Guidelines established by the General Revenue and Tax Act state that the monies are to benefit both the taxpayer and the tribal members. Land acquisition and tribal government, including programs (for example, Law Enforcement and road maintenance) and tribal administration (for example, business committee salaries), may be funded by tax monies. Emergency assistance to individuals has been given through Social Services since 1994.

The business committee appoints the members of the tax commission, which is composed of four tribal members chosen by district and which is chaired by the business committee treasurer. The tax commission and their staff are responsible for collecting and recordkeeping as well as making recommendations on allocations. In addition, the four-member tax commission staff is also working to develop a minerals management system whereby they can monitor severance tax collections on tribal wells and eventually develop a reporting system to audit allottee leases.

The Housing Authority

The Cheyenne-Arapaho Housing Authority is responsible for selecting the occupants of homes built through a H U D program and for collecting the monthly payments due on these mutual-help homes. There are five members on the board of commissioners of the housing authority, an executive and deputy director hired by the board, and about fifteen other employees. Board members are tribal members, selected by districts within the former reservation area. The business committee appoints the members of the board for three-year terms but cannot remove them without cause and without the consent of the Oklahoma Housing Authority. The board meets once a month, and the members receive per diem and mileage. The board controls the housing authority monies, which are used to build and repair homes for Cheyenne and Arapaho tribal members, selects the recipients of new or refurbished housing, and decides how to proceed against those in arrears—usually first through a negotiated payback agreement, then through eviction.

Each year the housing authority has obtained twenty new units. With business committee support they can apply for more. There are from two to three hundred applicants on the waiting list for homes. Families with housing often take in one or more other families, so there is severe overcrowding. The first one hundred homes that were built were substandard and are currently in very poor condition. The housing authority receives insufficient funds to make repairs. The minimum monthly housing payment is currently fifty-five dollars. The rate of arrearage is 60 percent.

There are several obstacles facing the housing authority in its efforts to obtain better housing for tribal members. The Cheyennes and Arapahos are at a disadvantage in obtaining units compared to other native peoples in Oklahoma because they have a one-fourth degree blood requirement. Other tribes may have a low Indian blood requirement or only a proof of lineage requirement and, with a larger population, qualify for more homes. One such tribe in eastern Oklahoma has a waiting list of one to two thousand applicants and received 250 units in 1993. There is a penalty for arrearage on the part of business committee members who have HUD homes, which, along with the penalty for the arrearage rate in general, adversely affects the tribes' ability to qualify for more housing. The housing authority has not resorted to payroll deduction or to garnishing general assistance or IIM income. It has been difficult to convince tribal members that they must pay the monthly payment, particularly since for sixteen years no action was taken against people in arrears. Recently, the housing authority has used the tribal court to force compliance through payback or eviction, and the rate of arrearage has gone down. Still, most of those in arrearage wait until they are compelled to negotiate a payback plan.

The Tribal Court

The tribal court system, which replaced the Code of Federal Regulations (CFR) court in 1988, includes a district court and a supreme court. A court clerk is responsible for preparing and monitoring the budget and is appointed by the five supreme court justices. The judges are Native American attorneys. District judges are selected by the business committee and can only be removed by the supreme court for commission of a felony, conflict of interest, or moral turpitude. Supreme court justices are selected by the business committee for a six-year term; the business committee cannot remove them, and reappointment is automatic unless a judge is convicted of a felony. The supreme court hears appeals on decisions from district court. The supreme court's rulings can be appealed to federal district court.[6]

About half of the court's budget is contracted from the BIA, and half is from tribal enterprises and taxes. This money is administered by the business manager. Recently, court fines, bonds, and costs have been taken out of the business manager's sphere and are now allocated by the court. There is a chief judge and an associate judge in the district court at Concho. The court has jurisdiction over cases involving Indians on trust land. Also, Cheyenne and Arapaho individuals and groups can bring suit against other tribal members. Non-Indians who wish to sue Cheyennes and Arapahos or the Cheyenne and Arapaho Tribes may have to bring suit in tribal court, as in the case brought by oil companies to avoid paying severance taxes. The court hears criminal, civil, and juvenile cases and operates by codes established by the business committee. The codes are modeled after the federally established codes used in the CFR court system that was operated by the

B I A. Adopting these codes facilitated the tribes' getting the contract. Decisions also are based on the 1975 constitution and the Indian Civil Rights Act of 1968. Many of the cases involve constitutional issues, that is, political disputes between the business committee and tribal council and between the business committee and election board. Litigants or defendants may bring attorneys to tribal court or represent themselves. Jury trials are possible but exceedingly rare.

Dilemmas of Dependency

Complaints and disputes about tribal government are not unexpected, given the existing constitutional ambiguities—for example, what authority rests with the tribal council and what with the business committee, and what authority does the business committee have to administer programs, enterprises, and tax funds? The constitution allows or requires the secretary of the interior to play a supervisory role in tribal politics. The secretary intervenes on some occasions and declines to do so at other times. Adding to the uncertainty about the constitution are the inconsistent court rulings. For example, when the C F R court ruled on whether business committee salaries from indirect costs were constitutional, the assistant secretary for Indian affairs overturned the decision, arguing that the constitution would have to be amended to that effect and that the C F R court had no jurisdiction over intertribal political disputes. Cheyennes and Arapahos also perceive the tribal court to be an unreliable source of redress for constitutional ambiguities. Among the most glaring problems with the constitution are its provisions about recall, which encourage constituents to frequently challenge tribal officials and employees. The amount of money the election board requires to deal with recall petitions and to hold recall elections often leads to their exceeding their budget, and much of the tribal court's resources are spent on these problems. A minority of voters can exert tremendous influence on the course of tribal business; only 30 percent of the electorate in a district can force a new election. Officials in the Department of the Interior helped write the constitution, and it was approved by the secretary at a time when the contracting of federal programs was imminent; yet an outdated constitution was approved.[7]

The problems with the constitution contribute to problems in fiscal management. With the exception of the housing authority funds from H U D, the business committee (or, more typically, the individuals on the committee who dominate it) exerts controls over virtually all tribal income—money from the tribal farming and grazing leases, tribal enterprises, tribal taxes, and direct and indirect costs from programs. The comptroller and business manager, whose salaries come from program and enterprise income and who are responsible for monitoring the use of tribal monies, are hired and can be fired by the business committee at will. The business manager or Finance Department can delay or deny funds to the election board, even though the constitution says that their funds are allocated through the tribal council budget. The use of program monies can be politicized, for the business committee can hire and fire program and administrative department directors and can appoint and refuse to reappoint board members (for example, on the tax commission and housing authority). Thus, constituents who oppose particular business committee members' actions potentially can be penalized financially. This can be devastating for people in an area as economically depressed as Cheyenne-Arapaho country.

One recourse available to constituents with complaints is the tribal court, where individuals and groups (such as the election board) can seek redress against the business committee. However, the funding for Law Enforcement and the tribal court also is controlled largely by the business manager and controller (and, therefore, by the business committee), and the personnel are selected, and in some cases can be fired, by the business committee. Personnel can be pressured in various ways by business committee members. With the judiciary branch of tribal government compromised, the only recourse for redress or the only means of reform is to appeal to the Department of the Interior, with uncertain outcome.

The tribal government depends on the federal government for at least half of its budget. Federal programs are designed to relieve the conditions of poverty and their consequences, and the Cheyenne and Arapaho community in the service area certainly needs relief. The most recent tribal survey showed that the per capita income for members ages nineteen and up was about $6,000. In the state of Oklahoma it was $15,444. Eighty-one percent of the Cheyennes and Arapahos are under the state average. Only 7 percent earn fifteen to twenty thousand dollars; 12 percent earn over twenty thousand dollars. Sixty-four percent qualify for and receive either food stamps or commodities. Sixty-eight percent of the tribes have graduated from high school, but in this rural region of Oklahoma jobs are in short supply. The unemployment rate was 62 percent in 1987 and 65 percent in 1990. Health conditions are much worse than in the state at large. The need for these programs is reinforced by the problems of discrimination that Cheyennes and Arapahos faced in the 1970s and subsequently. In 1977 the Oklahoma Human Rights Commission targeted western Oklahoma for discrimination in the public schools, law enforcement, employment, housing, and health care. In Blaine County, Cheyennes and Arapahos constituted 6.8 percent of the population and accounted for 63.9 percent of the arrests. The commission found that towns relied on fines and prisoner labor to supplement their budgets. The school dropout rate in Watonga was 25 percent; Geary, 34 percent; Canton, 58 percent; and Longdale, 86 percent. Tribal government seized the new opportunities for contracting to try to improve conditions for the Cheyennes and Arapahos, who were long neglected by the federal government and the wider society.[8]

Although there is a clearly demonstrated need for economic assistance, the programs are underfunded. Clients have to be turned away for lack of funds. Job training is not available for all who qualify. There are always more applicants for positions than can be hired. Ambulance service and programs for substance abuse are able to provide help to only a small sector of the population needing these services. There are not enough Headstart facilities for all the Cheyenne and Arapaho children who qualify. In addition, there is variation among the programs with respect to eligibility criteria. In the housing programs, payments and requirements vary among programs and there are long waiting lists for homes and for repairs. These conditions give rise to suspicions that some individuals or families receive favored treatment.[9]

A particular source of resentment is that tribal employees receive salaries that put them at the high end of the income range. Salaries of staff vary from $12,000 to $27,000; that of program and administrative department directors, from $18,000 to $38,000. In 1993 the business committee members received salaries of $35,000, and the business manager and comptroller received $35,000 and $32,700, respectively. With the exception of the comptroller these employees have usually been tribal members. Employees are under considerable pressure to help relatives and other tribal members financially, and there is pressure from tribal members for turnover in employee positions so that tribal income circulates. Turnover can be detrimental to program management and to the ability of the Finance Department to keep accounts properly. Employees sometimes ask for salary advances (treated as loans from the tribes) to be paid back by payroll deductions, which can create accounting problems.

People who live in the communities further removed from Concho may feel that they have less access to services than those living nearer Concho. Not only is the ambulance service limited in the amount of miles it can cover, but job development specialists do not have the means of transportation to visit the more rural areas regularly. Job training opportunities do not correspond to employment opportunities in the local community: welding and hairdressing are popular training programs, but neither is a promising source of employment. Most jobs continue to be seasonal, minimum wage, and part-time, not career oriented. People generally do not want to relocate to urban areas, where job opportunities are better, for they would have to leave behind family and ceremonial support and responsibilities.

Tribal contracting has meant that the number of Cheyennes and Arapahos hired for jobs in the programs has increased. On the other hand, the programs have less to spend, as the I H S and the B I A (both the area office in Anadarko and the Concho agency office) continue to receive some of the program money for administrative costs, even though most of the responsibility has been assumed by the tribes. Thus, after contracting, the program monies awarded to the tribes declined.

Program personnel argue very persuasively that the programs are run more effectively than when they were operated by the B I A and other nontribal agencies. Tribal employees give more personal attention to clients, spending hours helping them fill out applications for jobs or scholarships, for example. Clearly, B I A and state employees did not take this kind of interest. Tribal employees are more aware of cultural factors that shape their clients' expectations and behavior than were the people who provided services before the tribes contracted. Giving clients moral support generally is important to tribal employees, who are often friends and relatives of the clients, which facilitates communication. The Education Office is proud of the fact that, since the tribes contracted the college scholarship program, the college graduation rate has increased 100 percent. When the B I A ran some of these programs, they were operated out of the area office in Anadarko. Some Cheyennes and Arapahos observe that tribes in the Anadarko area received favored treatment then. Whether this is merely a matter of perception or a reality is difficult to determine. In short, educational levels and employment opportunities have improved since the late 1970s, but the expectations and needs of Cheyennes and Arapahos still cannot be met by tribal government.

Programs (contracts and grants) budget both direct and indirect costs. Direct costs are those that can be specifically identified with a particular grant or contract, something done for the benefit of clients (including salaries of the director and staff, supplies, program-related travel, and the cost of services for clients). Indirect costs serve programs, not clients. Indirect costs are reasonable costs incurred to benefit more than one program (for example, accounting, administrators' salaries, legal fees related to programs, cost of utilities for the tribal complex, and insurance). Because the governing body (in the case of the Cheyenne and Arapaho Tribes, the business committee is defined by the Office of the Inspector General [O I G] as the governing body) has responsibility for programs, as well as for other matters, O I G allows 50 percent of their compensation from indirect costs, but usually not more than 50 percent. The federal government imposes regulations and policies regarding all these costs that make deficits and mismanagement likely, if not inevitable.

The O I G in the Department of the Interior audits the department's programs (including those of the B I A) and negotiates with the tribes an indirect cost rate, which they apply to all programs, not merely those under the auspices of the Department of the Interior. The indirect cost rate is a percentage of the total direct costs of all the programs. It is based on the projected indirect costs budget and the projected sum of all direct cost budgets, adjusted for underrecovery or overrecovery on the budget of two years previously. The indirect cost rate is obtained by dividing the direct costs (the direct cost base) into the indirect costs (the indirect cost pool). For example, in preparing the 1994 budget, assume an estimate is made of indirect costs for the business committee and the Finance, Planning, and Personnel Departments in the amount of $100,000 and of direct costs for thirty contracts in the amount of $300,000. The indirect cost rate would be 33 percent. But assume the 1992 budget resulted in an overrecovery of $45,000. The following calculation is made: $45,000 is 15 percent of $300,000; 15 percent is subtracted from 33 percent. The indirect cost rate for 1994 would be 18 percent. In 1989 the tribes' indirect cost rate was 23.6 percent; in 1992, 36.6 percent.

The regulations applied by the O I G create difficulties for all tribes, for the recovery of these indirect costs is problematic. Tribes are faced with three kinds of recovery problems: nonrecovery, overrecovery, and underrecovery. Nonrecovery is caused by the fact that not all programs pay indirect costs and that some pay a percentage far below the rate set by the O I G. For example, assume an indirect cost rate of 24 percent and a total of four programs. Direct costs for the four programs are B I A—Higher Education, $100,000; I H S-C H R, $50,000; D O L-J T P A, $70,000; and H H S-J O B S, $30,000. While the B I A and I H S pay 24 percent in indirect costs, D O L and H H S pay only 10 percent. According to the indirect cost rate of 24 percent, the tribes should recover $60,000 for indirect costs, but they actually recover $46,000. This nonrecovery produces a shortfall of $14,000. Thus, the tribes do not receive sufficient funds to meet the legitimate expenses of the programs and are faced with the problem of making up shortfalls.

Overrecovery occurs in basically three ways. Assume, as in the above example, an indirect cost rate of 24 percent; four programs with direct cost budgets of $250,000; and a recovery of only $46,000 for indirect costs. Suppose the tribal administration attempts to cut expenses (for example, by creating layoffs or funding positions at salaries lower than those budgeted) and holds indirect costs to $46,000, even though, according to the negotiated indirect cost rate, they should receive $60,000. O I G computes this as a hypothetical overrecovery and subtracts $14,000 from the indirect cost budget that they subsequently negotiate. That is, O I G deducts the overrecovery from the projected indirect costs of an indirect costs budget that they negotiate in the future. In this example, the tribes' indirect costs were all legitimate, yet they are faced with a "debt" that will leave them with a shortfall in a subsequent budget year.

Another way that overrecovery occurs is in a situation where the tribes obtain additional grants subsequent to the negotiation of the indirect cost rate. These grants bring in additional indirect cost monies. For example, assume the negotiation of an indirect cost rate of 24 percent based on total direct costs of $250,000. The tribes would be entitled to $60,000 in indirect costs. But suppose an I C W grant subsequently is awarded in the amount of $100,000 for direct costs and $24,000 for indirect costs. According to the O I G, this produces an overrecovery of $24,000, even though the indirect cost expenditures were all legitimate. There may be a delay in approving the indirect cost rate because of lack of adequate staff in the office of the o i g, such that grants are received by the tribes after their indirect cost rate proposal is received by o i g but before it is formally approved. This situation produces an overrecovery of indirect costs as well.

There can also be an overrecovery of indirect costs if some of the indirect cost expenditures are disallowed, either because o i g staff members rule that an expenditure was not legitimate (for example, because the tribal administration did not submit adequate documentation of legitimate expenditures) or because other federal agencies fail to properly process the tribes' documentation of their legitimate expenditures. These are examples of disallowed expenditures that can result in an overrecovery. Problems of documentation are commonplace, in large part because there is so much employee turnover in the tribes' Finance Department or in other positions.

The problem of underrecovery is in large part the result of the fact that the o i g requires tribal programs (the enterprises, for example) to contribute to the indirect cost pool. For example, if an indirect cost rate of 24 percent is assumed and if the direct costs of the enterprises are $250,000, the enterprises should contribute $60,000 to the indirect cost pool. If not, o i g considers this an underrecovery of $60,000—in short, a deficit of $60,000. Yet, according to a common reading of the constitution, tribal funds in these amounts cannot be committed without tribal council approval. Tribal councils have been reluctant to approve the use of tribal income for matching funds for programs. Therefore, to use tribal funds to make up shortfalls due to nonrecovery or to avoid underrecovery makes the tribal administration that uses funds without tribal council approval vulnerable to a finding of disallowed costs when tribal funds are audited and also makes the business committee vulnerable to charges of abuse of power.

An additional problem for the tribes is that the indirect cost rate negotiated by o i g is a projected estimate that may prove inadequate for the program needs. The tribes may not have sufficient income to supplement programs or make up shortfalls even if tribal council approval could be obtained. Moreover, due to frequent delays in receiving program funds from Washington d c often a program must either operate without cash on hand or close. If the program operates by borrowing funds out of the direct cost pool, and if something should happen that withholds or cuts the anticipated funding for the program, then these program expenditures are disallowed costs.

Nonrecovery, overrecovery, and underrecovery can lead to shortfalls or disallowed costs that are treated as deficit spending by the o i g auditors. In other words, deficits occur that are not the result of misappropriation of funds by tribal employees or the members of the business committee. This is the case for most of the deficits.

Tribal administrations have tried to cope with these problems by using tribal funds for indirect costs without the consent of the tribal council, arguing that the constitution does not specify that enterprise profits and taxes cannot be allocated without tribal council approval. Or occasionally they have siphoned money from direct costs, hoping to replace it when they recovered more indirect costs. A common practice used to cope with delayed funding problems has been to charge expenditures against programs other than those that received the goods or services by pooling all monies so that programs can operate even when the funding has been delayed. When this pooling strategy is used, direct cost program expenditures may not be properly accounted for and some programs may not receive all the direct cost funding to which they are entitled. Such practices can result in disallowed costs that can show as deficits in an audit. Another option for the tribal administration is to refuse programs that will not pay the indirect cost rate prescribed by o i g—this, of course, would dramatically reduce services to the Cheyenne and Arapaho people. Another option is to cut staff in Finance, Personnel, Planning, and other administrative departments or to lower salaries of the business committee and other tribal employees in an effort to secure better cooperation from the tribal council in applying tribal funds to indirect costs. Already the tribes have difficulty getting qualified people for some of these positions; cutting employee salaries would make the tribes less able to compete for people with the needed expertise.

What is particularly galling to the tribal administration is that when these programs were contracted, the legislation (PL93–638) mandated that the program funding be at least as much as the funding prior to contracting. However, the tribes have not received funding at the same level the federal agencies did when they administered the programs. Federal agencies, such as the b i a, withdraw funds from the money allocated by Congress for programs in order to monitor the programs. And the b i a central office can alter budget requests by the tribes and thereby undercut the tribes' efforts to plan in the face of congressional budget cuts. Moreover, federal agencies such as the b i a and i h s do not have adequate staff to provide technical assistance to tribes struggling with these indirect cost and other budgeting problems. The federal government has also increased the requirements attached to contracts, which raised the level of expertise needed by tribal administrators, which in turn raised the indirect costs, as did new requirements such as meeting the special needs of handicapped persons or reporting to the i r s. At the same time, there has been an effort to cut the indirect cost rate for all the tribes as well as the direct costs of the programs.[10]

Another aggravation for the tribes is the fact that the Department of the Interior's o i g assumes no responsibility to help resolve the problems. The b i a has a direct responsibility to oversee its contracts with the tribes yet has a hands-off policy. Failure to properly monitor programs allows problems in financial accounts to multiply. The BIA, then, permits the tribes "to slip down," in the words of one councilman, rather than taking the time and resources to help resolve problems. The tribal administration complained bitterly when a recent OIG investigation put the blame for deficits solely on the shoulders of the business committee, overlooking the role of the BIA and other nontribal agencies in the problems. Business committee members argue that the BIA hides behind the Self-Determination Act rather than fulfilling the contractor's obligations, for example, to do an annual sit-down review of programs. One member characterized the problem in this way: "638 became a reason for the tribes to fail." In the tribal administration's view, the BIA has failed to live up to what tribal leaders perceive as its "trust responsibility" in regard to Indian-owned lands and resources.

Dependence on programs is encouraged by lack of access to other resources. Tribal income was roughly 5.5 million dollars a year before the law suit over severance taxes was settled. In 1994, up to 74 percent of this income was from programs, about 8 percent from oil and gas royalties, 16 percent from taxes, 2 percent from grazing leases, and 1 percent from enterprise profits. By the end of 1999, the income from programs was about 50 percent; from oil and gas, 10 percent; from taxes, 20 percent; from grazing leases, 2 percent; and from enterprises, 18 percent. The tribal council budgets the royalty money (usually for per capita payments to tribal members) and the grazing lease money (for the expenses of the tribal government— primarily for the election board, Health Advisory Board, and community halls).

The tribes' most important asset is land. It is from activity on tribal land that royalty and lease money and most tax monies come. If the tribes are to develop more business enterprises that hire tribal members, the tribes must acquire more land, particularly land along Highway 40, a main thoroughfare. The Fort Reno reserve, which is under the control of the federal government, adjoins the highway and was once part of the original reservation. The tribes have a longstanding claim on these lands. Efforts to secure their return have been made by the chiefs prior to the introduction of constitutional government in 1938 and by business committees since 1938. Land purchase is another option that has hitherto been forestalled by the reluctance of the tribal council to appropriate money for this purpose. Tribal leaders maintain that the BIA failed as trustee in encouraging the sale of allotted lands rather than consolidating or protecting the land for future development projects. The land base has shrunk dramatically during the last seventeen years. Congress passed the Indian Land Consolidation Act in 1983, ostensibly to ease the administrative problems of paying multiple heirs of allotments their small shares of income from the land. On the death of an owner of less than 2 percent of the allotment who earned less than one hundred dollars a year, that owner's share escheated to the tribe unless it was sold or willed to another party. Owners of land began to sell their individual shares; formerly all owners had to agree before the land could be sold. Mineral rights also could be sold. Since 1983, the pace of land sales has escalated, with no way to protect the sellers from selling below market value to obtain much-needed income. Since the business committee does not have access to funds to buy land, the land is being sold to non-Indians.[11]

Oil and gas revenue is another major source of income for tribal members. The federal government has responsibility for managing and monitoring this activity. Revenue from mineral leases is administered by the Department of the Interior through the BIA, the Bureau of Land Management, and the Minerals Management Service. The Anadarko Basin of western Oklahoma is one of the most prolific petroleum- and natural gas–producing regions in the United States in both development and new field discoveries. Tribally owned trust lands total 10,405 acres; individual allotments, 67,000 acres. The standard oil and gas royalty rate was 12.5 percent of gross and can be found on wells drilled in the 1960s and 1970s. This rate increased to 16.66 percent and, currently, to 20 percent. The tribes have forty-two active oil and gas leases and own royalty interest in nineteen gas and five oil wells.[12]

The tribes maintain that activity occurred under expired leases and that oil and gas were extracted from formations other than those specified in the controlling documents. In instances when the BIA had the option of supporting allottee efforts to monitor activity, assistance was usually for industry and at the expense of the royalty owner. In fact, illegal drilling and failure to pay bonuses on tribal land have been documented and successfully litigated in court by the business committee (*Cheyenne-Arapaho Tribes v. U.S. and Woods Petroleum Corporation*). Monetary recovery was forthcoming in this instance, but the tribes do not have the resources to pursue all of these cases through litigation. Tribal leaders also point out that when the revenue from oil and gas leases and royalties increased, rather than encouraging Cheyenne and Arapaho tribal members to invest some of the money (as the federal government did with many other tribes), the government allowed members to take 100 percent of the money in per capita. Moreover, the individual Cheyenne and Arapaho landowners have received less money than they were owed and have had their payments delayed, sometimes for months. Delays sometimes cause the repossession of cars, evictions, and postponed medical treatments. The BIA superintendent at Concho admitted in 1986 an error rate of 91 percent, with 54 percent being overpaid and 37 percent underpaid.[13]

There also are problems with surface, or farming and grazing, leases. In 1994 the tribes had nineteen farming and grazing leases on 4,027 acres (although leasing activity varies from year to year). Individuals who own shares in allotments lease their land as well. The BIA has allowed lessees of tribal land to neglect conservation practices, and the tribes maintain that the BIA is also negligent in collecting from lessees.[14]

The fact that individuals and tribes do not receive all the royalty and lease income to which they are entitled certainly stimulates the need for poverty programs and reduces the money available to the tribes for economic development. Of course, another problem hindering economic development is the tribal council's demand for per capita distribution of tribal income, a situation to be addressed in chapter 6. It is apparent that tribal government is constrained by economic and political dependency. Federal grants and programs are necessary to the local economy now, and, therefore, the tribes have to try to follow federal regulations for the administration of these programs, regardless of whether the regulations are fair and the required procedures are efficient and even though, because there are not enough program resources to meet the community's needs, constituents are inevitably dissatisfied. Despite the federal government's shortcomings as trustee, without federal protection of Indian land and resources—however inadequate— the Cheyenne and Arapaho people would be more vulnerable to attempts from the state of Oklahoma, business interests, or individual entrepreneurs to strip them of or siphon off their resources. Tribal government also is constrained by the legal authority of the Department of the Interior to arbitrarily intervene in tribal politics and to make unrealistic demands on tribal government, often in the guise of seemingly reasonable regulations. In short, tribal government is organized toward all sorts of problems that produce both the perception of powerlessness and institutions that prevent tribal government from working in a manner satisfactory to both tribal officials and constituents.

How constituents appraise the effectiveness of the business committees in serving their interests is impacted by the continuation of these forms of exploitation. Constituents' perception of business committee effectiveness is influenced by media reports of federal officials' characterization of tribal government and by the media accounts of tribal government generally. The *Watonga Republican* publishes a detailed report on what is said at tribal council and business committee meetings, including comments of people expressing grievances and complaints. Thus, Cheyenne and Arapaho constituents can read on a regular basis that, according to someone, business committee members do not work hard, an FBI investigation is impending, and mistakes are being made. Federal officials also make critical remarks to the press. For example, the area director of the BIA reportedly pleaded with the tribal officials to solve their problems or go "down the tubes." Another BIA official scolded tribal officials who asked for BIA assistance for not resolving their "own problems." An area director in 1987 threatened to take back the Social Services contract when he criticized a committee action. These stories reinforce the reservations Cheyennes and Arapahos have about the operation of programs and the ability of the business committee to protect the interests of tribal members.[15]

The trial of Viola Hatch and Juanita Learned took place in the context of publicity about the failings of tribal government in Oklahoma generally. The judge dismissed all charges of embezzlement and conspiracy; the prosecution had been unable to present evidence to support these charges. In Hatch's case, the jury deliberated on six counts of conversion, all based on the charge that she received expense money to attend six in-state meetings that she actually never attended. The jury acquitted her on two counts and found her guilty on four. In Learned's case, she was convicted of two counts of conversion with reference to out-of-state travel; here, the charge was not that she did not attend the meetings but that she received too much per diem, for example, in one instance, one hundred dollars more for a conference fee than its actual cost. The accounting practices of the Finance Department came under scrutiny in the trial. Since the inception of the contracting of programs, the practice was for the entire business committee to vote to authorize a trip. Then, because tribal employees did not have the financial means to pay their own expenses, the office would give the traveler a check for the anticipated cost of the trip. There was no procedure for an accounting of expenses after the traveler's return; no receipts were required. It also was the practice to issue a full day's per diem without regard for the actual time of departure and return, as is the practice in the federal government. This procedure was followed for all travel by tribal employees.

At the sentencing the judge characterized the women as inadequate leaders, arrogant, and corrupt. Hatch professed her innocence and presented herself as a victim of the dominant society, referring to an ancestor as "massacred by the United States army," characterizing Christopher Columbus as "getting lost and stumbling on our shores," and refuting the government's claim that the tribal office's accountings system was not up to standard. "The BIA is known to keep lousy records," she said. Learned's position was that the travel claim irregularities were errors and that she was unfairly singled out for persecution. But the judge, unmoved by testimony about their commitment to community and family, saw no reason to be lenient. Hatch lacked credibility, she thought, and Learned was "an authoritarian person" who, along with Hatch, "may not have known [about errors] but they should have." Addressing them, the judge remarked that they had "lack of experience and background in finance and government accounting." Yet, Hatch was sentenced to twelve months and Learned to fifteen months in prison "to provide an example." Their attorneys filed an appeal with the Tenth Circuit Court of Appeals at Denver, and they remained at liberty. In the *Watonga Republican,* the indictment had been reported as "conspiracy to embezzle funds through false travel claims." The newspaper reported that the four defendants were found guilty of "illegal travel vouchers" in the amount of approximately $18,000. At the time of sentencing, federal officials were reported to say that 744 employee travel vouchers were fraudulent, in the amount of $81,000, and they supposed that $67,000 could be the responsibility of the four defendants. The judge considered this "uncharged conduct" in determining the defendants' sentences.[16]

But how did it come about that only Hatch and Learned were indicted for financial practices that were widespread? What was the reaction of their constituents to the outcome of the trial? To understand all the ramifications of this case, we must examine the interpersonal dynamics of the business committee.

5
For the People

The business committees have continued the struggle of their predecessors, and they have continued to offer a critique of federal and local characterizations of Cheyennes and Arapahos and of tribal government. Yet they also have been preoccupied in recent years with undermining each other, and they have done this by drawing on a discourse that expresses themes of incompetence, abuse of power, and corruption. The mutual recriminations of committee members occur in a context in which there is general suspicion about tribal government derived from the failure of tribal economic programs to address all the problems in the community, from inadequate federal support for contracting, and from the intense media scrutiny of tribal government, which began in 1974 when tribal meetings and other events began to receive detailed coverage. Individuals who seek to serve on the business committee are aware of the atmosphere of suspicion and try to reassure constituents by addressing their concerns. They also use gossip and public criticism to generate hostility toward other committee members.

A Record of Resistance
As suggested by the overview of tribal government in chapter 4, business committees have faced serious challenges since 1975. Yet they have persisted in resisting detribalization, the irresponsible behavior of federal trustees, and the efforts of the surrounding society to discredit them as leaders. In so doing, these committees have taken actions to counter the economic marginalization and social stigmatization of the Cheyenne and Arapaho community by the larger society.

Much of the work of the business committee centers on protecting and expanding programs, trying to promote economic development in order to combat unemployment, prodding the B I A and other federal agencies that have trust responsibilities or other authority over Indian affairs to do their job more effectively, and protecting and developing tribal sovereignty. A look at the history of the business committee during the years 1977 to 1999 shows that there have been successes in these areas. Business committees have expended great effort in acquiring land, obtaining and constructing buildings for tribal use, contracting for programs and applying for grants to alleviate the community's problems, developing tribal businesses, generating more income for economic development and per capita payments, and affirming both tribal sovereignty and civil rights. Their accomplishments are generally the result of the work of successive committees, although a particular business committee generally does not acknowledge the contributions of predecessors.

Like their predecessors on pre-1977 business committees, Cheyenne and Arapaho committeemen who served during the years 1977 to 1999 vigorously defended the tribes' right to own land and property in common. The business committees have insisted that the lands reserved by the federal government at the time of allotment rightfully belonged to the tribes and should be returned to them in trust status. The struggle to obtain the agency and the Fort Reno reserves has occupied the committees from 1977 to the present. The tribes owned almost four thousand acres of land around Concho in 1977, but it was in fee patent status, which meant that the tribes had to pay state and local taxes on the land. The twentieth and twenty-first business committees (1977 and 1978–79) continued the work of previous committees to obtain restoration of trust status on these lands. They also worked toward the restoration of some land at Clinton that was formerly used by the federal government. The Concho lands were restored to trust status in 1978. The twenty-third committee (1982–83) successfully fought Canadian County's effort to collect taxes on the Concho land after it was restored to trust status. When the B I A closed the boarding school at Concho, this committee started the eventually successful effort by the twenty-fourth committee (1984–85) to get the 209-acre school site restored to tribal ownership. The twentieth through the twenty-sixth committees continued to work for the restoration of lands around Fort Reno as well. The twenty-seventh committee (1990–91) made Fort Reno a priority and obtained the support of key congressional leaders, hired a lobbyist in Washington D C, and obtained expressions of support from business and community leaders and the general non-Indian public in El Reno. Opposition from some non-Indians in El Reno persuaded a local congressman to withhold support, and this, coupled with a groundswell of constituent opposition to the members of the twenty-seventh committee, destroyed the momentum of the project. The twenty-eighth and twenty-ninth committees renewed efforts to recover Fort Reno.

The twenty-ninth committee (1994–95) struggled to defend the tribes' interests against state and local Republican politicians who supported non-Indian efforts to control this land. In 1994 in an effort to cut costs, the federal government announced the planned closure of the agricultural research station at Fort Reno. This action would enable the tribes to claim the land under the United States Surplus Property Act. Business committee members met with White House officials in 1994 to lobby for the return of the land. Senators and congressman from Oklahoma countered by obtaining funding for the station. When the Veterans Administration proposed putting a national cemetery at Fort Reno, the tribes (with the backing of the tribal council) offered support in return for title to the Fort Reno reserve; they offered to lease part of the site to the agricultural station. Again, the Oklahoma

Table 4

Cheyenne-Arapaho Business Committee Membership, 1977–99

1977 (20th)

Cheyenne	Arapaho
Art Hill	Winslow Sankey
Jasper Washa	Juanita Learned// (Unfilled)
Jerome Bushyhead// (Unfilled)	Saul Birdshead Jr.// (Unfilled)
Evelyn Redbird	Joe Pedro

1978–79 (21st)

Cheyenne	Arapaho
Art Hill*	Winslow Sankey*
Jasper Washa*	Willie Hail*// (Unfilled)
Ralph Beard	Albert Black
Evelyn Redbird	Joe Pedro

1980–81 (22nd)

Cheyenne	Arapaho
Ralph Beard*	Albert Black*
Evelyn Redbird*	Joe Pedro* / (Unfilled)
Guy Hicks Jr.	Vinita Sankey
Edward Wilson// (Unfilled)	Jerry Levi

1982–83 (23rd)

Cheyenne	Arapaho
Guy Hicks Jr.*	Vinita Sankey*# Allen Sutton Sr.
Murray Rhoads Sr.*	Jerry Levi*# Chet Learned
Don Eagle Nest	Viola Hatch
Fred Hoffman	Juanita Learned

1984–85 (24th)

Cheyenne	Arapaho
Fred Hoffman*	Juanita Learned*
Don Eagle Nest*	Viola Hatch*+ Don Reed
Wisdom Nibbs Jr.	Steve Birdshead
Floyd Black Bear	Clinton Young Bear Sr.+ Alton Harrison

1986–87 (25th)

Cheyenne	Arapaho
Wisdom Nibbs Jr.*	Steve Birdshead*
Floyd Black Bear*	Alton Harrison*
Don Eagle Nest~	Bill Blind
Evelyn Redbird + (Unfilled)	Juanita Learned

1988–89 (26th)

Cheyenne	Arapaho
Jonathan Burgess*~~	Bill Blind*+ George Sutton
Arleen Kauley*	Juanita Learned*
Floyd Black Bear	Alton Harrison
Edgar Heap of Birds	Viola Hatch

1990–91 (27th)

Cheyenne	Arapaho
Floyd Black Bear*	Alton Harrison*
Edgar Heap of Birds*	Viola Hatch*
Arleen Kauley	Juanita Learned
Jonathan Burgess	George Sutton

1992–93 (28th)

Cheyenne	Arapaho
Arleen Kauley*	Juanita Learned*+ Kris Little Raven
Jonathan Burgess*+ Moses Starr	George Sutton*
Edward Wilson	Alton Harrison
Leslie Medicine Bear	Saul Birdshead Jr.+ Viola Hatch

1994–95 (29th)

Cheyenne	Arapaho
Edward Wilson*# Elizabeth Thunderbull	Viola Hatch*# Edward Mosqueda
Leslie Medicine Bear*# Edward Starr Jr.	Alton Harrison*+ Yvonne Wilson
Glenn Starr# Lightfoot Hawkins	Charles Surveyor
Archie Hoffman	Robert Tabor

1996–97 (30th)

Cheyenne	Arapaho
Lightfoot Hawkins*// (Unfilled)	Charles Surveyor*
Archie Hoffman*	Robert Tabor*
Elizabeth Thunderbull$ Geraldine Warledo	Eugene Mosqueda$ Alonzo Sankey
Edward Starr Jr.	James Pedro

1998–99 (31st)

Cheyenne	Arapaho
Geraldine Warledo*	Alonzo Sankey*# Vinita Sankey Blind
Edward Starr Jr.*/ Eugene Black Bear Jr.	James Pedro*
Edward White Skunk	Robert Tabor// Donovan Birdshead
Diane Hawk	Bill Blind

KEY: // Resigned / Died # Removed by majority vote of business committee
* Holdover + Recalled $ Replaced in disputed election ~ Remained in office
during disputed election ~~ Seated after election dispute resolved

---

delegation opposed the tribes' plan and joined with El Reno residents to demand that the cemetery be placed at Fort Reno without tribal support. The Veterans Administration withdrew Fort Reno from consideration. In 1995 the business committee hired a public relations firm to develop television ads to make the case for the return of the Fort Reno reserve. The ads were initially stopped by a political ally of the Oklahoma politicians opposing the Fort Reno recovery; the tribes sued, and in an out-of-court settlement the ads resumed. Later in 1995 A B C news broadcast a program on the station at Fort Reno, portraying the work there as "pork," mismanagement, and graft. By the end of the year the committee began to focus on winning the support of the Democratic Party for the Fort Reno recovery.

The thirtieth committee (1996–97) became preoccupied with the recovery effort. Representatives met with Senators John McCain and Daniel Inouye and with Vice President Albert Gore and President Bill Clinton. Convinced by these conferences that the tribes' best hope for the recovery lay in their developing influence in Washington by participating in national politics and aware that local businesses made political donations to the Republican representatives, the business committee decided to use enterprise profits to make a donation to the Democratic Party and to work to increase the voter turnout among Cheyennes and Arapahos in the upcoming election. One member commented, "We have to make ourselves known, so we're in the ball game"; giving money to political leaders helps us "recognize our treaties." They noted that the eastern tribes in Oklahoma got most of the "attention" because they were "big donors." Media attention to the donation, amid the political parties' charges and countercharges of improper campaign practices, resulted in the tribes' donation being returned. The business committee chair was one of four Oklahoma tribal leaders to be invited to the presidential inaugural parade. Involvement in national politics also brought notoriety. Two committee representatives were asked to testify at congressional hearings on campaign finance in Washington; throughout these dealings the business committee continued to publicly air the case for the Fort Reno recovery.

The thirty-first committee (1998–99) repudiated the recovery work of the thirtieth committee but continued to push the federal government to transfer the land to the tribes. An N B C news broadcast (*Dateline*) in May 1998 gave publicity to the tribes' position. Representatives took their case to Congress and to President Bill Clinton, sponsored a rally at Fort Reno in support of recovery, and planned a demonstration and press conference in Washington, which was postponed because of impeachment hearings. In May 1999 Secretary of the Interior Bruce Babbitt, acting on information furnished by the tribes, determined that the Cheyenne and Arapaho Tribes had a credible claim to Fort Reno. In September the committee sponsored a rally in Washington; 150 tribal members went and held a press conference. Nonetheless, the Republican-controlled House of Representatives voted to provide funds for the agricultural station at Fort Reno. The *Watonga Republican* reported tribal members' views that Senator Don Nickles, a "modern-day Custer," had won. This committee also began working to get acreage at Elk City (to be purchased by the casino management company for the tribes in order to develop a truck plaza) put in trust, continued to negotiate with the state on the right of way for widening Highway 81 at Concho, and worked on buying allotted land in Seiling and other fee patent land at Concho, despite the lack of tribal council support.[1]

Taking full advantage of the federal government's self-determination policies, business committees attempted to expand their role in the communities and to make tribal government more visible by building tribal offices and centers in the communities where significant numbers of Cheyennes and Arapahos lived. The tribes acquired buildings as well as land after 1977, buildings that could help give tribal government increased visibility both with tribal members and nontribal members. Taking over buildings formerly owned by the B I A was a particularly powerful symbol of tribal sovereignty. The twentieth business committee continued the work of the previous committee to arrange for the construction of a new tribal office building, where all programs and governmental operations would be housed in a central location apart from operations of the B I A. This complex was finished during the term of the twenty-first committee in 1978, after much effort on the committee's part. The twentieth committee also planned and received a grant for a community center at Watonga (where a clinic and some tribal businesses were eventually established). The twenty-first committee continued to obtain funding for the project, and it was completed during the term of the twenty-second committee (1980–81) in 1981. The twenty-fourth business committee began working on building a senior citizens center in Clinton; the twenty-fifth committee (1986–87) got the construction going, and the center was completed during the tenure of the twenty-sixth committee (1988–89). The twenty-fourth committee also obtained the vacated school complex at Concho, which eventually became the site for a bingo operation and a clinic and which included houses that the business committee subsequently rented to tribal members. The twenty-sixth committee presided over the return of several buildings (lent to the local school district in 1948) at Colony to the tribes in 1988. The twenty-seventh committee accepted the transfer of the B I A office buildings at Concho to the tribes in 1990. The twenty-ninth committee supervised the construction of a food distribution warehouse in Watonga, a new water tower at Concho, and an E M s building at Clinton. The thirty-first committee began construction of day-care facilities at Concho.[2]

Business committees all have taken responsibility for creating jobs for Cheyennes and Arapahos by contracting programs, applying for grants, and establishing businesses. Tribal government is the main employer of Cheyennes and Arapahos, who have difficulty finding other kinds of employment in their local communities. Since 1977, when the only tribal program was funded by the Comprehensive Employment and Training Act (C E T A), the business committee has applied for and attained increasingly more contracts and programs. For example, Vocational Education was contracted by the twenty-first business committee, Social Services in 1982 and Food Distribution in 1983 by the twenty-third committee, and E M s and the Canton Headstart program by the twenty-fourth committee. The twenty-fourth committee began work on a T E R O office and a clinic at Concho; the twenty-seventh committee opened the T E R O office. The twenty-sixth committee started the Fire Suppression program, bought new vehicles for the C H Rs, and began work on the Youth Shelter, which opened during the tenure of the twenty-seventh committee. The twenty-eighth committee began planning a bus transportation program. The twenty-ninth committee expanded tribal programs, establishing a bus transportation system that linked all the communities with tribal service centers, Headstart programs in Hammon and Geary, and elderly nutrition services in Hammon and Concho. Considerable time was devoted to efforts to counter the new Republican Congress's efforts to cut programs ("Contract with America"). Planned cuts would have drastically reduced services for tribal members and diverted money from the tribes to the state of Oklahoma. Budget cuts had undermined the ability of I H s to provide health care to tribal members, and in 1994 the twenty-ninth committee developed a proposal to contract the hospital and clinics from I H s. The thirtieth committee obtained a new program, Stop Violence Against Indian Women. The thirty-first committee worked on getting funding for day-care centers.[3]

In contracting, business committees faced the continual problem of deficits and regularly had to negotiate with the federal government. Failure to account for expenditures or to secure indirect cost contributions would have resulted in the termination of programs. These problems began with the C E T A program, which was charged with a $500,000 deficit as early as 1977. Eventually tribal employees working for the twenty-fourth business committee were able to reconstruct the records and clear all but less than $10,000 of the deficit. By the tenure of the twenty-sixth committee, the tribes had documentation to show that the D O L actually owed the tribes several thousand dollars. The twenty-first business committee was charged with a deficit of upward of $400,000. About $52,000 of this was caused by the unauthorized use of tribal funds to pay back F I C A taxes that had accumulated apparently over several years on employee salaries; the I R S threatened to close tribal operations, so the committee used funds from leases on tribal land to pay the taxes. Eventually, the B I A referred to this action as a "grey area" of the tribes' financial management. About $388,000 also was borrowed from a local bank by this committee to complete the construction of the tribal complex and to pay C E T A workers, for federal funds in the first case did not materialize as expected, and in the second the D O L did not send the money on time. Paying off this debt became the responsibility of subsequent committees. The twenty-third and twenty-fourth committees faced a shortfall of $600,000 to $700,000 owed them for indirect costs from federal programs; cash flow problems threatened to result in layoffs or the problematic pooling strategy. This committee and the twenty-fifth committee also worked and succeeded in getting a waiver on a 25 percent matching requirement from the Department of Agriculture for the Food Distribution program, from which nontribal members benefited as well as tribal members. The twenty-fifth committee faced the problem of delayed funding for the Farm and Ranch enterprise, which had contract money from the B I A for soil conservation work; the cash flow problem put the operation in jeopardy. All tribal programs were undermined later that year as grants and contracts did not receive timely approval, creating serious cash flow problems. The twenty-sixth committee negotiated in-kind rather than monetary matching contributions for programs, which made more money available for per capita payments since matching costs had hitherto been taken from the tribal budget from leases on tribal land. The twenty-seventh committee continued to work on getting waivers on matching funds requirements. This committee also faced the problem of several thousand dollars in disallowed costs.

The twenty-eighth committee (1992–93) began its tenure facing the problem of the deficits that had accumulated over past years and that had been brought to the attention of the inspector general. Salaries and travel funds were cut and pooling was curbed by establishing separate accounts for different types of funds. Negotiations were begun with the I R S to pay off back taxes in a series of payments, and the B I A provided a technical assistant to the Finance Department. Still the problems continued. The twenty-ninth committee worked at documenting expenditures and succeeded in reducing a deficit of $175,000 to about $23,000. The thirtieth committee worked to pay back taxes to the I R S. In 1996 the B I A began close supervision of the tribes' financial affairs, designating them a high-risk contractor, and the thirtieth committee worked on clearing up program accounts in order to remove their high-risk status. The thirty-first committee joined the plaintiffs in *Ramah Navajo*

Chapter v. U.S. Department of Interior and the U.S.A. in an attempt to recover indirect costs and continued working on resolving the problems that led to the tribes' being declared a high-risk contractor.[4]

Since 1977 several tribally owned businesses have been established by successive business committees, and most are still in operation, although, with the exception of Lucky Star casino, profits generally are low. These businesses provide employment for at least 230 tribal members. The twentieth committee obtained a grant to start an hydroponic tomato farm (which failed by 1980). This committee also completed the work that resulted in an R V park and marina being built and a museum being opened at Canton. The twenty-second committee continued support for the marina, but it was not successful. The twenty-third committee contracted the marina out rather than attempting to have it operated by the tribal government after the tribal council refused to allocate funds for the project. The twenty-sixth committee reopened the marina, but activity there was short-lived.[5]

Other enterprises have been more successful. The twenty-first committee started a Farm and Ranch enterprise, which continues to raise cattle and grain. Its operations were expanded by the twenty-sixth committee. The twenty-first committee also established a smoke shop at Clinton. The twenty-third committee opened a high-stakes bingo operation in Watonga in 1983 and started working to develop a bingo enterprise at Concho that would be operated by a management company. The twenty-fourth committee eventually abandoned the effort to contract with a management company and planned a smaller-scale, tribally operated bingo operation at Concho. This committee opened a smoke shop at the Watonga center and worked on plans for a smoke shop at Concho. A bingo enterprise opened at Concho in 1986 during the tenure of the twenty-fifth committee.[6]

The twenty-fifth committee also set up an enterprise board that was supposed to manage the bingo, smoke shop, and Farm and Ranch enterprises independently of the business committee; they hired a nontribal member with an M.B.A. as director. The twenty-sixth committee disbanded the board, for profits were consistently low. After the business committee became directly involved in managing the enterprises, the problems continued, with audits revealing that federal taxes were not always withheld and that documentation of disbursements was often lacking. A major problem was that the bingo payout ratio was 85 percent, too high for the enterprise to make a profit. Despite the problems, the business committees have kept the smoke shops and bingo enterprises in operation so as to provide jobs for tribal members. The twenty-fifth committee also negotiated with Job Corps to lease the Concho buildings, which would have provided close to 120 jobs. They obtained consent from the tribal council, but the lease was never signed. The twenty-sixth committee worked to revive this project but without success. The twenty-seventh committee tried unsuccessfully to lease the buildings for an alcoholism rehabilitation center.

Late in 1991 the twenty-seventh committee began negotiating with a management company specializing in tribal bingo operations to take charge of a new, expanded bingo operation they planned for Concho. The twenty-eighth committee initiated new negotiations with another management company, with whom they eventually signed a contract, to operate a 1,250-seat bingo casino at Concho. They adopted required ordinances to obtain approval from the Indian Gaming Commission and began working on making a compact with the state to eventually expand the casino to include video machines, table games, and lotteries. Construction on the Lucky Star casino began in October 1993, and it opened in 1994. New businesses opened during the tenure of the twenty-ninth committee: a bingo enterprise in Clinton and, most significantly, the Lucky Star casino at Concho. The committee obtained tribal council consent to work on trying to obtain a Class III compact with the state to expand the gambling activities at the casino (which would produce more income). The Farm and Ranch operation expanded onto the Canton reserve, and the committee began negotiating with a mushroom farm company to build a plant at Concho. The thirtieth committee continued to negotiate for the mushroom farm, planned new smoke shops in Hammon and Seiling, and started to plan to purchase gas stations along Highway 40 and elsewhere.

The thirty-first committee made a bid on some allotted land that could be used for economic development, authorized compacts with the state on tobacco and fuel taxes, opened a gas station at Concho, and continued working on the plan for a truck stop at Elk City. The committee renewed the contract with the management company operating Lucky Star, which included getting the company's commitment to purchase land and help develop a truck plaza at Elk City, and continued to try to negotiate for Class III gambling status.[7]

Business committees promote economic development by working to produce more income on tribally owned land by collecting taxes from economic activity on those lands or by leasing tribal land. Subsequent to the Supreme Court's decision that tribes could collect severance taxes from oil companies that extract oil and gas on tribal land, Cheyenne-Arapaho business committees vigorously pursued levying taxes on oil companies and other businesses. This proved to be difficult, as businesses resisted paying the taxes to tribal governments. It also fell to the business committees to administer and collect these monies. The twenty-third and twenty-fourth business committees developed plans to collect a severance tax from oil companies doing business on tribal land and put the question to tribal members in a referendum. The twenty-fourth business committee developed severance tax ordinances for the allocation of the money, and the twenty-fifth committee set up a tax commission, which had responsibility for allocating tax monies. The twenty-sixth committee also got legal counsel to fight the oil companies that attempted to avoid paying the severance taxes (the *Mustang* case). (The taxes were paid but placed in escrow.) The twenty-seventh and twenty-eighth committees continued to work with attorneys against the oil companies. The twenty-eighth committee developed new ordinances to require employers (including building contractors and merchants) on Cheyenne and Arapaho land to pay retail taxes. The twenty-ninth committee began to license automobiles, and the tax revenue from the tags increased the tribes' income. As a result of the fuel compact made with the state in 1999 by the thirty-first committee, the tribes collected several hundred thousand dollars for the tax commission account.[8]

Cheyenne and Arapaho tribal government also has had to struggle against the state of Oklahoma's and the oil companies' efforts to appropriate tribal resources to which they are not entitled. The state has attempted to tax bingo and smoke shop proceeds and to regulate hunting and fishing on Indian or trust land—all challenges to tribal sovereignty. The business committee is responsible for hiring legal assistance, for helping their attorneys to resist these efforts, and for negotiating with the state on a settlement of the tax issue when income is obtained from non-Indian customers. Business committees have worked to compensate for the failure of the federal government to adequately protect Cheyenne and Arapaho land and resources and to develop those resources in the best interests of the tribes and their membership. More than 48 percent of Indian-owned oil and gas lands are in Oklahoma, but these lands produce only 2 percent of the oil and gas managed by the federal government; thus, Indian accounts are a low priority. The business committees have sent delegates to Washington DC to lodge complaints and make suggestions, attended conferences and written letters urging reform, and filed lawsuits. The business committee is responsible for obtaining a fair price for mineral, farming, and grazing leases on tribal land and making sure these rentals and the royalties and bonuses on mineral leases are collected. The twenty-second committee initiated a lawsuit (*Cheyenne-Arapaho Tribes v. U.S. and Woods Petroleum Corporation*) to challenge an oil lease on tribal land at Hammon. The BIA had approved the renewal of an oil lease before the tribes completed negotiations for more money. The twenty-second committee also negotiated and signed, and the twenty-third committee reaffirmed, an agreement with Long Royalty Company to jointly operate several wells. As part of the agreement, Long took responsibility for funding a minerals management office at the tribal complex and clearing some of the tribes' debts as well as helping the tribes in their effort to recover Fort Reno. Long stopped making the agreed-upon payments, and when the leases came up for renewal, the twenty-fifth committee did not resign. Long subsequently was not able to pay what he owed the tribes, and the twenty-sixth committee decided to file a lawsuit. The tribes reached settlement in the *Woods* case and continued to pursue their rights in the *Mustang* case during the tenure of the twenty-ninth committee. This committee also worked on establishing fees for right-of-way access on tribal lands.

The thirtieth committee presided over the distribution of a $145 per capita payment from the Woods settlement and joined with other tribes to counter the state of Oklahoma's efforts to resist making compacts with tribes in gambling and other business activity and to resist federal efforts to cut program funding and undermine sovereignty legislation. In 1997 the tribes won their *Mustang* oil case in the tribal Supreme Court (which gave them access to millions in severance tax monies). The thirty-first committee opposed state efforts to undermine tribal sovereignty in a number of areas, opposed B I A efforts to lease tribal land in ways disadvantageous to the tribes, and worked on appealing U.S. district court decisions that undermined their gambling enterprises.[9]

Money from the 1968 land claim award and another claim for interest on that fund has been put in trusts for education and burial costs. The business committees have tried to increase the interest earned from these accounts. The twentieth and twenty-second business committees worked on a burial fund plan that would assist tribal members with funeral expenses and investigated reinvesting the Education Trust Fund to obtain a higher interest rate. The twenty-third and twenty-fourth committees set up the Burial Trust Fund using the interest claim account, and the twenty-fourth and twenty-fifth committees got tribal council consent to build up the fund with money from mineral royalties. The twenty-sixth committee also tried to add money to the fund and to increase the interest earned; the committee finally began planning a tribally operated funeral service because the burial expenses have consistently exceeded the money available from interest on the fund. Subsequent committees continued to work on this problem. The twenty-seventh committee moved the Burial Trust Fund from a bank to a brokerage firm to earn higher interest. The twenty-fourth and twenty-fifth committees increased the Education Trust Fund with the consent of the tribal council. The twenty-eighth committee moved the Education Trust Fund from one bank to another that offered higher interest rates. The twenty-ninth committee worked to provide more support for the tribal burial program, making an agreement with a tribal member to provide a building at Concho and a start-up loan for a funeral home for more cost-effective funeral arrangements. Subsequently, however, the business failed.[10]

The business committees have assumed responsibility for providing support to the Cheyenne and Arapaho people, who face discrimination and other forms of stigmatization in the surrounding non-Indian society. Such facilities as senior citizens centers, clinics, and community recreation centers provide services that many tribal members would not otherwise be able to, or encouraged to, seek in the majority society. Social services operated by the tribal government are designed to be more culturally sensitive than the same services operated by non-Indian organizations. The Cheyennes and Arapahos clearly face legal discrimination in the local communities, a situation to which business committees have responded. The twenty-first business committee negotiated the establishment of a CFR court in 1979, which assumed criminal jurisdiction in cases involving Indians on Indian land and civil jurisdiction in cases where the defendant is a member of a tribe. This step was in response to a long tradition of discrimination against Indians in Oklahoma courts. As an illustration, in the Greenfield area in 1984, non-Indians who were leasing Indian land threatened to shoot several Indians who owned adjoining land and were there fishing. The local sheriff told the complaining Indians he could do nothing to help them. In 1985 in Geary an Indian home was broken into by a group of white men who, in a case of mistaken identity, proceeded to beat an adult male there. Cheyennes and Arapahos in Geary were outraged when the sheriff put off the investigation. One Arapaho man remarked at a community meeting about the incident: "Let's not put this aside like its another Indian dumped off." In 1986 in Geary a group of white men advanced on an Indian home, where there was an Indian man with whom they had had an altercation. The man's elderly mother fired a warning shot that ricocheted and hit one of the trespassing men in the leg. The local police filed assault charges on the woman. Tribal members also have expressed dissatisfaction with the BIA's administration of law enforcement on Indian lands. The twenty-fourth committee worked on a law-and-order code in preparation for the contracting of Law Enforcement from the BIA. One committee member emphasized that there were five intratribal killings awaiting investigation by the federal government, one that was two years old; yet, when a local farmer was killed by an Indian, he was indicted by the attorney general in a week. In 1998 the thirty-first committee protested police actions toward Cheyennes and Arapahos in Geary, calling for an investigation of several incidents.

Who should have legal jurisdiction on Cheyenne and Arapaho land is a sovereignty issue that has preoccupied business committees. While the tribes have concerns about activity of the state of Oklahoma, resentment of the federal government's role in law enforcement spurred business committees to contract Law Enforcement from the BIA. By 1986 there was great dissatisfaction with the CFR court. The twenty-fifth business committee began the groundwork for the establishment of a tribal court system. A tribal court was established and Law Enforcement contracted from the BIA by the twenty-sixth committee. The twenty-eighth committee obtained a grant to hire a public defender for the tribal court.[11]

With the passage of the Native American Graves Protection and Repatriation Act (NAGPRA), business committees had opportunities to act publicly to reaffirm the validity of Cheyenne and Arapaho culture, assert local views of history, and support the dignity of the Cheyenne and Arapaho people. The twenty-sixth business committee met with officials at the Smithsonian Institution and initiated a process that resulted in 1993 in the return of some skeletal remains tentatively identified as Cheyenne or Arapaho. The twenty-eighth committee participated in organizing the public ceremony when the remains identified as Cheyenne were interred at Concho. The twenty-ninth committee facilitated the repatriation and burial of Arapaho remains in 1994.[12]

Business committee members have consistently reaffirmed what Cheyenne and Arapaho leaders before them have affirmed—that their position in American society is based on the treaty relationship and on the concept of tribe as corporate entity and that the federal government, which agreed to protect the tribes, has not been a competent trustee. In fact, these leaders steadfastly have protested discrimination and insisted that they do not have real self-determination. They have protested demeaning stereotypes and argued for their own capabilities, despite the disparaging remarks of others.

Wisdom Nibbs, chair of the twenty-fifth committee, was a vocal proponent of tribalism and the treaty relationship. A member of the Bowstring Society and the Native American Church, he was employed by the tribes from 1977 to 1983; prior to that he was a teacher. Nibbs urged the tribal council to use at least some of the income from oil leases for land purchase and to support the Fort Reno recovery effort. He told the tribal council that they were "meeting on a historic issue" and should "consider the welfare of future generations": "I have heard about Fort Reno and how we were going to get it back since I was a child." He defended the tribes' treaty rights at every opportunity, countering the hostility of local non-Indians to the idea of treaty rights: "Some citizens say Indians should not have different treatment than Whites"; "sure, it's different because we were the ones who gave up the land. It wasn't what we wanted but these were the terms the government gave us." George Sutton, from the twenty-seventh committee, objected to his congressman's refusal to intervene in the Fort Reno recovery without the support of non-Indians in El Reno: "The land belongs to the Cheyenne-Arapaho people . . . ; again, the U.S. Government has breeched its promise to the Indian people." The members of the twenty-seventh committee also objected to the attempt of IHS to require cost sharing on the basis of their treaty right to health care. In 1994 and 1995, the business committee efforts to recover the Fort Reno lands led Oklahoma state officials to make personal attacks on the committee members and negative comments about the Cheyenne and Arapaho peoples. In both the Fort Reno effort and the resistance to budget cuts, committee members stressed the treaty relationship. When the congressional representative from El Reno scolded, "Isn't it about time we all became Americans?" Yvonne Wilson responded, "Isn't it about time to stop asking Indians to continue giving up our land?" Archie Hoffman (Fred Hoffman's son) stated, "Our delegation is pressing our tribes' longstanding claim to the Fort Reno lands, just as our parents and grandparents have done." Charles Surveyor, using the image of Custer attacking helpless families (as at Washita), criticized the "cavalry-like assault on tribal self-government" and the federal government's disregard of treaty agreements: "Through treaties, the U.S. undertook a trust responsibility." Similarly, the failure of I H S to provide adequate care was described by Robert Tabor as a violation of treaty guarantees: "Treaties say our health care will be provided."[13]

The competence of the B I A to act as trustee and to oversee tribal government has been an issue with all the post-1977 business committees. The twenty-fourth committee protested that their recommendation for B I A superintendent was ignored. The twenty-sixth committee pushed for the removal of the B I A superintendent, charging that he was responsible for long delays on peoples' lease payments, delays in program matters, and obstructing tribal operations through the C F R court. The twentieth business committee passed a resolution deploring discrimination at local hospitals and embarked on the contracting of programs to mitigate discrimination faced by their constituents. The twenty-fifth committee opposed the attempt by I H S to deny services to people less than one-fourth Indian. The twenty-seventh committee passed a resolution to oppose an attempt by Congress to impose the death penalty for first-degree murder on federal lands; such a law would disproportionately impact Native Americans.[14]

Business committees have been particularly insistent that federal regulations and incompetence make it difficult for them to manage programs effectively. Art Hill of the twenty-first committee told Congress this in 1978. Saul Birdshead, business manager of the twenty-second committee, insisted that federal officials wanted the tribes to fail: "They give us all the leeway but they never give us the guidelines we need." Alton Harrison, who had experience working in poverty programs before he returned to Geary, argued as a member of the twenty-fourth committee that the so-called deficit of over $300,000 was due to the failure of the B I A to pay the indirect cost rate for programs. Wisdom Nibbs charged that B I A delays in program matters amounted to harassment of tribal government. The twenty-sixth committee members concurred with their predecessors on the role of the B I A in the problems with programs.[15]

Business committee members also made it a point to counter negative stereotypes about Indian people. Juanita Learned did this often. When the twenty-sixth committee publicly objected to the dedication of an "End of the Trail" statue at the National Cowboy Hall of Fame in Oklahoma City by commenting on why they found it offensive, she told a reporter, "We're still here." She reported to the *Watonga Republican* that she attended the dedication of a new dormitory at the University of Colorado, where the building was named Cheyenne-Arapaho Hall, as opposed to naming it after a participant in the Sand Creek massacre, which took place nearby. When the Coalition of United Indians of Oklahoma declared "war on drugs," Learned told the press that "once again the Indians were first. We declared war on drugs three days prior to President Bush!" The twenty-sixth committee that she chaired also passed a resolution opposing President Ronald Reagan's characterization of Native American cultures as "primitive."[16]

Sensitive to the criticism they receive from constituents, committee members have tried to defend their efforts. Jasper Washa of the twenty-first committee, speaking of the opportunities that the contracting of programs offered, said the committee wanted "to blaze trails to show young people what can be done." Years later, Juanita Learned and Viola Hatch of the twenty-sixth and twenty-seventh committees tried to explain the connection between traveling to meet with officials and obtaining better services for the community. The trips "bring results," said Learned. We go "to find funds so you can have services," said Hatch. But, in the post–Self-Determination Act era, committee members had to counter not only the public criticism and ridicule of federal officials and local non-Indians but also that of their constituents. As Viola Hatch put it, "It's a hard thing for people to always talk down to you when you've helped them and you know you have and yet they turn right around and criticize you."[17]

While business committees since 1977 have made cumulative, significant accomplishments in protecting and developing tribal sovereignty—acquiring land, obtaining and constructing buildings for tribal use, contracting programs, developing tribal businesses, generating income for economic development and per capita payments, taking legal action to protect tribal interests—and have taken steps to improve the socioeconomic circumstances of the Cheyenne and Arapaho community, individual tribal officials, while they may speak positively about their own service to the tribes, generally do not acknowledge these accomplishments as cumulative. Individuals credit themselves and their allies of the moment but not those who have come before or colleagues who are not allies. In short, the political discourse is not congratulatory despite the gains in acreage in trust, tribal income, jobs, businesses, successful lawsuits, and expanded services.

"A See-Saw Battle": Intracommittee Conflict

Rather than crediting business committee members with defending tribal interests, tribal officials engage in a discourse that undermines predecessors and contemporaries. This occurs even though there are adverse consequences of this discourse for the tribes: projects initiated yet not completed or continued and negative characterizations about tribal government in the local press. From 1977 to the present, holdovers and newcomers on successive business committees have worked to undermine each other. Holdover or, incumbent, members are the two Cheyennes and two Arapahos who already have served the first half of their four-year term. The newcomers are the two Cheyennes and two Arapahos who are beginning their four-year terms (see table 4). Majority-minority conflict or a four-against-four division (which usually is based on a conflict between the holdovers and the newly elected representatives, not between four Cheyennes and four Arapahos) results in a great deal of effort spent on both sides to discredit the opposing group and to exclude them from participating in committee decisions. Sometimes the newly elected members agree among themselves to oppose the holdovers; other times, a hostility is gradually built up as individuals from both groups try to create suspicion between the holdovers and new members in order to solidify a division. For example, one holdover who initially did not have difficulty getting along with a particular new member explained, "People told him I said derogatory things about him. I challenged him for specifics and he didn't produce. He holds that against me."[18]

This conflict between holdover and newcomer members takes several forms. Gossip may be used to stir up opposition within the community and initiate a recall petition. Employees who one side feels are on the side of the other may be fired or in some other way disadvantaged. Ideas or projects proposed by one side may be opposed by the other without regard for the merits of the proposal. One group can boycott meetings in order to block a quorum so that business cannot be officially transacted. If the balance of power shifts (due, for example, to a successful recall) one side can undo what the other has done or has started to do. One group can encourage opponents to travel, thereby making them vulnerable to their constituents' resentment. There may be a struggle between sides to control the recall process by influencing the election board. And, finally, the position of authority given the chair—not by the constitution but by the B I A—can facilitate conflict, as it can enable a minority on the committee, or even the chair alone, to dominate decision making. A few examples drawn from the 1977–99 period will illustrate the pattern of conflict.

The twentieth business committee reversed the nineteenth committee's decision to build the tribal complex at Watonga and instead decided to locate it at Concho in order to comply with a constitutional requirement that tribal headquarters be at Concho. Animosity between holdover and new members prevented this committee from getting a quorum on several occasions, which limited what it could accomplish. The split on the twenty-first business committee between holdovers and newly elected persons was most pronounced in the struggle over a proposal for the tribes to contract the Concho School: the vote on the proposal was three to three, and the chair broke the tie (the eighth member resigned before actually being seated in January). In fact, the chair consistently broke tie votes. Throughout this committee's tenure, members of one side or the other refused to meet, thereby preventing a quorum and, as a result, preventing any business from being officially transacted. In a "see-saw battle of strength," as the *Watonga Republican* reporter put it, they alternated hiring and firing the same employees, particularly the business manager. Late in this committee's term, the new members initiated an audit and an F B I investigation of the holdovers' previous term.[19]

On the twenty-second committee there was a similar split between holdover and new members, which evolved into a situation in which the chair began to act unilaterally, to the point that the others eventually voted him out of the chair position. The new members reversed previous actions of the twenty-first committee and also initiated a lawsuit in federal court against the holdovers for unauthorized expenditures during 1979. (The suit was dropped in late 1981). The struggle for control of the committee was characterized by repeated boycotting of meetings by whatever group was in the minority on a given day, so that the quorum could not be reached, and by attempts to manipulate the recall process by trying to influence the election board's decisions, so that members of one's own group would not be removed and members of the other group would be. The twenty-third business committee had a similar struggle between the holdover and new members; in fact, the former chair locked the doors of the tribal complex to keep the newly elected members out. Eventually the committee had to have new locks put on the doors. The boycott of meetings continued throughout 1982, and so did the efforts to remove opponents from the committee, to rescind some past business committee actions, and to report publicly on suspected wrongdoing of the prior committee. When two holdover members were removed by a majority vote of the committee in 1982, the conflict subsided.[20]

The twenty-fourth business committee holdover and new members repeatedly split on key votes: eventually the chair, a holdover member, began voting with the new members. A proposed contract with a management company that offered to work on a contingency fee basis resulted in a split vote. Probably aided by the majority's failure to present the project to the community in local districts, the minority presented the contract to the community at large as a case of abuse of business committee power and allied with election board members who were charged with holding a referendum on the project and with conducting a recall election on one of the newly elected members. New members and the employees they hired accused the minority holdover members of starting a recall on one of the new members by blaming that member for the firing of an employee. The ex-employee, from a very large family, was able to generate much feeling against the newcomer members, and a recall petition was circulated that eventually resulted in the man's recall. The holdovers and the newcomers also traded accusations about past misuse of tribal funds, accusations that were published in the local newspaper. One new employee at the tribal complex remarked: "There is a war going on now, between them. [The leader of the holdover members] got one out and now has got a petition [started] on all the others [new members], shooting up the tribe."

Eventually, the majority voted to challenge the blood degree of the leader of the holdovers, so that person's children could not qualify for enrollment. The change would not affect the committee member's enrollment but was an affront, an attempt to discourage his participation in community affairs. Eventually, after an investigation, the B I A ruled that the committee's act was not legal. But perhaps one committee member, the newly elected replacement for a recalled member, expressed most people's views on the matter when he wrote in the tribes' newspaper that the action of the majority was "a personal, petty, and no useful purpose activity. . . . I have as much right to personally dislike [him] as anyone, for [he] has repeatedly circulated an untrue accusation that I am an ex-felon and other exaggerated and unsubstantiated gossip about me. But I didn't get elected to play 'king of the mountain' in gossip or to pass petty, get-even resolutions. Passing a resolution to reduce [his] blood will not paint a house, create one job or contribute to the development of tribal business. It will create some hard feelings and disunity." Subsequently, this individual was reelected for another term.[21]

On the twenty-fifth business committee a conflict between the holdover and new members emerged immediately after the new members were sworn in. Usually the chairmanship was rotated between Cheyenne and Arapaho committee members. Since the chair of the twenty-fourth committee was Cheyenne, the Arapaho leader of the holdover members expected to assume the chairmanship. However, one of the new members voted with the holdover group, and the chairmanship went to a Cheyenne. Split votes were the pattern on a number of issues, including the proposed Long Royalty Company lease and the firing of the manager of the Farm and Ranch operation. The minority, the newly elected group, attempted to ally with the election board by voting against limiting their activities so as to stay within budget limits. In response, the holdover group adopted defensive tactics. When one holdover member was late, the chair postponed the meeting until he arrived. When a recall petition came in on a member of the holdover group, the majority declared it invalid and defended this individual's position in C F R court. After a member of the holdover group died, the chair stopped holding meetings altogether (from July to December). The leader of the holdover group held his allies' loyalty by pressing the business manager and comptroller to give them salary advances.[22]

The twenty-sixth committee began their tenure in the midst of some controversy, for two allies from the twenty-fifth committee worked to mobilize opposition to the seating of two new members who had replaced their two colleagues from the twenty-fifth committee. At a tribal council meeting in February some members of the twenty-sixth committee made public charges of financial irregularities against the members of the previous committee and blamed the chair of that committee for delaying to sign the Job Corps lease (to lease buildings at Concho to a federal program) and thereby losing this opportunity for jobs and income. After the new members were seated, the committee members affirmed that the chair had no special authority and that decisions would be made by the full committee. Throughout the remainder of this committee's tenure, there was no split in the voting.[23]

Internal conflict began immediately after the twenty-seventh business committee took office, even though the new members had all served on the previous committee in relative unity. The vote on the chairmanship was a split vote, three to two; this vote returned the chair of the twenty-sixth committee to the chair's position. The newly elected treasurer of the committee, who had opposed the reelection of the chair of the twenty-sixth committee, requested full access to all financial transactions, made public his intent to publicize the figures, and refused to sign a signature plate, insisting instead on signing every check by hand. Split votes began to occur regularly over the treasurer's activity. By August four members of the committee voted to remove him as treasurer, but, since five votes were required constitutionally, they did not succeed. Two more unsuccessful efforts were made by members of the committee to oust this individual during the subsequent months. Late in 1991 a petition to recall the individual serving as chair was submitted from the chair's district; the majority of the business committee invalidated the petition despite the election board's decision that the petition had the required number of signatures in order to hold a recall election. A recall petition on a member who was supporting the treasurer was submitted without sufficient signatures, and the petition was not invalidated by the majority. One tribal member observed in frustration, "This business committee won't get reelected, then all their progress, including Fort Reno, will be out the window." This prediction was correct; in the midst of the turmoil, non-Indians in El Reno opposed the recovery, and the congressional representatives ceased to pursue the matter.[24]

The twenty-eighth business committee began its tenure embroiled in a legal dispute between two defeated members of the twenty-seventh committee and the newly elected members. The losing candidates filed to prevent the seating of the new members, who then got a court order to prevent the monthly business committee meeting. The February meeting did not materialize, as the holdover members boycotted, one commenting that she was now "on the outside looking in." The chair, a new member, commented that he did not have to "cater to" other committee members. Subsequently the new members publicized an OIG draft audit that was highly critical of the twenty-seventh committee's management of the Finance Department, and the tribal court agreed to their request to issue a restraining order to bar three holdover members from the March meeting. There was no quorum for this meeting; a fourth holdover member left the meeting, complaining that the chair refused to sign her travel authorization while traveling himself. Problems obtaining a quorum continued when one of the new members began criticizing the other new members, who then boycotted the meetings. In July three new members obtained a restraining order, preventing four other members from coming to the tribal complex. The four were accused of trying to overthrow the tribal government. They had changed the lock on the business manager's office. The restraining order was lifted, but three new members boycotted the July meeting.

Charges and countercharges escalated, and no business committee meetings were held August through November. When a federal monitor (with managerial powers) was proposed at a December meeting, three members voted "yes" and three voted "no"; the chair voted "no." Only a technical advisor (without managerial powers) subsequently was dispatched by the B I A. The chair and his allies attempted to remove his three opponents by a majority vote of the committee; but when a large group of constituents objected, the quorum was broken. The charges and countercharges continued throughout 1993. Two members of the committee filed a suit against a third to prevent him from impugning their honesty; the suit was dismissed. A new treasurer was elected from among the seated committee members after the occupant of that office was recalled; the vote was three to three, and the chair broke the tie. The chair and his allies refused to recognize the election of the representative who replaced the recalled member, and the business manager was instructed to withhold her salary. The tribal court dismissed her complaint, but after the fall 1993 election, when the balance of power shifted and there was a new chair, the court decided in her favor. The chair of the twenty-eighth committee did not convene a meeting from June through December in 1993.[25]

Among the first acts of the twenty-ninth committee was a removal action against two holdover members. In September, new members pushed for the removal of a third holdover member, who asked the tribal court for a restraining order. Supporters of the holdover members began to generate opposition to the new members. In January 1995 one holdover member was recalled, and in April the removal effort on a second succeeded. The indictments of Learned and Hatch happened in April 1995; at the same time the *Watonga Republican* reported that charges about "questionable financial doings" surfaced as frequently as ever among tribal members. One of the new committee members was removed by the others in May.[26]

The tenure of the thirtieth committee began with three defeated incumbents suing the election board, charging bias in the counting of ballots. The tribal court delayed the swearing-in of the three winning candidates and ordered new elections; the tribal supreme court delayed the new elections. The B I A took a position in opposition to the court. This disputed election was the source of much contention on the committee. By 1997 some holdover members of the committee attempted to remove other new members and promote recalls. Those opposed to removal actions boycotted the committee meetings so that the monthly public meetings fell short of a quorum during the spring and summer. Late in 1997 a new election was held, and two new members were seated.[27]

On the thirty-first committee several members new to the committee allied against one who had begun a second term. An effort was made in 1998 to remove the latter, but the committee could not muster a quorum. Eventually, this individual resigned. Accusations of illegal activity and voter fraud were made against those attempting to oust the member serving a second term. In retaliation, one of the accusers, a holdover, was suspended; the tribal court invalidated the suspension. Problems in getting a quorum plagued this committee, but, following the lead of the prior two committees, several members did tribal business through consensus rather than formal meetings, where a quorum was required.[28]

Boycotts and Bullsheets

As they maneuver for support, Cheyennes and Arapahos attempt to counter the attacks of rivals and the suspicions of constituents. Committee members and candidates for office attribute to themselves qualities that indicate humility, generosity, and competence. A candidate has to convey to the people that he or she is a person who is both one *of* the people and one *for* the people. A humble demeanor is important, for a person who is humble shrinks from exercising power and is unlikely to abuse the power that he or she reluctantly exercises. Acts of generosity on the part of a candidate, particularly a history of such acts, reassure others that the candidate will participate in the sharing network that defines much of Cheyenne and Arapaho social life and that he or she needs the help of others just as others require help from time to time. Being *for* the people means avoiding the appearance of siding with authorities that treat Cheyennes and Arapahos unfairly. Experience is a quality that voters say they want, for an experienced or educated person should be able to get tribal business done in a way of which people approve. Experience can mean anything from holding down a job with some managerial duties, to working in a bank or other business where money is handled, to having coursework in an academic or business field. Being able to speak effectively in public is also indicative of experience. One committee member accounted for his serving more than one term in this way: "People come to me. They know I know the system and I follow through. I know people in Washington and Oklahoma politics."

In campaigning, being able to speak persuasively about one's leadership qualities is essential. Both those persons running for election and those in office have several public forums in which to build support. The individuals who opt to pay their filing fee and register with the election board to run for election can attend public meetings, where someone has "put on a feed" and sponsored a candidates' meeting (usually a candidate does this), where each candidate speaks to the crowd and takes their questions. They can also campaign one-on-one, that is, visit potential voters in their homes or at gatherings. They can send campaign letters to the registered voters in their district. And, they can attend dances—benefit, honor, and memorial dances—and they or close family members can serve on head staff for these dances. In each of these different kinds of forums, candidates try to convey symbolically the ideals of leadership.

An examination of speeches at a candidates' meeting held for an Arapaho district in the 1990s illustrates how candidates convey these themes. There were nine candidates in this election, and a runoff election eventually was held between June W. and Bill H. Candidate June W. spoke eloquently at the candidates' meeting:

> *I reside here in Geary, raised my family here. . . . I'm really concerned about what's happening in the government. . . . I'm concerned we are not being informed about what took place. In the last tribal council, resolutions passed and these have not yet been enforced. They push them aside and not recognize what people want. . . . There is no revenue now from bingo and the smoke shop. What's happening to the money? I don't get any. Lots out here are having hard times. People in the communities don't benefit by what comes in. . . . Another problem is the deficit. We don't know where that stands. Where are the reports to show if they are paying it or are creating more deficit. They are hush hush. We can't meet with or talk with them. Every time people rise up and try to say something they try to hush us up. . . . I confronted different business committee [members]. I'm not afraid to talk to, ask anything, demand on behalf of people information or anything. . . . Put the people first. The business committee is supposed to be for everyone—we don't see that. A select few benefit. . . . I have never been rich. I work and exist. I don't have a lot but feed my family and do what I have to do on minimum wage. . . . They [the business committee] forgot us, our hardships out in the community.*

She situates herself in the community as one *of* the people who is subject to the same injustices and obstacles as other Indians who live in rural, western Oklahoma, where they are a minority and where they feel discriminated against. She has limited means and thus has had to participate in the network of mutual aid that defines socioeconomic relations in the Cheyenne and Arapaho community. And she sends a clear antiestablishment message that affirms her commitment to being *for* the people. Phrases such as "push aside," "not recognize," "we can't meet with or talk with them," "they try to hush us up," and "they forgot us" speak to clear resentments about being devalued as well as excluded from decisions that are rightly the prerogative of the tribal council, or the people. Challenges to abuse of power on the part of those in political office find a receptive audience among Arapahos, most of whom are ready to "rise up" in one fashion or another.

Suggestions that tribal resources are being hoarded by a "select few" speak to the importance of the ethic of sharing as well as the commitment to egalitarianism that is central to how Arapahos view their society.

Candidate Bill H., a tribal employee, raised similar issues:

> *I have a large family and I'm not ashamed of it. How do I take care of them—I do a lot of praying. . . . The elders say something must be done about what is going on. My kids could do better than the business committee. They get up and walk out, laugh at each other. I am not attached to a specific group. I can do what the tribal people tell me to do. I don't know who gave me the authority to speak for youth and elders. If it is not meant for me to be on the business committee, so be it. I will continue to work for the people. . . . I don't want to create hard feelings against any candidates. I try to get along with everyone. Even if I lose I want to work along with them. I met several who were fired by the present business committee. I got tired of hearing so and so will run and be on this side. I will run and be on the "C and A" side.*

He uses images of humility, particularly important for someone in an official position, such as his dependence on family and God and his commitment to the moral authority of elders and to Arapaho values of cooperation. The concept of respect is important in Arapaho life. This ideal, which one elderly woman explained to me as "noticing others," refers to putting value on—or, just as important, avoiding devaluing—the feelings, views, contributions, and physical being of others. And he states the antiestablishment theme: "do what the tribal people tell me to do." Alluding to the individuals who were fired—that is, treated unjustly or devalued, in their and probably many of their relatives' and friends' views—works to attract the disgruntled, largely opponents of the current business committee, to this candidate's effort.

Several other candidates used antiestablishment statements as well but for various reasons could not convince others that they were sincere. One spoke at length about his qualifications, stressing success in business ventures: "I have accumulated farms . . . have succeeded in my endeavors. I don't need a job. I'm well blessed. If elected I'll meet the people. I think the business committee is overpaid for what is done. . . . I looked Farm and Ranch over and asked questions. . . . They [some members of the business committee] gave me heck because I asked questions. . . . I'm not afraid to talk and will visit." He was not able to attract voters, for there was nothing in his previous behavior that indicated he would participate in the sharing network or that he subscribed to Arapaho values. Since he had not made it a practice to "visit" before, people were not confident he would be responsive to their concerns. Although people say that they value education and experience, what is most valued is identification with Indian people and commitment to their values and concerns. As one Cheyenne man put it, "It would be better if all [business committee members] had a management-administrative background, but we don't discriminate like white society."

While visiting people in their homes and sometimes in public meetings, individuals may reveal more personal experiences that communicate qualities of being one of and for the people. Although some view the run for office as a chance to increase their income if they are successful, others are motivated by a sincere desire to better conditions in the Cheyenne and Arapaho community, to help people deal with problems of poverty and discrimination. This ambition to work *for* the people is often stated, and, for some, working for the people may be linked to religious commitment.

One councilman who served more than one term explained his commitment this way: after years of concentrating on making a living for himself and behaving in ways that caused problems for his relatives, he began to ask himself, "What was I here [on earth] for?" He decided to work in the private sector to gain the experience, then to work in federal programs on a reservation to "pay them [Indian people] back for his early development." Then he wanted to come back to Oklahoma "to serve [his] people." He ran for business committee and won "by prayer" and by his "sincerity" and "humility." He explained, "I stood up and said 'I know people remember how terrible I was—drunk on the weekends, fighting.' I said I changed inside, was a different person." Another successful candidate explained his decision to run for office this way: "Three or four years ago I was not doing anything. I would walk every day, walk and pray. I prayed to God that I was getting old but had not done enough for my people. . . . Now things are happening because of God. . . . Others have tried to straighten out tribal government but they quit, because they were doing it themselves [instead of being an instrument of God]." Both of these individuals are regular participants in native ceremonies.

Letters are used by candidates and committee members to influence supporters. Letters can be particularly effective for a candidate who has been living away from the local community for a few years prior to running for office and who therefore does not have a track record. A letter that clearly expresses the right themes also can influence people who know the writer personally. One Arapaho woman explained her vote thus, "A lot thought they didn't care to vote for anybody. I felt that way. Then I read Roger's letter and was really impressed. I don't know him. He never had a tribal job, worked for the tribes. He worked outside [was employed in a city]. He said he would work for the people, the old and the young, rather than himself. Others were on before and just helped themselves." One candidate's success was explained in this way, "He wrote a letter saying he would prosecute a former committee member [for misuse of tribal funds]; that's what accounts for his making the runoff." The most effective message in a campaign letter is an attack on the perceived status quo. A sampling of campaign letters from 1991 to 1993 will illustrate how this is done.

Attacking privilege and promising to give everyone a share of tribal resources is a common theme. One candidate promised "assistance to the entire tribal membership (instead of a privileged few)" and to "stop selective delivery of program services" (1991). Another promised to be "respectful of the needs of all tribal members" (1992). Avowing commitment to giving the balance of power to the tribal council (which is often expressed in terms of "following the constitution") is another common theme. One candidate pledged support for "tribal council rights" (1992). Another wrote, "You the voter have been left out in the cold for too long regarding your in-put," and added, "the tribal council is the governing body" (1992). Another pledged to "stand up for you and your rights" (1993). And one appealed to his district's sense of being ignored: "We do not have a voice in tribal government. It is time that the voice of the people in District ____ be heard" (1993). One candidate in 1993 combined both of these themes with a flyer that promised in large print "Remember—No Salary." He stated that he was not asking for a salary and, thereby, complying with the constitution. Thus, he avoids the appearance of privilege and demonstrates commitment to the constituents' right to control the business committee representatives.

Individuals campaigning for support try to influence voters by talking to influential elderly members of families and sponsoring "feeds" for members of the community. They also show respect for Cheyenne and Arapaho ceremonies by their attendance or by playing a major role in these events. Much of economic, political, and ritual life has the extended family at its center, and women are at the hub of this family activity. Supporting one's family and, by extension, promoting community solidarity figure importantly in politics in efforts to attract and keep supporters in any political activity, whether it is serving on the business committee, the election board, the health board, or a community hall or powwow committee.

One committee member who served more than one term without being recalled explained how he campaigned one-on-one: "I go to the head of the household, sometimes a man and sometimes a woman. They tell family members how to vote. Some are honest, telling others how to vote. Some just sign the names [of the voters]." By convincing an influential family member that he or she is both one of the people and one for the people, a candidate may be able to persuade a large network of family members to support him or her. Another individual who served more than one term explained his campaign strategy: "The women really have a lot to say about politics. That's who I go talk to. . . . I [also] campaign by mailing out my resume. I go out to see women; they influence their kids." One elderly Arapaho woman explained how this worked in her family: "I got all my bunch and all my nieces and nephews to vote for Dan and so did Beatrice [another grandmother with a large family]." Although a candidate or office holder attempts to get support from family members, it would be simplistic to say that voters vote for their relatives. Individuals in the Cheyenne and Arapaho community have a vast network of people whom they consider "relatives," and they choose what kind of support in the form of money, property, labor, votes, and so on to provide each, depending on the circumstances. A network of friends also is important. These ties change over time. A voter may have to choose between several candidates, all of whom are relatives of the voter. In figure 4, the four candidates in this district were all classificatory relatives. Numbers one, three, and four were the voter's classificatory brothers, and number six was the voter's classificatory grandson. Voter number two made a choice between these four men depending on how convinced she was that they would be humble and generous; she also based her choice on how these four had treated her and others prior to the election and how effective she thought each would be as an advocate. Number five also chose between her three classificatory brothers and her "grandson." I frequently encountered situations where voters publicly supported a friend, or even someone they did not know well but whose presentation of self they liked, over a relative who was running for office.

Demonstration of generosity may take the form of promises of aid as well as participation in powwow activity and donation to the community in general. One candidate explained to me how he campaigned by promising assistance to individual voters: "One man had no running water or bathroom for two years. I said, 'Just vote for me and I'll get something done.' One month after I was in, it was done." Another committee member, with a reputation for helping, was described by a constituent in this way: "He is known for helping people, like if they have a problem with an employee at Concho he talks for them. Those whose electricity was cut off tried to get in touch with him." Another committee member received praise from his constituents for personally helping put out a brush fire and trying to keep vandals away from tribal property in his district. In another district, a constituent attributed their committee person's popularity to his successful effort to keep the community's bingo enterprise open. One woman, who had a health crisis, explained how she relied on committee people Rick T. and Betty S., who assisted her: "I was really sick in October and Betty dropped by and saw how sick I was. She said she would get me in [the I H S clinic] that afternoon. She called and said I H S would see me the next morning. . . . In December I ended up in Watonga hospital. Medicaid paid 70 percent. I H S wouldn't pay the rest. . . . Rick told me to come to the office on Monday and he would get something done. Rick talked to the I H S Area Director and got all the papers together and is sending it in. They paid."

Participation in ceremonies, at least at some level, is essential. Serving on head staff or even helping people during their "specials" (see chapter 7) is potentially

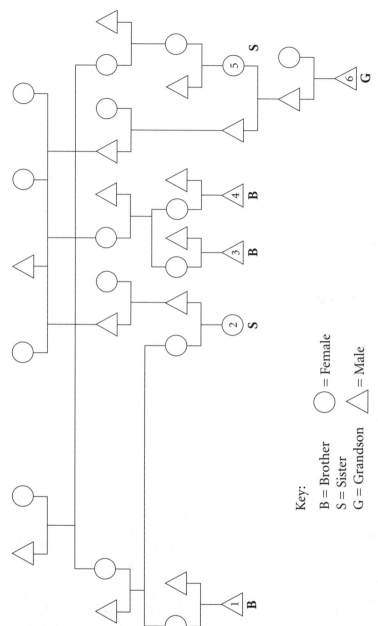

Key:

B = Brother   ◯ = Female

S = Sister   △ = Male

G = Grandson

4. Kinship Ties of a Voter and Candidates for a District Election, 1991.

helpful in recruiting or keeping supporters and in motivating people to cooperate on community projects once an individual is in office. One colleague of a successful Cheyenne candidate remarked of his campaign, "Traditional people, powwow people, have a lot of influence. That's why Francis started going to benefit dances, shaking hands, when he was running." Such participation demonstrates commitment to the extended family and its members and to the dignity and value of Arapaho and Cheyenne ceremonies. Participation in benefit dances is particularly helpful, as one establishes a bond of reciprocity with the other participants that may translate into political support. Benefit dances that support political ends are especially useful in building a core group of supporters. One candidate put it to me this way, "In politics, friends, relatives, powwow connections still prevail." Thus, business committee members frequently serve on head staff while they hold committee positions. The chair of the twenty-fifth committee was emcee for at least fifteen dances. The leader of the minority members of the committee was on head staff ten times. Four other committee persons served several times on head staff as well.

In sum, a candidate must campaign by convincing others he can live up to the community's hopes of being able to find someone who is both one of and one for the people. One particularly successful candidate described his method this way: "When I first ran, I did it the right way. I fed four of the chiefs. I sat down on the ground with them and said this is what I want to do. I asked for their advice. So I had all their families' support." Thus, in the act of giving hospitality to and soliciting advice from respected members of key families in his district, he demonstrated humility and commitment to a sharing ethos, in short, that he was one of the people. Convincing people that one will be for the people is a matter of campaigning against others who are perceived as abusive or greedy and of countering the same sort of insinuations from opponents.

Once a person is elected, retaining supporters and reassuring those who voted for someone else is a preoccupation, for a recall petition is always a possibility and reelection is the exception. Retaining support is complicated by the fact that the business committee role has three components, each of which can work against the others. A committee member is an intermediary between the federal bureaucracy and the tribes. This intermediary role involves acquiring knowledge of the rights that accrue to tribes as a result of the trust relationship and the Self-Determination Act and gaining an understanding of how the bureaucracy in Washington D C works. This bureaucracy is responsible for protecting these rights but generally acts in response to advocacy on the part of tribal leaders. The committee member has to establish personal contacts in Washington—with congressional staff and elected officials, with officials in the Department of the Interior, including the B I A, and with other Native American leaders who are fighting similar battles with the federal bureaucracy. The committee members have to pursue contracts and other opportunities to provide the services and employment their constituents expect. The intermediary role is potentially a source of constituent dissatisfaction, because of the travel associated with making these contacts and the difficulty of appearing humble in the face of the publicity that accompanies tribal business with officials in Washington. When attending meetings in or out of state, tribal officials may want to, or feel a social obligation to, entertain other tribal officials. If traveling in-state they may drive in the company of relatives or friends—a man may bring his wife and a woman may bring her husband or a woman friend. Children may accompany a caregiver. Given these conditions—the lack of financial resources of tribal members and the heavy financial obligations they have to constituents— travel per diem is perceived as a necessary supplement to salary as well as a perk. Generous travel per diem payments, however, can be highlighted by rivals or federal auditors.[29]

The second component of the committee member's job is responsibility for program management. Having to make decisions about hiring and having control over the program monies inevitably subject committee members to feelings on the part of at least some constituents that they are not being treated fairly. Problems in the fiscal management of these programs, regardless of the cause, inevitably become the subject of gossip that then is reflected in media accounts—all of which works to generate distrust toward business committee members.

The committee member is also expected by his constituents to provide personal services. A committee person is expected to use personal resources (salary) as well as tribal resources to help constituents. Committee people are on virtual twenty-four-hour call to assist people with a wide range of needs: rent and utility money, groceries, medicine, transportation, access to a telephone for local and long-distance calls, job hunting, home repair, car repair, problems with lease and royalty payments, coping with the death of a friend or relative, child custody and other legal matters, treatment for substance abuse, collection of money and property for a giveaway, and loans for other personal needs. Constituents routinely ask committee people to intercede on their behalf with the B I A and the I H S. Constituents also expect to be informed and solicited for their views through community meetings or home visits. These kinds of pressures put a strain on interpersonal relations, for it is difficult for a committee member to balance his constituents' expectations with his other responsibilities.

Cynicism is widespread among constituents, and rivals take advantage of the receptive climate to spread rumors and interpret events so as to cast each other as arrogant and greedy. Rumors and accusations about alleged greed in various forms and arrogance or disrespect toward others figure in elections as well as throughout the year. Allegations can be made by a candidate or committee member or by his or her supporters when visiting with others or by distributing "bullsheets" (anonymously circulated letters ridiculing or criticizing candidates or committee members). When these accusations become particularly widespread or numerous, constituents may take action, as described in chapter 6. Rumors about greed relate to travel abuse, outright theft, favoring relations, and, less frequently, criminal background.

A person who others believe spends money that belongs to others—money collected for an upcoming powwow or contributed during a benefit dance or tribal funds generated in a tribally owned business or from a program—or who appropriates tribal property (a vehicle, for example) puts his own interests ahead of "the people." Such behavior occurs from time to time in the community-at-large. Some recipients of tribal services take advantage of the tribe—for example, collecting scholarship money and not attending class—and some employees do not work all the hours for which they are paid. From time to time individuals abscond with funds raised at a dance or allocated for a community hall. These lapses are generally not prosecuted; individuals are rarely held legally accountable by the community. Exceptional tolerance is shown for these occasional lapses, and the community is very forgiving if the guilty parties eventually behave responsibly again, for example, by serving on a committee that sponsors a successful powwow. Thus, in a sense, behaving irresponsibly is being one *of* the people—but it is not being *for* the people. A candidate or committee member who can be portrayed as recently dishonest in relation to tribal or community funds or property is seriously compromised.

One of the business committee incumbents running for reelection in the 1990s was decidedly defeated. In the months before the election, numerous stories circulated about his use of tribal funds for unnecessary or illegitimate travel. One of his opponents asked at a public event, "Last week Jerod went to D.C. Who paid?" Another committee person was unsuccessful in a bid for reelection after he was the subject of rumors that he and his relatives stole from tribal funds: "He and his wife take money from the bingo for groceries and other things. Everyone knows it," one supporter of his opponent maintained. In one of the Arapaho districts, rumors about one candidate's exploitation of elderly relatives was a key factor in this individual's loss to the winning candidate. One voter, a supporter of a candidate, was visited by the candidate's rival. She reported to others of the visit: "Hendrick said 'I will tell the people what's going on; I'll work for all the people in the district, not just a few. I am one of the community.' . . . But I know him to be a crook—he lives off his aunt, getting his hands on the old lady's money [fraudulently]." In a Cheyenne district, at a public event, one of the candidates worked against a major opponent with the following remarks: "People in the district has found him out. Apparently he took the $1000 raised in the benefits [benefit dances]. There is a story of his getting in a fight with women in his family . . . ; apparently or maybe, it is that money [that was the cause of the fight]."

One example of how doubts about trustworthiness are generated by bullsheets is the following excerpt: "The tribal Election Board allowed a convicted felon to file . . . and now this candidate is in a run-off election. . . . If the Election Board is going to get away with their decision, are you going to let an ex-convict have access to your tribal trust monies? It would be better to vote for the incumbent." The attempt to defeat this candidate was unsuccessful, for his offense was not recent and he had obtained a pardon; thus, he had successfully reformed his life. In another district, a committee member just barely escaped being recalled. One of his constituents explained her views on the matter, which speak to the issue of forgiveness (a subject I return to in chapter 7):

> He was elected; I worked for him. He said he would get the business committee to help me, but he hasn't done anything. They have circulated a petition on him. I signed. These new ones that got on were supposed to see to it that someone from every family got a job. But instead they hired wives, sons, first cousins. They shouldn't have done that. . . . I signed the petition because he was drinking and not going to meetings. I voted for him because he was working and he and his wife weren't drinking. Then when he got in there and got that easy money he started in. He let it go to his head. I even told him to resign. So I signed the petition; it was for his own good. . . . Now he is doing right, going to meetings. I won't send in the recall ballot.

Another example of the use of a bullsheet that hints at greed is the following: "This candidate was once before removed by recall petition and election. Why does [he] want to be elected again? $? $?"

A member was recalled after many stories like this one circulated and received wide credence: he gave tax commission money to a powwow committee since his son was participating, and several of his family members took tribal cars on personal business, and when a tribal employee complained about it he was fired. One particular bullsheet was used by opponents of a certain committee member. It read, "How many family members has he employed since he went into office? Let's count them. Son, brother, sister, niece and two others for a grand total of seven people. How many more family members do you plan on putting to work? Don't H L care about anyone else?"

Individuals attempt to counter rumors. For example, one committee member told the *Watonga Republican* that he owned his house and car before he was elected. And, when one committee member was seen with a new car, his elderly grandmother went visiting; one of the women she visited explained the purpose of the grandmother's visit this way: "She felt sorry for him, not having good transportation, so when she got money she bought him that car. She said, 'Don't believe it when people say he got it with tribal money.'"[30]

Suspected arrogance and stories of disrespect also do damage to candidates and committee members. In one Cheyenne district, after a destructive fire, one candidate worked to discredit another by the following remarks: "He is not in good standing [in his community] now. . . . He didn't go around after the fire and tell the people his feelings." In an Arapaho district, people predicted successfully that a particular candidate would get only a handful of votes, for he never participated in community activities and lived elsewhere: "Vincent is not known here. He never comes around." He is in fact recognized by virtually everyone and spoken to by most when he is encountered elsewhere. But he had been criticized by opponents for not attending dances in the community. Another losing Arapaho candidate, Hendrick, was described as a person who "is often friendly and talkative but every other word is profanity." About Hendrick, another voter said, "He goes down the hall cussing everyone." Speaking to individuals in a rude, hostile, or profane way indicates lack of respect and undermines community cooperation. Hendrick, the person referred to earlier as living off of an elderly relative, generated suspicion as to commitment to relatives and to community cooperation and unity in general as well as to fiscal integrity. Voters in another district became increasingly alienated from their committeeman, a popular "powwow man," whom they thought became aloof from the people after his election. Among the stories circulated by his rivals was this one: "When he first got on he scheduled three community meetings and never showed. He doesn't want to face the people. At bingo he will go outside around the building to avoid facing people by walking through the room."

Instances in which a committee member is seen as being rude or arrogant in relation to constituents inevitably lead to a recall petition. In one case, a committee member was recalled after he responded in a public meeting to a constituent's complaint by remarking that if the constituent objected to his actions, "Sue me." Afterward, one man remarked of him, "His arms aren't long enough to scratch the sides of his head." Another incident involving this same committeeman was reported to me thus: "Alice went in to see him to help get her a job. He said go ask the one you voted for! She said she knew him all his life; he was dirt poor, no better than she." Another rumored encounter between this committee person and his constituents was, in the words of one constituent, "People told me they went to him for help and he said 'This constitution is my Bible. Where does it say I have to help you?' I took a recall petition around on him." All of these instances reportedly happened at the tribal complex, where the committee member's rivals could observe him closely and pass on stories that would discredit the man.

In a hearing held by the election board in the 1990s, where one candidate challenged the results of the runoff election in which she lost by two votes, the defeated candidate's sister complained about "a conspiracy," that is, gossip she thought was circulated by the other candidate's supporters: "They have all been talking about keeping her out. [One] asked people to say [she] bought ballots. [They] say [the business committee chair] gave [her] money." The charge that the chair of the business committee was financing this woman's campaign was potentially damaging (or, in her sister's view, actually devastating), completely effective in undermining her effort to convince the voters that she was for the people.

A return to events during the tenure of the twenty-seventh committee will illustrate how committee members appeal to their constituents' expectations at the same time they undermine their rivals. An antagonism between the chair and the treasurer began to be expressed openly in the summer of 1990. The chair was not only reelected for a second term as chair but serving on her eighth business committee, the most years on the committee anyone had served since 1975. She recently had been featured in several newspaper stories that highlighted her participation in a "prestigious conference," her invitations to speak at national conferences, and her national recognition as an outstanding Indian woman leader. Some on the committee and in the community were uneasy about the attention and the length of time she had been on the committee and chair of the committee. The treasurer demanded more authority in matters of tribal finance than was the custom and refused to sign a signature plate. He announced that he had requested a discovery audit from O I G and began to make public statements questioning the honesty of the holdover members on the committee, stating that excessive spending on travel was drawing money from programs, that is, reducing services for tribal members. Here the accusation (whether true or not) serves to portray his rivals as greedy and arrogant, for they appear to indulge themselves at the expense of those less fortunate. In a letter to the editor he wrote, "An elective body of vested interest individuals who rarely give consideration to what is good for the tribes" was taking excessive salary advances and "unrestrained" travel for themselves and "select staff." Subsequently, he suggested that his rivals "had something to hide," that they were guilty of illegal acts. The F B I raid on the bingo halls provided an opportunity for both the holdover group—including Juanita Learned and Viola Hatch—and the treasurer, Alton Harrison, and his supporters to accuse the other side of having knowledge of the machines that the F B I considered to be illegal. In the spring of 1991, the treasurer continued to question the holdover group's use of tribal funds: "If they have nothing to hide, why don't they invite in these auditors."

At the same time, the tribes became involved in a controversy over the election for governor of the state of Oklahoma. The headline in the *Watonga Republican* was "Tribal Officials Ask Return of Donation." Republican operatives had questioned a one thousand dollar contribution to the Democratic candidate. The check was sent by the controller, Mike Combs, and had the authorization of Viola Hatch (her signature plate), treasurer of the twenty-sixth committee. Republicans called for an investigation of the source of the funds and threatened to block Learned's reappointment on the Oklahoma Indian Affairs Commission. Both Learned and Hatch denied that they had approved the contribution. The treasurer accused the women of "circumventing the Cheyenne-Arapaho constitution" and "publicly embarrassing all of us by making us look like a bunch of financial incompetents waiting to be fleeced." Shortly thereafter, a petition, promoted by Harrison, was submitted to recall Learned. At the same time, Saul Birdshead, a former business manager terminated by the twenty-seventh committee, of which Learned was chair, told the *Watonga Republican* that he had notified the F B I of "gross mismanagement and possible fraud" in the tribes' Finance Department. The holdover members then began to accuse Harrison and Birdshead of improper use of tribal funds. Rumors that the F B I would close down the tribal program services spread through the community, and the *Watonga Republican* reported rumors of a major deficit. Harrison announced that the O I G would audit the tribes; the audit began at the end of August 1991.

Having tried several times to remove Harrison from the committee but failing to muster five votes, the other committee members voted to stop paying Harrison's salary because he refused to make treasurer's reports to the committee, arguing that he did not have complete records. This act generated further charges of abuse of power and failure to exhibit concern for the welfare of others in the community. Harrison, interviewed in the *Watonga Republican,* said, "They don't realize they're hurting my family and they are also hurting tribal members who come by to ask me for money to go to the hospital." When the committee agreed to resume paying his salary before Christmas, he refused to accept the offer and insisted on receiving all his salary with interest, announcing, "It will put a crimp in my Christmas but, like a lot of our tribal members, I'm used to doing without." That fall the accounting firm hired by the tribes released their findings: nothing of "a material weakness" was found, but the tribes were warned to follow carefully their policy on salary advances and to comply more closely with federal regulations on travel. Generally, the problems in the Finance Department were due to poorly trained personnel, insufficient numbers of personnel, and a high rate of turnover. Harrison predicted layoffs due to salary advances and excessive travel. There was an angry exchange in a business committee meeting—Harrison: "You're robbing the people." Learned: "You're the crook." [31]

The election for the twenty-eighth committee took place in the fall of 1991. With the exception of Alton Harrison, the incumbents were defeated, including Viola Hatch. The tribal court had ruled that the recall petition on Juanita Learned was not valid, but now in the minority on the committee, her term as chair came to an end. The tribes had concurred with their auditor's recommendations, promising to improve their compliance with accepted procedures and federal guidelines. But the F B I and O I G officials had the tribes' records, and these records were used to indict Learned, Hatch, controller Mike Combs, and the business manager from the twenty-seventh committee. Why were these two women singled out when the financial problems were long-term and widespread? The signature plates of the chair and treasurer are used on financial forms authorizing payment. Moreover, the statewide media attention the tribes received, both in stories relating to financial irregularities and in the charges concerning the political contribution (for which Combs was indicted—a charge of embezzlement, later dismissed by the judge in the 1995 trial), may have influenced the U.S. attorney general's decision to prosecute. In addition, Juanita Learned's name was associated in the media with the tribes' Fort Reno recovery and other self-determination initiatives opposed by state officials. On appeal the convictions of the four were overturned by the United States Court of Appeals for the Tenth Circuit in Denver in October 1996. The court ruled three to zero that the defendants did not have full control of the money in question and therefore could not have converted it. The overpayment had happened without anyone realizing it; the government had produced no evidence to show that the defendants committed the crimes for which they were convicted. Rather, laxity in tribal financial procedures caused accounting problems. Hatch commented, "We knew we were innocent of all charges and the Great Spirit really has answered prayer." While this brought relief to Hatch, her family, and the constituents who had participated in benefit dances to raise funds for her defense, it came too late for Learned, who died earlier in 1996.[32]

6
"A Line Has Been Drawn"
DISSIDENTS AND RADICALS

Despite the accomplishments of tribal government and the ways in which Cheyenne and Arapaho individuals clearly benefit from these initiatives, constituents generally disparage tribal government, denying that officials accomplish constructive work. Individuals generally insist that they do not benefit from the work of tribal officials. Constituents are both alienated from and engaged in tribal politics. Over the years 1977–99 by my observation there has been almost universal participation in tribal government in one or more of its dimensions: voting; working for or against a candidate or tribal official; serving on the election board, Health Advisory Board, or a community hall committee; working as a tribal employee; or participating in an organization that allies with tribal government for some purpose. Relatives of people participating also may be drawn into tribal politics. Over the long term, most individuals are also involved in dissident activity to some degree, opposing a tribal official or officials or attempting to undermine a particular project of tribal government.

In this chapter, I explore Cheyenne and Arapaho views about the relationship between individuals and tribal government and examine how these views influence the attitude of suspicion toward tribal government projects. I detail the pattern of opposition to tribal officials and consider the dissidents' use of discourse in their confrontations, particularly the way this discourse reflects hegemonic constructs that were introduced years earlier.

Getting One's Share

Cheyennes and Arapahos generally articulate the view that each tribal member is entitled to an equal share of whatever resources come to the tribes. In this perspective, which I refer to as individualism, there is not a general sense that tribal members have an obligation to contribute to the tribes' resource base. An opposing view, which I refer to as tribalism, considers the tribe or tribes as a corporate entity to which individuals should contribute in some way and encourages prosperous ones to help the disadvantaged. Much of the work of the business committees is based on this latter view, which has considerable historical depth. Cheyennes and Arapahos also view their tribal identity as reflective of an emotional and social bond between people who have shared a particular history (this view and its social expression are discussed in chapter 7). Individualism is expressed in a demand for the per capita distribution of tribal resources and in a rejection of tribal economic development. This perception of economic development is that a few committee members and tribal employees control it and that it may benefit (in the way of jobs) some but not all tribal members. An Arapaho woman reflecting on the importance of per capita payments explained it to me this way: "I am glad the oil money is in per capita. When it [tribal income from leases] went to the committee, the people saw no benefit from it. The per capita is the best way to handle the tribes' money as they never had anything to show for it before. This way the members benefit some way from it." One Cheyenne woman commented to me that tribal members "see the possibilities of more money. 'Why not me?' Everybody else is doing it [demanding a share]. It is power as well. It is me and myself." The perception that others are getting or may get a bigger share than oneself triggers opposition to proposed economic projects and to the proponents of such projects. Taking the individualistic view to the extreme, a woman whose husband's per capita check was one cent more than hers angrily protested at the tribal complex, demanding a new check equal to her husband's.[1]

Many constituents have opposed tribally owned businesses that have significantly improved opportunities for employment. An Arapaho man explained to me why people are critical of tribal government despite the creation of scores of jobs during the last few years: "Because they can't get jobs. Unless they are helped personally they don't give tribal government any credit." A constant source of complaint has been the bingo and smoke shop operations. The gross profits have been in the millions, but high overhead results in only marginal net profits for the small businesses (as opposed to Lucky Star casino). Jack T., a member of a Cheyenne ceremonial group and frequent recipient of program money, complained at a recent tribal council meeting: "You get millions out of the enterprises and people don't benefit unless employed at Concho. . . . Who is benefiting? . . . Does it go for trips? Support for other organizations? For parties? I would like to know. We get only a little per capita [from oil and gas royalties]. . . . Here no members receive anything unless they are business committee or employees." His speech received an outburst of applause.

Programs have critics as well. Eligibility requirements for federal programs restrict participation to people who live within the boundaries of the former reservation (the service area). An Arapaho man, experienced in tribal government, explained to me the attitude toward programs held by people who live outside the service area: "People don't want tribal money in programs [in contributions to indirect costs]. They say they want what's theirs [per capita distribution of tribal income] even if it's only five dollars. They can't see we should have programs for the people that are here." In a business committee meeting in 1989, a representative bemoaned the fact that "when tribal members hear someone else has received assistance, some demand the same regardless of need." Thus, many do not consider absence of need to be a reason not to receive any available assistance. Probably one of the more extreme examples is reflected in a letter to the editor, written by a tribal member objecting to the tribes' Social Services department's giving preference to families with children when funds were short. He complained that the tribes should "help people whether single or not."[2]

Constituents share the view that business committee members and any other tribal officials get more than their rightful share of tribal resources. They receive salaries or per diem, and many are able to travel using program or tribal funds. These monies are generally perceived by tribal members who do not have tribally funded jobs as more than a rightful share. Over time, most families have members who receive a share of enterprise, program, and tax money, but at any particular point in time some feel slighted and view tribal officials, especially the business committee members, as getting more than their share. The perception that committee members, tribal employees, and other officials use their positions to live at a higher standard than others is widespread. One Arapaho woman commented to me, "The business committee lives high while everybody else struggles." An elderly Cheyenne man (whose grandson was employed by the tribes for several years) remarked to me, "Now the business committee, all they do is take money for themselves. . . . This business committee helps their relatives. My granddaughter has an M.A. and can't get a job." There are constant accusations of favoritism in regard to services provided by tribal programs. As one Cheyenne man commented to me, "The business committee is abusive. They get money every year for a fuel program. That is supposed to go to districts but the first thing they do is give it to people at the tribal complex [employees], then folks in their district that support them." An Arapaho man commented, "People do not favor putting tribal money into programs like eyeglasses because they believe even if it is earmarked for that, the business committee would get access and use it another way." The implication here is that the committee would use the money to benefit themselves. It is in this context that one can understand Jack T.'s suggestion that bingo profits are being used to finance trips and parties for tribal officials, for the bingo enterprises at that time provided money for bingo employees' salaries and a small amount of support for tribal government operations. It is also in this context that tribal members often attribute candidacy for business committee positions to a desire to profit. One Cheyenne man actively involved in tribal politics commented to me, "They say 'Let's get in there and get our share.' I hear statements like that all the time."

Because constituents believe that tribal officials are getting more than their share by using money from enterprises, taxes, and programs (all of which are not specifically mentioned in the constitution), constituents link the idea that tribal officials misuse tribal funds with the idea that officials act in defiance of the constitution or that they are contemptuous of their constituents' views. In these constituents' view tribal members have not delegated authority to business committee representatives

Community Health Represen-
tatives Working at Health Fair,
July 1994. Photo by Loretta
Fowler.

Making an Identification
Card, Enrollment Office,
July 1994. Photo by Loretta
Fowler.

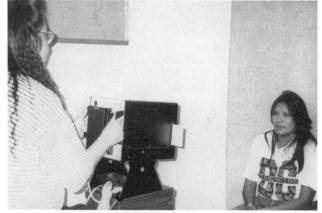

Smoke Shop, Concho,
July 1994. An employee
of the tribal enterprise
is helping a customer.
Photo by Loretta Fowler.

Feeding Tribal Buffalo, Concho, July 1994. An employee of the Farm and Ranch operation is providing hay for the tribal buffalo herd. Photo by Loretta Fowler.

Buying Pull Tabs at Lucky Star Casino, July 1994. Mary Webber (Arapaho) is purchasing a pull tab; generally, most of the customers at the casino are non-Indian. Photo by Loretta Fowler.

Opening of Lucky Star Casino, May 1994. *Left to right*: Archie Hoffman, Charles Surveyor, Robert Tabor (business committee members); Jim Druck (company president); Viola Hatch (business committee member, speaking); Fred and Kathryn Hoffman (elders and guests); Moses Starr (business committee member); Phoebe Blackowl (elder and guest); Fred Warner (bingo manager). Photo by Darrell Rice, Courtesy of *Watonga Republican*.

Twenty-sixth Business Committee Meeting with Senator Daniel Inouye, Concho, April 1989. *Left to right*: Minnie Goodbear (tribal secretary), Edgar Heap of Birds, Jonathan Burgess, Senator Daniel Inouye, George Sutton, Viola Hatch, Juanita Learned, Arleen Kauley, Alton Harrison. Committee member Floyd Black Bear is not pictured. Photo by Bill Wyrick.

Protest at Fort Reno, November 1994. In the foreground are veterans Joe Hicks and the members of an honor guard, *left to right*: Newton Old Crow, James Hawk, Melvin Whitebird, Charles Ruesch. Photo by Darrell Rice, Courtesy of *Watonga Republican*.

Gourd Dance during "One on One" at Barefoot Powwow, August 1986. During the "special" of a member of head staff, people from the crowd are putting money in the hat on the ground in front of him. Photo by Loretta Fowler.

to act on their behalf without consulting them. In the words of one woman, "The committee never tells the people what they are doing. . . . Even at tribal council in October, they adjourned before the people got a chance to talk about what they wanted." Another woman commented, "They [committee members] are supposed to do what the people want done but they are getting into management." At a tribal council in 1985, where the budget proposed by the business committee was rejected, a Cheyenne man leading a dissident organization stated, "We do not often have this opportunity to be heard, say what we feel." He was commenting on the fact that the dissidents outnumbered the business committee's supporters that day. The Cheyenne man who was elected to chair the tribal council that day reaffirmed, "This is a peoples' meeting." And one young Cheyenne woman commented on another occasion, "The committee never goes by the constitution. Not unless they think it is to their benefit. They just do as they please." Constituents often feel personally insulted by perceived elitism (a point to which I return in chapter 8).

Tribal members attempt to increase their share by appealing to the tribal council or the business committee, usually on behalf of a group or organization. Business committee members may support such efforts, particularly if supporters or potential supporters initiate them. In one case, related by a former Cheyenne business committee member, a fellow committeeman miscalculated: "He once told an old lady, a complainer, he would fix it for her organization to get money if she and the others would back his position at the tribal council meeting. He gave her the money then her group voted against him. I told him he let that old lady outpolitic him. He should have said he would get her the money after the vote." Tribal members may form alliances for the purpose of passing particular line items in the tribal budget. One election board member explained, "There is a trade off—like the Coalition [a dissident group active for a few years] backed money for the election board and they supported the Coalition [the group's effort to get a special audit, for example]." Some individuals are more adept than others at appealing for some kind of assistance at the tribal complex. If appeals are denied, accusations of wrongdoing on the part of tribal government may follow. One individual used a public meeting to express his concept of the relationship between tribal government and the individual: "I believe in fair government—the right to go to the complex and ask for services."

Tribal members also may attempt to use tribal funds in unauthorized ways. Sometimes the election board may try to inflate its budget and community hall committee members may use the allocated funds for personal rather than community benefit. One Cheyenne woman expressed to me such a suspicion about a particular election board: "The last election board wanted to make it a full-time job. Some were meeting every day. The business committee is not strong enough to say 'You make it work in seven meetings.'" Groups that sponsor powwows and dances or ceremonial activities may also divert funds intended for community benefit to personal use. Tribal employees may neglect job performance, use tribal property for personal benefit, or accept improper salary advances if the business committee members in control of tribal government need their political support. Program recipients may take benefits to which they are not entitled, some on a regular basis. For example, people may accept tuition money yet not attend classes or may accept start-up expenses for a new job yet fail to report for work. At the smoke shops and bingo halls there have been instances of employee embezzlement. One of the problems that the bingo operations have in showing a profit is that many of the checks the enterprises receive are returned for insufficient funds. The Canton marina, owned by the tribes, has problems with vandalism and with bad publicity; in an editorial of the tribes' newsletter tribal members have been scolded for "abusing privileges" by having rowdy drinking parties there. This is not to say that all or even the majority of tribal members attempt to misappropriate tribal funds or resources, but the Cheyenne and Arapaho view is that such behavior is not uncommon. Conning strategies are widely regarded as necessary in view of the depressed economy and the perception that nontribal avenues for improving one's lot are closed to Cheyennes and Arapahos. There is also the near universal perception that "everyone" employs such strategies in order to get "their share."[3]

Tribal members in general frequently abuse the housing program by not paying their rent, for example. Such behavior is viewed by many as not unjustified in view of the problems the Cheyennes and Arapahos face. In 1979, H U D complained to the tribes about a delinquency rate of 60–70 percent. In 1980, the housing authority director announced that there were four hundred applicants for housing but that no new houses could be built because of the arrears problem. Rather than take punitive actions, suggestions were made to use tribal funds to pay the outstanding rents. Following H U D policies, the housing authority proceeded with evictions, but because of public pressure the business committee asked them to delay. Fewer than ten families were evicted. The director complained that "deadbeats" had kept one hundred families from getting homes. In 1982 the director announced that there would be more evictions, as the rate of delinquency was 62 percent. Several of those in arrears were business committee members. In 1984 H U D told the housing authority that the tribes would receive no more new units until the delinquency rate was 15–30 percent. In 1985, the housing authority reported that 40 percent of 265 homeowners were in arrears; the monthly payments ranged from about forty-four to fifty-two dollars, and some people had never made any payments. There were 119 families on the waiting list for houses at the time. The C F R court approved thirteen evictions that year. In 1986, 159 out of 264 participants were in arrears. Fifteen houses were vacant because of evictions. By 1987 the housing authority had begun to turn things around so that the tribes obtained some new units and retained eligibility to apply for more in 1988. But by 1993 the rate of arrearage was back up to about 65 percent.[4]

A Cheyenne man remarked to me that people take advantage of tribal government because they see others doing it: "Now the new one [business committee] is fitting a rut. The new group sees how the old gets by with things wrong and so they go along." The "fitting a rut" characterization extends to tribal employees and tribal members in general. Some describe it as a domino effect: "The business committee should set an example, but they don't. It is a domino effect. The business committee asks for an advance, goes to a powwow. So the employees do it, too. And then others." Such a domino effect also would work to influence prospective business committee members: they observe people's economic strategies and apply them once in office.

"Nothing Will Come of It": Dissident Strategies

One of the predominant themes in Cheyenne and Arapaho conversations about tribal politics, aside from the concern about getting one's share, is the inability of constituents to have significant influence over tribal government. As one man put it, "There is an attitude among people, why should I care, why should I get involved." Yet, in actuality, the majority of tribal members participate by voting, influencing their representatives, and campaigning for or against individuals. A small minority is actually involved in opposing the committee at any particular point in time. How is it, then, that people are so pessimistic about tribal government, and how do opposition groups, as well as the general constituency, affect the sovereignty agenda of tribal government? Let us look first at the voting patterns.

Most middle-aged and elderly Cheyennes and Arapahos participate in politics on an irregular basis. That is, they may vote in two business committee elections and not vote in the third. Participation depends on the circumstances of the election and the individuals involved. Individuals usually draw into their political activity at least some of their friends and relatives. People with advanced education and high incomes, as well as people without employment or advanced education, and females as well as males run for office, attend political meetings, vote, and serve on the business committee and election board at least some of the time. Similarly, Arapaho and Cheyenne chiefs and ceremonial leaders run for office, attend political meetings, vote, and hold offices. Most of those who vote live within the former boundaries of the reservation; about half of the enrolled tribal members live outside the service area. From about 36 to 58 percent of the registered voters (about half of those eligible to vote) cast ballots in a particular election; most have voted at some time during the period 1977 to 1999. Even if an individual chooses not to vote, he or she defends vigorously his or her registration. Complaints against removal of names from voting lists (for example, because of an incorrect address) have been the source of a great deal of conflict and protest action against election boards. The voter registration list is revised (usually by adding names or transferring a person from one district to another) before each election. A closer look at a few districts reveals the way participation can fluctuate.

In Arapaho district 1 (Canton), in the fall of 1985, 59 percent of the 249 registered voters cast ballots. In 1993, 52 percent of 260 voters voted in a recall election. In the fall election 301 voters were registered and 58 percent voted. In this district, in 1993, 26 percent of the registered voters lived outside the local community (for example, in Oklahoma City). This is a district where the voters all know each other well; often the high voting percentage is explained as a desire to prevent a particularly objectionable individual or individuals from winning. In comparison, in Arapaho district 2 (Geary) in the fall of 1985, 55 percent of the 581 registered voters cast ballots. In a recall election in the same district in 1992, 38 percent of 591 registered voters cast ballots. In the fall 1993 election, 36 percent of 718 voters cast ballots. In this district 32 percent of the registered voters live outside the local community. The voters do not all know each other well, for this district is a large one that includes people who have moved from the rural communities to towns such as El Reno or Oklahoma City. In Cheyenne district 1 (Watonga), made up of small rural communities, in 1983, 50 percent of the 328 registered voters cast ballots in the fall election. In Cheyenne district 2 (El Reno), in a recall election in 1992, 49 percent of 382 voters voted. In that same district in the fall 1993 election, 43 percent of 545 registered voters cast ballots.[5]

Participation in referendums is far lower than in business committee elections. Often people do not bother to inform themselves on the issue under consideration, or they deliberately do not vote if they perceive the referendum as a way for the business committee to gain more access to tribal funds or if they believe it is useless to vote because the BIA officials will disallow the results of an election if the outcome is not favored by the BIA. If the parties in an election are behaving in a particularly acrimonious way, some voters may avoid participating—this is true in an election for the business committee as well as in a referendum. In a 1977 referendum on whether tribal funds should be used to construct new community halls, 1,120 ballots were mailed and 253 (23 percent) returned. During this time, ceremonial leaders were in conflict over access to tribal funds. In a 1979 referendum on contracting the school at Concho, 392 voted. In a 1980 referendum to amend the constitution to increase the powers of the tribal council relative to the business committee, 895 voted; the referendum failed 326 to 569. In the 1981 referendum to determine if the tribes would borrow money to retire a deficit and would distribute royalties per capita, 924 voted: 902 to 21 for a per capita payment. In 1984 2,500 ballots were mailed to tribal members for a referendum on a proposed contract with a bingo management company; only 550 ballots (22 percent) were returned.

In 1985, in a referendum to decide on another management contract, 2,299 ballots were mailed and only 610 people (27 percent) voted. In a 1989 referendum on whether tribal government should contract for programs, 2,777 ballots were sent out, 498 were undeliverable, and 662 (24 percent) were returned. In 1993 there was a referendum on changing the constitution so that the tribal council could prevent any particular business committee action. The B I A ran the election instead of delegating it to the election board. They required voters to register specifically for the referendum, and 835 out of 6,500 potential voters registered. Of these 835 ballots, 307 (37 percent) were returned.[6]

Attendance at tribal council meetings ranged from 87 to 326 during the 1977–99 period. Few Cheyennes and Arapahos have never attended a tribal council meeting, although attendance usually is low at these meetings because people believe that no significant business will be done and because the meetings are contentious. As one Arapaho observer noted, "People don't go because they think all they are going to do is fight and, besides, nothing will come of it. It never does." Nothing "comes of it" either because the motions made are unconstitutional, are not supported by business committee resolution, or are not recognized by the B I A. For example, frequently a motion is made that a particular employee be fired; there is no constitutional provision that allows the tribal council to fire employees. Thus, the business committee can choose to disregard the council's motion and the B I A will not approve the council's action. People who are determined to thwart the business committee's economic development goals resist discussion of such matters (on the agenda put forth by the business committee) and then insist that money from tribal leases all be distributed per capita. One Cheyenne woman expressed her frustration in this way: "I don't go to tribal council. There is never a result. The only thing approved is the budget and per capita. The rest is a gripe session." Often, if opponents of the business committee are in the majority, the tribal council refuses to approve the budget proposed by the business committee. It is in this context that Cheyennes and Arapahos say that people who attend tribal councils "just vote for spite." A Cheyenne man expressed it this way: "Now the tribal councils are for the wrong reasons. They are a general struggle between the business committee and the dissidents, no matter who they are." An elderly Cheyenne leader also remonstrated, "Once a year [before the 1975 constitution] there was a general meeting. The B I A superintendent presided. Now it is a free-for-all." Occasionally ceremonial leaders or elderly chiefs try to encourage people at tribal councils to live up to the ideals of cooperation and respect, but their efforts do not dissuade others from confrontation. For example, in a 1982 meeting, one Cheyenne chief remarked, "We lack unity. I can't put it in words, but there's something that is pulling us apart. We should be pulling together." An elderly Arapaho chief, remarking on the lack of influence of chiefs in contemporary times, noted, "In the past chiefs kept peace between people—now some chiefs are in the forefront of tribal controversies [be-cause they may join dissident groups]. Perhaps too many younger men are being put into chiefs positions now." Who are the dissidents referred to here?[7]

The tribal members who organize public demonstrations or attend the tribal council meetings to oppose the sitting business committee (or some of the mem-bers on it) are referred to as dissidents. They are consistent in pressing for the per capita distribution of tribal resources and in attempting to curtail the development of tribally owned businesses, taxation of business activity (for example, oil pro-duction), business committee salaries, and any expansion of business committee activity (including efforts to exercise sovereignty). From time to time, people may attend tribal councils to protest a particular action (such as the firing of a relative) or to support friends and relatives on the business committee or employed by the tribes. They attend "when it affects them personally," in the words of one Arapaho man. The tactics employed are the same as those used by dissidents who oppose the committee on principle. A Cheyenne man commented, "The ones that go [to tribal council] are those with a complaint, something came up. People don't like to go as they know it will be all arguing." Opposition groups appear at every tribal council meeting to confront business committee members. One long-term tribal employee explained the attendance at tribal council meetings in this way: "It is those that are for a particular committee versus those that oppose it. There are a few core radicals." The radicals referred to are a few individuals who lead dissident groups year after year. There were four individuals who led dissident groups in the late 1970s, the 1980s, and early 1990s. They are referred to later as Lester B., Wesley N., Aron P., and Jack T. (mentioned earlier). These individuals were particularly intractable in their opposition to tribal government (although they all stood for election to the committee at one time or another).

Over the 1977–99 period, dissidents tried to subvert the plans and actions of the committees through opposition in tribal council meetings, initiation of recall elections, and lawsuits. Often business committee members, who felt unfairly crit-icized, succeeded in thwarting them. Although the individual participants in these encounters changed through the years, there is a consistent pattern to dissident constituent activity, as briefly sketched in the next few paragraphs.

The twentieth business committee (1977), which was the first committee elected under the provisions of the new 1975 constitution, attempted to improve relations with constituents by selecting one member from each of ten communities to work with the business committee as an advisory board. This committee also budgeted money for Cheyenne and Arapaho ceremonial groups and decided to allow each district to decide how its share of the money for ceremonies would be used. The committee put the question of constructing community halls to the voters in a referendum that failed for lack of sufficient response and later in a tribal council meeting. At the tribal council meeting, the 1977 budget passed narrowly, although there were complaints about the high cost of tribal government. The tenure of the twentieth committee ended on a contentious note, as the C E T A program's financial troubles forced layoffs.[8]

The twenty-first committee (1978–79) succeeded in obtaining tribal council approval of the 1978 budget, which did not include money for tribal government operations due to indirect cost funds but did include funds for an organization with which some of the vocal dissenters in C E T A matters were affiliated. The controversy that came to consume this committee and generate widespread opposition was the business committee's effort to contract the boarding school at Concho. Some B I A officials wanted to turn the management of the school over to the tribes. With the support of other local B I A officials, the staff at the school, including non-Cheyenne and non-Arapaho employees, opposed contracting because they feared that they would lose federal government benefits. In May 1978 a petition with 264 names was presented, requesting a referendum on the contracting of the school. The business committee invalidated the petition and refused to call a tribal council on the matter. In October a dissident group led by Lester B., a Cheyenne headsman and former employee of both the federal government and the tribes, convened a tribal council in opposition to the meeting called by the business committee and also initiated recall petitions on some committee members. Neither meeting established a quorum, and the business was postponed until December. The business committee invalidated the recall petitions; the local B I A superintendent confirmed that there was not the required number of signatures. When the business committee signed the contract to operate the school, three Cheyennes, including Lester B., filed a lawsuit against the committee accusing the members of using C E T A layoffs to intimidate the opponents to the contracting of the school. Another petition, containing four hundred signatures, empowered the tribal council to oversee the business committee; the business committee invalidated this petition. Subsequently, at a tribal council meeting in December, tribal members voted to dispense $1.5 million in oil lease money in per capita payments. Business committee members argued that the tribal council did not have the authority to make such a decision. One of the leaders of the opposition, Wesley N., a Cheyenne whose brother unsuccessfully had sought employment with the tribes, described the impasse this way: "There is a line drawn between the tribal employees and the grassroots people."[9]

Early in 1979 a referendum was held, and the vote was 234 to 158 against contracting the school. When the tribes received $1.5 million in oil bonus money, the business committee wanted to use some of the money for economic development, but the dissident group and probably most tribal members wanted to distribute the income in per capita payments. The struggle between the business committee and the dissident group took the form of competitive tribal council meetings. In other words, the business committee would schedule a meeting and the opposition group would announce a different date for the meeting. A tribal council was held on 10 February, where the dissident group outnumbered the business committee supporters. As a result the council voted to distribute all the oil money in per capita payments and to reject the proposed budget for 1979. At another tribal council meeting held on 10 March, the council voted the budget down again. The business committee called another tribal council for 5 May, and this time they had enough supporters present to pass the budget, which (in deference to their constituents) included the allocation of oil bonus money for per capita payments and funds for ceremonial groups. The dissident group held a subsequent meeting, where people voted to overturn the decisions at the 5 May meeting, but the B I A refused to recognize a meeting not scheduled by the business committee (as the constitution specifies).[10]

At the October 1979 tribal council meeting, U.S. marshals were sent to keep order. Tribal members refused to pass the budget for 1980, which contained an increase in the amount allocated for tribal government, but voted for another per capita payment. Prior to the meeting, Lester B. announced publicly, "You can write yourself checks by being at the meeting and by being on time." The dissident group challenged the business committee's choice of site for a November meeting—characterizing it as "an act of tyranny"—but the federal district court upheld the committee's right to determine the site. At the 10 November meeting, tribal members passed resolutions calling for a referendum on a constitutional amendment to give the balance of power to the tribal council rather than the business committee and for the invalidation of the earlier tribal council meeting where the 1979 budget was passed, and they refused to pass the 1980 budget. The lawsuit that Lester B. and two other Cheyenne tribal members filed against the secretary of the interior to stop the contracting of the Concho school and, as amended, against the business committee for other acts of "abuse of power" was dismissed in federal court, but the plaintiffs filed a new suit.[11]

The twenty-second business committee (1980–81) scheduled a tribal council meeting to try to pass the budget for 1980, while constituents from Hammon delivered a recall petition on the Hammon representative, alleging failure to keep constituents informed, favoritism, and acceptance of a new H U D home to which she was not entitled. The business committee invalidated the petition. The tribal council met 23 February and did not pass the budget. Subsequently, Lester B. was hired as the housing authority director. The B I A agreed to hold a referendum to amend the constitution to increase the tribal council powers relative to the business committee. After the referendum failed, several members of a dissident group filed a new lawsuit charging that former business committee members were guilty of financial malfeasance. At a meeting on 29 March 1980, the tribal council also did not approve the budget for 1980 but approved a per capita payment from 60 percent of the oil and gas income. A tribal council was held on 26 July, and the vote was 326 to 0 for 100 percent of the oil money to be distributed in per capita payments, but the 1980 budget was not approved. The tribal council also voted to elect a new election board and to remove some of the business committee members from office. The B I A disallowed most of the actions taken at the 26 July meeting: until a budget was approved, allocations of tribal money could not be made, and the constitution specifies when the election board is to be chosen and how committee members can be removed. A tribal council was held 4 October, where a resolution was passed to hold a referendum on the 1981 budget, a budget that would provide for borrowing money to retire a deficit that had been accruing since the contracting of programs began and for paying all the oil money in per capita payments. During this fractious meeting, the council chair, who also chaired the business committee, and two members of the dissident group began struggling with each other for control of the microphone. Another resolution passed, 117 to 109, to have a referendum vote on whether to distribute all the oil money per capita or to use some to pay debts or for economic development. The business committee subsequently directed the election board to hold the referendum.[12]

In 1981 the proposed referendum to distribute all the oil money in per capita payments passed. The business committee invalidated a recall petition on the Cheyenne representative from Clinton, and a recall election was held on the Hammon representative, who was retained by a vote of seventy-one to fifty-seven. There were complaints from constituents that several business committee members were not attending the meetings yet still receiving their salaries. In order to prevent the tribes from losing program funding, the business committee contracted with Long Royalty Company to lease mineral rights in return for the company's paying off the tribes' deficit. A dissident group led by Aron P. (a self-employed Cheyenne man) began protesting the Long deal; some said the matter should have been presented to the tribal council. A tribal council meeting was held 12 September, where the council passed a 1981 budget that included a per capita payment, election board expenses, attorney fees, and money for a legal assistance organization that several members of the dissident group supported. Another tribal council was held 3 October in which the tribal members refused to vote on the 1982 budget. The council also elected a personnel committee for the tribal office, and they voted to replace the business manager and program directors. The business committee refused to certify the resolutions. Tribal members filed a lawsuit against the B I A to try to force them to approve the resolutions, but the B I A argued that the tribal council could not develop a budget from the floor.[13]

The twenty-third business committee (1982–83) held a tribal council in February, where the 1982 budget was passed, including operating expenses for the tribal government as well as a per capita payment and funds for an audit of 1981–82 tribal finances. The council also voted to allocate ten thousand dollars for ceremonial groups. A personnel committee, including some of the dissenters, was elected to screen people for tribal jobs. There was another tribal council in June, but the quorum failed. About this time, the tribal newspaper began publishing stories critical of the business committee—they were accused of "writing hot checks," and the editor was replaced. Recall petitions were submitted on the Geary Arapaho and Watonga Cheyenne representatives; the election board declared both petitions invalid. In July the scheduled tribal council again failed to draw a quorum. At a tribal council meeting in October, a budget for 1983 was adopted, with an allocation for per capita payments, and the Long Royalty Company lease was accepted. In 1983 conflict with constituents began over the site the committee chose for a tribal council meeting in February. In February a recall petition was submitted on the Watonga Cheyenne representative, but the election board found that it had insufficient signatures. At the tribal council meeting on 19 February, dissidents set up and allocated money for an oversight committee to supervise tribal finances and for another to stop business committee salaries. But the business committee refused to present the resolutions to the B I A because, they argued, there was no constitutional authority for the committees and no money allocated in the tribal budget to fund the committees. Another tribal council was held 23 April, where the business committee chair denied rumors that committee salaries were going to be raised and accused opponents of deliberately misleading the people. On 1 October, the tribal council refused to use tribal funds to retire deficits that were at least in part due to underrecovery of indirect costs and refused to vote on the tribal budget for 1984. Finally, at a council meeting on 19 November, with 396 in attendance, the budget was passed. The council allocated some matching funds for programs but voted against starting up a bingo operation at Watonga and against establishing a burial fund.[14]

The twenty-fourth business committee (1984–85) began the year with statements designed to reassure constituents. A new member, who had been an opponent of the twenty-third committee, maintained that tribal council actions would be "mandates." A recall petition was submitted on the Arapaho holdover representative from Canton. The election board subsequently validated the petition, and the member was recalled in April. A tribal council meeting was held in February, where a budget for 1984 was adopted that included $300,000 for retiring deficits. The council also voted approval for the business committee to continue trying to recover the Fort Reno lands. In their next meeting, the business committee gave reports on their trip to Washington D C and voted to approve the actions of the tribal council in February. They also decided to hold a referendum on whether the tribes should sign a management contract with a firm to operate a high-stakes bingo enterprise at Concho. In August 1984 a referendum was held on whether the tribes should contract with a management firm to operate a bingo casino, but not enough ballots were returned. A Health Advisory Board was organized to deal with tribal members' complaints about health care, and the business committee announced that it would try to pay the board members per diem. On 6 October, a tribal council was held. The council voted to take some of the money from the oil account to start a burial program and to use the rest for per capita payments. The budget for 1985 was approved. In October the business committee approved a management contract with another company to develop businesses in the community, with the company to take a commission on any profits they produced and to take a share of any new oil and gas development. This action led to active opposition against the committee and brought an end to the fairly amicable relationship between constituents and committee members. A small group of dissident tribal members delivered a petition with 279 names asking for a referendum on the "Hanes contract."[15]

In 1985, dissatisfaction with the contract led to Geary District's submitting a recall petition on their representative. The election board and the business committee then entered into a protracted struggle over this recall. The business committee sued the election board in C F R court, arguing that only the committee could validate a petition. A referendum was held in February on the Hanes contract, but not enough ballots were returned. The election board scheduled a recall election on the Geary representative, and the representative was recalled; but, the business committee refused to recognize the election results and filed an injunction against the election board. Subsequently, a recall petition came in on the Arapaho representative from Canton, and the business committee determined that the recall petition on the Canton representative was valid. The voters then cast fifty-eight ballots to retain him and fifty-four to remove him. The C F R court ruled that the election board had acted improperly on the recall petition on the Geary representative but allowed an election to proceed anyway. In July a dissident group led by Lester B. and Aron P. filed a lawsuit in federal district court to stop the business committee from receiving salaries from the indirect costs of programs. The tribal attorney challenged federal court jurisdiction. With only about eighty-seven people present at a tribal council meeting on 13 July, where the business committee hoped to pass a resolution to institute a severance tax on oil extracted from tribal lands and to establish a mineral management office to improve collections with oil and gas leases, the dissidents presented a series of their own resolutions: dismissal of the tribal attorney and more money for the election board to conduct recall elections. At the 5 October tribal council meeting, the council voted to hold a referendum on a constitutional amendment to authorize the tribes' collecting of severance taxes from oil companies. The dissident group protested that this tax collection would give too much power to the business committee. The budget was presented and tabled when the dissident group protested the allocation of money for matching program funds (that is, funds for tribal programs' indirect costs): one dissident said to the people in attendance, "It will come out of your pocket." Resolutions also passed for an audit and money for the election board; the business committee subsequently approved these. Also in October the c f r court judge issued a restraining order on the paying of salaries to the committee and scheduled a hearing after the federal district court referred the case to the c f r court. The tribal attorney appealed this ruling to the Court of Indian Appeals in Shawnee and also challenged this particular judge's right to sit on the court. Business committee members subsequently went to the Department of the Interior in Washington d c, where they successfully appealed the judge's ruling on the basis of tribal sovereignty. At a tribal council held 23 November, tribal members rejected the proposed 1986 budget and voted to fire the tribal attorney, despite frequent pleadings from the business committee, who called for them to "pull together."[16]

The twenty-fifth business committee (1986–87) took office at a time when the federal government was cutting program budgets and when oil prices were falling dramatically. The new chair urged that tribal members agree to use some of the oil money for educational and economic development, not just for per capita distribution. A tribal council was held 1 February at which tribal members passed a 1986 budget that included matching funds for programs and money for the burial program and the enrollment office as well as per capita payments. There were complaints from the dissident group. In February, the c f r judge decided that there would be a jury trial to hear a contempt of court action brought by the dissident group against the business committee after their salaries resumed in spite of the court's injunction. At their March meeting, the business committee decided in a close vote to set limits on the election board's use of the money budgeted them. Employees from the tribal Farm and Ranch operation also complained about layoffs. The dissident group's spokesperson complained that they did not have an adequate opportunity to present their grievances: "This is supposed to be a people's meeting." The appellate court (with judges from Montana, Washington, and Wyoming) heard arguments from both sides on the salary issue and affirmed the c f r judge's ruling that salaries were unconstitutional. An insufficient number of potential jurors answered the court summons, so the contempt of court trial of business committee members was indefinitely postponed. Subsequently, the assistant secretary of the interior for Indian affairs overturned the c f r court ruling, the appellate court ruling, and the b i a area director's support of those rulings, stating that the constitution does not prohibit salaries from indirect costs and that the c f r court has no jurisdiction over intratribal disputes. A tribal council meeting was held 31 May, and tribal members voted down the business committee's request to negotiate a new contract with Long Royalty Company to develop oil resources. The dissident group presented and tribal members passed resolutions to fire the business manager and to audit the 1985 tribal financial records—both beyond the scope of the tribal council powers. At the tribal council meeting on 4 October, the 1987 budget was approved by a vote of eighty-nine to thirteen; only one per capita payment (rather than two) was possible because of low revenue, but subsequently the local B I A superintendent refused to approve the payment because it would have been less than four dollars a person, not enough to justify the expense to distribute it. A recall petition was submitted against the representative from Clinton; the petition was invalidated.[17]

Early in 1987 the business committee chair began the first meeting by pledging better communication with tribal members, commenting that "petty bickering and infighting . . . hinder the growth of our people." He was promptly accused of "abuse of office" by a rival from his district for hindering the recall election in Clinton District. At a 7 March business committee meeting, the manager of the tribes' Farm and Ranch enterprise, with the assistance of a large group of tribal members, protested his firing, arguing that the committee wanted to replace him with their relatives or political allies. The chair refused to recognize tribal members who wished to speak on the manager's behalf, and the committee voted four to three to remove the manager. Efforts to recall the Cheyenne representatives from Hammon and Clinton continued. On request of the business committee, the C F R court judge granted a restraining order on the tabulation of recall ballots from Hammon District. Later that summer the business committee invalidated a recall petition on the chair (also the representative from Clinton). There was a tribal council meeting on 1 August, where, despite protest from the dissenter group, the tribal members approved a lease of the Concho school property to Job Corps (to be operated by the Cherokee tribe) as well as money for a new senior citizens center in Clinton and a new hall in Hammon. The election board chair accused the majority members on the business committee of impounding their money so they could not hold recall elections. Another tribal council took place on 3 October, where there was a slightly larger turnout, and the tribal members voted the 1988 budget down, forty-three to fifty-nine. Subsequently, the dissenter group filed a lawsuit in C F R court accusing all the business committee members of failing to provide information on audits, misappropriating funds and property, mismanaging the Farm and Ranch enterprise, and improperly holding up recalls. They requested the court to remove them and declare them ineligible to ever serve again. The election board counted the ballots in the recall election on the Hammon representative, after the B I A gave approval, and overruled the business committee's decision; the representative was recalled. By the time of the fall elections, constituents were furious that the business committee had not met since June. After the elections, the chair, who was defeated, got a restraining order from C F R court to prevent the seating of his opponent. And the recalled representative from Hammon vowed to file a court action to overturn the election results.[18]

The first meeting of the twenty-sixth business committee (1988–89) opened 2 January 1988, with the new chair denying rumors that some of the committee members were responsible for the per capita payment not being made in December. The business committee swore in the new members in defiance of a C F R court order. During 1988 the business committee held frequent community meetings to get constituents' opinions, published reports of trips and financial transactions in the tribal newsletter, and discussed proposed budgets in the districts before presenting them in tribal council. Relations between the committee and their constituents improved significantly. At their 6 February meeting, subsequent to the submission of a petition with 327 signatures, the business committee terminated a management agreement made in 1987 with a bank to operate the tribes' Farm and Ranch program. At the first tribal council on 20 February, the council passed two resolutions, one that called for the removal of two B I A officials at Concho for neglect of their responsibilities and one that directed the business committee to spend no funds from the enterprises and receive no salaries without tribal council approval. On 2 April the tribal council approved the 1988 budget; there was a light turnout. A per capita payment, money for the burial program, enrollment office, community halls, and health board, and matching funds for three programs were approved. In the spring the business committee continued to try to be responsive to tribal members' concerns. In the 2 April business committee meeting, the committee invited tribal members to attend their working sessions. The business committee rehired the manager of the Farm and Ranch program, who had been fired by the previous administration, and they sent a letter about that administration's supposed financial irregularities to the U.S. attorney. In a meeting on 2 July, the business committee decided that tax revenues (from bingo and smoke shop enterprises) were to be budgeted by the tribal council. People from Canton District delivered a recall petition; the business committee did not interfere when the election board validated it, and the representative from Canton was recalled. An economic development board was organized, and tribal members were appointed to sit on it and monitor the enterprises. At the tribal council held 1 October, tribal members approved the budget for 1989. The turnout was low, and the budget was lower than that submitted in previous years. Some constituents complained about the Health Advisory Board. Subsequently, that board was made elective. At the 1 October business committee meeting, the committee voted for relief money to flood victims in one of the districts. In a departure from their earlier deference to the tribal council, they also repealed the part of the Tax Act that required tribal council approval for appropriations.[19]

In 1989, relations between the twenty-sixth business committee and the constituents began to sour. When the committee dissolved the development board of
tribal members assigned to oversee the enterprises and put the business manager
in charge of investigating the problems in these operations, one of the discharged
board members (a member of the dissident group) threatened a lawsuit. Public opposition to the committee began to surface in May. There was a letter to the editor
from a relative of a member of the previous administration, challenging the right
of the business committee to set up a tribal court. At the 6 May business committee meeting, several tribal members complained about business committee travel.
One tribal member complained that her grandchildren did not get emergency assistance for utility bills, yet some tribal employees did. The committee admitted
that mistakes probably were made in distributing the emergency funds but stated
that they were trying to help. Apparently, one committee member, hoping to create
opposition to rivals on the committee, had photocopied the list of grant recipients
and circulated it, causing people to become upset when they saw that some people
got grants and they did not. He also circulated a list of trips the committee members had taken. Even those who did not see the list were critical of the committee.
One elderly Arapaho woman remarked, "There were a lot of complaints this winter. They had $16,000 for aid to the needy. The chair was away. Two committee
members took control of the money away from social services. They disbursed it
to people that weren't needy. One gave some to a sister to buy furniture. They gave
out $600 when they were supposed to give $200. And two old ladies at Canton had
no heat and light!"

In July, opponents of the business committee submitted a petition for a special
tribal council meeting and another petition to hold a referendum on the committee's efforts to contract more programs. The committee scheduled the tribal council
meeting for 29 July. One committee member explained the committee's lack of opposition to the petition this way: "We called their bluff. They expected the business
committee to sit on the petition. . . . If they had sat on the petition, it would have
stirred up people." At the meeting held 29 July, the three petitioners declined to
address the crowd; the committee's supporters outnumbered theirs. The referendum ballots were not counted, as less than one-third were returned. The business
committee met 2 September, and a member of the dissident group charged that
tribal members had received no information on money spent to try to recover Fort
Reno. The business committee's budget request for 1990 was the smallest in recent
years—money for the election board, tribal newspaper, Health Advisory Board,
community halls, and tribal events. All the oil and gas money was allocated for per
capita payments. Information on finances was mailed to constituents, and community meetings were held. The tax commission had allocated money for various

services—powwow expenses, flood relief, Head Start, tribal court, public works, and youth camps.

The 7 October tribal council meeting was described by the *Watonga Republican* reporter as "another Bedlam Series." The budget was never voted on. Instead, opponents presented a series of resolutions that passed, including one to pay tribal income out in per capita payments and another to audit financial records. The business committee chair became visibly angry during the meeting, lashing back at the critics with comments critical of their personal behavior. The council passed a resolution to cease contracting programs; the vote was 105 to 66. A business committee member pointed out that this would shut down the tribal complex. A resolution to fire the business manager and the tax commission director passed and so did another to create a committee of tribal members to develop constitutional amendments. A motion passed 88 to 57 to remove the election board; two members, both respected elderly women, told the crowd that they did their best and that tribal members should not judge them unless they were perfect. The election board had removed the names of people from the voters' lists whose ballots, the board said, were returned because of incorrect addresses. The board reported that the postage costs for 498 undeliverable ballots wasted tribal funds and that tribal members should take responsibility for keeping addresses current. Later, the business committee chair commented that all of the resolutions that passed were unconstitutional. The sponsor of the resolutions remarked that, nonetheless, "tribal officials would be well-advised to heed the majority's wishes." That fall, all the incumbent business committee members were reelected. Among their opponents were several of the most vocal critics of the committee, people who received very few votes. In their 25 October meeting the committee declared the tribal council resolutions unconstitutional and therefore invalid. One resolution, to extend services to tribal members in Oklahoma City, was invalidated because federal program guidelines do not permit services outside the area of the former reservation. At a 4 November business committee meeting, there were complaints about the business committee's efforts to make enterprises more profitable for the tribes; tribal members did not like the lower prize money nor the higher prices for cigarettes. The business committee removed one of the members of the Health Advisory Board in retaliation for her remarks at the tribal council meeting in October. Subsequently, she was reinstated after complaints from tribal members appeared in the *Watonga Republican* stressing that the woman's son was a decorated veteran. The last tribal council meeting of the year was held 9 December, at which time the budget for 1990 was approved 137 to 98, and the meeting was adjourned before opponents could voice their complaints.[20]

During the tenure of the twenty-seventh committee (1990–91), business committee minutes and travel reports still were published in the tribal newspaper but less frequently than before. The chair announced that the committee would try to get more programs to benefit tribal members and maintain an open-door policy. A policy of no firings would be implemented. Another member commented that leaders needed encouragement, too: "We need to talk good to one another." The treasurer announced that a resolutions committee would be formed to work with tribal members to develop tribal council resolutions that meet constitutional requirements. In February, the treasurer welcomed written, signed questions that could be answered in the tribal newspaper. And the committee set aside some tax commission funds for communities that organized elderly nutrition programs. In March, trouble began between the treasurer and other committee members (as discussed in chapter 5). A recall petition came in on the Canton representative, charging unfair dispersion of energy assistance checks, and the election board validated it. The election board set a filing fee of five hundred dollars for any recall petition in order to meet costs; then, tribal members protested the violation of their "constitutional rights." The Canton representative was not recalled in the close election that followed. A group of tribal members organized to challenge the tribes' severance tax on oil companies, fearing it would lower payments to individual landowners.

A major problem for the business committee at this time was the loss of momentum in their effort to recover the Fort Reno lands. Senator Daniel Inouye's office reported receiving "confusing calls" from some tribal members who objected not to the business committee's effort to recover the land but to the committee's composition. And some local non-Indians, hoping to profit from developing the Fort Reno site, convinced Representative Glenn English to withhold support for the tribes' effort. A group of about twenty-five tribal members picketed the entrance to the tribal complex, alleging lack of "accountability" by tribal officials and unconstitutional acts. The spokesperson for the group told the reporter from the *Watonga Republican* that a petition of 250 signatures would go to Senator Inouye asking for a federal grand jury investigation. At the business committee meeting on 1 September, the treasurer, Alton Harrison, presented a resolution to take funds spent on the tax commissioner's salary and use them for general assistance. The resolution was ruled out of order by the chair. A tribal council meeting was held 6 October, and the committee's agenda was disregarded in favor of a "peoples meeting." A motion for a per capita payment and an external audit passed 124 to 1, and the new election board was elected. The business committee reported that the bingo halls had lost money and that the tax commission had allocated money for elderly nutrition, a police car, tribal court, youth programs, cemetery work, preparation of powwow grounds, and forty thousand dollars for tribal government operations. Tribal members questioned the deletion of the requirement for tribal council approval of the allocation of tax commission funds. [21]

In 1991, the publication of business committee minutes and reports of trips all but ceased. The first meeting of the year set the tone for the next twelve months. There was a heated exchange between the committee chair and the election board chair. The business committee chair, visibly angry, accused the election board of being biased against and personally attacking her. The election board chair said she was filing a lawsuit in tribal court to change the location of the tribal council meeting. The tribal court dismissed the suit. At the 9 February tribal council meeting, the 1991 budget was approved. Shortly thereafter, however, the treasurer, still at odds with the majority of the committee members, announced that he and two tribal members, who were serving on the tax commission, would file in tribal court for an injunction to stop the committee from making expenditures from the tax commission funds, except for emergency assistance for tribal members. The judge dismissed the suit. Four members of the tax commission filed another petition with tribal court: to direct the committee to allow the tax commission records to be audited. The judge so directed. When the records were not produced, the judge cited the committee for contempt of court and scheduled a hearing. About the same time, a recall petition on Juanita Learned, the chair and a representative from Geary, was delivered to the business committee secretary, who gave it to the election board without first presenting it to the business committee (as the constitution prescribes). The election board validated the petition. Subsequently, the business committee invalidated it, and the chair told the board that no more funds would be provided for the board's expenses. The next few months were dominated by a struggle between the committee and a large group of tribal members in Geary over the effort to recall the chair. Tribal members asked the B I A superintendent at Concho to intervene, as he had the constitutional authority to do so, and direct that the recall election be held. He refused. The tribal court judge dismissed a contempt of court citation against the business committee for failing to turn tax commission records over to the board, ruling that there is no enforcement authority for contempt of court in the tribal law-and-order code. A recall petition was submitted on the business committee member from Hammon, but it did not have the necessary number of signatures. A recall petition came in on one of the representatives from Canton; it was subsequently declared invalid.

At the 5 October tribal council meeting, the 1992 budget was passed, but tribal members voted to increase the amounts allocated to the election board and the Health Advisory Board (which was attempting to prevent I H S from closing the Indian hospital at Clinton). The council also voted 119 to 0 for the election board to proceed with the recall election on the chair. Another resolution authorized the treasurer and another committee member to take control of the tribal monies until a new economic development board responsible to the tribal council could be established. The manager of the bingo hall subsequently resigned, stating that he could not work with conflicting pressure from the business committee and tribal council. Subsequently, the business committee cut off funds to the election board. The election board filed for a restraining order in tribal court to stop the committee from withholding their funds. The court denied the petition, and, instead, the court granted a restraining order filed by the chair to stop the recall election. The tribal court subsequently issued a permanent injunction against the election board's continuing with the recall on the chair. A large group of tribal members came to the tribal complex and succeeded in convincing the election board to proceed anyway. Ballots were mailed out to the voters in the chair's district. The El Reno Chamber of Commerce publicly opposed the Fort Reno recovery, and the business committee announced that the tribes would boycott merchants in El Reno. The stature of the business committee was further eroded when tribal members interviewed in the *Watonga Republican* indicated that they would not boycott. The year ended with the election board being subpoenaed into tribal court under a writ of mandamus obtained by the business committee chair, and the recall ballots (which had been mailed in by the voters) were kept under the protection of the court. Federal marshals took the ballots into custody. These events were televised, including twenty-five tribal members picketing the tribal court to protest its interference. And, finally, the chair filed in tribal court to invalidate the results of the fall election for four new representatives (all of the incumbents except the treasurer had been voted out of office).[22]

The tenure of the twenty-eighth business committee (1992–93) was marked by a bitter, all-consuming struggle between holdovers and newcomers and by an escalating conflict between the newly elected chair's supporters and a dissident group with a core membership from Geary, who referred to themselves as the "tribal council." In January a group of about eighty tribal members forced open the door of the bingo hall at Concho and declared a "peoples' " tribal council meeting. They passed resolutions to fire the business manager, recognize the new members of the business committee (several defeated candidates had filed in tribal court to overturn the election results), pay the former treasurer's back salary, allocate more money to the election board, hold a referendum to amend the constitution to allow the tribal council to restrict business committee actions by resolution, and replace the tribal court with the c f r court. At the business committee meeting of 7 January, several people from Geary District demanded that the business committee direct the election board to proceed with the recall of the former chair, still a representative from Geary. Tribal members in attendance at a 1 February business committee meeting again demanded that the business committee direct a recall election in Geary. In March the chair scheduled a tribal council meeting where tribal members were going to be asked to approve the use of tax commission and enterprise funds to reduce the deficit and the use of some of the burial fund principle (rather than merely the interest) to pay funeral debts. At the business committee meeting of 21 March, the members present voted to direct the election board to proceed with the recall election in Geary (despite the B I A's and tribal court's rulings to the contrary). They also voted to suspend the tribal court judge; but because his contract did not expire until 1995 the committee lacked the authority to remove him. A tribal council meeting was held 11 April, and the tribal members approved the use of burial fund principle and the use of Farm and Ranch income to hire an attorney but refused to approve the use of enterprise and tax money to reduce the deficit or to pay the portion of business committee salaries that could not be paid from indirect costs. They also approved increasing the election board budget by fifteen thousand dollars. The representative from the El Reno District filed in tribal court to stop a recall election in his district, charging that without a business committee resolution the election board could not proceed. The judge ordered the business committee to meet to consider validating the petition; the petition was validated by a four-to-two vote, and the representative was recalled by a vote of 132 to 34. Geary District recalled Learned, then elected a new representative. Subsequently, a recall petition was submitted on the new representative from Canton; the election board invalidated it. A week later a petition with 273 signatures was submitted, calling for a tribal council. One tribal member commented, "I feel the same frustration I felt when we tried to get our recall [against the Geary representative] through. I looked for something better when the new ones came in, and here we are and haven't accomplished a thing."

A tribal council was held 15 August, and a resolution passed 97-34-2 to hold a referendum on a constitutional amendment to allow the tribal council to overrule business committee actions. There also were complaints about the election board's alleged partiality to the newly elected members, their disregard of constitutional provisions and abuse of authority, and their expenditure of thousands of dollars without proper authority. The election board chair subsequently declined to hold the referendum, arguing that the business committee had not so directed. Two of the new business committee members retracted their earlier support for tribal council authority over business committee expenditures. In response, a tribal member announced a protest rally against the business committee and the business manager. A tribal council meeting was held 3 October. The turnout was very low, but the budget for 1993 was approved, 72-0-3. The budget increased the appropriation for the election board. With the public perceiving an alliance between the newly elected business committee members and the election board, the dissenting group continued to attract support. In October, O I G released findings on the fiscal management practices of the business committee in 1992. The committee had incurred a deficit, in large part because the election board had been overbilling, in the amount of at least $67,400. Personnel procedures were not being followed. O I G recommended that a federal monitor be assigned to oversee tribal operations. The

B I A agreed to provide the monitor. Subsequently, four new business committee members outvoted three holdovers and refused to accept a federal monitor.

The year ended with a very contentious tribal council meeting on 12 December. Tribal members approved bringing in a federal monitor, whom they wanted to report to them. They also approved a resolution not to allow the business committee to transfer the Education Trust Fund to another brokerage (which the committee believed would increase the interest earned on the principle), and they selected a subcommittee of four tribal members to oversee the business committee's actions with regard to the trust. Another resolution passed to reduce the salaries of the committee members. A new election board was elected, with all but one of the incumbent members being defeated for reelection. On 23 December, the business committee chair scheduled a removal hearing on his four opponents on the committee. About thirty tribal members arrived to protest this attempt, but the chair called for an executive, rather than a public, hearing and retreated into a conference room. The angry crowd followed him. Tribal police arrived but took no action. The new members of the election board accused the chair and business manager of withholding election records from them. Committee members fled the scene, so no vote on the removal question was held. Finally, the B I A announced that they would hold the referendum on amending the constitution.[23]

The year 1993 opened with a conflict between the old election board and the newly elected one. The former refused to step down, and the business committee majority, political allies of the old election board, withheld funds from the newly elected board. The business committee chair and his allies began putting pressure on the election board chair by criticizing her job performance on the housing authority. She responded: "I will not be politically harassed, threatened or intimidated to resign from my job or any board I serve on. If anything, such political actions make me more determined to stay on such boards." Subsequently, the business committee majority refused to approve the housing authority's application for more housing. Also, the tribal members elected by the tribal council as an education subcommittee to monitor the Education Trust Fund were "read their rights" by the criminal investigator at the tribal court (under the direction of the business committee chair) and threatened with jail, fines, and banishment for "obstructing tribal operations"; subsequently, criminal charges were filed against them. The election board continued to function, declaring the seat of one member of the committee's majority vacant due to election irregularities. The member sued, and the tribal court enjoined the board from recounting the ballots. The business manager denied the board access to the election board records. The new treasurer (from the newcomer group on the committee) confronted the tribal members at a committee meeting who were criticizing his actions: "I'm not going to sit here and debate it with you. . . . If you people don't like it, take it to court." A recall petition on this representative was immediately forthcoming and was validated by the election board. In May, the treasurer, a representative from Canton, was recalled by a vote of eighty-one to fifty-one. Another tribal member filed a suit in tribal court against three committee members to try to stop them from using tribal assets without tribal council approval; the petition was dismissed. A tribal council was held in response to a petition with 265 signatures, but the quorum failed before a resolution could be entered for a per capita payment. There were community meetings held by the management company with which the business committee was negotiating to run a new, large casino at Concho. A tribal member was told in response to his question that (despite business committee statements to the contrary earlier in the year) tribal council approval of the contract was not necessary. Meanwhile, constituent dissatisfaction was growing, for the business committee had not met since March. A tribal member filed in tribal court to force them to meet to transact tribal business, but the judge refused to so order. A tribal council was held 2 October, where tribal members demanded that the tribal council be consulted on the casino agreement, but to no avail.

The fall elections brought into office several of the supporters of the election board (opponents of the committee chair and his allies). Subsequently, the committee majority filed in tribal court to set aside the results, using tribal law enforcement personnel to obtain background information on some of the candidates' past legal troubles and publicizing the details. The B I A had already begun to register voters for a referendum on the constitutional amendment proposed by the tribal council, which would allow the council to override committee decisions. In July the referendum passed 231 to 65. The business manager, an ally of the chair, appealed to the B I A superintendent at Concho to overturn the results, pointing to "procedural difficulties" if the tribal council were allowed to limit business committee powers. The superintendent refused, and the appeal then was made to the B I A area director, who upheld the decision of the superintendent. The appeal was then sent to the Indian Board of Appeals in Washington D C. Finally, late in 1994, the Indian Board of Appeals ruled that the referendum results were valid.[24]

Opponents of the twenty-ninth committee (1994–95) attended their first meeting in January. Brenda R., a spokesperson from Oklahoma City, criticized the tribes' successful effort to require oil companies to pay severance taxes on tribal land, arguing that the tax would reduce the size of bonus payments to individual landowners. Another dissident, in a letter to the editor, complained that the casino contract would benefit only a few tribal members. At a meeting in February, the council approved the tribal attorney's contract and passed the budget, 193 to 0. There was a very small group of opponents present. Jack T. complained that tribal members did not benefit from the bingo and smoke shop enterprises. The council supported the business committee's goal of amending the casino contract to obtain better terms, although Wesley N. insisted that the tribal council should have approved the casino contract. At the March business committee meeting, the chiefs who attended expressed support for the Fort Reno recovery. In April, a recall petition was submitted on a representative from Geary, and the business committee invalidated it. In May the tribal court took custody of the recall ballots after a suit was filed by some of the signatories. In October the court instructed the election board to review the petition, and it was subsequently validated. By October there reportedly were petitions being circulated to recall all but one of the committee members. Foregoing the advice of the business committee, in October the tribal council, which was attended by about 125 tribal members, voted to distribute the Woods Petroleum Corporation settlement in per capita payments. Taking advantage of the recent amendment to the constitution, the tribal council also voted to reject the gaming board appointed by the business committee to oversee the casino enterprise and to appoint the members themselves. Another participant moved that bingo head tax money be budgeted by the tribal council rather than by the business committee (which had allocated most of the money for emergency assistance and the rest to programs, the election board, business committee salaries, the Fort Reno recovery, the Health Advisory Board, the enrollment office, ceremonies, legal bills, and burial expenses). No vote was taken on this or on the budget for the following year. After this meeting, dissidents began scheduling tribal council meetings to rival those scheduled by the business committee. A second tribal council meeting in October could not get a quorum, but those at the meeting voted to eliminate business committee salaries, reject the contracting of I H S services, remove members of the housing authority and appoint new members, increase the budget of the election board so that more recall elections could be held, make all tribal revenue subject to budgeting by the tribal council, subject the tribal court to tribal council supervision, and distribute oil and gas revenues in per capita payments. Dissident Wesley N. remarked, "The business committee is supposed to listen to us, not us to them." Influenced by rumors that members of the twenty-eighth committee would be prosecuted for embezzlement, the participants in a November tribal council meeting voted to deny salaries to business committee members and to deny them access to tax and enterprise money. In a December council meeting, tribal members approved the budget but voted against the business committee's proposal to buy land with the money earned from escheated properties.

In February 1995, the tribal council again repudiated various business committee actions, as the 1994 constitutional amendment permitted. They rejected the committee's effort to contract the hospital and clinics. Wesley N. argued that contracting would not be of benefit to him and that the business committee was not capable of contracting it successfully. That fall several of the dissidents ran for election but received few votes. In the October tribal council meeting, the council passed the budget but voted to use the Woods settlement money for per capita payments rather than reserve some of it for development or for services for children and elderly people, and they voted against charging fees for the right of way across tribal land. In a November tribal council meeting where the quorum was in doubt, the participants voted to organize an "economic authority," or oversight board, that would control all tribal funds. In a December meeting, dissidents complained about the contract with the casino management company, the Fort Reno recovery effort, and the tax collection effort, but there was no quorum.[25]

During the tenure of the thirtieth committee (1996–97), the tribal council met in January, April, May, and four times in November, each time failing to establish a quorum. A group of dissidents, many of whom had unsuccessfully run for business committee office and some of whom called themselves members of the Cheyenne separatist movement, took the lead in opposing the business committee. In February the tribal council attracted seventy-seven tribal members, who voted to fund the oversight committee, fire the business manager and the attorney working on the Fort Reno recovery, distribute all the Woods settlement money per capita, and give more funding to the election board. The B I A refused to take a position on which actions they would recognize, except to agree to validate council decisions on trust funds. The business committee argued that the decisions in the February council meeting should not be valid and called a tribal council meeting for October. The committee again asked for the council's support on granting an easement across land in which the tribes held an escheated interest (in return for damages amounting to several hundred thousand dollars and for other economic support). Dissidents at the meeting opposed the easement proposal, and their group persuaded a majority present to vote to instruct the business committee to supplement the burial fund from enterprise monies rather than from the Woods settlement, which they wanted distributed per capita. They also passed a resolution to request a federal investigation of I H S. Several dissidents criticized the committee for resuming paying business committee salaries in the amount of thirty-five thousand dollars. This action provoked one councilmember to argue that he worked fifteen-hour days. By July 1996 the dissident group, with Wesley N. and Brenda R. as spokespersons, had met with the state media to charge tribal government with ongoing abuses of power. About twelve dissidents accused the business committee of ignoring the tribal council and jeopardizing the programs, alluding to a $2.7 million deficit. In December 1996 the tribal council approved the budget but authorized the oversight committee selected by the tribal council to supervise all tribal monies. The council voted not to contract I H S and not to cooperate on the business committee's proposal for a mushroom farm, seventy-seven to zero. One participant urged that all programs be returned to the B I A.

The tribal council's oversight committee then embarked on a struggle with the business committee over control of the tribes' public relations that continued throughout 1997. Business committee members obtained a temporary restraining order from the tribal court against Eric A., the leader of the oversight committee, directing him to stop representing himself as a tribal official. In response he filed suit to gain control of tribal monies. This individual took the lead in stating to the state and national media that tribal members objected to the Fort Reno recovery activity of the business committee. He accused the business committee members of having unrealistic "visions of grandeur." In October, Eric A. and Brenda R. encouraged the tribal council to vote to fire the Fort Reno attorney and remove enterprise and tax money from business committee control. The council did not vote on the budget for 1998. In November and December, dissidents tried to reconvene the tribal council but could not get a quorum. Eric A. filed suit in tribal court to force the business committee to comply with the tribal council's decisions. At first the business committee provided financial reports to him, but after he made critical comments to the press, he received no more reports. Business committee supporters wrote letters to the editor in the *Watonga Republican* portraying the dissidents as "losers" who "can't get elected" and who were publicity seekers.[26]

The thirty-first committee (1998–99) asked the tribes' attorneys to speak at the first tribal council meeting in 1998. The lawyers stressed that loss of tribal sovereignty and, in fact, termination were real threats. The council approved the budget and the attorney contract. The meeting adjourned before a vote could be taken on continuing the oversight committee. The suit filed by Eric A. eventually was dismissed (the judge decided that constituents with complaints should vote representatives out of office). In September the tribal council approved 74-0-2 to hold a referendum on whether to proceed with a truck plaza project at Elk City. The referendum failed for lack of participation (745 ballots were undeliverable, but 635 out of 3,017 potential voters cast ballots; the majority voted against the proposal). During 1999, dissidents circulated recall petitions on committee members. By this time, the business committee was using the large income from Lucky Star and the taxes to operate an emergency assistance program for constituents— several hundred thousand dollars were distributed. Committee opponents, including several former employees, continued to charge employees with incompetence and embezzlement and blamed the business committee for the problems. State media reported their charges that emergency assistance money was used to reward supporters and that money was being wasted on the Fort Reno recovery. However, much of the potential discontent was relieved by liberal use of emergency assistance funds. Thus, the tribal council met in October and approved the budget and a per capita payment from the oil and gas account. The council also voted to instruct the attorney to apply to the National Indian Gaming Committee to distribute some of the Lucky Star profits in per capita payments so that everyone (not merely those applying for emergency assistance) would get a share of the profits. In November the tribal council approved granting an easement to the state for the widening of Highway 81 (which would bring the tribes a sizeable payment) and applying for trust status on the fifty acres at Elk City (purchased for the tribes by the casino management company) and some land at Seiling—land that would be used for a truck plaza and tribal programs, respectively.[27]

"Unqualified People": Criticizing Tribal Government

Critics of tribal government during the period 1977–99, particularly the dissidents at certain times, attempted to mobilize opposition by suggesting that tribal officials were incompetent, that they took more than their fair share, and that they arrogantly assumed more authority than that to which they were entitled. Dissidents also linked the victimization that Cheyennes and Arapahos felt at the hands of the federal government to actions of tribal government.

Constituents frequently expressed pessimism about tribal government. As one Cheyenne woman put it, "The tribe can't make a success of things." And an Arapaho woman also complained to me, "The C and A are the wealthiest tribe in Oklahoma yet the poorest. Everything they do flops." One of the most contentious issues during the late 1970s was the tribes' proposal to contract Concho school. At this time the tribes were just beginning to assume the operation of programs. A group of dissidents led by Lester B. and Wesley N. began to undermine the business committee in 1978, referring to them publicly, and sometimes within hearing distance of the press, as "incompetent." The suggestion that the tribes were not competent to operate the school shocked Joe Pedro, who stated that he was "heartsick" that "others don't share my confidence that we can play a role in our children's education." Opponents were given aid by local B I A officials and continued to question the competence of tribal members, one remarking that the tribes were "not ready" for contracting. By the 1980s, problems with program funding were routine, and the media exposure of these problems—for example, suggestions that these problems were deficits—was highlighted by opponents: Wesley N. charged in a letter to the editor that tribal officials were "unqualified people." They "tried to run a 1980 business on a 1930 mentality." A constituent, upset by rumors, suggested that tribal government be "turned back to the B I A." The severance tax issue gave rise to considerable opposition led by a group of dissidents whose spokespersons were Lester B. and Aron P. In 1985 one dissident wrote in opposition to the business committees' efforts to develop businesses and levy taxes that the business committee was "out of touch with the competitive business world." When the business committee tried to convince the tribal council to support the Long Royalty Company lease in order to aid the Fort Reno recovery, dissident leader Aron P. addressed the Fort Reno recovery effort: "We've heard this for years. That's the problem. It's the same story." He suggested that people no longer had confidence in the business committee's ability to successfully pursue the recovery. In a 1995 tribal council meeting, one dissident critical of the Fort Reno recovery effort remarked, "What would you do with the Fort Reno property if you did get it; you would probably just let it run down like the Concho school." Oklahoma politicians used dissidents' opposition to the recovery to justify their refusal to support the tribes' efforts. Throughout the years from 1977 to 1999, at tribal council meetings business committee members sometimes were referred to as "childish."[28]

Throughout the contention over contracting the school, operating programs, and levying taxes, dissidents suggested that the motive of tribal officials was to profit personally in ways other tribal members would not profit. As one woman put it, "The business committee lives high while everybody else struggles." In reference to the business committee's effort to convince the tribal council to budget money for indirect cost contributions to programs in 1980, one of the Arapaho dissidents from Lester B. and Wesley N.'s group charged, "These fat cats rip us off." There was the suggestion that if resources were not distributed per capita individuals would not get their share. Jack T. spoke against the tribes' contributing to programs this way: "This is your money. Do you want to pay off those bills [accumulated by others]?" Jack T. wrote a letter to the editor stating that deficits were due to negligence on the part of tribal officials: "We tribal members did not create this situation. Be strong, be individuals." He urged people to insist on per capita division of resources. Wesley N. also wrote a letter to the editor stating that tribalism was not feasible: "The white man's way of life has, in effect, placed individual survival over tribal survival." At a tribal council meeting in February 1984, tribal members adopted a budget that included money for the programs' disallowed costs. Speaking for the dissident group, one tribal member said, "Why does everyone have to contribute?" Led by Aron P. and Lester B., dissidents opposed the collection of taxes from oil companies and continued to oppose support for contributions to programs' indirect costs.[29]

Constituents saw a link between business committees' ignoring constituents' views and misuse of tribal money. One woman's views on the matter were stated to me thus: "The business committee has always been crooks. They take our money without asking and use it for what they want." Dissidents complained in 1986 that some of the tribal budget should not be allocated to programs: "These poor kids and a lot of poor people out there—after they [the tribes] get a little money, now they [the business committee] take it away from them." The suggestion was that affluent business committee members profited at the expense of the poor. At a business committee meeting in September 1986 the chair worried aloud about rumors that the per capita payment would be small because the business committee was spending the income on themselves; in fact, mineral income was down due to a fall in oil prices. One constituent who believed the rumor told me, "We only got thirty dollars per capita [last year]. Where's the rest of it; they [the business committee] got it. The money we voted for education [the Education Trust Fund] probably went to them." In 1987 one woman remarked about the decision to use tribal funds for a senior citizens program and a community hall, "The business committee spent all the per capita money for a center at Hammon and a van [for Clinton senior citizens]. They [the committee] are riding around in it at Clinton." In 1989 a constituent wrote a letter to the editor urging people to vote for a budget that would allocate all tribal income for per capita distribution because tribal members "never benefit," "never receive services." He wrote: "It's about time you and I got our fair share. The business committee members have had their share." In 1991 the O I G report encouraged rumors about the misuse of business committee funds. Aware of reports of deficits, the election board chair accused the committee of spending the board's budgeted funds on themselves. One woman told me that people were saying that the per capita fund was being used for committee traveling. At a tribal council in March 1992 the chair begged the people to support contributions to the programs from tax and enterprise money. A spokesperson for the dissidents insisted that tribal members should not have to pay for the needs of others when the business committee was not managing the programs well. In a letter to the editor, the business committee was criticized for delays in approving housing authority business: "Do they know how hard it is for our tribal members to survive? How could they know what it is like when they make a whopping $35,000 a year?"[30]

Most of the dissidents' actions took place in the arena of the tribal council meeting. When they made up the majority present at the meetings, they passed resolutions against economic development and against programs. The B I A would refuse to act on these resolutions, which would provoke frustration and anger among many constituents, not merely the dissident group. As Jack T. put it, "The B I A has always stood for Boss Indians Around." In a 1988 letter to the editor, a constituent complained, "The B I A has been making our leases for us and giving us the runaround for years and years that they have really got it in their heads that they're our mothers and fathers. I think it's about time for us to tell them! They work for us; we don't work for them." In response to the business committee's frequent encouragement of the B I A's actions in overriding tribal council decisions, dissidents publicly portrayed tribal officials as dictators or tyrants. Lester B. not only linked the business committee to the B I A's rejection of tribal council actions but associated the frustration of the tribal council with massacres, which still occupied a predominant theme in Cheyenne interpretations of their history: "We were told 'Here's your constitution' [here is your treaty]. We're using it and we have gathered under those instruments they gave us [we camped peacefully as prescribed by treaty]. And they're wiping us out [they violated the treaty and attacked us]."[31]

Many Cheyennes and Arapahos are aware that the federal and state governments create obstacles to gaining sovereignty and to improving their circumstances generally. One tribal member reflected on the problems this way: "Tribal sovereignty is like a jar of molasses with a label on it that says 'honey.' It's not honey." He, and many others, may be aware to some degree of how the federal trusteeship in constitutional, legal, and land matters and the regulations surrounding contracting contribute to the problems of tribal government. Yet the focus of constituents clearly is on pursuing an individual rather than a tribal agenda and on highlighting any lack of success tribal officials have in advocating for the tribes. Reinforced by negative media portrayals of native leaders, these views create a climate of suspicion and pessimism that works to undermine the sovereignty agenda—to thwart efforts to contract Concho school, to purchase land, to develop business enterprises, and to recover Fort Reno lands. Several chiefs still make speeches encouraging people to support the business committee and "pull together." But the Cheyennes and Arapahos are more successful at acting on values of cooperation in dance and powwow activities than in tribal government.[32]

7

Coming around the Drum

POLITICS IN RITUAL CONTEXT

While they may rail against the way they feel they are treated by the tribal government, Cheyennes and Arapahos also are outraged by the treatment they receive from the surrounding society. The B I A's control over their lives and the exploitation and discrimination they feel they must endure from the state of Oklahoma and the local towns are the subject of complaint and occasional protest and litigation on the part of individuals and groups of Cheyennes and Arapahos. Typical of the incidents that engender resentment is the recent refusal of an oil company to name the well they drilled on an Indian allotment after the original allottee, Crow Neck. Instead, the company named it after the non-Indian man who lived on an adjacent piece of land. Similarly, a letter written by a non-Indian resident of El Reno to the president of the United States found its way to the B I A and was brought to the attention of the tribal government. The El Reno resident complained about local Indians: "Most Indians do not and W I L L N O T W O R K. . . . Most Indians use their 'free money' to go out and get drunk on. Since these native Americans have been M O R E than paid back for the land the white man took from them (where would they be without us? Probably grinding corn with stones!), we should S T O P G I V I N G T H E M O U R M O N E Y!!!" Apparently, this individual believed that per capita checks from oil and gas royalties on tribal land were government welfare payments. Cheyenne parents in Watonga objected to the school program celebrating the "Land Run," that is, the opening of the reservation to settlement by non-Indians. They protested that they did not want their children participating in a celebration of the "theft of Indian lands." One parent commented that when he was in school he and his peers were "programmed to think stereotypes about Indians"; "not until the 1960s did we start thinking good about ourselves." Another parent sarcastically suggested that the school reenact the Dust Bowl run to California: "Let all the White kids run west and leave us here."[1]

In weekly dances and powwows, Cheyennes and Arapahos come together in rituals that express their commitment to a way of life that the surrounding society has not understood, valued, or tolerated. In these celebrations they also confront and repudiate experiences they have had as a subordinated people pressured to adopt the way of life of those that dominate them. In these celebrations they insist that extended kinship and the values they associate with kin relations are better than the Euro-American model of kinship, that generosity and sharing are better than the materialism of Euro-Americans, that an egalitarian social order is preferable to one where elites are privileged, and that native religion is of equal value to that of the non-Indian world. In this chapter, I describe the dance and powwow ceremonies, explore how these rituals express the meanings Cheyennes and Arapahos assign to their lives, and comment on the way these events are used as a critique of the colonial experience.[2]

Dances and Powwows: An Overview

Some dances are held in public buildings in towns, but most are at a community hall, and powwows take place at an outdoor arbor near a community hall. These sites are in the rural communities a few miles from the towns. The halls and dance grounds are nestled in clearings in groves of blackjack oak trees, where Cheyennes and Arapahos once camped for weeks at a time. Dances are organized and managed by a family or committee (referred to as the sponsor) and usually last one day. Powwows usually are organized and managed by committees and last throughout a weekend. Many of the people who participate camp on the powwow grounds in tepees and tents for the duration of the event; others drive to the site each day. The women of the families involved—sisters, mothers and daughters, and less often in-laws—do most of the work and make most of the decisions of the sponsoring groups. The organizers try to accumulate property that can be raffled off at the dance to raise money for the dance expenses (including the fee for use of a community hall or powwow grounds and, in the case of a powwow, the prize money for contest winners). The food that will be served to those attending the event is also the responsibility of the sponsors. They will recruit friends and relatives to cook or purchase the food and can expect them also to donate items to raffle.

Successful powwow and dance sponsorship involves political activity; that is, sponsors have to mobilize others to contribute time and money and to work toward consensus in decision making during preparations for the event. This activity may require negotiations with political rivals or with individuals and families that may not have close ties. Sponsors have custody of the money raised for the celebrations, and they have to decide how best to use it to accomplish their goals. A successful sponsor has to have maintained close ties or friendly contacts with a wide range of people in order to attract a head staff, a large crowd, and a network of friends and relatives to help with the cooking, errands, and other necessary activity.

Dances include those that recognize birthdays, graduations, and military service; those that memorialize deaths; and benefit dances that raise money for an organization or event, such as a powwow, a political advocacy group, religious ceremonies, or a young people's association. In the case of honor dances that recognize individuals (for their military service, for example), the ceremony is intended to encourage and protect the honorees as they undertake a new experience or role. Participants in these gatherings include both Cheyennes and Arapahos as well as a few people from other tribes. The powwows, however, generally are designated as either Cheyenne-Arapaho, Arapaho, or Cheyenne, regardless of joint participation. Several powwows are held annually, and others have been organized for a few years and then discontinued. The Cheyenne-Arapaho Labor Day Powwow, an annual event held at Colony, draws the largest crowd and, like most powwows, attracts a small number of non-Indians. The Oklahoma Indian Nations Powwow is also a Cheyenne-Arapaho powwow and has been held for the past few years at Concho. The Arapaho powwow of the longest duration is Barefoot Powwow at Canton. For a few years, there was a powwow in the Geary Arapaho community on the Fourth of July weekend. The Cheyenne powwow of the longest duration is Red Moon Powwow at Hammon. The Mollie Sheppard Memorial Powwow at Kingfisher was held for a few years in the 1980s.

The program of events is similar at both dances and powwows. At a dance, the afternoon or evening events begin with a prayer (usually in the Cheyenne or Arapaho language) by a respected elder or ceremonial leader, then a meal is served to those in attendance. The dishes of food (stew or soup, fried chicken, potato salad, beans, crackers, fried bread, pastries, canned fruit) are spread on a long table, and each person goes in line in front of the table with a paper plate and utensils, while the women who are helping the sponsor fill the plates. It is customary that something be offered from each of what are regarded as the four traditional food groups: meat, fruit, bread, and water (or more likely a beverage, such as coffee). After the meal, a drum is brought to the center of the room or arbor, and the singers assemble.

For the duration of the event, songs are sung that both evoke emotion and motivate people to contribute to the sponsors, and the sponsors and head staff have their "specials" (that is, giveaway ceremonies, in which people give certain kinds of property to others). First, there is a flag song, perhaps a memorial song, and, if any chiefs or headsmen are present, a chiefs song, then a headsmen song. At a benefit dance during a chiefs song, chiefs and their family members dance, and the sponsors then approach them and receive a donation. Similarly, headsmen make a donation. After this, there are honor songs for other respected categories of individuals, such as Native American Church members or veterans. These individuals and their families dance, then give a donation to the sponsors, who are standing with the emcee for the event. Throughout all dances and powwows, items are raffled or auctioned off to the crowd. Grocery baskets and shawls are raffled, along with rifles and Indian art. Shawls are most commonly sold to the person who makes the highest offer. The money that is raised will go to the honoree, in the case of a birthday, graduation, or soldier dance, or to the organization or activity, in the case of a benefit dance held for a political cause or a powwow.

A powwow will have an afternoon and an evening program. Sometimes a family volunteers to feed in the afternoon or evening to honor a relative—for example, the family of the deceased veteran whose flag is being flown at the event. Someone is always asked to pray before the meal. The singers at the drum spend the afternoon singing gourd dance songs, and men with gourd dance outfits and women in general gourd dance. Sometimes the program begins with gourd dancing and a meal is served in the early evening. Specials may be held during the afternoon and usually continue on into the evening program. After the dinner hour, the emcee calls for the "grand entry."

In the gourd dance, the male gourd dancers form a line and dance in unison. Their knees flex as they bounce slightly on their heels while standing in place and shaking their rattles in time to the song, tread in place, or advance forward toward the drum, depending on the musical cues in the gourd dance song. Gourd dance songs are sung in sets of eight, with the drum accent a loud-soft beat. The dancers flex their knees on the loud beat and straighten their legs, sometimes with a bump of the heels, on the soft beat. After the song is sung through once or twice, the beat gets louder, and the tempo and excitement build. At the end of the song there is a flurry of fast beats, and the dancers raise and shake their rattles. Women dance in place around the periphery of the arena. Male gourd dancers wear street clothes or possibly a ribbon shirt with dress pants or jeans, a beaded bandoleer with a silk scarf (containing "medicine") over the left shoulder, a red and blue woolen shoulder blanket around the neck, a long sash with beaded and fringed ends around the waist and tied on the right side, and Indian jewelry (such as a silver or beaded bolo tie). The dancer carries a shaker, made of a bead-decorated tin can with pebbles or shot inside, in his right hand and a feather fan in his left. There is no gourd dance outfit for women; they dance in war dance outfits or in street clothes and a shawl.[3]

The grand entry is a procession of all the people who will dance in outfits—women first, then men, organized according to the kind of dancing that they do—as well as the powwow sponsors and the head staff. The procession enters the arena from the east, led by an honor guard carrying the U.S. flag and other flags, including the Cheyenne-Arapaho flag. The honor guard dances around the arena once, then stands at attention while the rest of the procession enters and dances around the arena. Someone is asked to pray, then the emcee asks the head singer for a flag song (either the Northern or Southern Arapaho or the Cheyenne flag song, which were all composed during the time of World War II). Then a retreat song is sung while the flag is taken out of the arena. The crowd stands in respect during the flag song. One or two more songs, such as a victory song, are sung. After these preliminary songs, during the rest of the evening the emcee calls for particular kinds of songs (war dance, round dance, two-step, for example), presides over specials, announces during contest dances, and provides a commentary, including jokes of various types and statements about the significance and meaning of various activities, as he tries to keep people energized. The contests involve prize money, which is raised by the powwow committee largely from specials and raffles. There are contests for men (traditional and fancy dancers and sometimes straight and grass dancers), for women (cloth, buckskin, fancy shawl, and sometimes jingle dress dancers), and for teens and children. At the conclusion of the contests, relatives of the winners make a donation to the committee.

One of the first tasks of the sponsors of a dance or powwow is to select the head staff for the event. These individuals include a master of ceremonies (emcee), arena director, head singer, head man dancer (or head war, gourd, straight, grass, or traditional dancer), head lady dancer, head teen boy dancer, head teen girl dancer, head little boy dancer, head little girl dancer, and one or two co-host organizations. Of utmost importance is to select people whose families can be counted upon to participate in the process. Sometimes relatives of committee members are selected, but the goal of the sponsor, especially the powwow sponsor, is to involve people from as many different families as possible so as to draw a large crowd. Powwow committees also select a princess for head staff. The powwow committee for the Labor Day Powwow selects two head staffs, one Arapaho and one Cheyenne, and the flags used are alternately those of Arapaho and Cheyenne veterans.

The emcee is a man (for a powwow, two or three men may be chosen) who is good at public speaking, skilled at conveying local values, knowledgeable about interpersonal and kinship relationships so that he can joke properly, and able to handle the physical and social demands of announcing and commenting on events over as much as a twelve-to-fourteen-hour period for as long as three consecutive days.

The arena director is a man responsible for lining up the dancers for the grand entry, keeping the arena clear during contests, and lining up and grouping the contestants. He also carries the property that is given away during a special, if a recipient is unable to carry it easily, and he walks around the inner circumference of the arena carrying shawls or other items donated to the singers at the drum, auctioning them off to the crowd. He brings water, coffee, and carbonated beverages to the singers during the dance. The emcee can call on the arena director for assistance generally.

The head singer has custody of a drum and can recruit singers for the dance. He will invite the singers he wants; others will come to the drum during the dance or powwow. As one man frequently chosen as head singer put it, "If other singers have confidence in the head singer, like to sing with him, they come out." The head singer has to be able to motivate all the singers to work together harmoniously. He must know a wide range of songs and be able to coordinate the singing with other events at the dance. The head singer, who usually starts each song, has to be able to remember many family songs, flag songs, and songs with words in the native languages of the region and be able to sing the various types of songs that are called for during a dance. At a dance, the head singer takes his drum to the center of the arena or room; at a powwow, the head singer's drum is in the center of the arena and other drums ring the circumference of the arena; those singers, along with the head singer's drum group, take turns singing.

Songs are started (that is, repeated) several times. In "the Arapaho way" songs are started four or seven times, although the head singer may start a song additional times, if necessary. During a special, the family frequently asks for a "one-on-one," that is, a war dance followed by a gourd dance. The head singer will stop the repetitions in the war dance song when the family members leading the procession reach the spot where they will gourd dance. During the gourd dance phase of a special, if the stream of participants is ongoing, the singers will add repetitions until everyone is in place. Some types of songs have another part, a coda or "tail," that is sung after the drum stops, following the four or seven repetitions.[4]

Each type of dance has an appropriate type of song. One head singer explained it to me thus: "The style of the song suits the style of the dance. Some songs are used for buckskin dress and some for cloth dress. The songs are associated with, not required for, the buckskin dress. The buckskin dress style is graceful, slow; the drumbeat has to let them bend; there's a beat in the middle. With cloth, there is more movement, twists, steps, more variety, speed. The style of the song matches the style of the dance." During contests singers choose songs carefully to reflect the dance style featured in the contest (for example, the women's buckskin dress dance contest). During the war dancing that everyone does ("intertribal" dancing), singers do not have to be so selective. Most of the dancing at powwows and other dances is war and gourd dancing, but occasionally a round dance or two-step dance is announced.

In the round dance, males and females or groups of women move clockwise, perhaps holding hands or otherwise touching. They move in unison with the left foot lifted slightly higher than the right, either in half-time or stepping on every beat. Round dance songs differ from war dance songs; for example, they have a loud-soft rather than an even drumbeat. Dancers in war dance outfits and individuals not wearing outfits participate. The two-step is a partner dance, with males and females grasping hands in the skater's (or fox trot) position. In a line, they move their hands up and down and advance, then step back. At times, the male turns the female, lifting his arm up. (This is a stylized version of dances held on army posts and observed by Indians in the late nineteenth century.) The two-step songs have a loud-soft beat. This dance is usually led by male and female head dancers, who initiate minor changes in the footwork.

The head male dancer is expected to dance throughout the event, thus encouraging others to dance. Male dancers specialize in either gourd dancing or war dancing of the traditional, straight, grass, or fancy type. The outfits for each and the movements vary. The four men's war dance styles all are free style and individualistic. The dancers move around the center drum clockwise. Attitude is an important part of the style. Young men generally are fancy and grass dancers; middle-aged and elderly men, as well as young men, are straight and traditional dancers. The war dancers' steps coincide with the drumbeat and the tempo of the war dance song, which is usually composed of vocables. The drum beat is even and unaccented, except at certain transition points in the song, where it becomes louder.

The traditional dancer uses free style steps and motions and emphasizes movement of the head and shoulders that suggests the locomotion of certain birds, such as the prairie chicken. Facial expression is also emphasized. He wears a hair roach headdress of porcupine or, more likely, sisal fiber, which imitates the crests on birds. One feather bustle is attached to a beaded belt so that it stands out horizontally from the wearer. There is a cluster or rosette of feathers in the center of the bustle, two long side panels with feathers attached in rows, and two spikes or "horns" projecting out and up from the rosette. The bustle is patterned after a bird's spreading tail feathers. The dancer also wears arm "wheels" of feathers, which suggest wings, or beaded armbands. Beaded moccasins and a beaded front and back apron complete the most important parts of the outfit.

The straight dancer is restrained and dignified, with a more erect posture than the other war dancers, and he uses a walking step. He wears cloth tailored pants and a shirt, often ribbon trimmed, with two cloth-and-ribbon-trimmed trailers hanging from his neck and back rather than feathered bustles. He also wears a roach headdress with a feather, a silk kerchief, a long bandoleer, an apron and beaded belt, and moccasins.

The fancy dancer emphasizes footwork and speed. He spins, does knee-falls, and abruptly changes his posture. His outfit includes matching feather bustles, each with a large rosette in the center, at the dancer's neck and back. The back bustle attaches to a beaded belt, and some are "swing" bustles that open and shut like wings with the movements of the dancer. The feathers and beadwork are in a wide variety of bright colors. In addition to the two large bustles, the dancer wears a feathered roach as a headdress rather than a hair roach. Sometimes the headdress has a spreader so that the feathers move with the dancer. He also wears a beaded headband, a sequined and beaded front and back apron, a fringed cape or ribbon shirt, beaded cuffs and armbands (or arm feather wheels), a beaded shoulder harness, bells at the knees, anklets of white Angora fur, and moccasins.

The grass dancer puts emphasis on both the upper body and footwork. He shakes his shoulders, sways from side to side, darts quickly and changes directions, and appears to alternate between being off balance and recovering his balance. The grass dancer wears no bustle but, rather, heavily fringed cloth pants with long ribbons hanging from an apron. He also wears a fringed shirt, beaded belt, cuffs, armbands, head harness, shoulder harness, headband with a roach made from automobile choke cables, bells on his ankles, and anklets of Angora. He may wear a forehead rosette and beaded rosettes or feather clusters at the shoulders.

The head lady dancer also is expected to dance throughout the event. Women dancers have four dance styles (and occasionally a woman dances as a man in the fancy style). The traditional styles include the buckskin and cloth dress dancers. These dancers do a basic walking step. The buckskin dress has a beaded yoke and long fringe almost touching the ground. A woman wearing a buckskin dress also wears beaded leggings and moccasins, beaded and feathered hair ties, and carries a beaded bag and a shawl. The cloth dress dancer's dress reaches mid-calf and is often decorated with shells and made of broadcloth, cotton, or silk. She wears beaded leggings and moccasins and carries a shawl. Both these dancers wear beaded earrings and necklaces as well. The young fancy shawl dancers and jingle dress dancers contrast with the more conservative buckskin and cloth dress dancers, especially in the speed of their footwork. The shawl dancer has fast and elaborate footwork, spinning and manipulating the shawl she wears. This dancer wears a cloth dress just below or at the knee, usually made of satin, and beaded moccasins and leggings. Her shawl is elaborately decorated and trimmed with long fringe, and she also wears a beaded headband, hair ties, and a choker or necklace, or both. The jingle dress dancer uses a fast hopping step. Her cloth dress is mid-calf in length and is covered with horizontal rows of "jingles" made of the lids of snuff cans that clink when she moves. She wears moccasins and leggings, a headband, beaded jewelry, and carries a shawl. Children can choose from any of the dance styles.[5]

To participate in a dance as head dancer or in a powwow as one of the contest dancers, an individual must obtain an outfit, usually by calling on women who are kinspersons. They sew a shirt, bead moccasins and other regalia, and make cloth or buckskin dresses. Feather bustles worn by men and boys are usually purchased from one of the expert craftsmen who make these items, or a woman in the family may use old family bustles or headdresses to make a new one. Women who are not wearing outfits dance wearing a shawl over street clothes, and if a woman enters the arena—during a special, for example—it is proper for her to wear a shawl.

Host organizations include veterans, youth, ceremonial, and senior citizens groups as well as particular families. Sometimes an honorary elder is selected for a dance or powwow. At powwows, the flag of a deceased Cheyenne or Arapaho veteran is flown each day, and at the end of the day it is presented by an honor guard to the women of his family. Thus, relatives of the honorary elder and of the deceased veteran are drawn into supporting the event along with host organizations and head staff.

A powwow princess dances throughout the powwow and represents the pow-wow committee by appearing at other dances and powwows. The competition for this position involves a contest in which the families of the candidates try to raise money for the powwow; the girl whose family raises the most money is selected. Of course, the princess should be an individual who is in school and engaged in worthwhile community activities. She is expected to be unmarried and childless.

One of the most important ritual components during a dance or powwow is the special, a particular kind of giveaway ceremony. It takes two forms, a family giving away to the crowd in appreciation of an honor shown to a family member and the family of a head staff member giving away to other members of head staff. In a family's giveaway, at a dance or powwow, the family requests a particular song or type of song or songs from the head singer. During a war dance song, the family dances clockwise around the drum while people in attendance walk up and hand money to the honoree or a senior male member of the family. The donor may join in the procession, dancing with the family. During a gourd dance song, the men of the family form a line facing the drum and the women form a line behind them. People come up and place money in a hat on the ground in front of the honoree, or a shawl or Pendleton blanket is put on the honoree's shoulders. Sometimes one of a male honoree's female relatives will bring another woman up to dance behind the honoree, and the woman receives a gift, for example, a shawl that has been placed over the shoulders of the honoree.[6]

After the family dances, the honoree stands next to the emcee, and alongside of the honoree stand the senior women, with the younger women standing somewhat behind them. Males of the family may also be present, usually in the background. The women tell the honoree and the honoree tells the emcee who to call to come up and receive a gift. Shawls and dress or household goods are given away to women who have given gifts to members of the family in earlier dances or powwows. Shawls are made by women, and sometimes those received as a gift are refurbished by changing the fringe or adding decorative details, such as embroidery or appliqué. Women recognize shawls and often know who made or gave them away. These shawls circulate through the years, from giveaway to giveaway, until they look too worn to be suitable for a giveaway. At a memorial dance, items also may be given to persons who were helpful at the time of the death of the loved one. The family also will give away to the members of head staff at the dance, women receiving shawls, men blankets, and children baskets of candy and canned soda. At a benefit dance the family will give the sponsor cash or property (a basket of groceries or a shawl) that can be auctioned to the crowd to raise money. During the giveaway, the emcee will speak about the family and the individual being honored, pointing out, for example, their service to the community and their commitment to preserving Indian traditions.

In the special of a member of the head staff, the member's family gives a gift to each of the other members of the head staff: a blanket for the emcee, arena director, head singer, head male dancer or dancers, and head teen boy dancer; a shawl for the head lady dancer and head teen girl dancer; a basket of snacks and candies for the little boy and girl dancers; a shawl, blanket, and grocery basket for the host and co-host organizations. A shawl might also be donated to the singers at the drum, which they will have the arena director auction. Prior to the giveaway, the family requests a specific song or songs (usually a one-on-one). They dance clockwise around the drum, with the member of head staff and the senior women and usually a senior male from the family leading the procession. The honoree or a senior male usually holds a hat. While the family is war dancing, other relatives and friends, and especially relatives of other head staff, walk into the arena and place money in the hat or in the hand of the individual who is on head staff. They can then return to their seat or, more commonly, join the procession and dance with the family. A large group dancing behind the family reinforces the idea that they are important to the community and its traditions. In a one-on-one, after the war dance, the family and its supporters form horizontal lines for a gourd dance. The hat is placed on the ground, and people can come up at this time and put money in the hat and join in the gourd dancing. The money collected is donated to the sponsor at the completion of the giveaway.

"By Himself He Couldn't Do It": The Cultural Context of Dances and Powwows

Throughout all phases of the dances and powwows, cultural themes and values are expressed. Ritual symbols work to generate feelings of connectedness with others, that is, to create social and emotional bonds between the groups and individuals who participate in dances and powwows. One of the most important themes is that family connections and support are necessary and good. A good person helps his or her family and needs his or her family's help. A good person remembers his or her deceased relatives and their contributions to his or her well-being. Connections between families also are important, and all these social connections both facilitate and are facilitated by proper relations between people in the community and with supernatural forces.

"Family" is defined very broadly by Arapahos and Cheyennes. Arapaho terms for relationships are no longer used; English is the first language learned, and very few Southern Arapahos understand much of the native language. Only two or three can carry on a conversation with Northern Arapahos. A larger percentage of Cheyennes still speak their language, but they are generally elderly and decidedly a minority. But the ideas about kinship that informed the native terminology may still be present to a large degree. People who are referred to as "grandparents" include one's parents' parents and one's parents' aunts and uncles several degrees removed. These individuals refer to children of siblings and cousins as "grandchildren." "Aunts" include one's parents' siblings as well as their first cousins, second cousins, and beyond. "Uncles" are similarly defined. "Brother" and "sister" are terms often used to refer to first cousin, second cousin, and beyond. Of course, this network is a potential one; that is, not all relationships are activated. Just how emotionally close relatives are and how far they are prepared to go to help one another depends on many factors, including geographical proximity, past dealings, and marital ties. In addition to this collateral view of kinship, Arapahos and Cheyennes place great store upon "taking" (adopting) non-kin as relatives, which potentially enlarges the network of kin. People "take" one another as brothers and sisters and as parent and child. Most often this adoptive relationship is crosstribal.[7]

In Cheyenne and Arapaho life, much of the economic, political, and ritual activity has the extended family at its center. Individuals know they can potentially count on family members for a place to stay, loans, help getting work or benefits from government programs, support in native healing or other ceremonies, and, perhaps more important, nurturing in times of spiritual or social crisis. Individuals who want to start over, that is, change the course of their lives, will begin with attempting to repair or strengthen relations with close family members and with an appeal to relatives for help. Many people have to start over one or more times during their life spans, and extended family members help rehabilitate individuals' reputations and offer support when individuals attempt to change their lives.

Symbols of familial ties appear and are used by participants throughout all phases of dances and powwows. Particularly prominent is the symbolism inherent in dancing, standing in particular places, singing, using an American flag, giving away property, and sharing food. Dancing with an individual or a family is a public expression of commitment to the relationship and, ideally, of willingness to help "family" in material ways and to provide emotional support when needed. One can voluntarily dance with a family during a special or dance behind an honoree at the request of one of his or her relatives (in which case, the relative gives a gift to the one dancing with the honoree). Standing up with someone during a giveaway involves emotional support as well as a material contribution. The place one stands in relation to the honoree during a special reflects the nature of their kinship tie, and the recipient of a gift must come up to the honoree and shake his or her hand and usually the hands of the family members standing up with the honoree.

The use of a song associated with an individual, a family song, or a song composed by a family member can be highly charged emotionally, for in the Arapaho and Cheyenne view songs work to affect one's emotions, physical state, and spiritual essence and to connect people on all these levels. In this sense, then, songs are sung *with* as well as *for* deceased family members and for honorees. At one benefit dance, when the chiefs song was sung, the family of a recently deceased chief danced, then made a gift to the sponsoring organization. The chief's son had the emcee announce, "I still think about my dad. Honoring my dad like this, that's why I'm here and trying to help myself also [as he helps others by contributing to the benefit, he helps himself cope with feelings of loneliness due to the death of his father]." A song about a soldier killed in battle and composed by a relative reminds descendants of the loss they suffered, the pain of mourning, and the anguish experienced by the composer who "made" (composed) the song while mourning for his relative. Tears come easily to descendants when such a song is publicly sung. In other instances, pride in ancestors and commitment to the things that were important to them are expressed when relatives dance during a family song. When others help the family during an honor song, they express willingness to provide both social and emotional support.

The return of a veteran's flag to his female relatives is similarly charged emotionally. At one Fourth of July powwow, when a flag was being taken down by two veterans at the end of the day, the emcee (crying throughout) announced that the song being sung was made by the father of the deceased veteran. The man was killed in World War II, and when his father received the news, "he cried and cried. Maybe he made the song thinking about his son," one relative explained. The emcee interwove his own military experiences into the event, telling how when he was overseas he thought about home (and the possibility of not being able to return to his relatives). The flag was presented to the deceased veteran's daughter, who was also visibly moved. One of the emcee's duties is to verbalize these ideas about family and to praise people for living up to them in public, as well as in private, contexts. Veterans also may give speeches about camaraderie and about the pain of loss of comrades, in this way making an emotional connection to the veteran's family.

The giving of gifts to people to affirm or reaffirm a social bond is an important theme in all of these dances, and bonds are established among donors as well as between donors and recipients. When a family is having a special, people in attendance often say to one another as they get up to go out and dance with the family, "Shall we go help her?" Similarly, the emcee at an honor dance for a veteran addressed the people in attendance: "Fall in and help us out [get up and dance with the family]."

Individuals not part of an honoree's family often give away for the honoree during his special by placing a blanket or shawl around the shoulders of another dancer or setting money on the ground in front of that dancer and telling the recipient to go dance with the friend being honored. Thus, the donor publicly reinforces a bond with both the honoree and the recipient.

People giving away or having a special frequently have the emcee announce their feelings about family support. One woman, whose son was on head staff, had had a particularly difficult time trying to raise money for the powwow. Her mother and uncle had helped by contributing generously. She spoke to the crowd, saying she did not realize how important her relatives were in her life until this difficulty, then was overcome with emotion. Her mother rushed to her side, and they stood with heads bowed as the emcee continued to preside over the giveaway. At another powwow, one man, announcing for himself, thanked his relatives for help: "I can't afford this myself, but I consider myself very lucky because the Creator let me stay on this earth this long and because I got a lot of relatives. . . . I wouldn't be able to do this if I done it by myself. I have all this help from my friends, my relations, my brothers and sisters." The emcee also frequently mentions the names of the ancestors of head staff while they have their specials, reaffirming their ties to deceased as well as living relatives. It is obvious to all in attendance at dances and powwows that all the participants are representing not merely themselves but their family network and that whatever honor they receive, whether it is being chosen for head staff or winning a dance contest, they could not accomplish these things without the help of family.

The head staff special involves a gift exchange among head staff that is a completed transaction; there is no delay in a return, as in a family's special where recipients will give a woman in the donor family a shawl when they subsequently have a special at a dance in the future. In the head staff special the items are more likely to be quickly recirculated as well. The exchange symbolizes the unity of the members of head staff, how they work together for the common good. The extended family bond becomes a community-wide bond during the dance or powwow, as the members of head staff are generally drawn from different families. At the special for a powwow princess, who served on head staff for several dances other than benefit dances for the powwow she represented during her tenure, the girl's mother had the emcee announce that she was proud of her daughter "for the way she treats people who come around the drum," that is, for her support of many different families' efforts to express and support the community's values.

The monetary aspect of giveaways, and of dances and powwows in general, is downplayed by Arapahos and Cheyennes. When individuals are called to receive a gift, the emcee asks them to "come and shake hands" with the donor, not to come and receive a gift. As I discussed my observations about powwows with one man, he commented on my remarking that one dollar seemed to be the most common donation given to the honoree during a special: "People don't give 'one dollar.' That puts too much emphasis on money. It is any amount, large or small." The emphasis is rather on emotional support. An emcee speaking at a powwow expressed this theme thus: "The people of this community are very poor, as far as material things are concerned. It doesn't seem to bother them because whenever somebody needs help we're ready to do what we can to help them." After attending a benefit dance, I noted to some Arapaho and Cheyenne friends that the money spent by the sponsors was roughly equal to the amount they raised from the donations and raffles. My friends responded matter-of-factly that of course that was so, for the purpose was really social contact and social bonding (in this case, for a political cause), not profit. The monetary contributions one makes when dancing with the family are almost immediately given away by recipients to others in need, such as the sponsor of the dance. The shawls and blankets given away are distributed later to other kin, friends, or sponsors in need. This redistribution expresses empathy, a social bond with others, and a high regard for "family."

In speaking about sponsoring a dance or powwow, one frequent member of head staff remarked to me, "Food is the main thing." This is the general view—that the host or sponsor should "feed the people." Individual families also may prepare food and invite groups of people to come to their camp during a powwow in order to honor a relative or relatives. Those invited include elderly Arapahos and Cheyennes and often visitors. Again, the network of people who help and support each other is widened through the invitation to a meal. When a family or committee feeds, it is done without the public attention that a special brings. The emcee announces that the food is ready, and people form a line. The lack of attention paid to the generosity involved in feeding gives expression to the ideal that food is always to be shared freely. One should not be praised too much for that. Food is not to be refused, and whatever is not eaten should be carried away back to the recipient's camp or home, ostensibly to be eaten later.

An Arapaho orator serving as emcee expertly articulated how cooperation within and between families at the Barefoot Powwow expressed the ideals of unity and respect:

> Let's enjoy ourselves at this powwow. Take care of young children, your relatives, your friends. Talk to them. Say good things to them. If you've got something that you want to say that's bad about someone, just hold off; don't say it. Don't say anything bad about anybody. Pretty soon you're going to forget about it. And when you talk about people, talk good things to them, smile at them. Don't look for their faults, don't look for the problems that you might associate with them. Don't worry about it. That's what them old people used to tell me.

Quarrels in other contexts, political or familial, can affect and be affected by these dance gatherings. In one instance, there was a bitter recall election in one district; the vote was close, but the committee member was recalled. Attendance was down at that community's powwow, as people felt that the bitterness might intrude into the gathering itself. As one man observed, "The powwow wasn't well attended . . . because of what happened with the recall. . . . Families were split on the election. . . . People are upset so they avoided it." On the other hand, one family that had experienced a feud between two members used the occasion of a benefit dance to express reconciliation. A senior woman gave away for, or honored, the uncle who was embroiled in a dispute with her son, requesting the emcee to announce that she was giving away "so people can come back together and we can settle our differences." She and her brother embraced afterward.

As we have seen, women are at the hub of extended family activity in these gatherings. In the Arapaho and Cheyenne view, male and female spheres of authority and activity are found in most sociocultural institutions, not merely dances and powwows. These spheres are independent yet interdependent. One elderly Arapaho woman put this perspective succinctly: "Both men and women are needed to get things done. Each has a part. Women will push, where men won't. Women keep after something." What she means is that women take responsibility for executing things and initiating events in the lives of their relatives. They generally manage the household economy. They activate and reactivate family ties by visiting people whom they acknowledge as kin. Visiting takes place in homes but also at public gatherings. Public acknowledgment of kin ties is particularly important in a society where people may move away for a few years to find employment elsewhere. When they return, younger relatives may have had no personal contact with their kin.[8]

In general, women manage the life "careers" of their close relatives. They not only take the most responsibility for raising children but also initiate the ceremonies that facilitate the social development of children. For example, ceremonies such as the acknowledgment of public dancing for the first time, birthdays, graduations, aid for health crises—all are encompassed in the dances or religious rituals that women manage or for which they provide essential management skills. Adults seeking to, or eligible to, change status also are given a boost or even pushed toward these changes by women. An Arapaho man explained, "Women bring notice to people, call attention to them [by their activities in giveaways, singing, and suggestions]." They are central to their husband's position in society. They also influence the position of sons, brothers, and fathers. Often a man who loses his wife will retire from an active role, such as serving as a chief.

In chief initiations, the wife (or the woman who will support the man in his position—a mother, in a few cases) must participate in the ceremony. In Cheyenne chief initiations, "the wife sits behind the initiate on the outside of the tepee so she can hear the instructions," explained one Cheyenne chief. An Arapaho chief, telling how he was asked by two older chiefs to agree to be initiated, made it clear that "they asked us [his wife and him]." The wife of an Arapaho chief recalled, "Two chiefs came and asked him [to agree to be initiated]. He had a week to think it over. We talked about it. I thought it would be good for him to help his people more. I worked six months to get ready." "Getting ready" means to accumulate goods for a giveaway as part of the initiation ceremony as well as to prepare to feed the people in attendance. An Arapaho chief, recently a widower, had this to say about the chieftainship: "Women take care of everything in any home. We men just sit around and look on. When I was a[n active] chief, she cooked, gave things away. . . . There were others considered for chief but their wives wouldn't agree. Both must agree. The first time they asked me, I declined. Then they asked again. My wife said, 'Go ahead, we'll make out somehow.' I wouldn't be a chief if it weren't for her." Another Arapaho chief explained, "A chief does things with the support of his wife, mother, sisters. A man's family supports him. Some think that chieftainship runs in families. It's not hereditary but when a man's family supports him, it supports another family member. So they [the chiefs who select new chiefs] look for supportive families. What a chief does he does with the backing of his mother, wife, and sisters." Chiefs and their wives play key roles in dances and powwows, attending regularly and serving on head staff.

Religious ceremonies all have essential elements that can only be performed by women. This is true in both the Arapaho and the Cheyenne Sun Dance as well as in the Native American Church (peyote religion). One Native American Church leader explained it this way: "In Native American Church, in every fireplace, women always figured in. They handle the water and the last prayer in the morning. If the woman doesn't go along with the man, it's just half. You need both to make it complete. That's where the family comes from. Old-timers say when you have a family, children, grandchildren, you are ready to lead. Or you don't have nothing, you can do as you please. It revolves around family life; it has to. You [the man] have a purpose to sit down, advise, talk." He links the woman's sphere in social and spiritual life to her role as an essential partner to men in reproduction. In discussing the origin of the peyote religion, both Cheyennes and Arapahos say that the religion was brought to them by a woman. In general, then, the male and female roles, though different, were complementary. As one elderly Arapaho man put it, "Women were never excluded at any ceremonial event of the tribe. The laws they went by never excluded women because Mother Earth will bear a family when men can't. That is women's task [to generate life and, by extension, to nurture and to make things happen in the family generally]."

Giveaways are always viewed to be the work of women. As one woman explained, "Women give away because these are women's things [that are given away]." Women give away shawls and blankets and may also give money, as men do. The key role of women in giveaways is a favorite subject for the emcee. He makes comments, sometimes jokes, about the essential role women play in these public ceremonies as well as in the household and community in general. At one powwow, while the head singer was waiting for his wife, Lucy, and other female relatives to arrive with the goods the family was going to distribute, the emcee joked: "My friend up here always says 'He boss,' 'I'm the boss, what I say goes.' But he can't go until Lucy gets here, so we'll just wait around a bit longer. Boss man has to wait." Emcees often jokingly call for "the managers" (wives) to come up when it is time for a man's special.

In specials, a man and one or more women head the procession. The head staff always consists of both male and female dancers. Singing involves male and female contributions: women, many of whom are wives or relatives of the male singers, sit on the outer circumference of the drum and sing the female parts of the songs. Ceremonies involving veterans or veterans' flags require the participation of women, who, by doing so, offer testimony to the man's contribution and sacrifice, and in their emotional reaction to a deceased veteran's flag, they reaffirm his link to the community. Women commonly wear shawls that have their male relative's or husband's military record on the back. Shawls are painted with the man's name, rank, war in which he participated, time served, and emblem of service. The flag of a deceased veteran remains in the possession of one of his female relatives or his wife. At one honor dance for a veteran, the emcee gave this oration as the veteran danced around the drum carrying an eagle staff, proceeded by four women chosen to honor him: "Respect for our veterans, respect for our women, respect for our eagle staff. This is what we're doing, honoring our veterans, through these songs, through these womenfolk. Respect for our veterans, respect for our songs, respect for our every walk of life. These mothers, these sisters, these womenfolk do a lot of things for us."[9]

Thus, everyone in attendance knew the full implication and meaning of the emcee's words when he announced, in one instance for a family as the male honoree's mother gave away on his behalf, "She's still there with them, pushing and helping and picking up and helping out and carrying on. They want to say thank you publicly. That they appreciate you and your effort, your thoughts, your love for this family. May God bless you all the time you have left on this earth. They hope you have a nice way of life, good health."

Ideals about and attempts to connect with supernatural forces are evident in dances and powwows. One of the guiding premises of both Arapaho and Cheyenne religion is the concept of sacrifice, that giving up something attracts attention and pity or a favorable response from supernatural forces. Sacrifice of property is a prevailing theme in dances and powwows (in religious ceremonies, such as the Sun Dance and Native American Church rites, physical suffering is an additional way to sacrifice or give up something). A Cheyenne elder linked the giveaway to native religious and ethical traditions in this way:

The giveaway is an Indian custom by which an achievement or stage reached in life is recognized by the family giving away valued goods in honor of the occasion. It emphasizes that to Indian people material possessions are far less

268

important than family and friends and demonstrates the belief that the Creator will eventually replace what has been given, even if some hardship is felt at the time. In the Indian world to fail to be generous is to fail to show faith in life or respect for another and is considered a serious fault.

The special, then, in addition to connecting families, connects or facilitates good relations between the donors and supernatural forces. Giving to others is a way to receive aid from the Creator. Thus, one Arapaho man commented, "A giveaway is like a prayer to God." An elderly Arapaho woman explained, "They [Arapahos] believe in sacrificing their food; it always comes back." In other words, generosity brings a supernatural blessing.[10]

The other premise that underlies religious behavior is that human thought, especially when assisted by various mediums, can make things happen. It is in this context, then, that the emcee's urging of the crowd to suppress hostile thoughts and to think good thoughts must be understood. Prayer (including that with a pipe, steam, incense, and song) ascends to the supernatural world above. Both Arapaho and Cheyenne stories stress the role of thought and sound (songs) in the creation of the world and in the recreation or generation of states of being as well. In powwows and dances today, both these themes of sacrifice and the creative power of thought are expressed and acted out.[11]

"That's Where We're Different from Them": The Powwow as Critique

Dances and, especially, powwows, because they bring together large numbers of Cheyennes and Arapahos as well as people from other tribes and a few non-Indians, also are used as a forum in which Cheyennes and Arapahos can express their views on their colonial past. In these contexts, tribal members refute the idea that their celebrations are mere relics from the past, that their way of life is somehow inferior to that promoted by the wider society, and that the supervision and interference they experienced from the majority members of society have been helpful.

In Oklahoma, Native America is central to tourism. Indian imagery is used in tourist art and in the state's attempts to sponsor "Indian" ceremonies of various sorts for visitors. One such attempt was a "Sweat Ceremony Package for $39" to be offered at Roman Nose Lodge (named after the now deceased Cheyenne whose allotment is used for this state-operated recreational site). The ceremony was to be led by a member of the Creek Nation. Cheyennes made public protest of this attempt. In the words of Larry Roman Nose, "Our religion is being exploited." The charge of admission signifies to Cheyennes and Arapahos the commercialization of their way of life for the economic profit of non-Indians, and they make pointed reference to the fact that no admission is charged at powwows, for neither non-Indians nor Native Americans. Thus, from the Cheyenne and Arapaho perspective, the powwow is a gathering that stands in counterpoint to the town-sponsored events in the early twentieth century that showcased the tribes as relics from the past.[12]

One of the themes central to emcee oratory is that traditional ways, the teachings of Cheyenne and Arapaho ancestors or elders, have value and must be perpetuated. At one powwow the emcee made this statement: "A lot of them are gone, of those old people. But us younger ones have to continue the tradition that they left us. Because if we don't continue with these Arapaho traditions then we're going to become a part of this society, white society. And when we become part of it we're going to lose all of these good characteristics that stick with us as traditional Indians." He linked the valued teachings of the "old people" with repudiation of the life ways of "white society." This connection between powwow ritual and rejection of the pressure to assimilate into mainstream society is implicit in the emcee's statements about, and other symbolic expressions of, the importance of perpetuating Cheyenne and Arapaho traditions. The federal government targeted community gatherings in the effort to eradicate the Cheyenne and Arapaho way of life; the perpetuation of these gatherings with their associated giveaway ceremonies is viewed as evidence of the persistence of tradition in spite of the attempts made to repress it.

Like the camp circle, the circle of chairs surrounding the arena or room symbolizes the unity of the community situated in the midst of the wider society. In practical terms, the circle of chairs also works to exclude members of the dominant society. Arapahos and Cheyennes set up their chairs at powwows early in the day. In part they do this so that family members can reserve blocks of seats at convenient places. About the time that the evening program starts and non-Indians begin arriving, the new arrivals must put their chairs at the back of the ring of chairs or stand behind the seated Arapahos and Cheyennes. Thus, the setting up of chairs early in the day also allows the Indian community control over the spectator space outside the arena.

In the dances and powwows, Cheyennes and Arapahos affirm their own concept of kin or relations. In dancing with or standing up with an individual, the kin tie (regardless of the exact genealogical connection) is affirmed publicly. The Cheyenne and Arapaho view of gender relations, which was misunderstood and undermined by federal institutions, is similarly affirmed. Though undermined by the wider society, the roles of chief and headsman, of Native American Church member, and of native women are publicly honored in the context of the dance and powwow. The warrior's status—vilified in the Indian imagery of the wider society—is honored through the flag and honor guard rituals. The veterans who participate wear clothing that symbolizes both their service in the U.S. armed forces and their native warrior heritage (for example, honor guards sometimes wear war bonnets). There is also public affirmation of the important social and psychological work accomplished in the dance and powwow rituals, repudiating the Western notion that the celebrations are frivolous or primitive.

Singing is both a powerful symbol of community unity and a means to link humans and supernatural forces. The drum both symbolizes social unity and affects people emotionally so as to reassure them of their community's support. In many ways, songs and the act of singing itself can create and reinforce social ties between relatives (even between deceased and living relatives) and friends. Songs that are made for a veteran may be used by his or her relatives. When the song is sung in public, the family "is supposed to give away" to express their regard for the veteran and their appreciation to others for acknowledging both him and his family. Chiefs have songs that one Arapaho chief described as "pep songs" that talk *for* the chiefs and *to* the chiefs ("You chiefs, take care of this place" are the translated Arapaho words in one such song). The songs are said to urge the perpetuation of Indian ways.

The act of singing is supposed to take place in an atmosphere of goodwill and cooperation; this kind of unity radiates out on the crowd and contributes to the success of the event. One head singer explained it publicly through the emcee at a powwow in this way: "He is honored to be chosen as head singer, as head singer not only has to be a good singer but to know Arapaho songs and to be able to get along with the people at the drum." Occasionally the head singer feeds the people sitting at the drum sandwiches or a meal at his camp to show them that "by himself he couldn't do it; he always needs help," explained one singer. Thus, singers stress that, as one man put it, "Around the drum there is good feeling. At the Arapaho drum someone can ask someone to start a song and out of respect for the head singer ask him. Or the person asked could tell them to ask the head singer if it is o ᴋ."

In Arapaho and Cheyenne belief, songs link humans and supernatural forces or beings. For some, this belief is a vague understanding that they have from listening to others, older relatives or peers. For others, singing is an experience that puts them in direct contact with the supernatural. Individuals who make, or compose, songs do so as a result of a dream or vision or by intense concentration and meditation ("hard thinking"). This other-world experience is viewed as direct contact with the supernatural world, sometimes represented by an animal (that is, by the spiritual essence of an animal). Histories of types of songs and dances involve stories about encounters between humans and supernatural beings. Thus, songs and the act of singing them—in the past, as it is understood by Arapahos and Cheyennes today, and in the present—represent two-way communication between humans and supernatural forces. Songs are both a prayer for help and a message from helpful supernatural forces. The message is one of reassurance, for listeners as well as singers. As the crowd listens to the singing around the drum, people feel better if they are troubled, feel comforted if they are in distress. The singing is viewed by many, particularly singers and those knowledgeable about Arapaho and Cheyenne community life in the early twentieth century, as having a healing quality. People who are physically ill or troubled psychologically may be helped by the singing. Similarly, a dance may be sponsored for the purpose of helping an individual change the course of his or her life.

An elderly singer, who has made many songs and who was trained by old Arapaho singers in the early twentieth century, explained it this way: "At a gathering the beat of the drum was like a healing or prayer. It would pick people up; the sound of the drum made people feel better if they had sickness or a troubled mind. They danced around clockwise and when they completed the circle they were better." He connects the making of songs with a dream or vision experience in which a supernatural, usually in animal form, teaches the song to the recipient after he has made some sort of sacrifice: "In the old days they inherited songs through dreams. In the old days birds and animals understood all in general. Old people dreamed and put words in; it's a prayer song. Indians inherit that." For this man, specific songs and dances are linked to certain events with supernatural significance. Thus, he explains, "The gourd dance started from the Sun Dance. When they cut poles, the leaves would shake, make a sound: 'I think I'll gather a gourd.' The origin was from the sound of leaves. It comes from the Sun Dance. They felt so good doing it they wanted to dance from that." He also described how drums were once made: "A strong thinking, strong believing person hollowed out a trunk and stretched hide over one log. This was the first drum." His drum was made by an older man and given to him: "The person who originally had that, everything meant something. The deer was the being he had a relationship with—the way the rawhide is tied [laced through the drum] looks like deer ears. Now anyone makes a drum. But it used to be you had to sacrifice. . . . Everything used to have meaning. But if a tree is to grow it must be trimmed. So the restrictions are removed."

Middle-aged singers have the same understandings, if not the same experiences. A Cheyenne singer remarked to me that "the drum is a living thing. It has a spirit in it. . . . People who are sick go to the drum and soon they start moving to it and the sickness goes away. People who have emotional problems go to the drum and they start moving to it and they feel better. People who are mad at others go to the drum and they start moving and they forget and start dancing with the person they were mad at." One middle-aged Arapaho singer explained publicly at a powwow, "When I make a song I don't sit down and write; it just comes to me. My philosophy is that it is just up around me; I absorb it. . . . These songs that singers have put out, my philosophy is that these songs belong to the holy spirit, that just pass down here for us to use. So when we sing these songs around here, everybody that listens to them songs they get a blessing out of it. . . . That song is a contact between you and that holy spirit." And from another Arapaho singer: "Traditional songs talk. They talk to

God. There are other, social songs. . . . There is a link between thinking, the song, and things that happen. When Arapahos sing they are relaxed. People hear songs and it helps them deal with problems, feel better. This is because the songs link them to the holy spirit. Singers don't make people feel good, the songs do." The knowledge of the older singers is understood by their juniors, even though their songs generally come from "God" or a generalized supernatural force rather than from an animal spirit. Another middle-aged Arapaho singer explained, "They used to get songs from animals and imitate their sound. The first part is the animal's cry and as it gets lower the song starts." A young Arapaho singer explained how the blessing inherent in a song is transferred from the singer to the people: "The feelings of the singers when they sing affect the people." Thus, it is important that they have goodwill toward the other singers and "think hard" when they sing.

Individuals may experience a kind of transformation when they begin to sing at the drum. One case concerned a man who was often hostile and violent toward others, or headstrong. He was asked by a man and wife to be head singer at a dance for their son. The man was "changed"; "like a flower he bloomed," the man's friends said.

Songs have a structure that expresses the circularity of life. The starting phrase of a song is usually repeated four or seven times. The number four conveys the idea of the four directions (up, down, and center make the number seven) and the four seasons. The circular procession and the circle of the drum circumference represent unity. This idea is a virtual platitude among Cheyennes and Arapahos today. The circle represents the unity of all life, of society in the ideal, and of the generations (the circle of life). Sitting or moving in a circle reinforces the feeling of belonging, of unity with others, and helps motivate feelings of goodwill toward others. Even in the rectangular community halls, the dance participants' chairs are arranged in a circle and the drum is always in the center of the room.

The opening prayer at Blue Sky Powwow, held in Geary on the Fourth of July in 1992, was given by an elderly Arapaho man: "Bless this drum, all these songs they sing. You gave them to us in our minds so we could express them through our voices, praising you in every way. Things [that] take place around this arena, will be [he "thinks hard" so that they will be] a blessing to each and every one of us." He attempts here to fuse supernatural power, the good thoughts of everyone present, and the symbols of connectedness inherent in the arena or camp circle to create both social unity and healing for individuals. The symbolism surrounding the camp circle, drum, and songs all reinforces the idea of the dance gathering as a healing event that is considered to have religious implications by the Cheyennes and Arapahos, implications that they are aware their non-Indian neighbors do not understand. Like Cheyennes and Arapahos in the past, people today affirm their own perspective on religion through participation in dances and powwows and in overt statements like that of a Cheyenne man who told the *Watonga Republican,* "We pray for the same things as other churches, and we all pray to the same supreme being."[13]

The giveaway ceremonies and the public feasts affirm the generosity of Cheyennes and Arapahos and contrast that generosity with the lack of it in the wider society. Giving away property and sharing food are publicly proclaimed as virtues, not signs of weakness or immorality (as federal officials suggested in the past), and the quality of generosity is contrasted with the character of the "white people" who have been and continue to be so critical of Cheyenne and Arapaho life ways. The emcee often speaks on this theme. As an example, the following is one emcee's speech at a powwow:

We're not in love with that money; we're not in love with material things. That's what those old people taught us. They told us, don't ever fall in love with that money. Don't even hold that money up to a very high standard. . . . That type of character belongs to the dominant society. White people like to have lots of things. They like to have lots of furniture. They like to have two cars, maybe a boat. They don't like to give anything away unless they're going to get something back in return. That's where we're different from them. We might seem poor to them. But we're rich in our heart. . . . We're still able to feel sorry for people. We're still able to show empathy and sympathy for people. . . . We don't worry too much about trying to get rich material-wise, because we know that type of character is not very good in terms of our religion.

This emcee also is affirming the emotional rather than material emphasis that "giving away" has in the context of a powwow—that donors have empathy for other Arapahos and Cheyennes.

The head staff giveaway ceremony is a particularly significant development. As discussed in chapter 3, this ritual developed in the context of the urbanization of the dance and powwow organizations. That is, in the 1960s the local communities were undergoing an economic transformation with the return of many individuals who had pensions or who had advanced training that prepared them for new positions in tribal government. Economic differentials developed at the same time the florescence and revitalization of dance traditions were taking place. In the head staff giveaway, each individual, regardless of economic means, receives one standard gift from each of the other members of the head staff group and gives one standard gift to each of the others. Those who are not able to afford to buy these gifts receive help from friends and relations. Thus, for example, an affluent head dancer is not able to give more generously than an impoverished arena director. The head staff giveaways take most of the time relegated to giveaways at dances and powwows, such that this representation of equality gives expression to the value placed on egalitarianism by Cheyennes and Arapahos—the idea that each individual is entitled to respect from other Cheyennes and Arapahos regardless of his or her economic circumstances. The custom also ensures a broad-based network of participants that includes elderly and young, rural and urban, those with years of powwow experience and relative newcomers to community dances. In these specials, individuals put various amounts of money in the honoree's hat; the exact amount contributed by each individual is not known, so, again, all donors are equal in the view of the participants.

Dance and powwow activity is not merely the expression of "Indian" or tribal identity. The giveaway ceremony is not merely a way to maintain social ties. These ceremonies both publicly confront the ideology with which Cheyennes and Arapahos have had to contend and reinforce among Cheyennes and Arapahos the spirit of defiance and resistance that has helped them perpetuate their way of life as it is historically constructed at any particular point in time. A Cheyenne tribal member wrote to the editor of the *Watonga Republican* that, despite the fact that "our careers were planned out by the [federal] government . . . we mean to hold on to our identity through our religion, cultural ways, language and art." That awareness and repudiation of supervision by the dominant society is frequently expressed during dances and powwows by the emcee's joking about Cheyenne and Arapaho subordination. One example is the following, told to a large crowd at a powwow by one gifted emcee: "An Indian, Whiteman, and Blackman were trying to get in heaven. The Whiteman said, 'I went to church all the time and gave ten percent of my income.' The Blackman said the same. The Indian said, 'I didn't do anything; I was under the B I A.' Saint Peter said, 'Let him in; he's already been through hell.' "[14]

8
"Looking for High-Up Places"
HEGEMONY, CONSCIOUSNESS, AND
HISTORICAL EXPERIENCE

Many times during the course of my fieldwork I heard Cheyennes and Arapahos tell the story about the crabs in the bucket—always with reference to political contexts. Narrators reflecting on why the metaphorical crabs were bent on dragging each other down suggested that individuals with aspirations to reach "the top" saw others as a threat to their ambitions. Narrators also suggested that it was the nature of individuals when they perceived themselves insulted to fight back in kind. Careful attention to the discourse in quarrels between business committee members and between committee members and dissidents shows a focus on defending perceived self-worth. Defense of personal valuation is linked to efforts to accomplish something that would bring public recognition. Both the desire to accomplish things in tribal politics on behalf of the people and the belief that others will challenge one's worth have developed from the historically specific experiences of the Cheyennes and Arapahos as subordinated populations in western Oklahoma. What began as a sense of personal devaluation by the wider society in the nineteenth century now includes the expectation of potential devaluation from tribal officials as well as non-Indians. This theme is reflected in the speech of a business committee candidate running for office in the 1990s: "We are the underdog. It makes me want to prove to the outside world, I'll make my way to the top, so people in the district can hold their heads up and say we are going somewhere. We have been ran down, trampled on for years. We have just taken it. I'm not that kind of person." The message to potential voters is that the candidate will defend constituents not only from being "trampled on" by the dominant non-Indian society but also from being abused in some way by the business committee. Let us look at these linked themes—the aspiration to achieve great things and the apprehension about being devalued—as they are expressed today.

In talking about their experiences on the business committee, members and former members stress that they resorted to offensive tactics against other committee persons in response to being attacked in some way. One committee member justified his vote to withhold the salary of another by saying that that individual once voted to withhold his pay. Another member explained his boycott of a committee meeting as retaliation for denial of a trip authorization when others were traveling. One member, widely regarded as vindictive toward opponents, commented, "The new bunch that got on treated me like a step-child. They would start their meetings without telling me." Another member of this committee remarked that the other business committee members "really were abusive toward" and apt to "make fun of" this member. Another committee member, who became a business committee opponent, complained that the others on the committee treated him "like a step-child" by not putting him on important subcommittees. One feud between two members of one of the business committees began when one man gave unsought advice to the other and the latter responded by rudely telling his colleague to keep his opinions to himself. Attempts to remove a member or to support recalls of members impress the target of such action as personal attacks that deserve retaliation.[1]

Business committee members experience their constituents' criticism and opposition as a personal attack and express outrage at the way some constituents treat them. A committee member was quoted in the tribal newspaper thus: "I have been accused of stealing toys for the children. I was told that someone saw me putting the toys in my car. I did put the toys in my car and brought them to the tribal complex, as there was not very many left. That's the thanks you get for trying to do something for the C & A people. We have many that complain, but they don't try to help. So I'll let someone else do something for the children this Christmas." Another complained, "Abuse from people is a haphazard [sic] of being on the business committee. Verbal and physical abuse. It makes a person retreat from visibility. A lot of people have a put-down attitude." The sense that constituents attack committee members unfairly encourages members to retaliate, for example, through lawsuits in the tribal court or invalidation of recall petitions.[2]

Constituents explain that they oppose tribal officials because these officials devalue them. In other words, an individual feels insulted or slighted, then joins or organizes a dissident group in opposition to individuals on or projects of the business committee. Individual constituents describe their dissidence as emanating from being personally picked on, dominated, insulted, or ignored. When the business committee decided to go to tribal court to challenge the election board's right to validate a recall petition in 1985, a member of the board urged the committee to "not sue me"—the lawsuit was perceived as a personal attack. One tribal member remarked to me that an individual, who as the leader of dissident activity in the 1980s was an avid opponent of contracting the Concho School, was originally in favor of contracting: "Then he got fired [from a tribal job] and he was opposed [to it]." When the candidacy of an individual was challenged in a 1993 election board hearing, a tribal member commented to me, "The election board is just picking on [this candidate]." Another tribal member, explaining why he agreed to serve on the election board, pointed to the business committee's "hassling" the Health Advisory Board, on which he served. He got on the election board: "That was the only way I could fight back," he said. Even though the business committee is constrained by federal guidelines, dissidents who live in Oklahoma City (a large segment of the potential electorate) may feel personally undermined when their efforts to obtain services are denied. To give one more example, individuals who present a recall petition that is subsequently invalidated frequently protest that action and expand their opposition into other spheres of committee activity.[3]

Complaints of constituents in general frequently center on the perception that tribal officials dictate to or dismiss tribal members. For example, one Arapaho woman at a community meeting in 1993 argued passionately, "We have to take things shoved down our throats. We should shove back. We are the tribal council, the governing body." Another tribal member, one of the dissidents in a 1988 meeting, put it this way, "We shouldn't have anyone dictating to everyone. This place [the tribal office] should be shut down." At a business committee meeting where the committee could not make a quorum, a tribal member in attendance angrily commented, "We have to wait and wait for them . . . to make their grand entry. The only difference between them and us is they are drawing $25,000." The allusion to the grand entry, which in the powwow context is a legitimate way for Cheyennes and Arapahos to be honored, here is used to express the feeling that committee members were claiming a status they did not merit. At a tribal council meeting in 1993, when a group of business committee members and their supporters left the meeting and, in so doing, broke the quorum, a woman grabbed the microphone: "See what the tribal council means to them! We are the people. They just walk out on us!" A dissident, quoted in the *Watonga Republican* in 1980, explained why compromise and cooperation were not possible between the committee and opponents: "It would be good if we could all work together. But a line has already been drawn. . . . When we try to meet with the business committee, they don't show up. When you call long distance, they put you on hold and forget about you." One member of the opposition in the 1980s explained his involvement this way: He [a business committee member] had to be put in his place in the general meeting [tribal council]. I was tribal council chair, against him. In his district he was so sure of himself he was not paying attention to his people. . . . He ignored people. There was also envy. . . . People were jealous and he didn't associate like he used to. . . . He was a bigshot." In all these constituents' comments, the suggestion is that the committee members are guilty of elitism, of not respecting their fellow tribal members. The commitment to getting one's share, or to receiving per capita, is an expression of the desire to have one's worth recognized, thus, the intense emotional commitment to per capita even though the actual amount of these payments is usually only a few dollars. Tribal officials may be accused of elitism if the views of a minority dissident group do not prevail, if tribal council resolutions are not approved by the BIA, if committee meetings are canceled or delayed, or if people attending a tribal council meeting are denied time to speak (because the meeting adjourns or the comments are ruled out of order). The perception of being ignored provokes accusations of dictatorship or abuse of power.[4]

When opposition tactics are successful, individuals feel that their own abilities are affirmed. One man spoke to this point by telling the story about the two fishermen with buckets of crabs. Afterward he commented, "People *build themselves up* with this criticism. When they see someone trying to make it, trying to do good, there is jealousy" (italics mine). Another man, describing a ceremonial group that was publicly criticizing his own, remarked: "They want to be known [for] doing something great." At a tribal council meeting in 1986, a dissident urged the others not to support a particular business committee proposal, arguing that if they were to give the committee authority to do something, "We're not going to have anything left" (that the "outs" will lose face through bestowing authority on tribal officials). A dissident leader in another meeting in 1980 told the crowd to support the dissidents so that the business committee "will be nothing." One other tribal member reflected, "Our people resent people, think people 'try to be better' than they. Instead of being supportive, they want to pull you down. They say you are moving too fast, getting too much recognition. Yet they don't try to help; they just want to be 'the one' without doing the work. A lot of time people will run around tearing people down to build up their ego." A committee member said of a dissident group in 1986, "They want recognition—that's what it's about." In conversing with me, an elderly man, who previously had served on the business committee, bemoaned the results of antagonism between constituents and tribal officials: "When there is a good one crawling up [again, the crab image], they drag him back down."[5]

An observation about business committee members, made by themselves as well as by tribal employees and others, is that, while a committee member may assume office with the intention of staying in touch with his constituents and following their wishes, he or she soon begins to ignore his constituents and colleagues in order to pursue individual ambitions. One tribal member summarized thus: "People think 'Nobody has the answer but me.' " Or, to return to our two fisherman analogy, one tribal member made this complaint in a public meeting during an election: "We have enough people saying 'I, I, I did.' That person stands alone, for himself. It's a cycle for our tribes. A bunch of crabs pulling each other down in the bucket." One long-term tribal employee characterized the business committee members' attitude this way: "They act very arrogant, all of them. They [voters] take [elect] them off the street [that is, they are not better qualified than the other tribal members], but, even so, they begin acting superior. They become like your mother-in-law [that is, bossy and arrogant, according to this individual]. . . . The committee members all challenge program directors' decisions, even when they know nothing about it." An individual who is elected to the committee often feels that he or she can make a contribution that he or she has been prevented from making by the non-Indian society. If other tribal members are critical of these aspirations, the committee member may come to feel that he or she is being treated disrespectfully, and this, Cheyennes and Arapahos often say, leads to the committee member's ignoring constituents or treating them rudely. In characterizing committee members' behavior in general, each committee member attributes these traits to others but not himself or herself.

Others point out that the nature of the job itself encourages individuals to feel self-important. One committeeman's wife explained, "When a person gets on the business committee they go to high-up places [for example, congressional offices, the office of the B I A area director, lavishly appointed corporate offices, workshops and training sessions where the accommodations are more luxurious than what most people have encountered] and start thinking it's them [who are important], not the tribe. They forget about the tribe." Another individual, experienced in tribal government, pointed out, "The business committee today is bolstered, made to feel [unrealistically] important by the federal agencies that say they must attend various meetings ["high-up places," in the words of the committeeman's wife]. This helps justify the agencies' existence and budgets."

The only opportunity to make one's way to the top, or so it seems to many local Arapahos and Cheyennes who do not want to leave their relatives, home communities, and associated traditions to live in urban areas, is to become a tribal official or to become prominent in the arena of tribal politics in some other way, such as leading groups of dissidents. Political discourse reveals that tribal officials and dissidents alike call for public recognition of their worth and are committed to defending it. In defending personal valuation, constituents try to thwart the committee's aims, but they do not make a serious challenge to the institution of the business committee. Dissidents, particularly leaders, frequently run for election, and they usually become committee supporters when a close relative or close friend becomes an official. When there is denial of a job, house, or emergency assistance, when a motion in tribal council is ruled unconstitutional, or when an individual is denied the right to vote or run for election, then opposition groups form. When committee members deal with opposition by criticizing opponents personally or blocking avenues of redress through the privileges of office (such as through their control over the budget or over employees or their influence over law enforcement), dissidence becomes more fervent and widespread. Most tribal members change affiliation over the years, from supporting officials to opposing them, perhaps with periods of "standing back." Tribal members often characterize this pattern as a cycle. One man described this cycle in a letter to the editor in the fall of 1989: "Every new election we get new members and the same problems—the business committee against the tribal members." Reflecting on recent political events, another tribal member said, "Before these [current] business committee members got on, they were hustling for gas like the rest of us. When they get off they are whining about the business committee, too. I even saw one at a [dissidents'] meeting (laughs)." A tribal employee commented to me, "It is just a cycle. Whatever good these ones [current business committee] do will be undone by the next. People see something good being done and someone doing good. Then they think, 'I can do better,' and try to knock him off." Again, the crabs-in-a-bucket image.[6]

The seeming preoccupation of Cheyennes and Arapahos with personal valuation is understandable, given their position within the western Oklahoma social context. To accommodate settlers, the federal government opened the reservation and transferred most of the land to them. Federal officials rationalized these actions, and the subsequent sale of the allotted lands that remained, by characterizing Indians as incapable of making good use of their land. Economic exploitation in the form of low wages, substandard education, and discrimination in employment also was justified by negative characterizations of Indian character and ability. As Cheyenne and Arapaho poverty worsened, federal agents increased their supervision over the remaining property and income, even inspecting individual households for efficiency and cleanliness. Federal operatives refused to acknowledge the local discrimination faced by the Cheyennes and Arapahos when they tried to compete economically with their settler neighbors. As the settlers took over the Cheyennes' and Arapahos' land base, leaving them in possession of small parcels of land surrounded by settler farms and towns, they transformed the social landscape so as to make Cheyennes and Arapahos a small preyed-upon minority. Cheyennes and Arapahos interacted daily with settlers, and in public dialogue settlers demeaned them on virtually a daily basis. Routinely ridiculed and insulted in face-to-face contacts and cheated in business matters, they found their treatment rationalized in a settler discourse that characterized them as incompetent and morally deficient. The participants in tribal politics in the 1960s and 1970s had experienced these conditions growing up in rural Oklahoma. The Arapaho leader Lime spoke to their experience when he tried to explain to federal officials in 1926 that Cheyenne and Arapaho children were "kept back and are considered as inferior and all the white children are considered superior and so it is impressed in the minds of our children."[7]

In postwar years, Cheyennes and Arapahos understood that the high expectations raised by New Deal reforms had not been realized. Still stalked by poverty and closely supervised, instructed, and interfered with by federal and local authorities, they also faced being characterized as less advanced than their non-Indian neighbors. Public schools continued to expose children, who later would be participants in post-1975 tribal politics, to ridicule and to the message that they were not as capable as non-Indians. In 1989 a parent in Watonga explained it in terms quite similar to Lime's: they were "programmed to think stereotypes about Indians," not to think "good about ourselves." In the 1950s the federal government transplanted many Cheyennes and Arapahos to more "civilized" communities, away from their homes in the rural districts. In urban areas they faced exposure to a generalized negative Indian imagery. Now, in the 1990s, demeaning characterizations are less overt but persist nonetheless. From time to time specific statements or actions from officials or non-Indian neighbors are directly challenged, but, from the Cheyenne and Arapaho perspective, prejudice against Indians remains a factor in their daily lives. In this context, Cheyennes and Arapahos have developed great sensitivity to devaluation, and they aspire to reach the "high-up places" from which they feel they have been excluded. In the words of one participant in business committee politics, they want to "prove to the outside world" that they are making their way "to the top," "going somewhere."

Throughout this process of devaluation, the federal government also directly attacked the institutions of chiefdomship so as to encourage Cheyennes and Arapahos to rely on individual enterprise and to lose confidence in tribal leaders. At first federal officials were unsuccessful. Individuals realized ambitions and achieved prestige by conforming to the Cheyenne or Arapaho authority structure and cooperating economically with other members of their band under the direction of headmen. From the time when Cheyennes and Arapahos settled on the reservation to the turn of the century, when land sales began, leaders "earned" their positions in agreed-upon ways, and Cheyennes and Arapahos evaluated their performance according to how successful they were. Men became influential by achieving recognition for war honors, attaining economic prosperity through owning cattle and freighting (which required the possession of large horse herds), and demonstrating the ability to persuade others to cooperate—all of which they achieved with supernatural assistance.

In fact, the federal government helped reinforce the authority of headmen and intermediary chiefs. Headmen distributed federally issued rations, cattle, and annuity goods, in this way continuing to provide for others and to coordinate group work efforts. Intermediary chiefs (as a rule, chosen from the ranks of headmen) were advocates for treaty relations, working to persuade federal officials to honor agreements. Chiefs were subject to review (or mockery, as they put it) by people in their bands, but generally they were perceived as successful until sometime after the opening of the reservation to the settlers. Cheyennes and Arapahos were aware of the Americans' negative characterizations of their way of life, and chiefs took responsibility for rejecting those characterizations publicly. They refuted American claims that supervision was in the Indians' best interest and challenged the demeaning representations of Cheyennes and Arapahos. They compared their way of life with that of the Americans and found the latter to be incompetent, corrupt, and immoral.

Beginning in the 1890s, tribal funds were distributed to individuals and some individuals collected lease payments. Still, individuals could only achieve personal valuation by accepting the authority of the chiefs and ritual authorities and by contributing to the needs of others in the district. Gradually, however, the opening of the reservation resulted in the loss of much of the land base used for agricultural and herding activities and reduced the need to freight supplies by wagon; therefore, headmen had greater difficulty organizing group labor projects or supporting large numbers of followers.

During the first three decades of the twentieth century, Cheyenne and Arapaho political life began to be transformed in a way that encouraged individuals to rely less on others in their community for economic support and to conform less to the traditions associated with values of cooperation and sharing. The loss of an adequate land base for agriculture made headmen less able to provide for others and made it impossible for individuals to make an adequate living by working cooperatively. All individuals relied on wage work and cash payments from leases and sales of allotted land, and this dependence on cash precipitated competition among relatives as well as Cheyennes or Arapahos generally. Headmen and chiefs struggled against other individuals for access to income. This struggle over access to money, much of it in the context of heirship hearings, generated mutual suspicion and undermined ties between individuals and their extended kin and family members in a particular district. Some got more than their share, Cheyennes and Arapahos believed.

Federal officials had little need to ally with chiefs; instead they "negotiated" with individuals over land and income matters. By the 1920s, many Cheyennes and Arapahos had come to understand that the federal government rejected the legitimacy of chieftainship, and, therefore, while chiefs still were respected for past accomplishments as advocates (as well as warriors), they could no longer defend Cheyenne and Arapaho interests. At the same time, chiefs expanded their role in the ceremonial life of their districts, where they could be effective in organizing these rituals. People in the districts continued to provide a critique of the ideology Americans used to support exploitation of Cheyennes and Arapahos, but it was subtler than the public statements of the previous century that directly criticized Americans. Desperately poor now, and needful of the goodwill of townspeople, native critics made their views known in places like the little-noted Indian column in a local newspaper and in the ceremonial camps.

Elderly chiefs publicly articulated the Cheyenne and Arapaho view of the history of colonization and continued to struggle to refute ideologies of individualism that demeaned tribalism and chieftainship. As we saw in Tobacco's debate with the commissioner of Indian affairs, chiefs insisted that the history of treaty relations be remembered, recognized, and respected. They refuted the federal officials' characterization of assimilation policy as helpful and honorable. This view of history was a charter for chiefs in their dealings with federal agents and was discussed in council meetings in the large camps, where many younger men learned it.

By the 1950s, a large group of Cheyennes and Arapahos was residing away from the rural communities, encouraged by the federal government to relocate in order to obtain employment and become part of mainstream America. For these people, new ways of attaining personal valuation developed in this urban context, including working toward a military career, higher education, and civil service employment. The Civil Rights movement (including the message of "Red Power" advocates) affected many, particularly those born in the 1940s and 1950s, encouraging a spirit of resistance to perceived injustice and an appreciation for native ritual tradition. Because of the employment opportunities in Oklahoma or nearby Kansas and Texas, many tribal members were able to return to western Oklahoma periodically to participate in tribal politics and ritual activities (in contrast to remote reservation communities such as the Northern Arapaho, where urban relocation meant moving far away).

Earlier, in the late 1930s, the federal government had succeeded in pressuring the Cheyennes and Arapahos to accept an elective form of government that would administer funds and make decisions about the allocation of tribal resources. In the 1930s and 1940s, district councils still made major decisions and committee members articulated their districts' views. Old and young men in the districts tried to compromise so that the interests of both could be addressed, and several young men studied the history of treaty relations. New Deal funds were channeled to the Cheyenne and Arapaho business committee but in inadequate amounts, so that the committee had difficulty convincing people it was successful and addressing constituents' suspicions about whether some tribal members were getting more than their share. In the mid-1950s, the committee finally succeeded in winning a legal claim for monetary damages for treaty violations, and the publicity surrounding this development attracted the attention of urban Cheyennes and Arapahos, who became involved in tribal politics and challenged the business committee's leadership and the treaty model of tribal government (or tribalism). The self-identified outsiders who won seats on the committee showed others how political activity could be used both to defend one's worth and to do "great things."

These "outsiders" introduced a different view of the relationship between individual and tribe and of how business committee affairs should be conducted. Individualism, expressed as the per capita distribution of tribal assets, served as a model for their political activity. These individuals had not apprenticed themselves to the old committee members to learn the tribes' "historical background," as one old Arapaho man put it. Many had not grown up in the districts, where social pressure moved individuals toward consensus and civility. Relying on the local media, they also promoted a discourse about the old committee members that I have argued was hegemonic. That is, negative characterizations of tribal government that were being advanced in the wider society were appropriated and used in confrontations with committeemen. Local media accounts that referred to the business committee as "needing help" and lacking "integrity" portrayed tribal government negatively and ignored the role of the federal government in creating problems for tribal government. Federal officials' characterizations of native leaders (not "business-like," not financially "responsible," incompetent, not doing "real work") were part of the individualism then promoted in the 1950s, and in these characterizations the BIA avoided accepting responsibility for the tribes' economic problems. The rhetoric of Red Power proponents (for example, American Indian Movement discourse) portrayed the business committee form of government as a group of "BIA yes-men" who were corrupt. Thus, constituents were encouraged to view abuse of power, political incompetence, and graft as inherent in tribal government: from this perspective, the old tribal leaders were backward, incapable of doing tribal business effectively, and guilty of taking more than their fair share (for example, in advocating the programming of claim money, which the business committee would administer). Sensitive to devaluation, people suspected that programming was a way to disadvantage or ignore tribal members.

In the rural districts, many people, already suspicious of the business committee, were receptive to these characterizations. The arrival of War on Poverty funds in the 1960s and 1970s, never adequate to meet people's expectations, encouraged their suspicions that some individuals took more than their fair share. In the 1970s, constituents began to overtly oppose not only a paternalistic federal government but also the Cheyenne and Arapaho business committee activity, characterizing that activity negatively with the same descriptions used by outsiders. This new discourse encouraged overt resistance to devaluation and dovetailed with developments in the Civil Rights movement and with the spirit of individualism that arose from the contention over the claim and the constitution. The outsiders provided leadership in the revision of the Cheyenne-Arapaho constitution, revisions that incorporated the concept of the tribe as a collection of individuals rather than a corporate entity.

Cheyenne and Arapaho intermediary leadership was to a large extent a casualty of federal policies. But what of ritual leadership? Federal officials also attempted to use economic sanctions to destroy Cheyenne and Arapaho ritual traditions, and they and many settlers in western Oklahoma demeaned native ceremonies. How did ritual authorities fare under these conditions, and how did Cheyennes and Arapahos respond to negative characterizations of their ceremonial life?

Federal officials were less successful in undermining ceremonial gatherings than the headman and chief traditions. Local communities did not need federal recognition of ceremonial authorities, and they developed institutions of sub-terfuge that mitigated repressive sanctions. Though opposed by federal agents, camp life was not as subject to surveillance and sanction as property management and formal education, which were the focus of federal activity in the late nineteenth and early twentieth centuries. Moreover, army officers in the reservation era and residents of settler towns in western Oklahoma actively encouraged gatherings and old-time dances and feasting, even though they also disparaged these ceremonies. Thus, ritual life was both encouraged by some sectors of non-Indian society and ineffectively opposed by federal officials. The perpetuation of activities in the rit-ual sphere did not depend on obtaining resources from the dominant society but rather on the extent to which these rituals met deep-seated emotional needs of Cheyennes and Arapahos.

The extensive social transformations of the late 1950s and 1960s also had reper-cussions for ceremonial life. The Red Power movement and the return of hundreds of veterans to Cheyenne and Arapaho communities worked to create a revitaliza-tion of dance activity and a significant increase in numbers of participants. The cer-emonies no longer focused on relationships within the rural districts but reflected the urbanization of the population—people traveled long distances to participate, and powwow committees had a pan-district and urban composition. The powwow activity offered an outlet for individuals to gain recognition and could be pursued in urban as well as rural contexts. The dance organization and opportunities for recognition therein became stronger at the same time chieftainship was being re-defined as a position with ceremonial rather than political authority. In fact, dance activity became a focal point for many new chiefs. In the early twentieth century, holiday camps lasted for a few weeks at a time, and there was reciprocal entertaining between districts. During the camps, people engaged in gift giving, councils, and other activities that reinforced both the authority structure based on chieftainship and values of cooperation and sharing in everyday activities. In contrast, in the late 1950s the powwows lasted two or three days and served as a means for individual recognition and a way to symbolically reinforce values associated with traditional life. Chiefs figured in these ceremonies, often serving on head staff.

From the Cheyenne and Arapaho perspective, the perpetuation of gift giving and dances and the associated beliefs about supernatural sanction for these activ-ities served as testament to the success of native leadership and the value of Chey-enne and Arapaho traditions. These dance rituals are the product of cooperative political activity in which authority roles have broad community acceptance and contributions of others are publicly acknowledged without challenge. Individuals and groups in cooperation are publicly praised. Dance and powwow activities sym-bolize generalized respect for others, connectedness between tribal members, social equality, and appeal for supernatural support. These symbols generate powerful emotions that help to move people to cooperate in the context of public ritual. The affirmation of individual and group value is celebrated in dances and powwows and serves as a counterpoint to American views about Cheyenne and Arapaho kinship, gender relations, leadership, economic relations, and religion. Perpetuation of the dance organization served as a form of resistance to the colonial encounter and was reproduced generation after generation. The idea that Cheyenne and Arapaho people have survived as a distinct community with culturally specific values and institutions is generally embraced and is prominent within public discourse, particularly in the context of dances and powwows.

Why is there confrontational conflict in tribal government and cooperation in the powwow arena? Why is so much of the political discourse in the tribal government sphere hegemonic, yet counter-hegemonic discourse is common in dance and powwow activity? This complex pattern developed in the context of western Oklahoma, where the expansion and consolidation of U.S. interests in collusion with settler interests stripped the Cheyenne and Arapaho people of the means to be economically self-sufficient and denied their political intermediaries the means to organize the community to prosper economically. In conjunction with this was a discourse that attributed the poverty of natives to character flaws, to the "natural" incompetence of both leaders and individuals. Through these historical experiences, the Cheyennes and Arapahos came to suspect that their chiefs and elected leaders were inept or corrupt and that economic cooperation would be less successful than individual entrepreneurship. Small victories in prior decades kept alive a nonhegemonic tradition that lends support to the sovereignty movement, and officials attempt to draw on this tradition, but hegemonic influences also gained a foothold in the sphere of tribal government. In the ritual context, individuals poor or not could be publicly recognized for accomplishments as well as for opposition to attempts to undermine native ways. In fact, Cheyennes and Arapahos developed new rituals through which they rejected the ideology of the dominant society.

Cheyennes and Arapahos have interpreted their historical experience and articulated it in a discourse about the past that influences contemporary political views and behavior. Their interpretations of the past reflect the coexistence of accommodation and resistance to dominant institutions and discourse. Cheyennes and Arapahos tell stories in each other's presence about a time when they were united. These memories affirm and encourage cooperative bonds as an aspect of identity. An elder expressed this perspective in 1982: "The way it is now people don't understand each other anymore very well. It's hard to get along together like we used to. . . . One thing is that we still hold on to what we remember—our prayer and our ways and remembering our relations. These are happy ways." He links Cheyenne and Arapaho tradition to prayer and "ways of remembering" relations and associates these with the perpetuation of dance activities and with both proof of and hope for the perpetuation of the Cheyenne and Arapaho as peoples. Several leaders draw from the discourse of their parents and grandparents in an effort to remind Cheyennes and Arapahos of historic themes, as one business committee chair put it. These themes are, first, that the treaty relationship defines the federal trustee's duties and obligates the federal government to protect the tribes in various ways. Second, the tribe consists of ancestors and future generations, as well as Cheyennes and Arapahos still living, and the interests of all these people take precedence over the individual's interests. The perception that the federal government has reneged on its treaty obligations is given expression in the use of the Custer metaphor in public discourse, and this belief gives the Cheyennes and Arapahos the moral high ground. These understandings are used to refute negative characterizations of Cheyennes and Arapahos by the wider society, and leaders try to mobilize supporters by giving expression to them.[8]

Critique of the ideology used by the federal government and of the Indian imagery in the local media that demeaned tribalism and native leaders once was prominent in the Cheyenne and Arapaho public discourse. Now it is overshadowed by themes of abuse of power and malfeasance on the part of native leaders. What began as criticism of business committee policy regarding the Judgment Fund in the 1950s by an urban interest group became in the 1980s and 1990s a common-sense characterization of native leaders. That is, the demeaning ideology about leaders was assumed to be true. The problems in constitutional ambiguities, contracting regulations, level of funding for programs, legal remedies for redress, and federal irresponsibility in the role of trustee all emanate from and are under the control of the federal, not the tribal, government. Yet, these constraints are de-emphasized in negative characterizations of tribal government; thus, negative portrayals of native leaders were a featured part of Cheyenne and Arapaho political discourse in the 1980s and 1990s. Recently, a state official who disagreed with a committee member's position on a sovereignty matter (the recovery of Fort Reno) and had no knowledge of business committee matters suggested in statewide media accounts that the committee member lacked "integrity" and "competency." Business committee opponents and dissidents who viewed this committee member as one who attacked them personally drew from these press accounts to attack their rival's character and to mobilize support for the recall of this individual. Today most Cheyenne and Arapaho interpretations of Cheyenne and Arapaho history focus on the loss of a tradition of cooperation and unity in tribal government. As one man, referring to tribal government politics, told it in 1980, "History has taken its toll on our people. . . . The white man's way of life has, in effect, placed individual survival over tribal survival." Thus, he suggests that cooperation in tribal government and tribalism are not possible. In the public discourse about the post-1975 business committee (and the tribal government generally), one sees leaders described as "unqualified," "childish," and "fat cats"—images that echo the descriptions given by federal officials in earlier times. In the frequent accusation that tribal leaders would not make good use of recovered lands, one is reminded of the federal and settler discourse that rationalized land sales.[9]

Individuals came to resist dominance by political cooperation in the ritual context and by confrontation in the context of tribal government. Cheyennes and Arapahos understood that both activities enabled personal valuation and allowed rejection of at least parts of the subordinating discourse. In the sphere of tribal government, political discourse is framed in terms of resistance to personal devaluation through confrontation; defense of personal valuation is linked to the ideal of political reform. In the ritual sphere, discourse is framed in terms of personal valuation and linked to the ideal of social and spiritual unity. Thus, both forms of dominance and forms of resistance have risen from local constructions of history in articulation with wider forces of power and meaning. In the Cheyenne and Arapaho experience of colonial and postcolonial processes, ritual cooperation and public protest against tribal and nontribal officials have come to coexist, and both have come to serve as vehicles of personal valuation. Over time a local focus on personal valuation emerged and found expression in political individualism and ritual communalism.

This study has shown how Cheyenne and Arapaho political consciousness has been constructed historically and how political consciousness has been a factor in Cheyenne and Arapaho response to colonial and postcolonial processes. Generalizations based on the Cheyenne and Arapaho case (for example, about Indian-settler relations within Oklahoma or about differences between Oklahoma and reservation communities) must await ethnographic and historical studies in other communities. What also is clear is that Cheyenne and Arapaho constituents currently play a role in the development of a sovereignty agenda and that they influence how successful tribal officials can be in pursuing that agenda at state and federal levels. At the very least, opponents of Cheyenne and Arapaho sovereignty are bolstered when dissidents undercut tribal government efforts to contract for services that are poorly delivered by others or to recover or purchase land that could be instrumental in the development of the local economy. Potentially useful projects are delayed or aborted by protests and by high turnover in employees and elected positions. While the self-determination legislation probably has had similar effects in Native American communities generally, the shape of tribal politics varies locally. In any case, ethnographic studies of the sovereignty movement at the local level are needed if we are to understand the impact of the self-determination legislation on Native American communities.[10]

Comparative work on the issue of how relations between constituents and intermediary leadership bear on the sovereignty movement has not been done in other

Fourth World contexts. Fourth World sovereignty studies (primarily Australian Aborigines, Canadian First Nations, Sami, and Maori) focus on the relationship between the state and native leaders who represent regional or pan-tribal interests. The achievement of sovereignty goals largely is discussed in terms of legal decisions, legislation, representation in regional or national organizations, and manipulation of public opinion. The emphasis is on constraints placed on sovereignty movements by states and on the effects of different colonial histories on state policies toward Fourth World peoples.[11]

Disguised dominance is an important issue in Fourth World studies. Without the development of political consciousness in subordinate communities about how structures of dominance work, state and other interests encounter weak resistance as they chip away at tribal resources, legal protections, and self-image. Thus, problems in government are not just about colonial domination but also about the development of political consciousness in native communities. My study of Cheyenne and Arapaho politics speaks to the issue of political consciousness, both for scholarship on the sovereignty movement and for local-level political advocacy. That is, of clear importance are efforts of native leaders to focus attention on the ways in which ideologies of self-determination promoted by federal representatives work to misrepresent and hinder tribal government projects that benefit native peoples in significant ways. To return to the metaphorical crabs in the bucket, perhaps the story could be interpreted differently. Perhaps the problem with tribal politics lies not with the crabs but with the bucket.[12]

Notes

The following abbreviations are used in the notes:

BC   Mennonite Library and Archives, Bethel College, North Newton, Kansas

BIAA   Office Files, Bureau of Indian Affairs, Anadarko, Oklahoma

C & A   Office Files, Cheyenne and Arapaho Tribes, Concho, Oklahoma

CC   *Calumet Chieftain*

CFAA   Central Files, 1950–67, Anadarko Area Office, RG 75, Records Relating to Tribal Committees, Federal Archives, Regional Center, Fort Worth, Texas

CFC   Central Files, 1907–39, Cantonment Agency, National Archives, Washington DC

CFCA   Central Files, 1907–39, Cheyenne-Arapaho Agency, National Archives, Washington DC

CF-Concho   Central Files, 1926–47, Concho Agency, RG 75, Records of the Bureau of Indian Affairs, Federal Archives, Regional Center, Fort Worth, Texas

CFSP   Central Files, 1940–57, Southern Plains Agency, RG 75, Records of the Bureau of Indian Affairs, National Archives, Washington DC

CR   *Canton Record*

CT   *Cheyenne Transporter*

CVR   *Canadian Valley Record*

DD   Doris Duke Oral History Collection, Western History Collections, University of Oklahoma, Norman, Oklahoma

DO   *Daily Oklahoman*

ERA   *El Reno American*

FMC   George Dorsey Collection, Field Museum of Natural History, Chicago, Illinois

FN   Loretta Fowler, Field Notes, Southern Cheyenne and Arapaho, 1984–94, personal possession

GB   *Geary Bulletin*

GJ   *Geary Journal*

HME   *Home Mission Echoes*, Union Theological Seminary, Columbia University, New York

I R	Inspection Division, Reports, 1881–1924, R G 48, Records of the Office of the Secretary of the Interior, National Archives, Washington D C
L B - C	Letterpress Books, Cantonment Agency, Oklahoma Historical Society, Oklahoma City, Oklahoma
L B - D	Letterpress Books, Darlington Agency, Oklahoma Historical Society, Oklahoma City, Oklahoma
L B - E R	Letterpress Books, Darlington Agency, Carnegie Public Library, El Reno, Oklahoma
L R	Letters Received by the Office of Indian Affairs, 1881–1907, R G 75, Records of the Bureau of Indian Affairs, National Archives, Washington D C
L R, Cen Supt	Letters Received by the Office of Indian Affairs, 1824–81, Central Superintendency, R G 75, Records of the Bureau of Indian Affairs, National Archives, Washington D C
L R C A	Letters Received by the Office of Indian Affairs, 1824–81, Cheyenne-Arapaho Agency, R G 75, Records of the Bureau of Indian Affairs, National Archives, Washington D C
L R P R - C S	Letters Received, Post Records of Camp Supply, R G 393, Records of the U.S. Army Continental Commands, 1821–1920, National Archives, Washington D C
L R U A	Letters Received by the Office of Indian Affairs, 1824–81, Upper Arkansas Agency, R G 75, Records of the Bureau of Indian Affairs, National Archives, Washington D C
L S P R - C	Letters Sent, Post Records of Camp Cantonment, R G 393, Records of the U.S. Army Continental Commands, 1821–1920, National Archives, Washington D C
L S P R - C S	Letters Sent, Post Records of Camp Supply, R G 393, Records of the U.S. Army Continental Commands, 1821–1920, National Archives, Washington D C
Menn	*The Mennonite,* Mennonite Library and Archives, Bethel College, North Newton, Kansas
M J	Mary Jayne Diaries, Western History Collections, University of Oklahoma, Norman, Oklahoma
M L S-Canton	Miscellaneous Letters Sent, Cantonment Agency, 1902–14, Oklahoma Historical Society, Oklahoma City, Oklahoma

M L S-Darl   Miscellaneous Letters Sent, Darlington Agency, 1900–1914, Oklahoma Historical Society, Oklahoma City, Oklahoma

N A F W   Federal Archives,, Regional Center, Records of the Bureau of Indian Affairs, R G 75, Concho Agency, Fort Worth, Texas

O H S   Oklahoma Historical Society, Oklahoma City, Oklahoma

R C I A   "Upper Arkansas Agency" (1869–74) and "Cheyenne and Arapaho Agency" (1875–1906), in *Reports of the Commissioner of Indian Affairs*, 1846–1906, Government Printing Office, Washington D C

S C   Special Cases, 1821–1907, R G 75, National Archives, Washington D C

S C A N N   *Southern Cheyenne and Arapaho Nation News*

S N R - C A   Superintendent's Narrative Reports, 1907–38, Cheyenne-Arapaho Agency, R G 75, Records of the Bureau of Indian Affairs, National Archives, Washington D C

S N R - C   Superintendent's Narrative Reports, 1907–38, Cantonment Agency, R G 75, Records of the Bureau of Indian Affairs, National Archives, Washington D C

W H   Western History Collections, University of Oklahoma, Norman, Oklahoma

W R   *Watonga Republican*

Introduction

1. "Indian Self-Determination and Education Assistance Act," pp. 2203–13. The Department of Education and the Department of Health and Human Services replaced the Department of Health, Education, and Welfare.

2. See Esber, "Shortcomings"; Barsh, "Indian Policy." Esber argues that the effect of the Self-Determination Act was to rid the federal government of responsibility in Indian affairs.

See Nicholas, "Factions: A Comparative Analysis"; Burja, "Dynamics of Political Action"; Salisbury and Silverman, "An Introduction: Factions and the Dialectic"; Bailey and Nicholas, "Rules, Resources, and Groups"; Boissevain, "Of Men and Marbles." An example of the use of the factionalism model, particularly as introduced by Bailey and Nicholas ("Rules, Resources, and Groups"), in a study of native North America is Bee, *Politics of American Indian Policy*.

Factions also were seen not merely as conflict groups but as a mode of organizing political relations and performing political functions, particularly in situations of rapid change. These studies were of the "process approach" in political anthropology (see Vincent, *Anthropology and Politics*). More recently, Elizabeth M. Blumfiel argues that the action or agent-centered approach of early factionalism studies can be adapted to "practice theory," wherein individuals similarly positioned within society compete for resources and positions of power and local competition has regional effects that serve as a mechanism of social transformation. Thus, agent-centered and system-centered analyses are integrated in a single framework ("Factional Competition and Political Development").

The treatment of factionalism as a type of shady tactics and as an expression of political pessimism appears in Bailey, "Definition of Factionalism." Prior to Bailey's work on factionalism, Bernard J. Siegel and Alan R. Beals characterized factionalism as a potentially pervasive process, leading to social breakdown, particularly in situations of colonialism or Westernization, where disorganization follows rapid change ("Pervasive Factionalism"). Studies of Native American political activity that employed this approach include French, "Ambiguity and Irrelevancy in Factional Conflict." See also Bee, *Politics of American Indian Policy.*

On progressive-conservative factionalism, see Fenton, "Factionalism at Taos Pueblo, New Mexico" and "Factionalism in American Indian Society." Others have argued that "progressive" and "conservative" labels can misconstrue political disputes. Edward P. Dozier argues that precontact divisions at Santa Clara got articulated in terms of progressivism and conservatism but in actuality did not represent different perceptions on change ("Factionalism at Santa Clara Pueblo"). Peter Whiteley makes a similar point, on one level, about Friendly-Hostile factions among Hopi (*Deliberate Acts*), as does Shuichi Nagata, who argues that Hopi individuals played off Friendly and Hostile groups against each other ("Opposition and Freedom in Moenkopi Factionalism"). Annemarie Anrod Shimony notes that Iroquois factionalism is more complicated than a simple progressive-conservative schism; she points out that the Confederate Council, which is opposed by supporters of the Elective Council, was composed of proponents of both the Longhouse (or conservative) religion and the Christian religion (*Conservatism among the Iroquois*). Characterization of progressive-conservative conflict as ideological—by outside observers or native participants—is problematic and should be a matter for investigation.

3. As Fourth World peoples, the Cheyennes and Arapahos experienced, and to some degree still experience, internal colonialism, that is, cultural and political subordination and economic exploitation within a nation-state.

4. "Indian Self-Determination and Education Assistance Act," pp. 2003–13.

5. Scholars have argued that the effects of state imposition of identities include disruption of native alliances and victimization of individuals and groups who are denied access to resources (see Sawchuk, ed., *Readings in Aboriginal Studies*). Most studies of the impact of imposed identities have been regionally, rather than local-level, focused. The collection of essays in Sawchuk's volume focuses on Canada and Australia; for a treatment of this subject in the United States, see Sider, *Lumbee Indian Histories* (see Blu, *Lumbee Problem*, for another perspective). See also Biolsi, "Birth of the Reservation," and Smith's work, "Emergence of 'Eskimo Status,'" on how forms of "governmentality"—in this case, bureaucratic systems of identifying and tracking native peoples—constrain those people's options.

For examples of how state and corporate interests combine to undermine native leadership traditions and further deplete resources in native communities, see Waldram, *As Long as the Rivers Run*, and Jorgensen, *Oil Age Eskimos*.

Sally Weaver discusses representivity of native organizations as a political resource that state governments can assign and withdraw from native organizations in order to serve state interests ("Political Representivity"). Thomas Biolsi makes essentially this argument with regard to Lakota political organization (*Organizing the Lakota*). (But, see Feit, "Legitimization and Autonomy," and Loretta Fowler, *Arapahoe Politics*).

Studies that focus on how government funding works to constrain native political activity include Sawchuk, "The Métis, Non-Status Indians and the New Aboriginality"; Watson, "Reification of Ethnicity"; and Driben and Trudeau, *When Freedom Is Lost*.

6. Comaroff and Comaroff, *Ethnography*, p. 235; Comaroff and Comaroff, *Of Revelation*, pp. 21–22, 28; Comaroff, *Body of Power* (see especially p. 185). Pierre Bourdieu views the creation of bureaucratic policies and procedures as not necessarily malevolent in intent but having a net social impact of "symbolic violence" in underprivileged, overregulated, and overcontrolled populations. Symbolic violence is "the gentle, hidden form which violence takes when overt violence is impossible" (*Outline of a Theory of Practice*, p. 196).

7. See Berkhofer, *White Man's Indian*, for an excellent discussion of the use of Indian imagery in the colonial context.

8. Comaroff, *Body of Power*, p. 1; Comaroff and Comaroff, *Ethnography*, p. 115.

9. Scott, *Weapons of the Weak*; Comaroff, *Body of Power*, p. 234; Comaroff and Comaroff, *Of Revelation*, pp. 21–23. See also Sturm, "Blood Politics."

10. See Hale, *Resistance and Contradiction*, p. 26. See also Sturm, "Blood Politics," pp. 22–35. This approach to hegemony is based on the views of Gramsci, *Selec-*

tions. After Gramsci, contradictory consciousness occurs when oppressed peoples react to their world with a mixture of tacit accommodation to the hegemonic order at one level and expressions of resistance at another. There is a discontinuity or tension between the world as hegemonically constituted and the world as practically apprehended and ideologically represented by subordinated people. Thus, hegemony is intrinsically unstable (Comaroff and Comaroff, *Of Revelation*, p. 26–29). The Comaroffs characterize this as a chain of consciousness, a continuum between the unrecognized and the cognized. Some of the meanings and actions of resistance may become conventionalized among a subordinated people; others are matters of contest (see Comaroff, *Body of Power*, pp. 185, 195, 263). Subject peoples may internalize alien cultural forms while taking issue with an ideological argument; transparent and mystified modes of domination are not mutually exclusive (pp. 43, 173).

11. Berthrong, *Southern Cheyennes*, pp. 345–47. The Medicine Lodge Creek Treaty guaranteed the Cheyennes and Arapahos an agent, schools, medical care, blacksmiths, and other technical assistance, in addition to annuity goods for twenty-five years. The Cheyennes and Arapahos also signed the Fort Laramie Treaty of 1851, in which the federal government guaranteed them rights to their territory in Wyoming, Colorado, Nebraska, and Kansas and promised them economic support (see Loretta Fowler, *Arapahoe Politics*).

12. The tribes do not keep two membership roles; rather, there is one Cheyenne-Arapaho roll. Probably most individuals identify themselves as either Cheyenne or Arapaho, at least in some social contexts. In 1999 there were almost eleven thousand enrolled Cheyenne-Arapahos. The information in the next three paragraphs and in map 1 is taken from "Cheyenne-Arapaho Tribes Base Studies, 1993," C & A, pp. 8, 10–12, 30, 66.

13. See Kan, "Clan Mothers and Godmothers"; Harkin, "Engendering Discipline"; Sturm, "Blood Politics." Also, Hopi commodification of culture in the service of intellectual sovereignty is discussed in Whiteley, *Rethinking Hopi Ethnography*, p. 3.

1. "To Be Friendly with Everybody"

1. R. Dodge to Assistant Adjutant General (hereafter A A G), 9 January 1880, v. 1, L S P R - C.

2. Fred Eggan's research on Arapaho and Cheyenne kinship is the best summary of nineteenth-century kinship organization. See Eggan, Field Notes, 1933; "Cheyenne and Arapaho Kinship System." See also Straus, "Northern Cheyenne Kinship Reconsidered," pp. 147–71; Moore, *Cheyenne Nation*.

3. J. Miles to W. Nicholson, 28 February 1876, L R C A. In 1871 the Arapahos remained near the agency in May while the army stalked the Northern Cheyenne who were in the area. They camped but three miles from the agency "to avoid trouble" (B. Darlington to E. Hoag, 22 May 1871, L R U A and R C I A 1871). Again, in 1872, the Arapahos moved toward the agency "to avoid trouble" while the Kiowa and Comanche were engaged in conflict with the army (J. W. Davidson to A A G, 30 June 1872, L S P R - C S). In 1875 Agent Miles arranged for troops to accompany the bands when they went hunting so that they would not be drawn into the fighting (Miles to E. P. Smith, 19 January 1875, and Nicholson to Smith, 27 May 1876, L R C A). After Agent Miles's tenure, there were four agents until the reservation was allotted in 1892: D. B. Dyer (1884–85), J. M. Lee (1885–86), G. D. Williams (1886–89), and C. Ashley (1889–91).

4. Miles to Hoag, 3 February 1873, L R U A. The source for map 2 is Ben Clark Collection, W H; base map provided by Robert Brooks, Oklahoma Archaeological Survey.

5. On ration distribution, see Miles to Nicholson, 9 November 1876, L R C A. On the headmen's receipt of annuities, see Darlington to Hoag, 7 April and 11 July 1870, L R U A; R C I A 1871 and 1872. On the beef issue, see Nicholson to Smith, 7 July 1876, L R C A. On the use of beef, see Capt. Henry Alford's Report, R C I A 1872.

6. Truman Michelson, "Narrative of the Old Moccasin Society," by Little Left Hand, 1932, in Smithsonian Institution, Truman Michelson Collection. Miles to Nicholson, 28 February 1876, L R C A. On Arapaho societies, see Kroeber, *The Arapaho*; Lowie, *Plains Indian Age Societies*; Fowler, *Arapahoe Politics*.

7. On the soldiers' supervision of camp movements, see John Williams to Miles, 10 April 1873, L R U A. On war parties, see Darlington to Hoag, 9 February 1871, L R U A; R C I A 1871; Darlington to Williams, 20 September 1871, L S P R - C S; J. A. Covington to Miles, 30 June 1873, and Miles to Hoag, 11 July 1873—both in L R U A.

8. Miles to Smith, 16 June 1874; Miles to Smith, 20 June 1874; Miles to Smith, 26 May 1874—all in L R U A; Covington to Smith, 16 August 1875, L R C A.

9. On Cheyenne societies, see Clark, *Indian Sign Language*, p. 355; Mooney, "Cheyenne Indians"; Dorsey, "The Cheyenne"; Grinnell, *Cheyenne Indians*, 2:48–86.

10. Miles to Hoag, 11 April 1873, and John Rush to A A G, 26 September 1873—both in L R U A; Rush to A A G, 10 October 1873; Davidson to Williams, 20 September 1871; Rush to A A G, 18 May 1874—all in L S P R - C S; R C I A 1871, 1874.

11. Grinnell, *Cheyenne Indians*, 2:211–84; Hugh L. Scott Ledger Books, 1889–97, Fort Sill Museum Archives, v. 2, p. 3.

12. On robe sales see Miles to Nicholson, 31 October 1876, v. 1, L B - D. On the horse epidemic, see Miles to Nicholson, 27 April 1876, L R C A; Miles to Hoag, 4 February 1876, v. 1, L B - D; R C I A 1877. On the decline of the buffalo, see J. A. Covington to E. A. Hayt, 12 January 1878; Miles to Hayt, 26 January 1878; Covington to Miles, 1 July 1878—all in L R C A; R C I A 1878 and 1879.

13. R C I A 1877 and 1878.

14. Nicholson to Smith, 5 August 1876, and Miles to Nicholson, 20 August 1876, L R C A; R C I A 1877; Miles Report of August 1878, v. 1, L B - E R. See Freight and Transportation File, O H S, for a list of wagon owners. On opposition to freighting by Cheyennes and Arapahos, see C. E. Campbell to Hayt, 10 December 1878, v. 1, L B - E R; Miles to Hayt, 19 September 1878, and Miles to Commissioner of Indian Affairs (hereafter C I A), 24 September 1878 in L R C A; John McNeil, 9 September 1878, I R 917.

15. On the increase in wagons, see R C I A 1880; Miles to C I A, 25 May 1881, L R 1881-9143; R C I A 1881; C T 10 May 1881, 10 September and 25 October 1881, 25 June 1882; R C I A 1887; Williams to C I A, 9 October 1888, L R 1888-22844; R C I A 1889. Miles to Covington, 7 August 1882, v. 5, L B - D, and Covington to O. J. Woodard, 13 November 1882, Freight and Transportation File, O H S; William Hodgkiss to J. Blair, 15 September 1886, v. 16, L B - D.

16. Ben Clark to J. K. Mizner, 16 May 1877, Ben Clark Collection, W H.

17. Arapaho Enrollment, Enrollment Lists, 1880, O H S; Land Transaction Files-Concho Agency, Entry 12, N A F W. James Mooney reported that there were five Southern Arapaho bands in 1892: Bad Faces (Left Hand's band), Pleasant Men (settled along the South Canadian River, their principal headman was Powder-face); Blackfeet (settled southeast of the Darlington agency, their principal headman was Row of Lodges); Wolves; and Looking Around (*Ghost-Dance Religion*, p. 951).

18. C T 28 October 1883, 10 May and 30 August 1884; R. Gardner, 29 June 1887, I R 3507.

19. R. Gardner, 29 June 1887, I R 3507; H. R. Voth, *Menn*, Feb. 1888, pp. 74–75.

20. R C I A 1876; J. Williams to James Rhoads, 14 July 1876, v. 1, L B - D; on Yellow Bear, see Miles, 17 May 1876, v. 1, L B - D; R C I A 1878; Miles to Hayt, 20 March 1878, and Mizner to A A G, 17 July 1878—both in L R C A; Robert Gardner, 24 November 1883, I R 4871; Frank Armstrong Report, file 29393-1885, S C; Lee to Seth Clover, 6 May 1886, v. 13, L B - D; J. Kliewer to Voth, 10 January 1888, Board of Missions, General Correspondence, box 6, f 65, B C.

21. Conference with President Grant with Northern and Southern Cheyenne and Arapaho, 17 November 1873, L R U A; R C I A 1876 and 1877; on tolls, see Miles to

Hayt, 18 September 1878, and Miles to Mizner, 18 September 1878; W. L. Clark to CO, Camp Cantonment, 18 June 1880; Miles to Hayt, 20 September 1878—all in LRCA; C. Hood to Miles, 27 May 1882, v. 3, LSPR-C; Dickey Brothers to CIA, 30 July 1883, LR 1883-13970.

22. RCIA 1880; CT 10 September 1880, 26 February 1883, and 12 July 1883; Miles to H. Price, 22 November 1881, v. 3, and Miles to P. B. Hunt, 9 May 1882, v. 4—both in LB-D. The Kiowas and Comanches also leased land to cattlemen and cultivated an alliance with them to postpone the allotment of their reservation and to strengthen their local economy (see Hagan, *United States-Comanche Relations*).

23. Miles to Hayt, 7 February 1878, LRCA; CT 10 February 1883 (see also H. Voth to J. Moyer, 3 October 1884, Henry Voth Collection, box 14, f 2, BC); Miles to CIA, 20 January 1883, LR 1883-1682 (see also RCIA 1883); Williams to John Seger, 29 August 1887, v. 21; W. DeLesdernier to W. Pulling, 23 April 1890, v. 31; Ashley to CIA, 8 November 1889, v. 27; Williams to CIA, 9 March 1888, v. 20—all in LB-D.

24. RCIA 1877; on the grass payment, see CT 27 June 1883 and 25 May 1885.

25. Miles to Hayt, 2 January 1879, v. 1, and D. B. Dyer to Price, 9 October 1884, v. 4—both in LB-ER; Miles to R. E. Trowbridge, 18 August 1880, LRCA; Miles to Price, 7 January 1882, LR 1882-1024; Ben Clark to J. Wade, 2 January 1890, LR 1890-5112.

26. CT 10 June 1881, 25 June 1882; Dyer to J. Atkins, 15 June 1885, LR 1885-1415; Dyer to CIA, 22 July 1884, LR 1884-14238. On scouts, see Williams to Atkins, 18 April 1887, v. 19, LB-D; J. Wade to Adjutant General (hereafter AG), 21 January 1890, LR 1891-7055.

27. RCIA 1884; *Menn*, November 1889, pp. 26–27.

28. See RCIA 1871. I use the term "intermediary chief" (see Fowler, *Arapahoe Politics*). In the documents, the term "principal chief" is closest in meaning to this. Yellow Bear was probably expressing the Arapaho and Cheyenne concept of intermediary chief when he told officials in council in May 1875, "I am the peacemaker between white man and red man" (LR, Cen Supt, p. 31).

29. See Mooney, "Cheyenne Indians," p. 403; Dorsey, "The Cheyenne"; Grinnell, *Cheyenne Indians*, 1:336–44; Moore, *Cheyenne Nation*. When the main camp of Cheyenne, numbering 820, came to a council to negotiate their return to the reservation in 1875, forty-nine principal chiefs reportedly sat in a semicircle facing the government officials. Behind them were the other men, and behind them the women and children in concentric circles (Thomas Neill to AAG, 7 March 1875, LRCA).

30. The following sources identity intermediary chiefs, that is, spokesmen: Darling-

ton to Hoag, 26 March, 7 April, and 9 November 1870; A G to C I A, 23 August 1870; Darlington to Hoag, 23 January 1871—all in L R U A; Hoag to J. Pope, 25 March 1871; Davidson to A G, 4 January 1872—both in L S P R - C S; R C I A 1872, 1875; Ben Clark to Mizner, 1 October 1879, L R C A; Miles to Hayt, 11 November 1879, v. 1, L B - E R; Davidson to A A G, 30 June 1872, L S P R - C S; Covington to Miles, 30 June 1873, L R U A; R C I A 1873; Miles to Smith, 4 June 1874, L R U A; War Department to C I A, 24 February 1885, L R 1885-4459; J. H. Potter to C. C. Augur, 22 June 1885, L R 1885-16697. On council chiefs, see Powell, *People of the Sacred Mountain*.

31. Council of 14 July 1870, Miscellaneous Records, 1873–1912, Post Records, Fort Sill Museum Archives, Fort Sill, Oklahoma; A. Nelson to W. G. Mitchell, 23 September 1870; Davidson to A A G, 30 June 1872—both in L S P R - C S; R C I A 1872 and 1873; Covington to Miles, 30 June 1873; Report of Council, 1–18 November 1873; Miles to Smith, 23 May 1874—all in L R U A; War Department to C I A, 24 February 1885, L R 1885-4459.

32. Cyrus Beebe to Smith, 20 October 1873, L R U A; Miles to Price, 13 December 1882, L R 1883-7594; Miles to C I A, 26 January 1883, L R 1883-2141; Miles to C I A, 20 March 1884, L R 1884-5886. The money for the grazing leases arrived in silver dollars. The thirty-one thousand dollars in silver was arranged on long tables, and the distribution was made by ration ticket, about five dollars each (C T 27 June 1883). In effect, the land was leased at two cents per acre, far less than it was worth (Gardner, 24 November 1883, I R 4871; Frank Armstrong Report, file 29393-1885, S C 9). Four semiannual payments were made before President Grover Cleveland canceled the leases (R C I A 1886). As a result of the leases, many camps relocated closer to the agency and lost much of their stock (T. A. Bland to President, 29 June 1885, file 14580-1885, S C 9).

33. R C I A 1871, 1872, 1873, 1876, 1884; see also C T 24 December 1880 and 13 February 1884; Hoag to H. R. Clum, 1 November 1871; Hoag to F. A. Walker, 3 December 1872; Miles to E. P. Smith, 10 November 1874—all in L R U A; C. E. Campbell to Hayt, 10 October 1879, L R C A. See also Entry 1327 and 1328, Student Folders and Student Information Cards, Carlisle Indian Industrial School Records, Records of the Bureau of Indian Affairs, R G 75, National Archives.

34. General Council Proceedings, Okmulgee, May 1875, L R, Cen Supt; R C I A 1875 and 1886; Miles to H. Price, 7 January 1882, L R 1882-1024; Principal Chiefs to C I A, 18 December 1888, L R 1888-31520; Proceedings of Delegation, 1 December 1891 in L R 1891-42868. Leaders' strategy of presenting themselves as supportive of the civilization policy was in practice elsewhere (see, for example, Fowler, *Arapahoe Politics* and *Shared Symbols, Contested Meanings*; Hoxie, *Parading through History*).

35. R C I A 1873 (see also C T 30 April 1885); Miles to Smith, 18 February 1875, L R C A; C T 24 December 1880. On houses, see R C I A 1885 and 1886; *Menn,* July 1891; Ashley to C I A, 29 December 1891, L R 1891-46104. For background on the civilization policy, see Hoxie, *A Final Promise*; Prucha, *Great Father*; Hagan, *American Indians*.

36. R C I A 1872 and 1881; Miles, Monthly Report for Jan.–Feb. 1873; Miles to Hoag, 12 March 1873; C & A Delegation to C I A, November 1873; Report of Council, November 1873—all in L R U A; C T 25 August 1880, 25 September 1880, and 28 January 1886; H. M. Teller to President, 2 January 1885, Council with Cheyenne and Arapaho, in Letters Sent to the Secretary of the Interior, Indian Division, v. 38, pp. 263–66, R G 48, National Archives, Washington D C (see also Frank Armstrong Report, 22 July 1885, file 29393-1885, S C 9); Ashley to C I A, 21 November 1891, L R 1891-420634; William Junkin to C I A, 23 September 1891, L R 1891-35027; Proceedings of Delegation, 1 December 1891, L R 1891-42868; Ashley to C I A, 2 January 1891, v. 30; Ashley to N. Polson, 18 April 1891, v. 32—both in L B - D.

37. Miles to C I A, 3 July 1882, L R 1882-12454; Miles to H. Price, 13 December 1882, L R 1883-7594; Cheyenne Chiefs to Indian Department, December 1887, L R 1887-33603; C T 13 June 1884 and R C I A 1884. On the Northern Arapaho incident, see Miles to E. P. Smith, 5 November 1875, L R C A; E. M. Hayes to Post Adjutant, 14 November 1875; G. Gordon to A A G, 27 November 1875—both in L S P R - C S. On the shooting of John Holloway, the physician's son, see Miles to Nicholson, 9 June 1876, L R C A; Miles to Mizner, 8 June 1876, v. 1; Miles to Nicholson, 9 June 1876, v. 1; Miles to Nicholson, 17 June 1876, v. 1—all in L B - D. Miles to Nicholson, 5 January 1877, L R C A; C T 25 May 1882; R C I A 1891; Charles Ashley to Secretary of Interior, 31 August 1891, v. 24, L B - D.

38. B. Clark to Miles, 22 July 1873, L R U A; George Bent to C I A, L R 1889-36576; Thomas Neill to A A G, 7 March 1875, L R C A; J. M. Lee to C I A, 1 September 1885, v. 9, L B - D; J. H. Potter to A A G, 18 July 1883 in file 14817-1883, S C 9. On Little Raven, see R C I A 1886.

39. Report of Jerome Commission, Irregularly Shaped Papers 78, R G 75, National Archives, Washington D C, and *Menn,* July 1891.

40. On the Ghost Dance, see Ashley to C I A, 7 August 1890, L R 1890-24229; R C I A 1890 and 1891; C. H. Carlton, 11 January 1891, L R 1891-7055; F. J. Hardin to P. B. Plumb, 13 May 1891, L R 1891-18043; Report of Jerome Commission; Ashley to C I A, 17 December 1890, L R 1890-39382.

41. On 2 May 1890 Congress created the Territory of Oklahoma, and the Jerome Commission was appointed to negotiate with tribes to allot lands to Indians and to purchase unallotted reservation land. The Cheyennes and Arapahos were to

be paid $1.5 million, $500,000 in per capita payments and $1 million deposited in the U.S. Treasury at 5 percent interest. Part of the fund for per capita payments (about $67,000) was paid to a group of businessmen under conditions the tribes' spokesmen have maintained to be fraudulent (see Berthrong, *Cheyenne and Arapaho Ordeal*, pp. 33–34). The cession itself is widely regarded as fraudulent; that is, many of the signatures on the agreement were illegitimate. On the allotment act generally, see Hoxie, *A Final Promise*; Prucha, *Great Father*.

42. Ashley to Richard Pratt, 15 May 1891, v. 32, L B - D.

43. On the allotment clusters, see William Junkins, 18 February 1892, I R 1308; A. E. Woodson to Secretary of Interior, 5 December 1894, v. 48, L B - D; R C I A 1893 and 1894. On farming districts, see Woodson Circular, 24 July 1897, v. 70, L B - D. And see C. C. Duncan, 13 July 1896, I R 5018; *Menn*, v. 8, July 1893; Paul Faison, 23 December 1895, I R 9092; Woodson to C I A, 2 May 1894, L R 1894-1697/3; F. L Benson to Woodson, 13 January 1897, v. 66; Woodson to George Coleman, 9 November 1894, v. 47—both in L B - D. On Cantonment, see also C. Briscoe to Woodson, 4 June 1895, v. 3, L B - C and Woodson to J. Thompson, 13 March 1896, v. 60, L B - D. On Twelve Mile Point, see M J, 28 January 1901. Population figures are from George Stouch to Employees, 29 May 1901, v. 98, L B - D. Map 3 is based on a map provided by John Moore.

44. On houses, see C. F. Neslen, 30 October 1897, I R 7965; R. Hamilton, "Among the Cheyennes," *H M E*, February 1899, v. 3, no. 2.

45. Woodson to C I A, 4 January 1894, L R 1894-979; Woodson to C I A, 5 December 1893, L R 1893-45425; C. C. Duncan, 13 July 1896, I R 5018; Woodson to Caleb Brooks, 31 December 1894, v. 48, L B - D; Woodson to C I A, 21 November 1893, file 43947-1893, S C 147; R C I A 1900 and 1902.

46. Woodson to C I A, 5 December 1893, L R 1893-45425; Woodson to C I A, 4 January 1894, v. 38; Stouch to C I A, 8 January 1900, v. 92; Stouch to Farmers, 12 November 1901, v. 100; Woodson to District Farmers, 29 July 1896, v. 63—all in L B - D; E. F. Mitchell to D. M. Browning, 5 May 1893, L R 1893-17373; Woodson to C I A, 4 September 1896, L R 1896-34162.

47. R C I A 1897, 1899; Stouch to Farmers, 2 May 1900, v. 87, L B - D. On the beef issue, see Woodson to George Coleman, 21 August 1896, v. 63; Stouch to H. Wilson, 16 August 1901, v. 99; Woodson Circular, 13 November 1896, v. 65—all in L B - D; Fred Winterfair to Woodson, 19 November 1898, v. 5; Winterfair to Stouch, 14 July 1900, v. 6—both in L B - C. On farming, see Woodson to J. O. Thompson, 13 March 1896, v. 60; Stouch to C I A, 30 April 1900, v. 92; Woodson to C I A, 1 October 1894, v. 47; Woodson to R. Druley, 11 February 1896, v. 59; Woodson to Secretary of Interior, 10 December 1894, v. 48; Woodson to ?, 2 July 1894, v. 49;

Woodson to William DeLesdernier, 5 July 1894, v. 45; Property Clerk, 30 August 1894, v. 42—all in L B - D; M J, 14, 16, 24 April and summer and fall entries for 1898 and 13 April 1900 entry; Stouch to C I A, 11 February 1901, L R 1901-9536; William Pulling to Woodson, 15 March 1894, v. 2; Stephen Janus to Woodson, 7 September 1896, v. 4; Pulling to Woodson, 31 March 1894, v. 2—all in L B - C.

48. R C I A 1895; M J, 9, 14, 16, 24 April 1898, 12 July 1900, 21 January 1901, and 12 February 1902; J. S. Krehbiel to Board of Missions, 4 January 1896, box 9, f 49, B C; Janus to Woodson, 7 February 1896, v. 3; Winterfair to Woodson, 12 June 1899, v. 5—both in L B - C; Woodson to Coleman, 25 May 1896 and 11 June 1896, v. 62; Woodson to David Day, 13 July 1896, v. 63; Woodson to H. Brown, 24 August 1893, v. 39—all in L B - D; G B 10 and 17 October 1901. Assembling for camp ceremonies during national holidays was common in other Native American communities (see, for example, Hoxie, *Parading through History*, p. 210).

49. R C I A 1899, 1902. The funds from income from allotted lands were deposited in the U.S. Treasury and distributed at the direction of the agent, who determined the amount of money and the kind of purchase that should be approved for distribution to the allottee (Stouch to Coleman, 5 January 1900, v. 86, L B - D).

50. The following sources all document disputes between kinsmen and in-laws along the lines discussed: Janus to Woodson, 8 February 1897, v. 4; Pulling to Ashley, 9 February 1892 and 11 June 1892, v. 1; Kingsley to Stouch, August 1902, v. 8; Little Raven to ?, 1900, v. 7; Ashley to Seger, 10 April 1893, v. 36; Woodson to Seger, 13 July 1894, v. 45; Woodson to Seger, 17 April 1895, v. 55; Woodson to F. Winterbottom, 20 August 1897, v. 71; Ashley to Potter, 18 March 1891, v. 32— all in L B - D; Stouch to E. Kingsley, 23 June 1902, v. 55, M L s-Darl; Henry Roman Nose to C I A, 12 May 1891, in Ashley to C I A, 29 May 1891, L R 1891-20032.

51. See, for example, Ashley to C I A, 10 March 1892, v. 33, L B - D; Janus to Woodson, 15 August 1896, v. 4; Fred Winterfair to Woodson, 31 May 1898, v. 5; Winterfair to Stouch, 13 September 1900, v. 9—all in L B - C; Jesse Bent in T. Ryan to C I A, 26 April 1899, L R 1899-19988; Horace Wilson to Stouch, 12 and 15 September and 4 October 1901, Cantonment Superintendents' Letters, v. 2; J. Witcher to Agent, 31 July 1902, Indian Customs File—both in O H S.

52. Pulling to Woodson, 1 January 1894, v. 2; Kingsley to Stouch, 28 April 1900, v. 6—both in L B - C; Stouch to P. Sisney, 6 August 1900, v. 89, L B - D.

53. Charles Meserve to C I A, 21 June 1892, L R 1892-22757; Dorsey, *Arapaho Sun Dance*; Stouch to John Sams, 17 October 1902, v. 57, M L s-Darl; T. Ryan to C I A, 26 April 1899, L R 1899-19988.

54. L. D. Davis to C I A, 18 July 1893, R C I A 1893; Proceedings of meeting between delegates and C I A, 31 December 1898, 27 January and 1 February 1899 in L R 1899-

502 and L R 1900-502; Pulling to Ashley, 11 May 1893, v. 1; C. Briscoe to Woodson, 16 and 18 September 1895, v. 3—both in L B - C; R. Pratt to C I A, 24 April 1896, L R 1896-15984; Thomas Smith, 24 March 1894, I R 2436. The selection of "chiefs" probably included many society leaders as well as council chiefs.

55. On fulfillment of the Jerome Agreement, see Ashley to C I A, 6 April 1892, L R 1892-13880. On the attorney contract, see Council Proceedings, 3 May 1892, L R 1892-17445; Council Proceedings 9–10 May 1892, L R 1892-19355, enc. 1; Woodson to C I A, L R 1894-5995; Woodson to C I A, 2 May 1896, L R 1896-17070. On the separation of the tribes, see Woodson to C I A, 24 October 1894, v. 47, L B - D; Mc Cormick, 3 December 1896, I R 7777 and H. Roman Nose to Browning, 5 March 1897, L R 1897-9120; Proceedings of Delegation, 20 March 1898, L R 1898-14669 1/2. The Comanches, Kiowas, and Plains Apaches also charged that their cession agreement was fraudulent (see Hagan, *United States-Comanche Relations*, pp. 251–52).

56. On Woodson's interference, see F. Glasbrenner to C I A, 11 March 1895, L R 1895-10810; Woodson to C I A, 10 October 1896, v. 64, L B - D; Woodson to C I A, 15 February 1898, L R 1898-7949. On Woodson's opposition, see Woodson to C I A, 2 May 1896, L R 1896-17070; Woodson to C I A, 15 March 1898, L R 1898-12754; Talks with Arapahos, 20 March and 4–6 April 1898, L R 1898-14669 1/2; Proceedings of Delegation, 30 November–1 December 1898, L R 1900-502; Proceedings of Delegation, 27 January and 1 February 1899, L R 1899-502.

57. Woodson to E. P. Pearson, 21 May 1897, v. 69; Woodson to C I A, 20 September 1893, v. 38; Woodson to Isaac Durie, 20 September 1893, v. 42—all in L B - D; Proceedings of 1895 Delegation, S C 147, 1891-13100; R C I A 1893, 1901; Ashley to C I A, 18 May 1893, L R 1893-18546; Briscoe to Woodson, 14 April 1895, v. 3, L B - C. Black Coyote's statements are in Charles Meserve to C I A, 21 June 1892, L R 1892-22757. Anthropologist George Dorsey supported the chiefs' requests, assuring the agent that the ceremony was not harmful. At Darlington were the Arapaho Manual Labor and Boarding School (also referred to in the official record as the Arapaho Boarding School) and the Cheyenne Manual Labor and Boarding School (also referred to as the Cheyenne Boarding School).

58. Proceedings of 1895 Delegation, S C 147, 1891-13100; in the Proceedings of the Delegation of 20 March 1898 (L R 1898-14669 1/2), Left Hand stated that he represented a district, that "each of them is from a separate district"; Proceedings of Delegation of 3 November–1 December 1898, L R 1900-502; Proceedings of Delegation of 27 January and 1 February 1899, L R 1899-502.

59. Secretary of Interior to C I A, 20 April 1892, L R 1892-14792; 9–10 May Council, L R 1892-19355, enc. 1; R. Gardner, 18 May 1893, I R 4066; R C I A 1893; Glasbrenner to

Woodson, 14 March 1895, v. 54, L B - D; Woodson to C I A, 15 March 1898, L R 1898-
12754; Winterbottom to Woodson, 15 March 1898, v. 5, L B - C. On schools, see
R C I A 1892; Ashley to C I A, 18 May 1893, L R 1893-18546; Wilson to Stouch, 8 June
1901, Superintendents' Letters, Cantonment, v. 1, O H S. On attorney conflict, see
Stouch to C I A, 14 July 1900, v. 93, L B - D.

60. Woodson to R. Davis, 14 February 1895, v. 53, L B - D; Stouch to C I A, 5 February
1900, L R 1900-7091 and 7234. And see Woodson to C I A, 14 November 1894, v. 47;
F. Glasbrenner to C I A, 7 March 1895, v. 54; Woodson to Briscoe, 7 June 1895, v.
50—all in L B - D; Interior Department to C I A, 28 February 1895, L R 1895-9388;
Woodson to C I A, 23 October 1895, L R 1895-44265; Woodson to C I A, 17 August
1896, L R 1896-32849; Stouch to C I A, 5 February 1900, L R 1900-7233; Kingsley to
Ruckman, June 1902, v. 8, L B - C.

61. R C I A 1893, 1896; Woodson to Black Coyote, 10 October 1893, v. 40; Woodson
to White Horse et al., 27 October 1893, v. 41; Woodson to Chief Left Hand, 23
January 1895, v. 48; Woodson to J. B. Woolsey, 16 October 1895, v. 57; Woodson
Circular, 14 December 1896, v. 66; Woodson to Coleman and Woodson to C I A,
3 July 1899, v. 82; Woodson Circular, 6 May 1895, v. 49; Woodson to C I A, 6 April
1895, v. 52—all in L B - D; Woodson to C I A, 8 May 1895, L R 1895-20329.

62. *Menn*, February 1891, pp. 73–75; May 1890; September 1895; April 1896.

63. R C I A 1871, pp. 459–69; 1872, p. 249; 1877, p. 86; 1882, p. 64; 1884, p. 71; 1885, pp. 75,
80; 1893, p. 249; 1898, p. 235; C T 10 April 1882; 11 January 1883; *Menn*, November
1891; December 1892, p. 22; July 1894.

64. R C I A 1888, p. 93; 1894, p. 235; 1895, p. 245; 1896, p. 246; 1897, p. 225.

65. R C I A 1871, pp. 459–69; 1872, p. 135; 1885, p. 80; 1886, p. 126; 1894, p. 231; 1895, pp.
245–46; C T 26 December 1882.

66. H. T. Weiss, July 1894, Board of Missions, General Correspondence, box 8, f. 44,
B C.

67. R C I A 1871, p. 470; 1892, p. 250; 1901, pp. 316–17; *Menn*, March, June, December
1891; February 1888, pp. 70–71; October 1894, p. 6.

2. "They Are Trying to Make Us Stingy"

1. *Menn*, March 1894; Berthrong, "Legacies of the Dawes Act," p. 52 (see also pp.
35–37). The Dead Indian Land Act refers to the Indian Appropriations Act of
1902. Subject to political pressure from Westerners to sell Indian allotments and
desirous of reducing the appropriations for Indian support, Congress passed
legislation in 1902 to allow adult heirs of a deceased Indian allottee, who had
been issued a trust patent (containing restrictions on the sale or taxation of

said land), to sell these inherited lands. Minors' heirs could sell inherited land through a court-appointed guardian with the approval of the secretary of the interior (32 U.S. Stat 245, 275). In 1906 Congress passed the Burke Act (34 U.S. Stat 182-83), which allowed "competent" Indians, with the secretary of the interior's permission, to obtain a fee patent on their allotments, allowing said allotments to be sold and taxed. Only Indians with fee patents on their allotments would be granted citizenship. In the 1907 Indian Appropriations Act, noncompetent Indians were given permission to sell their allotments. The commissioner of Indian affairs was to supervise the expenditure of the land sale funds (34 U.S. Stat 1015, 1018). See also R C I A 1903, 1904, 1906. On pressure from Americans, see C V R 31 October 1907 and C C 7 May 1909.

2. R C I A 1892; G B 19 June and 11 December 1902.

3. R C I A 1903; Charles Shell to C I A, 18 October 1909, C F C A 127-83067-1909; S N R - C 1920; Horace Wilson to George Stouch, 11 April 1902, Superintendents' Letters, Cantonment, v. 2, O H S; Stouch to M. Gates, 20 December 1902, v. 58, M L S-Darl; Stouch to Farmers, 3 September 1902, v. 56, M L S-Darl; Conference with Agent, 24 April 1914, C F C A 150-48369-1914.

4. Statistics on income differentials are from a research project, "Aging in Historical Context," funded by the National Endowment for the Humanities, in which I was the principal investigator. This research will be published at a later time. During the early twentieth century, Indians employed by the federal government received $1.25 per day's work (R C I A 1903). Map 5 is based on B I A records.

5. Statements from Jess Rowlodge, T235, 4 April 1968, and Myrtle Lincoln, T588, 23 October 1969, D D. Julia Jordan, interviewer.

6. O. M. McPherson, C. R. Trowbridge, and W. W. Scott, Journal of Cheyenne and Arapaho Competency Board, Entry 485, January–February 1917, Records of the Bureau of Indian Affairs, R G 75, National Archives.

7. E. J. Bost to C I A, 20 January 1925, Industrial Survey, 1922–25, C F C.

8. R C I A 1903; Charles Shell to C I A, 18 October 1909, C F C A 127-83067-1909. And see S N R - C 1920.

9. Transcript of hearings between Delegation and C I A, June 1912, C F C A 056-59814-1912. In 1910 Congress gave the secretary of the interior the authority to determine the heirs of dead allottees (36 U.S. Stat, 855). All of these cases are documented in heirship hearings found in the Land Transaction Files-Concho Agency, N A F W (files 1690, 3215, 1763, 2343, 1311, 2224, 2210, 1624, 1203, 1427, 1771, 2246, 2316) except for the Mrs. Sore Thumb case (B. White to J. Seger, 26 March 1903, M L S-Canton, v. 1, p. 210). And see Conference with Agent, 24 April 1914, C F C A, 150-48369-1914. For Goodwin's comments, see W. D. Goodwin to C I A, 31

October 1914, in file 1084, and 22 January 1915, in file 1289, in Land Transaction Files-Concho Agency, N A F W. All the names of the parties in the heirship cases have been changed except those of well-known intermediary chiefs White Shirt, Sitting Bull, Bird Chief Jr., and White Eyed Antelope. Quotations are from the heirship files.

10. There is little published information on inheritance practices of Arapahos and Cheyennes during the nineteenth century. Alfred Kroeber, reporting on Arapaho customs, noted that a man's horses were taken by his brothers and sometimes by his sisters, although it was considered generous for them to give some to his adult children (*The Arapaho*, pp. 11, 317). Karl N. Llewellyn and E. Adamson Hoebel concluded that brothers of a deceased Cheyenne usually took his or her horses but that they might wait for the widow to send for them. Generosity to the deceased's children was encouraged. If the deceased were elderly, a son might take or distribute the horses. A father usually took or distributed a youth's horses. A husband might take some of his deceased wife's horses but also would give some, along with her other property, to her female relatives (*The Cheyenne Way*, pp. 212–21). In both Arapaho and Cheyenne society, there were no fixed rules of inheritance; rather, distribution of the deceased's property depended on social circumstances and personalities.

11. For references to prominent men's camps, see Farmers File 1907, 1911, O H S. On efforts to form Indian villages, see Wolf Robe et al. to C I A, 28 May 1909, C F C 056-15976-1909; Proceedings of Conference, 11 February 1911, C F C 056-14461-1911; and Hearings, 22 January 1917, C F C 056-7692-1917. On younger men working on the farms of their elders, see Farmers File 1911, O H S, and the *Carrier Pigeon*, 28 February 1913, C F C A 100-38580-1913. On the halls, see Farmers Weekly Reports for 1922, O H S.

12. Scott to C I A, 30 August 1918, Indian Dances File, O H S; L. S. Bonnin to C I A, 8 October 1923, C F C A 062-64212-1921.

13. Bonnin to C I A, 8 October 1923, C F C A 062-64212-1921; J. B. Edigre to J. W. Smith, 17 December 1918, Indian Celebrations File, O H S; Shell to C I A, 11 April 1907, L R 36598-1907.

14. Cleaver Warden Notebooks, 1903, 1906, F M C.

15. *H M E*, February 1906, May 1906, and March 1907; Bonnin to Bost, 14 July 1923, and Bost to Bonnin, 17 July 1923, Indian Dances File, O H S.

16. *C V R* 6 June 1907; Farmers Weekly Reports, 29 December 1917, O H S; Bonnin to E. J. Bost, 14 July 1923, and Bost to Bonnin, 17 July 1923, Indian Dances File, O H S; Fowler, F N; interview with Laura Big Horse and Gladys Mann, February 1968, T256, D D.

17. Program for Third Annual Cheyenne and Arapaho Indian Fair in C F C A 047-83974-1912; William Freer to C I A, 16 October 1913, C F C A 047-121195-1913; S N R - C and S N R - C A 1914.

18. M J 1903; H. G. Wilson, Inspection Report, 20 December 1916, C F C A 150-1916; Scott to C I A, 27 March 1918, C F C A 126-28053-1918; S N R - C A 1919 and 1920.

19. S N R - C A 1915, 1917, 1918, 1924. For an overview of Native American efforts to perpetuate their way of life during these difficult times, see Hoxie, "Reservation Period."

20. S N R - C A 1915; Phelps, *Tepee Trails*, p. 64.

21. R C I A 1903; C. F. Hauke to Gov. Lee Cruse, 17 February 1912, Indian Dances File, O H S; Scott to C I A, 7 June 1915, C F C A 063-64697-1915; R. D. to Chester Westfall, 22 July 1918, Indian Celebrations File, O H S; R. Daniel to J. W. Smith, 14 July 1918; Daniel to W. W. Scott, 13 August 1918; Scott to Daniel, 29 July 1918—all in Indian Dances File, O H S.

22. Interview with Jess Rowlodge, T458, 4 June 1969, D D. Julia Jordan, interviewer.

23. *H M E*, January 1909, p. 7.

24. *Carrier Pigeon* 1911, C F C A 047-79155 and 86634-1911.

25. W. W. Scott to C I A, 7 July 1914, C F C A 054-76272-1914. On Middleman, see F. Sweezy to Agent, 1 March 1907, Farmers File, O H S; Cloud Chief to C I A, C F C A 056-96296-1907; J. Ijam to Freer, 5 January 1911, Farmers File 1911, O H S; J. Logan to Freer, 12 October 1912, Farmers File, O H S.

26. *H M E*, December 1907, v. 10; F. E. Leupp to Secretary of Interior, 28 August 1907, C F C A 127-70596-1907; Shell to Whom It May Concern, 1 January 1907, M L S-Darl, v. 2, p. 357; Freer to C I A, 17 November 1910, C F C A 047-45400-1910; George Hoyo to F. E. Farrell, 18 November 1912, and John Logan to Farrell, 7 December 1912, Farmers File, O H S; Report of William Freer, 12 July 1913, C F C 150-33424-1913; Meeting with Asst. C I A E. B. Meritt, 26 October 1916, C F C 056-112404-1915; Cut Finger in 17 January 1917 meeting, C F C A 056-5805-1917 (see also Cut Nose's talk against liquor in *H M E*, May 1906); Yellow Hawk to C I A, 25 May 1922, C F C 110-13991-1922.

27. Hearing between Arapaho Delegates and C I A, 26 October 1915, C F C 056-112404-1915; Ella Bates to Bost, 28 September 1925, Land Acquisitions Files-Concho Agency (file 2306), N A F W. On Cheyennes, see Mower to Victor Evans, 17 February 1920, C F C 056-16919-1920; Petition to C I A, 11 November 1919, C F C A 056-14620-1920; and Bonnin to C I A, 9 May 1925, C F C A 056-20073-1925.

28. Cloud Chief to C I A, 22 November 1907, C F C A 056-94102-1907; G. Stouch to C I A, 11 May 1906, L R 42843-1906; Conference with agent, 24 April 1914, C F C A 150-48369-1914; Scott to C I A, C F C A 054-76272-1914.

29. C. H. Dickson to C I A, 20 January 1903, L R 5356-1903; Cloud Chief to C I A, 22 November 1907, C F C A 056-94102, and Shell to C I A, 6 December 1907, C F C A 056-96296-1907; Shell to C I A, 18 January 1908, C F C A 056-4520-1908; Wolf Robe et al. to C I A, 28 May 1909, C F C 056-15976-1909; Transcript of Meeting, 11 February 1911, C F C A 056-14461-1911; Talk of Delegation, 13 June 1912, C F C A 056-59814-1912; Hearing between Delegates and E. B. Meritt, 26 October 1915, C F C 056-112404-1915; Petition to President, 1 November 1915, C F C A 127-116286-1916, and Hearings with Delegation, 22 January 1917, C F C 056-7692-1917; Report on Cheyenne and Arapaho Delegation, 2 February 1924, C F C A 056-8777-1924; Bonnin to C I A, 9 January 1926, and Hearing of 15 January 1926, C F C A 056-1828-1926.

30. Stouch to C I A, 21 March 1906, L R 26581-1906; Wolf Robe et al. to C I A, 28 May 1909, C F C 056-15976-1909; Transcript of Meeting, 11 February 1911, C F C A 056-14461-1911; Hearing of 15 January 1926, C F C A 056-1828-1926; E. M. Goss to Scott, 22 February 1917, Farmers File, O H S; Hearings with Delegation, 22 January 1917, C F C 056-7692-1917; Report on Cheyenne and Arapaho Delegation, 2 February 1924, C F C A 056-8777-1924.

31. C C 7 May 1909; Transcript of Delegation, 11 February 1911, C F C A 056-14461-1911; Talk with Delegation, 13 June 1912, C F C A 056-59814-1912; Conference with Agent, 24 April 1914, C F C A 150-48369-1914.

32. Stouch to C I A, 30 March 1906, L R 26581-1906; Wolf Robe et al. to C I A, 28 May 1909, C F C 056-15976-1909; Transcript, 11 February 1911, C F C A 056-14461-1911; Talk of Delegation, 13 June 1912, C F C A 056-59814-1912; Hearing of 17 January 1917, C F C A 056-5805-1917, and Hearing with Delegation, 22 January 1917, C F C 056-7692-1917; Hearing, 12 February 1920, C F C 056-14620-1920; Hearing, 25 January 1924, C F C A 056-8777-1924; Little Raven to C I A, 20 February 1926, C F C A 056-8933-1926; Hearing, 15 January 1926, C F C A 056-1828-1926.

33. Wolf Robe et al. to C I A, 28 May 1909, C F C 056-15976-1909; Transcript, 11 February 1911, C F C A 056-14461-1911; Hearing, 17 January 1917, C F C A 056-5805-1917, and Hearing, 22 January 1917, C F C 056-7692-1917; Transcript, 15–16 February 1926, C F C A 056-1828-1926.

34. Wolf Robe et al. to C I A, 28 May 1909, C F C 056-15976-1909; Hearing, 12 February 1911, C F C A 056-14461-1911; Hearing, 17 January 1917, C F C A 056-5805-1917, and Hearing, 22 January 1917, C F C 056-7692-1917; Mower to Evans, 7 February and 18 March 1920, C F C 056-16919, and Hearing, 12 February 1920, C F C A 056-14620-1920; Transcript, 15–16 February 1926, C F C A 056-1828-1926; Little Hand to C I A, 30 September 1919, C F C 056-27292-1918, and Talk with Delegation, 1

June 1926, C F C 056-29615-1926. In 1927 the Canton school closed and the agency consolidated with Darlington (Concho).

35. Little Man et al. to C I A, 27 August 1914, C F C 056-93812-1914; Scott to C I A, 20 September 1916, C F C A 056-110618-1915; Big Nose et al. to C I A, 11 November 1919, C F C A 056-14620, and Mower et al. to Evans, 17 February and 18 March 1920, C F C 056-16919-1920; Transcript, 25 January 1924, and Bonnin to C I A, 19 January 1924—both in C F C A 056-8777-1924; Transcript, 15–16 February 1926, C F C A 056-1828-1926; Transcript, 1 June 1926, C F C 056-29615-1926.

36. Conference with Agent, 24 April 1914, C F C A 150-48369-1914; Hearings, 11 February 1911, C F C A 056-14461-1911; Talk with Delegation, 13 June 1912, C F C A 056-59814-1912; Scott to C I A, 7 July 1914, C F C A 054-76272-1914; F. E. Brandon to C I A, 10 August 1921, C F C 063-61493-1921; Grant Left Hand et al. to Bonnin, 5 August 1921, Bonnin to C I A, 1 August 1921 and 11 June 1923, and Turkey Legs to C I A, 2 October 1922—all in C F C A 062-64212-1921; Bonnin to Grant Left Hand et al., 25 July 1922, and Bonnin to Owen, 20 July and 27 July 1927, Indian Celebrations File, O H S; S N R - C A 1922; S N R - C 1924; Bonnin to C I A, 6 March 1924, C F C A 062-64212-1921; Little Raven to C I A, 20 February 1926, C F C A 056-8933-1926.

37. Information on the Arapaho delegates' lodge careers comes from the field notes of Cleaver Warden, 1903 and 1906, F M C.

38. W. Dickens to Freer, 1 July 1910, Fairs File, O H S; Constitution, Cheyenne and Arapaho Fair Association, C F C A 047-79155-1911; Scott to C I A, 27 March 1915, Farmers File, O H S; S N R - C A 1921, 1922, and 1923; Hearing before E. D. Meritt, 12 February 1920, C F C 056-14620-1920.

39. Hearing, 12 February 1920, C F C A 056-14620, and Mower et al. to Evans, 17 February and 18 March 1920, C F C 056-16919-1920; Bonnin to C I A, 19 January 1924, C F C A 056-8777-1924.

40. R C I A 1904, p. 63; R C I A 1906, p. 30.

41. R C I A 1903, p. 244; R C I A 1904. (In 1903 there were four agencies for Cheyennes and Arapahos; these were consolidated in 1927.)

42. S N R - C A 1910, 1911 (*Carrier Pigeon*, 1 June 1911), 1912.

43. S N R - C A 1910, 1914, 1915, 1916, 1917, 1919, 1920.

44. S N R - C A 1921, 1926, 1927, 1928; Industrial Survey, 20 January 1925, Central Files-Cantonment, National Archives, Washington D C.

45. S N R - C A 1916, 1917.

46. Wolf Robe et al. to C I A, 28 May 1909, C F C 056-15976-1909; Hearing, 11 February 1911, C F C A 056-14461-1911; Meeting with Indians, 17 January 1915, C F C A 150-10746-1915; Transcript, 15–16 February 1926, C F C A 056-1828-1926; Talk with

Delegation, 13 June 1912, C F C A 056-59814-1912; Conference with Agent, 24 April 1914, C F C A 150-48369-1914.

47. Transcript, 11 February 1911, C F C A 056-14461-1911; Mower to C I A, 1 February 1922, C F C 063-10246-1922.

48. Hearing, 17 January 1917, C F C A 056-5805-1917; Hearing, 12 February 1920, C F C 056-14620-1920; Talk with Delegates, 1 June 1926, C F C 056-29615-1926.

49. Conference with Agent, 24 April 1914, C F C A 150-48369-1914; Hearings with Delegation, 22 January 1917, C F C 056-7692-1917.

50. Little Raven et al. to C I A, 2 February 1914, C F C 127-14794-1914; Hearing, 7 July 1914, C F C A 054-76272-1914; Transcript, 17 January 1917, C F C A 056-5808-1917; Proceedings of Council, 12 February 1920, C F C 056-14620-1920; Proceedings of 15–16 February 1926, C F C A 056-1828-1926.

51. Quoted in C C 6 October 1911; R C I A 1903.

52. C V R 25 November 1909; C C 6 April 1917; G B 30 January and 24 April 1902. "Mixed blood" is a native cultural (not biological) category.

53. C V R 7 September 1905, 1 March 1906, 14 October 1926, 11 April 1912, 3 February 1927.

54. C C 22 September 1911, 20 September 1912, 18 June 1915.

55. G B 20 February 1902, 22 July 1903, 20 August 1903, 23 July 1908, 27 June 1907.

56. C R 27 November 1924, 1 April 1926, 22 April 1926; C C 9 April 1909; G B 23 January 1902, 20 February 1902, 8 January 1903; G J 29 December 1910.

57. G B 14 August and 23 October 1902; 8 March, 13 September, and 27 September 1906.

58. C R 21 September and 21 October 1911; 23 November 1905; 17 September 1908. In the vicinity of Hammon, settlers in the 1890s expressed hostility to Cheyennes by armed attacks (see Berthrong, *Cheyenne and Arapaho Ordeal*, pp. 184–89).

59. C V R 5 January and 6 April 1911, 7 July 1921, 12 June 1924, 9 August 1926.

60. C C 11 September and 25 August 1911, 30 August 1912, 24 September 1915.

61. G B 28 August and 4 September 1902, 13 August 1903.

62. C V R 13 June 1907; C C 11 June 1909, 23 July 1915; G B 23 July 1903.

63. C R 12 February 1925, 4 March 1909; C C 16 April 1903, 4 March 1910. In 1937, many of the settlers were interviewed about the histories of their communities. The majority of those in Blaine, Canadian, and Kingfisher Counties did not mention their Cheyenne and Arapaho neighbors. Interviewees who did so frequently remarked that Indians constantly begged for food and other help, sometimes in

the form of advances on lease payments. In some of these accounts, interviewees mentioned that Indian dances attracted visitors to the towns. The social world of Cheyennes and Arapahos appears to have been hidden from or ignored by the settlers. Cheyennes and Arapahos mentioned by name are those who own the land being leased by the settler (see Indian Pioneer Papers, w H). In 1990 I interviewed descendants of the settlers in one of the Canadian County communities. Common themes in these interviews were that Indians constantly begged, received settler and federal largess, and were too lazy to work.

64. G B 2 January 1902, 4 April 1907; G J 10 June 1909.

65. C R 17 April 1924.

66. C R 6 April, 4 May, 9 and 30 November 1922.

3. Toward a New Deal

1. Minutes, 14 March 1933, C F-Concho 064.

2. E. V. Downing to A. L. Miller, 14 July 1953, 2483-1953-077, box 124, C F S P 68; Extension Narrative and Statistical Report (hereafter Extension Report), Anadarko Area 1953, 031-7811-1954, box 120, C F S P 59; Extension Report, 1953, 7021-1954-031, box 76, C F S P 59.

3. E. V. Downing to A. L. Miller, 14 July 1953, 2483-1953-077, box 124, C F S P 68; minutes, 1 December 1950, C F C A 054-17127-1946. On Indian participation in World War II, see Bernstein, *American Indians and World War II.* On relocation, see Fixico, *Termination and Relocation.*

4. C R, "Indian News," 18 April 1929; 24 March 1932; 16 November 1933; 3 January 1935; 28 October 1937; 22 December 1938; 31 October 1940; 3 April 1941; minutes, 6 December 1939, C F-Concho 064.

5. C R 29 December 1942; 25 February 1943; 10 May 1945; E R A 20 December 1951; 23 April 1953; 12 July 1956; 29 March 1956.

6. On district dances, see E R A 14 January 1954; 3 March 1955; 22 October 1953; C R, "Indian News," 5 June 1947. On individually sponsored dances, see E R A 22 October 1953; 3 June 1954; 13 January 1955; 19 January 1956; C R, "Indian News," 19 June 1947. On powwows, see C R 2 July 1942; 25 February 1943; 24 August and 21 September 1944; 7 and 28 June 1945; 26 June and 3 July 1947; 19 August and 14 September 1948; 5 August 1954; 8 August 1957; 21 August 1958; 6 August 1959.

7. Some communities also continued the holiday dances. For example, in the town of Watonga, a committee formed that held benefit dances and raised money for Christmas, Easter, and Thanksgiving dances. The chiefs in the area selected the committee members and helped raise money (w R 23 and 30 December 1965; see

W R 7 February 1974 on Hammon); chiefs functioned this way in other districts as well (*W R* 13 January 1966). In 1965 the *Watonga Republican* reported that there were "weekly powwows," for example, at "Dogpatch" in Clinton (*E R A* 30 June 1955) and Hub City in Clinton (*E R A* 25 June 1965). Clinton's powwow was called a homecoming powwow in 1954 (*E R A* 8 July 1954). A powwow princess is mentioned in 1964 (*E R A* 3 October 1964), although this custom was part of the American Indian Exposition (see below in this note and in note 9). The Clinton powwow is mentioned in 1947 (*C R* 3 July 1947) and Colony in 1953 (*E R A* 16 July 1953). Head staff positions are mentioned in the context of the Armed Forces Day powwow in 1963 (*E R A* 2 May 1963). Canton Arapahos began holding an annual Barefoot Powwow in 1954 (*W R* 19 August and 2 September 1954 and *C R* 5 August 1954), but this community held dances referred to as powwows in 1943 with assistance from the town of Canton (*C R* 25 February 1943 and see *C R* 26 June 1947). In 1949 the program included war, rabbit, buffalo, two-step, and snake dances (*C R* 14 September 1949). In 1958 this powwow was advertised as "all Indian managed" with no admission fee (*C R* 21 August and 4 September 1958). The Kingfisher Cheyennes held a powwow in 1947 (*C R* 5 June 1947), but it was a local affair. The C & A powwow of 1956, held in El Reno, had a committee made up of people from all the districts (an all-tribal committee)(see minutes, 2 May 1956, *C F C A* 64, 2402-1957-053, box 16, and *E R A* 9 February and 29 March 1956). Benefit dances are reported for the Geary powwow in 1957 (*E R A* 16 May 1957) and the C & A Colony Powwow is mentioned in 1962 (minutes, 11 January 1962, *C F C A* 64, 2402-1957-053, box 16). Meat's Rodeo (and powwow) began in 1929 in the Canton area and attracted non-Indians as well as Cheyennes and Arapahos (*C R* 31 January 1935, 25 February 1943). The Southwestern Indian Fair, which became the American Indian Exposition, held at Anadarko drew Cheyenne and Arapaho participants beginning in 1931 (see minutes, 28 July 1934, *C F*-Concho 064).

8. *W R* 5 May 1966.

9. On the political agenda of powwows, see minutes, 18 April 1950 and 18 April 1951, *C F*-Concho 064; *C R* 5 August 1954. The American Indian Exposition began with an effort of Kiowas and others to wrest the fair away from the control of federal officials and settlers. The powwow trend in Cheyenne and Arapaho country was a similar expression of a commitment to self-determination. See Gaede, "American Indian Exposition: Reciprocal Commodification" and "American Indian Exposition, 1933–1998." J. M. Haigler's nickname was Barefoot, after his habit of wearing no shoes.

10. *C R* 28 July 1932; 6, 13, and 20 October 1938; 7 August 1941; 3 August 1946; 14 August 1947; 11 August 1949; *E R A* 29 July and 12 August 1954; 28 June and 26

July 1956; 10 May and 14 June 1956; 25 August 1955; 15 August 1957; W R 8 July 1965; 20 June 1974; 8 August 1974; 9 June and 31 July 1975; 8 January 1976. On the Cheyenne Sun Dance, see Moore, *Cheyenne,* pp. 214–28.

11. E R A 14 January 1954; 24 May 1956; 20 June 1957; W R 28 October 1965; 10 February 1966.

12. Interview with Birdie Burns, 27 May 1968, T260; 30 November 1967, T152; 21 November 1967, T162—all in D D; Fowler, F N. On chiefs, see also Moore, *Cheyenne,* pp. 160–67.

13. Fowler, F N.

14. L. S. Bonnin to C I A, 10 May 1928, C F-Concho 064.

15. J. Rowlodge to Bonnin, 18 January 1932, C F-Concho 064.

16. Delegation Hearing, 2 March 1928, C F-Concho 064. The Arapahos' original contract with the attorney was approved on 13 June 1924, and the Cheyennes' contract was approved on 14 December 1923. The contracts were renewed in 1928 and 1929, respectively, and were to expire in June 1931 (Bonnin to C I A, 3 January 1931, C F-Concho 064).

17. Bonnin to C I A, 5 May 1931, C F-Concho 064; tribal council minutes, 26 June 1931, C F-Concho 060.1.

18. Tribal council minutes, 22 December 1930, C F-Concho 064.

19. Bonnin to C I A, 11 June 1930, and tribal council minutes, 15 December 1931, C F-Concho 064. My summary of the history and activity of the General Council is based on documents in C F-Concho 064.

20. Petition from Chiefs and Headmen to C. H. Rhoads, 12 December 1931; tribal council minutes, 22 December 1930 and 27 January 1932—all in C F-Concho 064.

21. Tribal council minutes, 22 December 1930; 30 January 1931 and 15 December 1931; 27 January, 4 March, 9 and 25 November 1932; 14 March 1933; Jess Rowlodge to Bonnin, 28 January 1932, and C. J. Rhoads to Sen. Elmer Thomas, 29 February 1932—all in C F-Concho 064.

22. Tribal council minutes, 30 January 1931; 9 November 1932; 14 March 1933—all in C F-Concho 064.

23. Documents that record much of the tribal council's response to the B I A's presentations on the New Deal are found in C F-Concho 020. See especially tribal council minutes, 17 February 1934 and 3 February 1934; Berry to C I A, 5 March 1934—all in C F-Concho 020. For background on the New Deal and its effect in Native American communities, see Taylor, *New Deal,* and Philp, *John Collier's Crusade.*

24. Tribal council minutes, 3 February 1934, C F-Concho 020; tribal council minutes, 22 October 1934, C F-Concho 064.

25. Tribal council minutes, 22 October 1934, 8 December 1934, and 26 January 1935, C F-Concho 064; 3 February 1934, C F-Concho 020.

26. See files in C F-Concho 020, and minutes, 4 April 1935, C F-Concho 064.

27. Minutes, 8 June 1935, C F-Concho 064.

28. Tribal council minutes, 3 November 1934 and 8 December 1934, C F-Concho 064.

29. Tribal council minutes, 8 February and 8 December 1934, C F-Concho 064; tribal council minutes, 3 February 1934, C F-Concho 020.

30. John Otterby to Charles H. Berry, 15 March 1935; Minutes of Geary and Greenfield Local Council, 4 December 1935; tribal council minutes, 29 April 1936; Proposed Amendment to the Constitution—all in C F-Concho 064.

31. Tribal council minutes, 19 March 1937, and James Curry to C I A, 28 April 1937; H. D. Milburn to C. Berry, 12 July 1937; tribal council minutes, 8 May 1937—all in C F-Concho 064, box 26.

32. Collier to Berry, 17 June 1937, C F-Concho 064.

33. Berry to C I A, 23 September 1937, C F-Concho 064. See also interview with Birdie Burns, 27 May 1968, T261, D D.

34. Collier Circular, 19 February 1934, C F-Concho 020; minutes, 22 October and 3 November 1934; C. Berry to Fred Daiker, 1 June 1936; Berry to Adult Members of the Cheyenne-Arapaho Tribe, 20 August 1937; Berry et al. to Sen. Thomas, 5 February 1935—all in C F-Concho 064.

35. Minutes, 3 February 1934, C F-Concho 020 (see Little Raven and Turkey Leg speeches); minutes, 19 March 1937; Chief William Goodsell speech, 21 January 1937; minutes, 3 November 1934—all in C F-Concho 064.

36. Business committee minutes, 1 June 1938, and Ben Dwight to Monahan, 7 October 1938, C F-Concho 064.

37. Business committee minutes, 2 March, 6 April, and 7 December 1938, 14 June 1939; Ed Burns to John Collier, 4 August 1939—all in C F-Concho 064.

38. Business committee minutes, 1 June, 6 July, and 7 September 1938, C F-Concho 064.

39. Business committee minutes, 2 October 1940, C F-Concho 064.

40. Business committee minutes, 7 August 1940 and 6 August 1941, C F-Concho 064; Oscar Chapman to Guy Hobgood, 11 December 1941, and Hobgood to C I A, 20 February 1942, C F-Concho 068.

41. Business committee minutes, 23 February, 17 April, and 12 July 1946; 5 February and 5 March 1947; 23 April and 3 December 1948; 17 November 1950; 3 January, 7 March, and 2 May 1951; 2 April and 3 September 1952; 4 February, 11 March, 28 April, and 1 July 1953—all in C F C A 054-17127-1946; W R 30 December 1948 and 26 May 1949; W. J. Pitner to C I A, 20 March 1957, 056-7091-1953, box 76, C F S P 59. See Act of January 29, 1942, 2 Stat 21, and Act of August 10, 1946, 60 Stat 976, *U.S. Statutes at Large.*

42. Business committee minutes, 3 March 1948 and 6 February, C F C A 054-17127-1946.

43. Business committee minutes, 19 May and 6 August 1947 and 3 December 1948, C F C A 054-17127-1946; W R 29 January 1948 and 3 May 1948; Progress Report on Reduction of Bureau Services by Termination, 30 June 1952, 2483-1953-077, box 124, C F S P 68; business committee minutes, 3 January 1951; 3 December 1952; 15 January, 4 February, 4 and 11 March, 1 July 1953; 27 January and 11 February 1954—all in 7091-1953-056, C F S P 59; Glen Emmons to C I A, 8 April 1954, and W. B. Greenwood to Chair, Cheyenne-Arapaho Business Committee, 31 March 1954, 8924-1953-806, box 81, C F S P 59.

44. Dover Trent to Albert Hamilton, 4 May 1949; Trent to C I A, 18 October 1949, Cheyenne-Arapaho Correspondence—both in C F A A; business committee minutes, 6 July 1938, and memo from B. Dwight to A. C. Monahan, 7 October 1938, C F-Concho 064.

45. Business committee minutes, 7 December 1938; 4 June, 6 August, and 1 October 1941—in C F-Concho 064; business committee minutes, 5 May and 3 December 1948, and R. Boynton to W. A. Brophy, 20 April 1946—both in C F C A 054-17127-1946.

46. E. V. Downing to A. L. Miller, 14 July 1953, 2483-1953-077, box 124, C F S P 68; business committee minutes, 1 December 1950; 4 April and 2 May 1951; 9 July and 5 November 1952; 1 March and 3 June 1953; 6 February, 3 and 31 March, 5 May, 11 December 1954—all in C F C A 054-17127-1946.

47. Business committee minutes, 1 February 1939, C F-Concho 064, and 25-27 June 1940, C F-Concho 060. The larger committee of 1938–41 also was composed of men, except for one woman who served in 1939 and was a member of a relatively well-off Cheyenne family from Canton.

48. On district petitions, see business committee minutes, 1 June, 8 October, 7 December 1938; 14 January, 1 February, and Resolution of 29 April 1939; business committee minutes, 3 January, 6 March, 1 May 1940—all in C F-Concho 064. On polling, see business committee minutes, 8 October, 7 December 1938, C F-Concho 064; 1 May, 6 November 1940; and 7 May 1941; and in C F C A 054-17127-

1946, see business committee minutes, 7 October 1953; 27 January, 11 February, and 3 March 1954. On donations, see minutes, 4 May 1938; 5 April and 13 May 1939; 6 August 1947, C F-Concho 064. On chiefs, see business committee minutes, 6 March 1940; 7 May 1941; 5 February 1947; 23 January 1948—all in C F-Concho 064; business committee minutes, 1 September 1952; 11 March, 3 June, 1 July 1953; 27 January 1954; 7 December 1955—all in C F C A 054-17127-1946.

49. C & A Tally Sheet, 18 September 1937, and Election Tally in C F-Concho 064, and Election Returns of 7 January 1953 in C F C A 055-49543-1943; E. V. Downing to A. L. Miller, 14 July 1953, 2483-1953-077, box 124, C F S P 68.

50. Business committee minutes, 3 July 1940, C F-Concho 064; minutes, 1 May and 12 July 1946; 5 May 1948; 3 October 1951; 3 September 1952; 4 February and 25 August 1953; 5 May and 3 November, and 1 December 1954; 14 October 1955—all in C F C A 054-17127-1946; W. Payne to C I A, 16 March 1954, 5288-1954-720, box 81, C F S P 59; E. V. Downing to A. L. Miller, 14 July 1953, 2483-1953-077, box 124, C F S P 68.

51. Business committee minutes, 2 February, 7 March, 3 October and 7 November, C F C A 054-17127-1946; Sam Dicke to Secretary of Interior, 27 July 1953; Dicke to Robert S. Kerr, 19 August 1953; and W. B. Greenwood to Dicke, 10 September 1953, 7091-1953-056, C F S P 59.

52. Business committee minutes, 8 May and 5 August 1953; 27 January, 6 February, 3 March, 13 October, 1 December 1954, C F C A 054-17127-1946.

53. Business committee minutes, 1 June and 14 October 1955, C F C A 054-17127-1946. In later years, the integrity of attorney Payne was questioned by some business committee members.

54. *E R A* 3 and 10 November 1955.

55. Business committee minutes, 4 January 1956, C F C A 054-17127-1946.

56. T. Reld to Chair, 22 January 1958; W. B. Greenwood to Chair, 29 April 1957; and Glenn Emmons to Chair, 29 May 1956—all in 7091-1953-056, box 76, C F S P 59; *E R A* 19 January, 7 and 14 December 1961. The 1961 delegation was W. Wilson, Sam Buffalo, J. Pedro, and H. Haury.

57. *E R A* 19 April 1956; 23 January, 24 April, and 5 June 1958; 4 June 1959; 22 September and 13 October 1960; E. J. Utz to V. Wickersham, 7 August 1957, 1427-1954-211, box 77, C F S P 59.

58. *E R A* 16 March, 13 and 27 April 1961. Rumors circulated, for example, that claim money was being withheld by the B I A and the business committee (W. B. Greenwood to V. Wickersham, 11 January 1956, 1427-1954-211, C F S P 59).

59. Business committee resolution, 20 September and 5 June 1957, Cheyenne and

Arapaho Tribal Council, C F A A; Tribal budget, 1961, Tribal Government Records, C & A; business committee minutes, 6 June 1956, 00-1953-054, box 76, C F S P 59.

60. E R A 10 November 1955 and 19 March 1959; business committee minutes, 6 June and 6 July 1956, 00-1953-054, box 76, C F S P 59; business committee minutes, 2 May and 6 June 1956, C F C A 17127-1946-054; on the amendment referendum of November 3, 1959 and ordinance of May 4, 1961, see file 2402-1957-053, box 16, and Anadarko Area Office Report, 8 December 1959, 00-1956-032, box 113—both in C F A A 64; Chair's Report, 7 October 1967, C & A.

61. E R A 7 and 14 December and 26 July 1961. The delegation of November–December 1962 was W. Wilson, Sam Buffalo, Ed Burns, J. Fire, E. Woolworth, and Dave Williams (L. Gay to General Office Staff, 4 December 1962, B I A A). The delegation of 1963 was Wilson, Buffalo, Burns, Walter Hamilton, Woolworth, Fire, Williams, and H. Haury (W. Pitman to C I A, 12 March 1963, B I A A).

62. E R A 12 August, 7 October, 11 November, 23 December 1965; D O 11 November 1965.

63. E R A 13 and 20 January, 17 and 24 February, 18 March 1966; 10 January 1967.

64. E R A 13 January 1966 (also on the eleventh business committee, two Cheyennes served as chair and vice-chair); Resolution 18-R15, 6 April 1966, C & A.

65. E R A 16 June, 13 November 1966; Chair's Report, 7 October 1967, and Proceedings of General Council, 29 October 1966, C & A; W R 17 August 1967.

66. E R A 16 June 1966; business committee resolution 19, 22, 23, 19-R15, 6 April 1966, and Chair's Report, 7 October 1967, C & A.

67. Fowler, F N; business committee resolution 67-R15, 6 July 1966, and Chair's Report, 7 October 1967, C & A; E R A 19 October 1967.

68. E R A 24 October 1968 and 27 February 1974; business committee minutes, 3 October 1972 and 13 April 1974, C & A; W R 26 September 1974; 9 January, 6 February, 10 April, 12 June, 7 August, 11 December 1975; 2 September 1976. See Castile, *To Show Heart*, on War on Poverty programs in Indian communities.

69. Report of Delegation, 16–19 August 1971; minutes of General Council, 3 October 1970 and 21 July 1973—all in C & A; E R A 26 October 1968; Fowler, F N.

70. Fowler, F N; business committee minutes, 3 October 1970, and Report of Delegation, 16–19 August 1971, C & A.

71. Business committee minutes, 13 April 1974, C & A; W R 24 April, 19 June, 24 July 1975.

72. W R 30 October 1975; 13 May and 9 December 1976.

73. *E R A* 9 February 1956; 26 September 1963; *W R* 7 April 1966; 6 February 1975.

74. *E R A* 2 June 1955; 22 September 1960; 13 and 20 January, 16 June 1966; *D O* 11 November 1965; *W R* 7 November 1974 and 18 December 1975.

75. *W R* 5 May 1966; 9 January, 6 February, 7 August, 11 December 1975.

76. *W R* 25 June 1965; 1 July 1965. In the late 1940s and early 1950s, "Indian News" columns by Ralph Beard in *W R* and by Charles Wicks in *E R A* reported on visits and the health of individuals and, while giving some insider information, did not directly challenge media imagery.

77. Harold Cameron to Mrs. Fred R. Harris, 25 July 1966, file 27, box 282, Fred R. Harris Collection, Carl Albert Center, University of Oklahoma. For background on Oklahomans for Indian Opportunity, see Cobb, " 'Us Indians Understand the Basics.' "

78. *W R* 5 May 1966; Fowler, F N.

79. *W R* 28 October and 9 December 1965; 10 February 1966; 18 September 1975; 30 October 1975; interviews with Howard Goodbear, 3 February and 3 March 1968, T201, D D; minutes, 20 April 1974 and 28 August 1975, C & A.

80. *E R A* 23 December 1965; interviews with Jess Rowlodge, 2 November 1967, T158, and 16 April 1968, T239, and interview with Birdie Burns, 30 November 1967, T171, D D.

81. Fowler, F N.

82. Fowler, F N.

83. *W R* 20 April and 7 November 1974, 8 May and 18 December 1975.

84. *W R* 20 April and 17 October 1974, 9 January, 18 December, and 30 October 1975; Fowler, F N.

85. *W R* 30 September and 16 December 1965.

4. "A Reason to Fail"

1. Transcript of Proceedings, 17 July and 26–30 October 1995, *U.S.A. v. Mike Shadaram; Juanita Learned; Michael Alan Combs; and Viola Hatch*, C R-95-37C, U.S. Court Clerks Office, U.S. Federal Court Building, Oklahoma City, Oklahoma.

2. The information in this chapter is based on my observations at the tribal office, tribal court, and in the community from 1984 through 1994 and on interviews with business committee members; election board members; directors of administrative departments, programs, and enterprises; and tribal employees generally. I also was allowed access to many of the materials filed and produced by the tribal office. Most of the information on programs is from 1994; since that time, the tribes have instituted additional programs.

3. Constitution and By-Laws of the Cheyenne-Arapaho Tribes of Oklahoma, "Cheyenne-Arapaho Tribes Base Studies, 1993," C & A.

4. In 1997 the Cheyenne and Arapaho Tribes made a compact with the state of Oklahoma to pay a percentage of the tobacco sales to reflect the purchase of products by non-Indians. Tobacco prices still are somewhat cheaper than at other locations. The thirty-first business committee opened a gas station, which also pays some state tax.

5. The General Revenue and Tax Act followed the American Indian Tax Act passed by Congress in 1982.

6. In the C F R court, established at Concho in 1979, the B I A could affirm or reverse the decisions of the court.

7. W R 7 August 1986.

8. "Cheyenne-Arapaho Tribes Base Studies, 1993," C & A; W R 8 September 1977; 21 June 1979.

9. Elizabeth S. Grobsmith reached the same conclusion with regard to the housing program at Rosebud Reservation (*Lakota of the Rosebud*).

10. Congress passed revisions to the Self-Determination Act, which the tribes feel have not done enough to correct problems with the legislation, in large part because Congress does not give adequate funding to the B I A. Recently, the Cheyenne and Arapaho Tribes were part of a class action suit (*Ramah Navajo Chapter v. U.S. Department of the Interior and the U.S.A.*) that will result in some recovery of indirect costs for past years.

11. W R 20 March 1986.

12. "Cheyenne-Arapaho Tribes Base Studies, 1993," C & A.

13. W R 27 October and 3 November 1983; 9 February 1984; 8 May 1986.

14. "Cheyenne-Arapaho Tribes Base Studies, 1993," C & A.

15. W R 9 March and 17 August 1978; 1 February 1979; 18 September 1980; 7 April 1983; 12 February 1987.

16. Transcript of Proceedings, 26–30 October 1995, *U.S.A. v. Mike Shadaram et al.*; W R 20 April, 3 August, 26 October 1995. The non-Indian comptroller and business manager, Mike Combs and Mike Shadaram, also were tried and convicted for their involvement in the tribes' financial irregularities.

5. For the People

1. W R 9 and 16 June, 16 October 1977; 2 February 1978; 25 June 1981; 29 April, 7 October, November 1982; 14 July and 10 November 1983; 6 and 11 September 1984; 6

March and 12 June 1986; 7 July and 6 October 1988; 8 February, 8 March, 24 May, 7 June 1990; 17 October and 21 November 1991; 11 March 1993; 10 and 24 February, 17 November, 15 December 1994; 7 September, 5 October, 8 November, 10, 22, and 27 December 1995; 15 January, 3, 9, 17, and 24 July 1996; 19 March, 3 September, 8 and 29 October, 2 November, 10 December 1997 (see also *Newsweek,* August 1997); 6 May, 13 and 17 June, 14 October, 9, 16, and 23 December 1998; 10 March, 19 May, 8 August, 22 and 29 September, 6 and 27 October, 10 and 24 November 1999; s c a n n 15 January and 20 November 1985 and August 1987; *C & A Bulletin* March and October 1988; 12 January, 23 February, 9 November, 7 December 1989; February and May 1989; April 1990; February 1993; March 1994.

2. w r 18 April 1985; 18 February 1988; 19 April 1990; 22 June 1995; 9 December 1998; s c a n n 15 January and 25 February 1985; July 1987; *C & A Bulletin* April, June and July 1988; April 1989.

3. w r 10 September, 29 October, 12 November 1981; 9 February, 4 and 11 March, 6 and 20 May, 26 August 1982; 10 February, 21 April, 9 June, 25 August, 15 December 1983; 8 November 1984; 7 August 1986; 8 June 1989; 12 September 1991; 5 and 12 March 1993; 6 and 13 October 1994; 30 March, 27 April, 3 August, 21 September 1995; 23 October 1996; 17 June 1998; *C & A Bulletin* April and May 1989; March 1990; December 1994.

4. w r 13 and 20 March, 29 May, 31 July, 9 October 1980; 10 September 1981; 29 September, 6 October 1983; 9 May, 12 December 1985; 6 March, 7 August 1986; 7 July 1988; 29 June and 9 November 1989; 5 April 1990; 12 and 19 September, 3 October 1991; 20 August, 19 and 26 November 1992; 22 June, 7 September 1995; 10 September, 2 and 23 October 1996; 5 February, 10 September, 8 October 1997; 6 May, 9 August 1998; s c a n n 3 May and 12 December 1985; 27 February 1986; November–December 1986; *C & A Bulletin* December 1889; April and July 1992; December 1994.

5. w r 28 April and 7 July 1983.

6. w r 15 September, 24 November, 8 December 1983; 12 April, 8 November, 6 December 1984.

7. w r 8 September and 6 October 1977; 7 June and 13 September 1979; 7 May, 16 July, 6 August 1981; 25 February, 6 May 1982; 7 July and 24 November 1983; 8 and 30 November; 6 December 1984; 7 August 1986; 11 June and 6 August 1987; 11 February, 7 April, and 23 June 1988; 2 March 1989; 7 February, 12 and 19 September, 12 and 19 December 1991; 4 June 1992; 7 January, 8 April 1993; 21 July and 29 December 1994; 12 January, 30 March, 6 July, 13 December 1995; 5 June and 17 July 1996; 15 October and 10 December 1997; 8 April, 17 June, 19 August 1998; 7 April, 9 June, 18 August 1999; s c a n n 15 January, 20 November

1985; 25 March 1986; November–December 1986; *C & A Bulletin* October 1987; February–April 1988; October 1993.

8. W R 16 August 1984; 9 June and 6 October 1994; 3 February 1999.

9. W R 13 January, 10 February 1977; 11 June, 16 July, 6 August, 10 September 1981; 8 April, 29 July, 7 October 1982; 9 February, 15 March, 12 April, 9 June, 12 July, 6 August, 8 November, 11 and 29 December 1983; 12 October 1984; 18 July, 15 August 1985; 6 February, 8 May, 11 September, 11 December 1986; 12 February 1987; 7 April, 12 May, 9 June, 6 October, 10 November 1988; 10 May, 6 September 1990; 17 December 1992; 10 June 1993; 9 June 1994; 11 May, 7 September, 12 October, 29 November 1995; 5 June, 3 and 24 July, 23 October 1996; 18 March, 13 August, 10 September 1997; 8 April, 27 May, 19 August, 9 September 1998; S C A N N 15 January, 17 May, 31 July, 2 December 1985; 29 May, 27 February, and 25 August 1986; July 1987.

10. W R 6 November 1980; 24 December 1981; 29 July 1982; 9 February 1984; 10 February and 3 November 1994; 1 January 1997.

11. W R 3 March, 8 September 1977; 7 June, 16 August, 23 August 1979; 21 January, 11 July, 18 July, 7 November, 14 November, 12 December 1985; 7 August, 11 September 1986; 15 January 1987; 15 September, 3, 10, and 17 June 1988; S C A N N 9 November 1984; 17 May, 20 November, 24 December 1985; 31 July 1986; *C & A Bulletin* February 1989; August 1993.

12. *C & A Bulletin* August 1988; March 1989; W R 14 October 1993; D O 27 June 1994.

13. W R 9 January, 12 June 1986; 16 April 1987; 8 March 1990; 12 September 1991; 3 March 1994; 30 March, 7 September, and 19 October 1995.

14. W R 7 July and 10 March 1977; 16 August 1984; 11 September 1986; 25 February 1988; 12 September 1991.

15. W R 16 February 1978; 18 September 1980; 18 July 1985; 7 August 1986 (see also 12 March 1987); 12 February 1987; 10 March 1988.

16. W R 9 June 1988; 13 July, 28 September, and 19 October 1989.

17. W R 12 April 1979; 7 February and 9 November 1989; 11 April 1991.

18. Fowler, F N. Most of the observations, interviews, and conversations on which this chapter is based come from my fieldwork from 1984 through 1994. I relied on newspaper accounts for subsequent years. I have 528 recorded interviews with Cheyennes and Arapahos from a representative sample. I spoke with 116 Cheyennes and Arapahos; in addition to these interviews, I also spoke with B I A officials, individuals from other tribes, local non-Indians, and other knowledge-able parties. Quotations are from recorded observations, interviews, and written materials I collected during my fieldwork. I use pseudonyms throughout

unless the material used is from published media accounts. On occasion, I have disguised identities in published accounts where comments might be embarrassing to individuals. Incorporated in the interviews with Cheyennes and Arapahos are conversations with business committee members who served on the first through the twenty-ninth committees, a total of thirty-one individuals, sixteen Arapahos and fifteen Cheyennes. For the early years, few former committee members were still living, but I was able to talk to David Fanman, Joe Antelope, Henry Whiteshield, Pete Birdchief, Bill Tall Bird, and George Levi (see table 2).

19. W R 13 January, 15 December 1977; 12 January, 3 and 6 April, 11 May, 13 July, 7 December 1978; 25 January, 8 February, 12 April, 27 September 1979.

20. W R 10 January, 7 and 14 February, 27 March, 8 May, 24 July 1980; 19 February, 19 March, 21 May, 11 and 25 June 1981; 7 January, 25 February 1982.

21. W R 12 January, 27 December 1984; 15 August, 12 September, 17 October 1985; S C A N N 26 October 1984; 25 February, 12 April, 28 June, 24 December 1985.

22. W R 9 January, 6 March, 10 April, 11 September 1986; 12 March, 28 May, 17 December 1987; S C A N N May–June 1987.

23. W R 4 and 25 February, 10 March, 7 April, 7 July, 11 August 1988.

24. W R 11 January, 22 March, 2 April, 9 August, 6 September 1990; 21 March, 8 August, 26 September, 10 October, 28 November, 19 December 1991.

25. W R 9 January, 6 February, 12 March, 7 and 21 May, 9 and 16 July, 20 August, 10 and 17 December 1992; 20 and 27 May, 10 June, 18 November, 9 December 1993; C & A Bulletin February 1992.

26. W R 10 February, 22 September, and 22 December 1994; 16 and 20 April, 11 and 18 May 1995.

27. W R 3, 10, and 17 January, 28 February, 6 March, 17 April, 8 and 22 May, 3 July 1996; 1, 8, 15, and 22 January, 9 April, 7 May, 9 July, 6 August 1997.

28. W R 8 May 1998; 14 and 21 April, 12 May, 16 June, 28 July, 18 August, 8 and 22 September 1999.

29. Robert L. Bee provides the best account of the importance of travel for tribal officials (*Politics of American Indian Policy*). In his work the focus is on travel to Washington D C.

30. W R 12 January 1984; Fowler, F N.

31. W R 7 September 1989; 12 April, 10 May, 9, 16, and 23 August, 6 September 1990; 21 March, 9 and 16 May, 13 June, 4, 11, and 18 July, 1 August, 12, 19, and 26 September, 3, 10, and 17 October, 21 November, 12 and 19 December 1991.

32. W R 23 October 1996; D O 17 October 1996.

6. "A Line Has Been Drawn"

1. Quotations from Cheyennes and Arapahos throughout the chapter are taken from my field notes (1984–94) or, where cited, from the *Watonga Republican* or the tribal newspapers (s c a n n or *C & A Bulletin*).

2. w r 7 September 1989; 18 October 1990.

3. On misuse of funds by members of the community, see w r 11 July 1985; 25 February 1988; 26 January and 2 March 1989; 12 September and 21 November 1991; s c a n n 12 April 1985; June 1988.

4. w r 13 September 1979; 17 July, 11 and 18 December 1980; 2 December 1982; 12 September 1985; 11 December 1986; s c a n n 24 August 1984; August 1988.

5. w r 20 October and 17 November 1983; 2 April, 11 June, and 20 August 1992; 11 November 1993; s c a n n 21 June, 12 July, and 20 November 1985; *C & A Bulletin* November and December 1993.

6. w r 7 April and 4 August 1977; 11 January 1979; 27 March 1980; 2 April 1981; 17 August 1989; 29 July 1993; s c a n n 24 August 1984; 28 February 1985. About half of the eligible voters do not register to vote. Thus, in February 1986, 2,300 out of 4,700 eligible voters registered (w r 6 February 1986).

7. w r 9 September 1982. In recent years, a small group of Cheyenne chiefs and soldier society members has met periodically to consider issues involving repatriation; in fact, the business committees have deferred to this group rather than directly involving themselves in matters associated with Cheyenne religion. The general view is that the politics of religion and tribal government are distinct spheres. Thus, there are frequent clashes between competing groups of Cheyenne religious authorities, who may or may not try to involve tribal officials; but, these officials (including the tribal court) attempt to avoid getting involved in these disputes (see Moore, *Cheyenne,* pp. 242–43).

8. w r 13 and 20 January, 10 February, 21 April, 4 August, 6 October, 3 and 24 November 1977.

9. w r 25 May, 22 June, 13 July, 14 and 21 September, 30 November 1978.

10. w r 12 October, 7, 14, and 28 December 1978; 11 and 25 January, 15 February, 15 March, 10 and 17 May 1979.

11. w r 12 April, 24 and 31 May, 13 September, 18 and 25 October, 1, 15, 18, and 22 November, 6 December 1979.

12. w r 7, 14, and 28 February, 27 March, 3 April, 31 July, 21 and 28 August, 9 October, 11 December 1980.

13. w r 19 March, 2 April, 25 June, 16 and 23 July, 17 September, 8 and 15 October 1981.

14. *WR* 25 February, 10 and 17 June, 22 July, 5 and 19 August, 7 October 1982; 13 January, 3 and 24 February, 10 March, 28 April, 6 October, 24 November 1983.

15. *WR* 12 January, 9 and 23 February, 8 March, 12 April, 10 May, 16 August, 11 October, 6, 20, and 27 December 1984; *SCANN* 24 August, 11 September, 12 and 26 October, 10 December 1984.

16. *WR* 4 April, 16 and 30 May, 18 July, 3, 10, and 17 October, 21 and 28 November 1985; *SCANN* 28 January, 28 February, 31 May, 29 July, 20 November, 24 December 1985.

17. *WR* 9 January, 6 and 27 February, 6 and 27 March, 17 April, 1 May, 12 June, 7 August, 2 October, 6 and 16 November, 11 December 1986; *SCANN* November and December 1986.

18. *WR* 15 January, 12 February, 12 March, 23 April, 28 May, 6 August, 8 October, 12 November, 31 December 1987.

19. *WR* 7 January, 11 and 25 February, 7 April, 12 May, 9 June, 11 August, 8 September, 6 and 13 October 1988.

20. *WR* 2 March, 4 and 11 May, 6 July, 17 August, 7 September, 12 October, 9 and 23 November, 7 and 14 December 1989; *C & A Bulletin* September 1989.

21. *WR* 11 January, 8 February, 8 March, 3 May, 7 June, 9 August, 27 September, 11 October 1990; *C & A Bulletin* February and April 1990.

22. *WR* 17 January, 7, 14, and 21 February, 13 and 27 June, 4 and 11 July, 1 August, 26 September, 10, 24, and 31 October, 7, 21, and 28 November, 12, 19, and 26 December 1991.

23. *WR* 9 January, 6 February, 12 March, 2 and 16 April, 11 June, 9 and 16 July, 6 and 20 August, 17 September, 1, 8, and 19 October, 10, 17, 24, and 31 December 1992.

24. *WR* 14 and 28 January, 4, 11, and 25 February, 18 March, 1 and 22 April, 6 and 20 May, 29 July, 12 August, 16 September, 7 October, 21 and 25 November 1993.

25. *WR* 15 and 29 January, 10 February, 10 March, 7 and 14 April, 26 May, 28 July, 6, 20, and 27 October, 10 November, 8 December 1994; 9 February, 3 August, 12 October, 8 November, 20 December 1995.

26. *WR* 17 January, 7 and 14 February, 13 March, 17 July, 4 and 24 September, 9 and 16 October, 6 November, 11 and 25 December 1996; 19 March, 2 April, 12 August, 8 and 10 October, 5 November, 10 December 1997. The separatist movement originated from a partnership between a businessman and a group of dissidents, who sought to bypass the business committee in the establishment of business enterprises. Some sentiment exists, as in the past, for separating Arapaho and Cheyenne affairs, but the reasons against such a change have prevailed in the minds of most Cheyennes and Arapahos.

27. *WR* 25 February, 4 and 10 March, 29 April, 1 July, 19 August, 23 September, 4 November, 9, 25, and 30 December 1998; 6 January, 10 February, 7 April, 4 August, 22 September, 6 October, 24 November 1999.

28. *WR* 5 and 26 October 1978; 15 February and 30 August 1979; 24 July and 1 December 1980; 12 June 1986; 8 October 1987; 7 January 1988; 14 September 1995; *SCANN* 15 January 1985. On Oklahoma politicians, see *WR* 21 September 1995 and *DO* 6 and 15 December 1995.

29. *WR* 27 March, 3 April, 9 October, 1 December 1980; 23 February 1984; 5 October 1989.

30. *WR* 6 March and 11 September 1986; 3 and 10 October 1985; 5 October 1989; 12 March and 13 August 1992.

31. *WR* 25 May, 22 June, 13 July, 9 November 1978; 18 and 25 October, 1 November 1979; 18 September 1980; 30 March 1985; 2 January 1988.

32. *WR* 7 September 1989.

7. Coming around the Drum

1. *SCANN* 30 November 1984. Unless otherwise cited, all quotations are from my field notes.

2. Studies of the powwow (and what I refer to as dances) at first accepted the view that powwows were a form of Pan-Indianism, that is, that these events, including songs and dances, represented an amalgamation of tribal traits, an expression of "Indianness" rather than tribal tradition (Corrigan, "Plains Indian Powwow"). These studies generally embraced James H. Howard's argument that Pan-Indianism was a stage of assimilation, that the amalgamation of tribal traits was a step toward loss of Indian identity ("Pan-Indian Culture of Oklahoma" and "Pan-Indianism in Native American Music and Dance"; see also Margaret Sanford, "Pan-Indianism, Acculturation and the American Ideal," who argues that Pan-Indianism allowed for integration into American society, for it provided a positive image of ethnic identity). Corrigan and later Howard, in his discussion of the gourd dance ("Plains Gourd Dance"), viewed the Pan-Indian powwow complex of innovations as a revitalization movement, a way for native peoples to express identity in a hostile social environment and to underscore the differences between Indians and non-Indians (see Ellis, "Truly Dancing").

Reassessments of the Pan-Indian interpretation have emphasized that tribal customs have survived and coexist with those that are common to several tribes and that the powwow complex is not a product of assimilation but of revitalization of local native sociocultural institutions. William K. Powers ("Plains Indian Music and Dance" and *War Dance* [pp. 10–11]) argues that intertribal developments (such as the diffusion of songs and dances) have stimulated revivals of local traditions and precipitated innovations compatible with those traditions. Much of this literature on the powwow focuses on the expression of ethnic identity in the context of the powwow complex. Loretta Fowler *(Shared Symbols, Contested Meanings,* [pp. 141–95]) focuses on the way in which powwow rituals and the symbols therein allow for the expression of a range of identity constructs—Indian, tribal reservation or community, gender, kinship, and age group.

Another approach to understanding persistence, innovation, and revival has been to put ritual life in historical perspective—to document that native peoples have managed to perpetuate institutions and values despite colonial repression (Kracht, "Kiowa Powwows") and to examine the ways in which native communities have changed their ritual symbols (see Fowler, *Arapahoe Politics*) and organization (see Foster, *Being Comanche*).

Studies of the powwow complex also have emphasized its contemporary social, economic, and political aspects. Kracht writes that the powwow (especially its dances) is a vehicle for the Kiowa to forge a unity as a people, despite social differentiation, through the evocation of emotional ties. Foster views the powwow as a vehicle for the construction of social organization in an era when the Comanche community is fragmented and dispersed. John H. Moore ("How the Giveaways and Pow-Wows Redistribute the Means of Subsistence") employs an economic interpretation, arguing that the Southern Cheyenne and Arapaho powwow complex, that is, its giveaway ceremonies, is the product of poverty— of a marginal and uncertain local economy—and that it functions primarily to redistribute resources over the long term (see also Corrigan, "Plains Indian Powwow", who discusses the creation of "exploitable" ties between people of different reservations or Bands). Noel Dyck ("Political Powwow") examines a case in which organizing powwows facilitated success in native politics in western Canada.

The issue of how the powwow complex evokes emotions has been largely ignored. (But see William K. Powers, "Foolish Words," who discusses how the texts of Lakota love songs evoke emotion and work to help men deal with rejection.) While Kracht refers to the creation of a common identity through the shared experience of emotions of sadness and happiness, I will be examining who specifically shares what emotions, under what circumstances, and how these emotions work together with ideas about connectedness in the Cheyenne and Arapaho community. What I also explore (and what has not been addressed in the literature) is the coexistence of a ritual symbolism in dances and powwows that focuses on the theme of unity and alliance, on the one hand, and intertribal and intratribal rivalry outside the context of the powwow, on the other (although the powwow is not without expressions of rivalry; see Kracht, "Kiowa Powwows," and Moore, "How Giveaways").

3. For a discussion of the history and diffusion of the gourd dance, see James H. Howard, "Plains Gourd Dance." See also Ellis, "Truly Dancing," and Kracht, "Kiowa Powwows."

4. William K. Powers provides a good introduction to the structure of the war dance song (*War Dance*, pp. 32–38) and a discussion of Plains music in general. The war dance is a modern version of the Omaha Dance, or grass dance. The term "war dance" may have come into use as a result of the popularity of Wild West shows. See Hatton, "In the Tradition," for a discussion of women's singing groups, a few of which are active on the northern Plains.

5. There is a large literature on Plains Indian dance and costume, too numerous to cite in its entirety here. My description is drawn from James H. Howard, "Pan-Indian Culture," and William K. Powers, *War Dance*. See also selected passages and references in Koch, *Dress Clothing of the Plains Indians,* and Laubin and Laubin, *Indian Dances of North America.*

6. The giveaway in various forms is an aspect of the Plains powwow complex that has received attention from anthropologists. Everywhere on the Plains, gift giving is a means to prestige; other functions have been identified as well. The giveaway has been viewed from the perspective of exchange theory, that receipt of a gift requires a return gift, that reciprocal exchange promotes alliances between non-kin and communities, and that relatives are expected to assist each other, which promotes family bonds (Grobsmith, "Lakhota Giveaway"; Weist, "Giving Away"). Both Grobsmith ("Changing Role of the Giveaway") and Weist ("Giving Away") also point to the giveaway as a marker of Indian and of Lakota and Northern Cheyenne identity, respectively. Others emphasize economic functions. Mary Jane Schneider ("Women's Work") points to the giveaway's promotion of craft production (quilts that are given away, for example), the items of which are sold by local Mandan, Hidatsa, and Arikara producers to other tribal members, many of whom earn a living off the reservation. These more affluent participants bring in money to the reservation for distribution during giveaways. Moore ("How Giveaways") argues that reciprocal exchange is a way to recognize others who help throughout the year with subsistence needs, such as food, gas, fuel, and telephone calls. Alice B. Kehoe ("Giveaway Ceremony of Blackfoot and Plains Cree") argues against viewing the giveaway as primarily an economic institution or an alliance mechanism. She views the ceremony as an "announcer" of ethnic affiliation, individuals' and families' social networks, and status rankings. The donors claim a new social status for the honoree and, at the same time, express their membership in an idealized rather than a bounded net-

work. In this ritualized context they give expression to the idea that, in contrast to non-Indians, Indians are generous and not motivated solely by goods accumulation, despite their participation in the market economy. Kehoe's position is closest to my own. The Southern Cheyennes and Arapahos do not always know or activate a social relationship with a recipient of their gift, nor do they always, or even frequently, request or receive economic assistance from a recipient.

7. Generally, scholars have concentrated on analyzing kinship terminology and organization before native societies began to experience the constraints of reservation life that led to changes in the kinship system (in the case of Cheyenne and Arapaho kinship, see Eggan, "Cheyenne and Arapaho Kinship Systems"; Moore, *Cheyenne Nation*; and Hilger, *Arapaho Child Life*). Straus ("Northern Cheyenne Kinship Reconsidered"), however, discusses changes in Northern Cheyenne terminology since the 1930s. Her findings appear consistent, in large part, with developments among Southern Cheyennes and Arapahos. Straus builds on Eggan's work, contrasting his findings with the contemporary tendency on the part of some Cheyennes to use the native term for mother's brother for the father's brother, and the native term for father's sister for mother's sister. Eggan found that the latter category of relative was classified as father and mother, respectively, and that their children were classified as sons and daughters. The children of father's sister and mother's brother were distinguished from sons and daughters in native terminology. Father's male cousins were classified with father's brothers, and father's sisters with father's female cousins. Brothers and sisters-in-law are no longer classified as siblings. Speaking English, the terms "aunt" and "uncle" are used to distinguish father and mother from their siblings. But "brother" and "sister" are often used rather than "cousin," and "grandparent" and the reciprocal "grandchild" are used for collateral, as well as lineal, relatives. In Oklahoma, "grandparent" and "grandchild" refer to collateral as well as lineal relatives, but few Cheyennes and no Arapahos use native terms. In the first ascending and descending generations, the "father" and "mother" are distinguished from "aunt" and "uncle" in the case of a parent's siblings, and the terms "niece" and "nephew" are used for the children of siblings.

Straus attributes these changes to the fact that the nuclear family and neolocal residence have become far more important than the localized extended family. Thus, there has been some shift toward a lineal system. But, how then to explain the use of "grandparent" and "grandchild" terms for collateral relatives? Or, the tendency for many to refer to the children of their "aunts" and "uncles" as "sisters" or "brothers"? Possibly the sibling bond is still important because of the frightening and often hostile environment faced in boarding school, then public school, during the twentieth century, where relatives were a source of protection and comfort. The elderly have always played an important role as caretakers and in recent years as instructors and mentors in Indian tradition for nonrelatives. This brings us to the question of the use of kinship terminology as a strategy, another subject generally ignored in the context of contemporary Native America. Straus touches on this point, but like change in kinship organization it remains an important subject for future research.

8. Marla N. Powers has studied gender symbolism in the powwow context, arguing that changes in dance patterns and costume reflect sociopolitical changes in Lakota life during the twentieth century ("Symbolic Representations of Sex Roles").

9. An eagle staff (a staff, often crooked, with eagle feathers attached) is sometimes carried by a veteran in an honor dance or grand entry, but there is no tribal staff as at Fort Belknap (see Fowler, *Shared Symbols, Contested Meanings*).

10. *WR* 24 January 1976. This statement is taken from an interview of Charlie Yellow Calf by Darrell Rice.

11. The best discussion of the relationship between creation and singing is Hatton, " 'We Caused Them to Cry.' " This is a study of religion and song among Gros Ventres (an Arapaho subdivision), but it is also representative of Southern Arapaho tradition and is informative on Cheyenne tradition.

12. *WR* 6 April 1989.

13. *WR* 6 April 1989.

14. *WR* 6 April 1989.

8. "Looking for High-Up Places"

1. *WR* 7 November 1991; 12 March 1992. Other statements from Cheyennes and Arapahos are taken from my field notes.

2. *SCANN* October 1987.

3. *SCANN* 25 February 1985.

4. *WR* 10 March 1988; 10 April 1986; 18 September 1980.

5. *WR* 12 June 1986; 21 February 1980.

6. *WR* 26 October 1989.

7. Talk with Delegates, 1 June 1926, *CFC* 056-29615-1926.

8. *WR* 21 January 1982.

9. *WR* 1 December 1980; 16 May 1991.

10. Thomas Biolsi's interesting study of Pine Ridge and Rosebud reservation communities in South Dakota is a good point of comparison (*Organizing the Lakota*). Here competing corporate groups emerged and each developed its own political consciousness, expressed in competing forms of government. This work covers Lakota political history through the 1930s. Biolsi concludes that some constituents rejected the Indian Reorganization Act business committee because they rejected federal dominance. More generally, Fowler discusses how different colonial contexts led to different strategies of resistance on the part of Gros Ventres and Northern and Southern Arapahos ("Civilization Strategy").

A staff member of the Tribal Relations division of the B I A in Washington, who discussed my research with me, noted that the highest number of complaints about tribal government come from tribal members in Oklahoma and California—both places where native groups were engulfed and personally ridiculed by settlers.

11. On studies of Fourth World sovereignty, see Cassidy and Bish, *Indian Government*; Dyck, *Indigenous Peoples*; Hylton, ed., *Aboriginal Self-Government*; Mawhiney, *Towards Aboriginal Self-Government*; Fleras and Elliott, "*Nations Within*"; Boldt, *Surviving as Indians*; Armitage, *Comparing the Policy of Aboriginal Assimilation*; Michael C. Howard, *Aboriginal Politics* and *Aboriginal Power*; Brennan, *One Land, One Nation*; Goodall, *Invasion to Embassy*; Bennett, *Aborigines and Political Power*; Fletcher, *Aboriginal Politics*; Jull and Roberts, eds., *Challenge of Northern Regions*; Long and Boldt, *Governments in Conflict?*; Coombs, *Aboriginal Autonomy*; Tonkinson and Michael C. Howard, *Going it Alone*.

In Canada, native political organization exists at several levels: First Nations (small local communities, perhaps no more than five hundred in population); tribal councils, composed of representatives from a province or territory (there are eighty tribal councils that link First Nations); tribal organizations (based on tribal, language, or treaty affiliations—such as the Anishnabek Nation); and provincial and national organizations (Warry, *Unfinished Dreams*, pp. 52–61, 107–9, 236–39). Warry discusses how suspicion and competition between First Nation communities and tribal councils affect the level of success on contemporary self-government projects and how they are a "major obstacle to self-government." But this problem, and the fact that native leadership at the regional and national levels is regarded as elite, from which First Nation communities feel estranged, has been ignored ethnographically (Boldt, *Surviving as Indians*; but see Salisbury, *A Homeland for the Cree*). There is recognition that differences in "quality of leadership" and "factionalism" have led to some native governments working "better than others," but there are no ethnohistorical studies from which comparisons can be made (see Buckley, *From Wooden Ploughs to Welfare*).

In Australia, studies of local councils examine the ways in which these councils are subject to external bureaucratic control and explore how these controls have hindered Aboriginal self-determination (see Michael C. Howard, *"Whitefella Business,"* and Rowse, *Remote Possibilities*). Rowse reviews studies that show how councils are considered alien to Aboriginal life: centralization is not compatible with kin and other group relations at the local level; councils may not have authority to speak for others or be able to mobilize support for projects; brokers or council members help insulate local groups from non-Aboriginal social institutions, and, in fact, council business ("Whitefella business") may be threatening to the Aboriginal sense of autonomy ("Blackfella business"). David S. Trigger explores how white racism and paternalism affect Aboriginal sense of worth and how consciousness is constrained by domination (*"Whitefella Comin"*). Thus, councils have difficulty articulating with the Australian state. Rowse suggests that, given there is a new political elite working to organize the pursuit of land rights and economic gains as a means to power, ethnographic studies are needed to explore the relationship between old (ritual knowledge) and new forms of power (for example, the manipulation of government subsidy). The question of how local councils articulate with regional and other Aboriginal organizations (such as Land Councils) in the pursuit of self-determination has not been explored.

12. Wayne Warry, writing about First Nation governments in Canada and the problems created by state imposition of Western forms of government, extols the ability of community members and First Nations leadership to create programs that contribute to the native community and suggests that Canadian society holds First Nations to unreasonably high standards. There are media reports about First Nation deficits suggesting that Aboriginal leaders are incompetent. These accounts fail to place deficits in the context of provincial and federal deficits, "which have been considered a natural part of doing business for decades." Warry suggests that native leaders urge First Nation peoples to begin to examine how colonization has contributed to the ill health of communities, to community divisions. He urges them to consider developing new forms of representation less based on state-imposed models. This awareness is necessary to the process of "community healing" (*Unfinished Dreams*, pp. 126–27, 215–16, 233–38).

Works Cited

Archival Sources

Bethel College. Mennonite Library and Archives. North Newton, Kansas (B C).

Board of Missions, General Correspondence.

Henry Voth Collections.

The Mennonite (Menn).

Bureau of Indian Affairs. Office Files. Anadarko, Oklahoma (B I A A).

Carnegie Public Library. El Reno, Oklahoma.

Letter Books, Darlington Agency, 5 vols., 1879, 1881, 1883–85 (L B - E R).

Cheyenne and Arapaho Tribes. Office Files. Concho, Oklahoma (C & A).

"Cheyenne-Arapaho Tribes of Oklahoma Base Studies, 1993." Planning Office, Cheyenne and Arapaho Tribes.

Tribal Government Records.

Columbia University. Union Theological Seminary. New York, New York. *Home Mission Echoes* (H M E).

Federal Archives. Regional Center. Records of the Bureau of Indian Affairs, Record Group 75. Concho Agency. Fort Worth, Texas (N A F W).

Central Files. Anadarko Area Office. Records Relating to Tribal Committees, 1950–67 (C F A A).

Central Files. Concho Agency, 1926–84 (C F-Concho).

Land Transaction Files, 1904–87, Entry 12.

Field Museum of Natural History. George Dorsey Collection. Chicago, Illinois (F M C).

Fort Sill Museum Archives. Fort Sill, Oklahoma.

Hugh L. Scott Ledger Books, 1889–97.

Miscellaneous Records, 1873–1912. Post Records.

National Archives. Washington D C.

Records of the Bureau of Indian Affairs, Record Group 75.

Central Files, 1907–39. Cantonment Agency (C F C).

Central Files, Cantonment Agency, Industrial Survey, 1922–25.

Central Files, 1907–39. Cheyenne-Arapaho Agency (C F C A).

Central Files, 1940–57. Southern Plains Agency. Entries 59A and 68A (C F S P).

Letters Received by the Office of Indian Affairs, 1824–81.

Central Superintendency (L R, Cen Supt).

Cheyenne-Arapaho Agency (L R C A).

Upper Arkansas Agency (L R U A).

Letters Received by the Office of Indian Affairs, 1881–1907 (L R).

Irregularly Shaped Papers. Report of the Jerome Commission, 1891–93.

Journal of Cheyenne and Arapaho Competency Board, 1917. Entry 485.

Special Cases, 1821–1907 (S C).

Student Folders and Student Information Cards. Carlisle Indian Industrial School.

Superintendent's Narrative Reports, 1907–38. Cheyenne-Arapaho Agency (S N R - C A).

Superintendent's Narrative Reports, 1907–38. Cantonment Agency (S N R - C).

Records of the Office of the Secretary of the Interior, Record Group 48.

Inspection Division, Reports, 1881–1924 (I R).

Letters Sent to the Secretary of the Interior, 1881–1907, Indian Division.

Records of the U.S. Army Continental Commands, 1821–1920, Record Group 393.

Post Records of Camp Cantonment: Letters Sent (L S P R - C).

Post Records of Camp Supply: Letters Sent (L S P R - C S).

Post Records of Camp Supply: Letters Received (L R P R - C S).

Oklahoma Historical Society, Archives and Manuscript Division (O H S).

Cheyenne-Arapaho Records. Oklahoma City, Oklahoma.

Enrollment Lists.

Fairs File.

Farmers File.

Farmers Weekly Reports.

Freight and Transportation File.

Indian Celebrations File.

Indian Customs File.

Indian Dances File.

Letterpress Books, Cantonment Agency, 8 vols., 1892–1902 (L B - C).

Letterpress Books, Darlington Agency, 100 vols., 1875–76, 1881–1900 (L B - D).

Miscellaneous Letters Sent, Cantonment Agency, 1902–14 (M L S-Canton).

Miscellaneous Letters Sent, Darlington Agency, 85 vols., 1900–1914 (M L S-Darl).

Superintendent's Letters, Cantonment Agency, 2 vols., 1899–1902.

Smithsonian Institution. National Anthropological Archives, Truman Michelson Collection. Washington D C.

University of Oklahoma. Norman, Oklahoma.

Western History Collections (W H).

Ben Clark Collection.

Doris Duke Oral History Collection (D D).

Indian Pioneer Papers.

Mary Jayne Diaries (M J).

Carl Albert Center. Fred R. Harris Collection.

U.S. Federal Court Building. U.S. Court Clerks Office. Oklahoma City, Oklahoma. Transcript of Proceedings, *U.S.A. v. Mike Shadaram; Juanita Learned; Michael Alan Combs; and Viola Hatch.* C R-95-37C.

Newspapers

C & A Bulletin

Calumet Chieftain (C C)

Canadian Valley Record (C V R)

Canton Record (C R)

Cheyenne Transporter (C T)

Daily Oklahoman (D O)

El Reno American (E R A)

Geary Bulletin (G B)

Geary Journal (G J)

Southern Cheyenne and Arapaho Nation News (S C A N N)

Watonga Republican (W R)

Federal Documents

"Indian Self-Determination and Education Assistance Act." *U.S. Statutes at Large* 88 (January 4, 1975), Public Law 93-638, pp. 2203–13.

Reports of the Commissioner of Indian Affairs. Washington D C: Government Printing Office, 1846–1906 (R C I A).

Books and Articles

Armitage, Andrew. *Comparing the Policy of Aboriginal Assimilation: Australia, Canada, and New Zealand.* Vancouver: University of British Columbia Press, 1995.

Bailey, F. G. "The Definition of Factionalism." In *A House Divided?: Anthropological Studies of Factionalism,* ed. M. Silverman and R. F. Salisbury, pp. 21–36. Social and Economic Papers 9. Institute of Social and Economic Research, Memorial University of Newfoundland. Toronto: University of Toronto Press, 1977.

Bailey, F. G., and Ralph W. Nicholas. "Rules, Resources, and Groups in Political Contests." In *Local-Level Politics,* ed. Marc J. Swartz, pp. 271–/9. Chicago: Aldine, 1968.

Barsh, Russel Lawrance. "Indian Policy at the Beginning of the 1990s: The Trivialization of Struggle." In *American Indian Policy: Self-Governance and Economic Development,* ed. Lyman H. Legters and Fremont J. Lyden, pp. 55–69. New York: Greenwood, 1993.

Bee, Robert L. *The Politics of American Indian Policy.* Cambridge: Schenkman, 1982.

Bennett, Scott Cecil. *Aborigines and Political Power.* Sydney: Allen and Unwin, 1989.

Berkhofer, Robert F., Jr. *The White Man's Indian: Images of the American Indian from Columbus to the Present.* New York: Vintage, 1979.

Bernstein, Alison. *American Indians and World War II: Toward a New Era in Indian Affairs.* Norman: University of Oklahoma Press, 1991.

Berthrong, Donald J. *The Cheyenne and Arapaho Ordeal: Reservation and Agency Life in the Indian Territory, 1875–1907.* Lincoln: University of Nebraska Press, 1976.

———. "Legacies of the Dawes Act." In *The Plains Indians and the Twentieth Century,* ed. Peter Iverson, pp. 31–53. Norman: University of Oklahoma Press, 1985.

———. *The Southern Cheyennes.* Norman: University of Oklahoma Press, 1963.

Biolsi, Thomas. "The Birth of the Reservation: Making the Modern Individual among the Lakota." *American Ethnologist* 22, no. 1 (1995): 28–53.

———. *Organizing the Lakota: The Political Economy of the New Deal on the Pine Ridge and Rosebud Reservations.* Tucson: University of Arizona Press, 1992.

Blu, Karen I. *The Lumbee Problem: The Making of an American Indian People.* New York: Cambridge University Press, 1980.

Blumfiel, Elizabeth M. "Factional Competition and Political Development in the New World: An Introduction." In *Factional Competition and Political Development in the New World,* ed. Elizabeth M. Blumfiel and John W. Fox, pp. 3–13. New York: Cambridge University Press, 1994.

Boissevain, Jeremy. "Of Men and Marbles: Notes Towards a Reconsideration of Factionalism." In *A House Divided?: Anthropological Studies of Factionalism,* ed. M. Silverman and R. F. Salisbury, pp. 99–110. Social and Economic Papers 9. Institute of Social and Economic Research, Memorial University of Newfoundland. Toronto: University of Toronto Press, 1977.

Boldt, Menno. *Surviving as Indians: The Challenge of Self-Government.* Toronto: University of Toronto Press, 1993.

Bourdieu, Pierre. *Outline of a Theory of Practice.* Cambridge Studies in Social Anthropology 16. Cambridge: Cambridge University Press, 1989.

Brennan, Frank. *One Land, One Nation: Mabo, Toward 2001.* St. Lucia, Queensland: University of Queensland Press, 1995.

Buckley, Helen. *From Wooden Ploughs to Welfare: How Indian Policy Failed in the Prairie Reserves.* Montréal: McGill-Queen's University Press, 1992.

Burja, Janet. "The Dynamics of Political Action: A New Look at Factionalism." *American Anthropologist* 75, no. 1 (1973): 132–52.

Cassidy, Frank, and Robert L. Bish. *Indian Government: Its Meaning in Practice.* Lantzville B C: Oolichan Books, 1989.

Castile, George Pierre. *To Show Heart: Native American Self-Determination and Federal Indian Policy, 1960–1975.* Tucson: University of Arizona Press, 1998.

Clark, W. P. *The Indian Sign Language.* Philadelphia: L. R. Hammersly, 1885.

Cobb, Daniel M. " 'Us Indians Understand the Basics': Oklahoma Indian Participation in Community Action Programs During the War on Poverty." Paper presented at Western History Association Conference, 14 October 2000, San Antonio T X .

Comaroff, Jean. *Body of Power, Spirit of Resistance: The Culture and History of a South African People.* Chicago: University of Chicago Press, 1985.

Comaroff, Jean, and John Comaroff. *Of Revelation and Revolution: Christianity, Colonialism, and Consciousness in South Africa.* Vol. 1. Chicago: University of Chicago Press, 1991.

Comaroff, John, and Jean Comaroff. *Ethnography and the Historical Imagination.* Boulder: Westview, 1992.

Coombs, H. C. *Aboriginal Autonomy: Issues and Strategies.* Cambridge: Cambridge University Press, 1994.

Corrigan, Samuel W. "The Plains Indian Powwow: Cultural Integration in Manitoba and Saskatchewan." *Anthropologica* 12 (1970): 253–77.

Dorsey, George A. *The Arapaho Sun Dance: The Ceremony of the Offerings Lodge.* Field Columbian Museum Publications 75, Anthropological Series 4. Chicago, 1903.

———. "The Cheyenne." *Field Museum, Anthropological Series* 9 (1905): 1–186.

Dozier, Edward P. "Factionalism at Santa Clara Pueblo." *Ethnology* 5 (1966): 172–85.

Driben, Paul, and Robert S. Trudeau. *When Freedom Is Lost: The Dark Side of the Relationship between Government and the Fort Hope Band.* Toronto: University of Toronto Press, 1983.

Dyck, Noel, ed. *Indigenous Peoples and the Nation-State: "Fourth World" Politics in Canada, Australia, and Norway.* St. John's, Newfoundland: Institute of Social and Economic Research, Memorial University of Newfoundland, 1985.

———. "Political Powwow: The Rise and Fall of an Urban Native Festival." In *The Celebration of Society: Perspectives on Contemporary Cultural Performance,* ed. F. Manning, pp. 165–84. Bowling Green, Ohio: Bowling Green University Popular, 1983.

Eggan, Fred. "The Cheyenne and Arapaho Kinship System." In *Social Anthropology of North American Indian Tribes,* ed. Fred Eggan, pp. 35–95. Chicago: University of Chicago Press, 1955.

———. Field Notes. Oklahoma, 1934. Personal possession.

Ellis, C. "Truly Dancing Their Own Way: Modern Revival and Diffusion of the Gourd Dance." *American Indian Quarterly* 14, no. 1 (1990): 19–33.

Esber, George S., Jr. "Shortcomings of the Indian Self-Determination Policy." In *State and Reservation: New Perspectives in Federal Indian Policy,* ed. George Castile and Robert L. Bee, pp. 212–23. Tucson: University of Arizona Press, 1992.

Feit, Harvey. "Legitimization and Autonomy in James Bay Cree Response to Hydro-Electric Development." In *Indigenous Peoples and the Nation-State: "Fourth World" Politics in Canada, Australia, and Norway,* ed. Noel Dyck, pp. 27–66. St. John's, Newfoundland: Institute of Social and Economic Research, Memorial University of Newfoundland, 1985.

Fenton, William. "Factionalism in American Indian Society." *Actes du Congrès International des Sciences Anthropologiques* 2 (1955): 330–40.

———. "Factionalism at Taos Pueblo, New Mexico." *BAE Bulletin* 164, Anthropological Papers 56, Smithsonian Institution (1957): 297–344.

Fixico, Donald L. *Termination and Relocation: Federal Indian Policy, 1945–60.* Albuquerque: University of New Mexico Press, 1986.

Fleras, Augie, and Jean Leonard Elliott. *The "Nations Within": Aboriginal-State Relations in Canada, the United States, and New Zealand.* Toronto: Oxford University Press, 1992.

Fletcher, Christine. *Aboriginal Politics: Intergovernmental Relations.* Carlton, Victoria: Melbourne University Press, 1992.

Foster, Morris. *Being Comanche: A Social History of an American Indian Community.* Tucson: University of Arizona Press, 1991.

Fowler, Loretta. *Arapahoe Politics, 1851–1978: Symbols in Crises of Authority.* Lincoln: University of Nebraska Press, 1982.

———. "The Civilization Strategy: Gros Ventres, Northern and Southern Arapahos Compared." In *North American Indian Anthropology: Essays on Society and Culture,* ed. Raymond J. DeMallie and Alfonso Ortiz, pp. 220–57. Norman: University of Oklahoma Press, 1994.

———. Field Notes. Southern Arapaho and Cheyenne, 1984–94. Personal possession. (F N)

———. *Shared Symbols, Contested Meanings: Gros Ventre Culture and History, 1778–1984.* Ithaca: Cornell University Press, 1987.

French, David H. "Ambiguity and Irrelevancy in Factional Conflict." In *Intergroup Relations and Leadership: Approaches and Research in Industrial, Ethnic, Cultural, and Political Areas,* ed. Muzafer Sherif, pp. 232–43. New York: John Wiley and Sons, 1962.

Gaede, E. R. Jethro. "The American Indian Exposition: Reciprocal Commodification of the Image of the Indian." Paper presented at the Plains Anthropological Conference, 22 October 1999, Sioux Falls S D.

———. "The American Indian Exposition, 1933–1938: An Abridged History and Critique." Unpublished paper.

Goodall, Heather. *Invasion to Embassy: Land in Aboriginal Politics in New South Wales, 1770–1972.* St. Edwards N S W: Allen and Unwin, 1996.

Gramsci, Antonio. *Selections from the Prison Notebooks of Antonio Gramsci.* Trans. Q. Hoare and G. N. Smith. New York: International Publications, 1971.

Grinnell, George Bird. *The Cheyenne Indians: Their History and Ways of Life.* 2 vols. New Haven: Yale University Press, 1923.

Grobsmith, Elizabeth S. "The Changing Role of the Giveaway in Contemporary Lakota Life." *Plains Anthropologist* 26, no. 91 (1981): 75–79.

———. "The Lakhota Giveaway: A System of Social Reciprocity." *Plains Anthropologist* 24, no. 84 (1979): 123–31.

————. *Lakota of the Rosebud: A Contemporary Ethnography.* New York: Holt, Rinehart, Winston, 1981.

Hagan, William T. *American Indians.* 3d. ed. Chicago: University of Chicago Press, 1993.

————. *United States-Comanche Relations: The Reservation Years.* Norman: University of Oklahoma Press, 1990.

Hale, Charles R. *Resistance and Contradiction: Miskitu Indians and the Nicaraguan State, 1894–1987.* Stanford: Stanford University Press, 1994.

Harkin, Michael. "Engendering Discipline: Discourse and Counterdiscourse in the Methodist-Heilsuk Dialogue." *Ethnohistory* 43, no. 4 (1996): 643–61.

Hatton, Orin T. "In the Tradition: Grass Dance Musical Style and Female Pow-Wow Singers." *Ethnomusicology* 30, no. 2 (1986): 197–221.

————. " 'We Caused Them to Cry': Power and Performance in Gros Ventre War Expedition Songs." Master's thesis, Catholic University, 1988.

Hilger, Inez M. *Arapaho Child Life and Its Cultural Background.* Bureau of American Ethnology Bulletin 148. Washington D C: Smithsonian Institution, 1952.

Howard, James H. "The Pan-Indian Culture of Oklahoma." *The Scientific Monthly* 18, no. 5 (1955): 215–20.

————. "Pan-Indianism in Native American Music and Dance." *Ethnomusicology* 27, no. 1 (1983): 71–82.

————. "The Plains Gourd Dance as a Revitalization Movement." *American Ethnologist* 3, no. 2 (1976): 243–59.

Howard, Michael C., ed. *Aboriginal Politics in Southwestern Australia.* Nedlands, Western Australia: University of Western Australia Press, 1981.

————. *Aboriginal Power in Australian Society.* Honolulu: University of Hawaii Press, 1982.

————. "*Whitefella Business*": *Aborigines in Australian Politics.* Philadelphia: Institute for the Study of Human Issues, 1978.

Hoxie, Frederick E. *A Final Promise: The Campaign to Assimilate the Indians, 1880–1920.* Lincoln: University of Nebraska Press, 1984.

————. *Parading through History: The Making of the Crow Nation in America, 1805–1935.* Cambridge: Cambridge University Press, 1995.

————. "The Reservation Period." In *The Cambridge History of the Native Peoples of the Americas,* ed. Bruce G. Trigger and Wilcomb E. Washburn, pp. 183–258. Vol. 1, pt. 2, *North America.* Cambridge: Cambridge University Press, 1996.

Hylton, John H., ed. *Aboriginal Self-Government in Canada: Current Trends and Issues*. Saskatchewan: Purich Publications, 1994.

Jorgensen, Joseph G. *Oil Age Eskimos*. Berkeley: University of California Press, 1990.

Jull, Peter, and Sally Roberts, eds. *The Challenge of Northern Regions*. Casuarina, Northern Territory: Australian National University, North Australia Research Unit, 1991.

Kan, Sergei. "Clan Mothers and Godmothers: Tlingit Women and Russian Orthodox Christianity, 1840–1940." *Ethnohistory* 43, no. 4 (1996): 613–41.

Kehoe, Alice B. "The Giveaway Ceremony of Blackfoot and Plains Cree." *Plains Anthropologist* 25, no. 87 (1980): 17–26.

Koch, Ronald P. *Dress Clothing of the Plains Indians*. Norman: University of Oklahoma Press, 1977.

Kracht, Benjamin R. "Kiowa Powwows: Community in Ritual Practice." *American Indian Quarterly* summer 1994: 321–48.

Kroeber, Alfred L. *The Arapaho*. Bulletin of the American Museum of Natural History 18 (1902–7).

Laubin, Reginald, and Gladys Laubin. *Indian Dances of North America*. Norman: University of Oklahoma Press, 1977.

Llewellyn, Karl N., and E. Adamson Hoebel. *The Cheyenne Way*. Norman: University of Oklahoma Press, 1941.

Long, J. Anthony, and Menno Boldt. *Governments in Conflict?: Provinces and Indian Nations in Canada*. Toronto: University of Toronto Press, 1988.

Lowie, Robert H. *Plains Indian Age Societies: Historical and Comparative Study*. Anthropological Papers of the American Museum of Natural History 11 (1916).

Mawhiney, Anne-Marie. *Towards Aboriginal Self-Government: Relations between Status Indian Peoples and the Government of Canada, 1969–1984*. New York: Garland, 1994.

Mooney, James. "The Cheyenne Indians." *Memoirs* (American Anthropological Association) 1 (1907): 357–442.

———. *The Ghost-Dance Religion and the Sioux Outbreak of 1890*. Fourteenth Annual Report of the Bureau of American Ethnology. Washington D C, 1896.

Moore, John H. *The Cheyenne*. Cambridge M A: Blackwell, 1996.

———. *The Cheyenne Nation: A Social and Demographic History*. Lincoln: University of Nebraska Press, 1987.

———. "How the Giveaways and Pow-Wows Redistribute the Means of Subsistence." In *The Political Economy of North American Indians,* ed. John H. Moore, pp. 240–69. Norman: University of Oklahoma Press, 1993.

Nagata, Shuichi. "Opposition and Freedom in Moenkopi Factionalism." In *A House Divided?: Anthropological Studies of Factionalism,* ed. M. Silverman and R. F. Salisbury, pp. 146–70. Social and Economic Papers 9. Institute of Social and Economic Research, Memorial University of Newfoundland. Toronto: University of Toronto Press, 1977.

Nicholas, Ralph W. "Factions: A Comparative Analysis." In *Political Systems and the Distribution of Power,* ed. Michael Banton, pp. 21–61. Association of Social Anthropologists Monograph 2. London: Tavistock, 1965.

Phelps, G. L. *Tepee Trails.* Atlanta: Home Mission Board, 1937.

Philp, Kenneth R. *John Collier's Crusade for Indian Reform.* Tucson: University of Arizona Press, 1977.

Powell, Peter John. *People of the Sacred Mountain: A History of the Northern Cheyenne Chiefs and Warrior Societies, 1830–1879.* 2 vols. San Francisco: Harper and Row, 1981.

Powers, Marla N. "Symbolic Representations of Sex Roles in the Plains War Dance." *European Review of Native American Studies* 2, no. 2 (1988): 17–24.

Powers, William K. "Foolish Words: Text and Context in Lakota Love Songs." *European Review of Native American Studies* 2, no. 2 (1988): 29–34.

———. "Plains Indian Music and Dance." In *Anthropology on the Great Plains,* ed. W. Raymond Wood and Margot Liberty, pp. 212–29. Lincoln: University of Nebraska Press, 1980.

———. *War Dance: Plains Indian Musical Performance.* Tucson: University of Arizona Press, 1990.

Prucha, Francis Paul. *The Great Father: The United States Government and the American Indians.* 2 vols. Lincoln: University of Nebraska Press, 1984.

Rowse, Tim. *Remote Possibilities: The Aboriginal Domain and the Administrative Imagination.* Darwin: Australian National University, North Australia Research Unit, 1992.

Salisbury, Richard Frank. *A Homeland for the Cree: Regional Development in James Bay, 1971–1981.* Kingston: McGill-Queen's University Press, 1986.

Salisbury, Richard F., and Marilyn Silverman. "An Introduction: Factions and the Dialectic." In *A House Divided?: Anthropological Studies of Factionalism,* ed. M. Silverman and R. F. Salisbury, pp. 1–20. Social and Economic Papers 9. Institute of Social and Economic Research, Memorial University of Newfoundland. Toronto: University of Toronto Press, 1977.

Sanford, Margaret. "Pan-Indianism, Acculturation, and the American Ideal." *Plains Anthropologist* 16, no. 53 (1971): 222–27.

Sawchuk, Joe. "The Métis, Non-Status Indians, and the New Aboriginality: Government Influence on Native Political Alliances and Identity." *Canadian Ethnic Studies* 17, no. 2 (1978): 135–46.

———, ed. *Readings in Aboriginal Studies.* Vol. 2, *Identities and State Structures.* Brandon, Manitoba: Bearpaw, 1992.

Schneider, Mary Jane. "Women's Work: An Examination of Women's Roles in Plains Indian Arts and Crafts." In *The Hidden Half: Studies of Plains Indian Women,* ed. Patricia Albers and Beatrice Medicine, pp. 101–21. Washington D C: University Press of America, 1983.

Scott, James C. *Weapons of the Weak: Everyday Forms of Peasant Resistance.* New Haven: Yale University Press, 1985.

Shimony, Annemarie Anrod. *Conservatism among the Iroquois at the Six Nations Reserve.* Syracuse: Syracuse University Press, 1994.

Sider, Gerald. *Lumbee Indian Histories: Race, Ethnicity, and Indian Identity in the Southern United States.* New York: Cambridge University Press, 1993.

Siegel, Bernard J., and Alan R. Beals. "Pervasive Factionalism." *American Anthropologist* 62 (1960): 394–417.

Smith, Derek G. "The Emergence of 'Eskimo Status': An Examination of the Eskimo Disk List System and Its Social Consequences, 1925–1970." In *Anthropology, Public Policy, and Native Peoples in Canada,* ed. Noel Dyck and James B. Waldram, pp. 41–74. Montreal: McGill-Queen's University Press, 1993.

Straus, Anne S. "Northern Cheyenne Kinship Reconsidered." In *North American Indian Anthropology: Essays on Society and Culture,* ed. Raymond J. DeMallie and Alfonso Ortiz, pp. 147–71. Norman: University of Oklahoma Press, 1994.

Sturm, Circe Dawn. "Blood Politics: Racial Hybridity and Identity in the Cherokee Nation of Oklahoma." Ph.D. dissertation, University of California at Davis, 1997. In press, University of California Press.

Taylor, Graham D. *The New Deal and American Indian Tribalism: The Administration of the Indian Reorganization Act, 1934–45.* Lincoln: University of Nebraska Press, 1980.

Tonkinson, Robert, and Michael Howard. *Going It Alone: Prospects for Aboriginal Autonomy.* Canberra: Aboriginal Studies, 1990.

Trigger, David S. *"Whitefella Comin": Aboriginal Responses to Colonialism in Northern Australia.* Cambridge: Cambridge University Press, 1992.

Vincent, Joan. *Anthropology and Politics: Visions, Traditions, and Trends.* Tucson: University of Arizona Press, 1990.

Waldram, James B. *As Long as the Rivers Run: Hydroelectric Development and Native Communities in Western Canada.* Winnepeg: University of Manitoba Press, 1993.

Warry, Wayne. *Unfinished Dreams: Community Healing and the Reality of Aboriginal Self-Government.* Toronto: University of Toronto Press, 1998.

Watson, Graham. "The Reification of Ethnicity and Its Political Consequences in the North." *The Canadian Review of Sociology and Anthropology* 18, no. 4 (1981): 453–69.

Weaver, Sally. "Political Representivity and Indigenous Minorities in Canada and Australia." In *Indigenous Peoples and the Nation-State: "Fourth World" Politics in Canada, Australia, and Norway,* ed. Noel Dyck, pp. 113–50. St. John's, Newfoundland: Institute of Social and Economic Research, Memorial University of Newfoundland, 1985.

Weist, Katherine M. "Giving Away: The Ceremonial Distribution of Goods among the Northern Cheyenne of Southeastern Montana." *Plains Anthropologist* 18, no. 60 (1973): 97–103.

Whiteley, Peter. *Deliberate Acts: Changing Hopi Culture through the Oraibi Split.* Tucson: University of Arizona Press, 1988.

———. *Rethinking Hopi Ethnography.* Washington D C: Smithsonian Institution Press, 1998.

Index

Whiteley, Peter, 294 n.2, 296 n.13
whites: and relations with Cheyennes and
    Arapahos, 23, 120, 173, 195–96, 198, 280. *See
    also* dominance, ideological forms of;
    settlers, American
Wichita Indians, 10, 13
Wichita κ s, 13, 94
Wicks, Charles, 124
Williams, Dave, 133, 318 n.61
Williams, G. D., 297 n.3
Williams, John, 10
Wilson, Alfred, 100, 110, 114, 121
Wilson, Woodrow (President), 72
Wilson, Woodrow, 114, 125, 126, 133, 139, 317
    n.56, 318 n.61
Wilson, Yvonne, 197
Wolf Chief, 10, 23
Wolf Face, 14, 23, 24, 28, 41
Wolf Hair, 15
Wolf Robe, 25, 26, 28

Wolves band, 298 n.17
women, 3–6, 11, 12, 13, 18, 19, 20, 28, 33, 34, 35,
    44, 46, 50, 52, 55, 70, 94, 95, 96, 97, 98, 101,
    107, 133, 209, 238, 253, 259, 260, 266, 267,
    268, 270, 316 n.47, 328 n.4 n.6, 330 n.8
Woodson, A. E., 33, 39, 40, 42, 44, 45, 46, 80
Woolworth, Arnold, 36, 71, 73, 74, 75, 82, 100,
    103, 108
Woolworth, Eugene, 318 n.61
World War I, 67–68, 79, 88, 94, 97, 124
World War II, 92, 93, 94, 96, 97, 98, 125, 141, 255

Yaqui Indians, 86
Yellow Bear (Arapaho), 10, 13, 14, 15, 16, 17, 18,
    19, 22, 24, 26, 69, 71, 74, 299 n.28
Yellow Bear (Cheyenne), 39
Yellow Calf, Charlie, 330 n.10
Yellow Hawk, 70, 74, 76
Young Bull, 64